SHAKESPEARE IN AN AGE OF ANXIETY

SHAKESPEARE IN AN AGE OF ANXIETY

NEVILLE GRANT

Greenwich Exchange
London

Greenwich Exchange, London

First published in Great Britain in 2023
All rights reserved

Shakespeare in an Age of Anxiety
© Neville Grant, 2023

This book is sold subject to the conditions that it shall not, by way of trade or otherwise, be lent, resold, hired out or otherwise circulated without the publisher's prior consent in any form of binding or cover other than that in which it is published and without a similar condition including this condition being imposed on the subsequent purchaser.

Printed and bound by imprintdigital.com
Cover design by December Publications
Tel: 07951511275

Greenwich Exchange Website: www.greenex.co.uk

Cataloguing in Publication Data is available
from the British Library

ISBN: 978-1-910996-73-7

To Jane, Tom, Alex and Tara

CONTENTS

Preface: The Birth of a Book *13*

Introduction *17*

1 Who was Shakespeare? *24*

2 The Early Years *37*
Sonnets 153 & 154

3 The Family Man *50*
Sonnet 145

4 More Lost Years: Leicester's Men *61*

5 The Queen's Men *73*
Locrine

6 London *83*

7 Enter, Shakespeare *96*
Two Gentlemen of Verona. Arden of Faversham. Titus Andronicus

8 Lord Strange's Men *109*
2 Henry VI. 3 Henry VI. 1 Henry VI.

9 The Battle of the Sexes *123*
The Taming of the Shrew. The Dark Lady Sonnets 127-144, & 146-152

10 Power Play *136*
Edward III. Richard III

11 Friends, and enemies *148*
Venus and Adonis

12 Unto Southampton do we shift our Scene *162*
The Rape of Lucrece. Sonnets 61-77, & 87-103

13 A Little Light Relief *176*
The Comedy of Errors. Love's Labours Lost

14   The Lord Chamberlain's Men *189*
     Richard II

15   What Fools these Mortals Be *202*
     Romeo & Juliet. A Midsummer Night's Dream

16   Courting Controversy *216*
     King John

17   Bad News *228*
     The Merchant of Venice

18   Pride Comes Before a Fall *242*
     Henry IV first draft

19   Game of Thrones *254*
     1 Henry IV. 2 Henry IV.

20   The Price We Pay for Love *268*
     Sonnets 18-60. The Reproduction Sonnets 1-17

21   Much Ado on and off Stage *281*
     To the Queen. Much Ado About Nothing

22   Wherefore War? *294*
     Henry V. Julius Caesar

23   Friends, and Rivals *310*
     The Rival Poet Sonnets 78-86. The Spanish Tragedy (rewrite)

24   From Comedy to Tragedy *322*
     As You Like It.

25   Humouring the Queen *338*
     The Merry Wives of Windsor

26   The Food of Love *349*
     Twelfth Night

27   War and Lechery *361*
     Troilus and Cressida

28 The Queen is Dead, Long Live the King! *375*
   Sonnets 104-126

Select Bibliography *385*

Notes *389*

Index *413*

Images *429*

PREFACE

THE BIRTH OF A BOOK

> 'A writer's reputation is two-fold, what we think of his work, and what we think of him. What's more, we expect the two halves to relate: if they don't, then one or other of our opinions alters until they do.'
> – Philip Larkin (1975)

Both Henry VIII and his daughter Queen Elizabeth I were born in Greenwich, and so in a sense was this book. It seemed more than appropriate, therefore, that this book should be published by Greenwich Exchange.

Looking through an old history of Greenwich I stumbled on the comment that 'some say the Dark Lady of the Sonnets lived here', on Crooms Hill,[1] in the centre of Greenwich town. This was a reference to Emilia Lanier (or Lanyer), née Bassano, the daughter of an Italian Jewish musician who played for the queen. Allegedly, she was Shakespeare's 'Dark Lady'. Emilia became the mistress of Queen Elizabeth's cousin Henry Carey, Lord Hunsdon. Looking though the archives at the Greenwich Heritage Centre, I discovered that Emilia probably did briefly live on Crooms Hill. Some readers may recall a performance of the play *Emilia* at the Globe Theatre in London in 2018: an entertaining play, though it is definitely not history.

As I embarked on the hunt for the Dark Lady, I began to wonder whether Emilia Lanier was the real one? Indeed, was the Dark Lady even real? The jury has not even been sworn in, let alone been called on to reach a verdict, because of the almost total lack of evidence. The answer could not be found in any documents, and for a time I thought that the answers to these questions could perhaps lie in hints to be found in the life of William Shakespeare, in whose sonnets the Dark Lady has been immortalised. This in turn moved me to a wider investigation of the man himself, which turned into this book: Emilia, and any other dark lady then became a side-show, as Shakespeare entered, centre-stage. Talking of dark ladies, we also look at the case for arguing that a woman wrote some of his work.[2]

I have read, acted in and been a spectator of Shakespeare's plays all my life, and have indeed taught him in three continents; and have always assumed that I knew him, and his works, thanks to my professor at Bristol university, L.C. Knights, author of the essay 'How Many Children had Lady Macbeth?'[3] But so much has been unearthed about Shakespeare in the last two decades – the last ten years, even – to make it clear that a great reset was required: recent research by an impressive array of dedicated Shakespeare scholars – a veritable Shakespearian stage army of them, in fact – led me to a re-assessment of his life and work. What better time than the 400th Anniversary of the publication of Shakespeare's First Folio?

Many of the investigations carried out by these researchers have been based on computer-based stylometric analysis of the language used by Shakespeare and his fellow playwrights, their linguistic 'fingerprints', to determine how far the works of Shakespeare were his and his alone, and when they were written, and who may have collaborated with him. Shakespeare himself was fully aware that one could identify a writer through his words: in Sonnet 76 he notes that 'every word doth almost tell my name'.

This book does not inflict on the reader a mass of computer-generated data, for, in Wordsworth's words, 'we murder to dissect'. This literary biography will, I hope, generate enjoyment of Shakespeare, and to this end it is important not to reduce him to an accumulation of stylistic information. This book provides an account of what the research has uncovered so far, much of it recent; however, any study of Shakespeare still remains a fascinating exercise in detective work. Accordingly, readers will, I hope, enjoy following the trail, and exploring the paths that lead off it, and perhaps reaching their own conclusions. On offer, then, is a lay-person's guide to what the research can tell us, together with a chronological account of Shakespeare's life and work, noting how they reflected the *zeitgeist* of the

Elizabethan age. This book also offers a personal perspective on, and an appreciation of, each of his major poems, and his plays, written during the reign of Elizabeth, in what I call an Age of Anxiety. This approach will, it is hoped, generate renewed interest in, and enthusiasm for, the extraordinary artistry of William Shakespeare, and a fuller awareness of the times he lived in.

Shakespeare had many reasons to be anxious – political, religious, professional and highly personal, including, not least, the plague pandemic, social unrest, and security threats at home and abroad. Members of his own family were regarded by the Elizabethan secret service as 'persons of interest', as MI5 would have it, and some paid a heavy price. As one looks at his life and times, one cannot fail to see there are extraordinary parallels between the first Elizabethan Age of Anxiety, and those of us who live still in a similar state on 'this sceptred isle'; thus making Shakespeare as relevant as he has ever been. Perhaps, too, we can learn from his survival strategies.

I have many people to thank in the writing of this book: for their valuable comments on early drafts, to Hester Grant, Anita Mir, Paul Ryan, Alex Grant and my wife Jane; to Greenwich Heritage Centre, the Greenwich Public Library Service, the British Library, the Shakespeare Birthplace Trust, the Wren Library at Trinity College, Cambridge, the Museum of London, and the Folger Library, Washington DC. Thanks to the National Maritime Museum in Greenwich, and the National Portrait Gallery, among many other sources, for permission to reproduce pictures and art work; and to my long-suffering publisher, James Hodgson of Greenwich Exchange. Above all, to the many scholars who are cited in this book: may their invaluable work continue to refresh and inform Shakespearian studies, and to enthuse new generations of Shakespeare-lovers.

Neville Grant
Greenwich, London,
September 2023

Unless otherwise indicated, all Shakespeare quotations are from *The New Oxford Shakespeare: The Complete Works*, edited by Gary Taylor, John Jowett, Terri Bourus and Gabriel Egan (OUP, 2016)

INTRODUCTION

> The applause, delight, the wonder of our stage!
> My Shakespeare, rise! I will not lodge thee by
> Chaucer, or Spenser, or bid Beaumont lie
> A little further, to make thee a room:
> Thou art a monument without a tomb,
> And art alive still while thy book doth live
> And we have wits to read and praise to give.
>
> – Ben Jonson

Why yet another book on Shakespeare, readers may well ask. More books have been written about William Shakespeare and the works he wrote – or is supposed to have written – than any other author, whether living or dead. All this despite – or because of – the fact that very little is known about his personal life: there are no private letters, or diaries, and most of the anecdotes and reminiscences about him emerged years – sometimes many years – after his death, and are of dubious provenance. George Steevens, the eighteenth-century Shakespearian scholar wrote:

> All that is known with any degree of certainty concerning Shakespeare, is – that he was born in Stratford upon Avon, – married and had children there, – returned to Stratford, made his will, died, and was buried.[1]

Steevens' comments are often repeated as if they were true, especially by those who doubt whether Shakespeare was the man who wrote the plays. I refer particularly to those who signed up to a petition, started in 2007, called 'The Declaration of Reasonable Doubt about the Identity of William Shakespeare', and who have since joined 'The Shakespeare Authorship Coalition' – 'the SAC'. This petition, as the American Shakespeare scholar James Shapiro has observed, appears by its very wording to give credibility to a seriously unsustainable claim that there are plausible grounds for believing that someone else, unspecified, wrote his plays and poems – in short, that there can be, for a hypothetical jury, 'reasonable doubt'. Their claim, untrue, is that we have so little definite knowledge about Shakespeare that he couldn't possibly be the man that successive generations have claimed he was: an incredibly gifted playwright and poet. The SAC also suffers from the fatal flaw that no plausible alternative author has ever been nominated. Those interested in a demolition job on this petition should read *Shakespeare Beyond Doubt* by Paul Edmondson and Professor Stanley Wells.[2]

This book is a literary biography that makes it clear that the SAC is seriously wrong in suggesting that Shakespeare was not the author of his poetry and plays. While the truth is that although we have virtually no firm information about Shakespeare's inner life – his personal thoughts, his feelings, his politics, his religion, even his sexuality, we still know a great deal about Shakespeare, and a great deal more about him than we know about almost all of his contemporary playwrights. (The exception is Ben Jonson.) About Webster, for example, we know virtually nothing, and no one doubts that Webster was indeed Webster. In short, we know enough about William Shakespeare to be sure that he could not have been anyone else but Shakespeare, the playwright and poet.

In a year celebrating the 400th anniversary of the First Folio of Shakespeare's plays, published in 1623, seven years after his death, this book aims to give the general reader access to the findings of the most recent research carried out by a host of devoted Shakespearian scholars. Much of this has been produced in the current century – and casts new light on the man and his works, exploding many myths. To these scholars we owe a huge debt of gratitude. Crucially, their research forces us to reconsider the order in which his works were written, and the extent to which Shakespeare collaborated with other playwrights. The book also provides a brief critical study of each of his plays, and his main poems, in the order in which they were written, hoping to whet the appetite of anyone not familiar with each of the works considered. This chronological approach enables one to trace his development as a playwright and poet. In this book, readers will be asked to consider who he was, who he knew, who he loved, what he did, or may have done, and what he did, or didn't write. There will be times when both author, and readers, will find themselves sleuths in a kind of literary detective story.

In reassessing the life and work of William Shakespeare, this book also looks at why the Elizabethan era can be described as 'an age of anxiety'. Of course, anxiety is part of the human condition, and one could claim that all of humanity has always lived in a state of anxiety. However, those who were born in, and lived through, the Elizabethan era had special reasons to be anxious, even terrified, and some of these still resonate in today's society. In the words of Nicholas Pevsner (echoing Hegel), 'No artist can live against his century. The Zeitgeist must come out.'[3] The Elizabethan Zeitgeist (we can define it as 'spirit of the age') – was largely dominated by anxiety at all levels of society, from day labourers to dukes. As well as social tensions, there were serious political threats, both at home and abroad, with numerous plots to kill Queen Elizabeth. Religious conflict continued throughout the queen's reign, and had a direct impact on Shakespeare's family.

Europe, too, was undergoing poisonous religious tensions, which at times erupted into extreme violence between Catholics and Protestants. Small expeditionary forces from England fighting in the Protestant cause did little to reduce threats from France, and in particular Spain, whose armies threatened to overwhelm the Protestant inhabitants of the Low Countries, and there was a persistent threat of invasion – most pressingly with the Spanish Armada of 1588, which could so easily have gone the other way: without denigrating their courage and skill, Elizabeth's sailors sent only one of Philip II's ships to the bottom – the Armada was defeated by divided leadership, and fierce gales. In the words of the chronicler John Speed, 'We were onely delivered by His owne most gracious providence, and not by any policy or power of our owne.' Nevertheless, various paintings of the event, such as the 'Armada portrait' in the National Maritime Museum in Greenwich, the NPG, and Woburn Abbey, glorified an English victory – hardly decisive, given the fact that the Spanish put to sea not just one Armada, but five, at different times over the years. Two other Armadas were also only defeated by the weather.[4]

Enemies of the state were not just from abroad: in 1569 the Northern Earls' rebellion was a serious threat; and there were numerous plots by Catholics to kill the queen and overthrow the state – in one year alone, 1596, there were three such plots. There were also many other issues – religious, political, social, economic, that were a threat to the whole of society, and which also have strong echoes today. Moreover, there were serious health risks, not least the plague, which, terrifyingly, hit both randomly and often. Such issues – compounded by a pitiless and often brutal authoritarian government, supported by a ruthless secret service, and presided over by an unpredictable queen – will emerge as this book unfolds, and will force us to consider how accurate is the mythos of 'Good Queen Bess'.[5] These were just some of the threats that Elizabethans had to learn to live with. This book will show how such issues had an effect on Shakespeare's life and work.

Shakespeare also had strong professional reasons for feeling anxious: there were occasions when his survival hung by a thread – at one point, he faced bankruptcy; on at least two other occasions, he risked the wrath of the authorities; one of his patrons was poisoned; another was imprisoned in the Tower of London, under sentence of death; a fellow-playwright was murdered; another was jailed and narrowly escaped the gallows; a third was brutally tortured so badly that he never recovered. Plays could be censored, banned or burnt, and playwrights could be jailed, or worse. Shakespeare learnt to make sure that what he wrote could be interpreted in different ways, in a process he called *equivocation* – what in this book is called *creative ambiguity*: this meant he could baffle the thought-police by claiming that the meaning was quite different from what they might have thought. The words that Princess Elizabeth cannily wrote when still a teenager, around 1548, when she could have been seen as a possible threat to the reigning incumbents, at a time when to have some claim to the throne could be a death sentence, could have been written by Shakespeare himself:

> It is ... rather characteristic of my nature not only not to say in words as much as I think in my mind, but also, indeed, not to say more than I think.[6]

Creative ambiguity also plays well aesthetically: audiences, or readers, could enjoy untangling the inferences that could be drawn – and indeed arguing over them. They could also enjoy choosing what they would like a text to mean.

There were features of his private life, too, which would have induced anxiety: apart from the natural worry that any absent father and husband would have, he had serious relationship problems, as evidenced from his sonnets. He would also have concerns about his family's safety, for some of his relatives were perceived as having strong Catholic connections, and were not well-placed, with a rabid Catholic hunter on their doorstep. His own father was 'a person of interest', as MI5 now has it, for being a recusant – one who broke the law by not attending church; and his family ties with the Catholic Ardens created a strong feeling of vulnerability; especially when Edward Arden was arrested, and was then hanged, drawn and quartered. His crime: to be a suspect.

How, then, did Shakespeare cope with all these pressures, both public and personal? In his Four Quartets, T.S Eliot declared that 'Humankind cannot bear very much reality'. If that were so, one might think that Shakespeare saw theatre as a way to escape the pressures. There may be elements of truth in this glib explanation: but the more one sees of his work, both his poems and his plays, the more one realises that he deals with anxiety, not by denying, or escaping, reality, but by confronting it. One could say he both speaks truth to power, especially perhaps in his history plays, where he exposes the brutality, greed, ambition and self-interest of Tudor politics. But he also seeks power in facing the truth: acknowledging the existence of all the multiple causes of anxiety that face humanity, as he does, and fighting back, if only by staying alive, becomes an act of defiance.

In doing so, Shakespeare speaks for all of us – we can certainly agree that, in the words of his friend and rival, Ben Jonson, 'He was not of an age, but for all time.' There are many ways in which he remains relevant and important today. Living in the present century, I think that we can claim a special affinity with Shakespeare and our Elizabethan forebears, because we too, have special reasons to be anxious: do they need spelling out? Well, for example, he had the plague; we have had Covid. Elizabethan England did not have to cope with global warming – but a series of bad harvests especially in the 1590s caused immediate hardship. Now, as then, there is an ongoing internal security threat, from different quarters; as in Shakespeare's time, there are also divisions in our society – whether social, political and religious, and even cultural. For example, the yawning gap between haves and have-nots, now, as then, resulting in sporadic outbreaks of discontent, and even violence. As with the Tudors, there are also serious problems in creating a stable relationship with sister nations in mainland Europe. The Tudors had to deal with the refugee issue, as we do; and while no Armada threatens our shores, the shadow of nuclear weapons still lurks.

However, what we share with Shakespeare, above all, is a consciousness of our humanity. The central argument of the great tome *The Invention of the Human*, by the American literary critic Harold Bloom, is that 'Shakespeare invented the human as we continue to know it.'[7] From kings and queens to tinkers and barmaids, fools and knaves, heroes and cowards, victims and survivors, the whole panoply of human diversity is laid before us: Henry V and Falstaff, Hamlet and Hotspur, Romeo and Juliet, Macbeth and Malvolio, Cleopatra and Mistress Quickly, Rosalind and Portia, Shylock and Othello, his rich cast list goes on and on, and every one of them speaks to us all, across all cultures. The first chapter of Bloom's book is justly called 'Shakespeare's Universalism'.

However, the present work is not merely an exercise in 'Bardolatry'. This book looks at the man, his life, his family and contemporaries, and in particular at his works, in the order in which they were written, and the times, politically, when they were written. In this way, readers can trace his development as a playwright and poet: in doing so the book offers a brief treatment of each of Shakespeare's plays and major poems. For those who are not as familiar with Shakespeare as they would like to be, the book offers an overview of his life, and 'tasting sessions' for each of his works; for those who know Shakespeare well, the book offers some surprises, and some different perspectives. It is hoped that readers will receive a renewed impetus to see his plays performed, and to read his poems and plays.

The First Folio: the first collected edition of Shakespeare's plays, collated and published in 1623, seven years after his death

1

WHO WAS SHAKESPEARE?

' ... he that filches from me my good name
Robs me of that which not enriches him,
And makes me poor indeed.'

– Othello

Visitors to London's National Portrait Gallery often head straight for the Tudors and Stuarts collection. Among the wonderful images on display in 'the NPG' is the Ditchley portrait of Queen Elizabeth by Gheeraerts the Younger, circa 1592, her virginal white dress studded with jewels and pearls, her feet firmly planted on a map of England. There are also numerous portraits of her courtiers and royal apparatchiks, including the grand image of William Cecil, First Baron Burghley, exuding power and authority in his flowing red robes, a sinister representation of the spy-master Walsingham, dressed in black, and glamorous paintings of sundry earls and grand ladies – among them leading members of the dramatis personae on the cast-list of Shakespeare's life. Amid this magnificent array of pictures, it is easy to overlook one smaller image, neither grand nor glamorous, of William Shakespeare.

So exactly how did this man, once a mere schoolboy from a small country town manage to become the greatest playwright of his age, if not of all time? How did he acquire the knowledge and skills that anyone writing the great works attributed to him would certainly have needed? Whence came the words that created some of the most subtle poems in the English

The Shakespeare memorial on the wall of Holy Trinity Church, Stratford-upon-Avon

language? Was he really the sole author of these great works? Or, as some believe, was he the greatest literary fraud the world has ever known? This book seeks to answer these questions. First, some hard facts.

The parish register of Holy Trinity Church in Stratford-upon-Avon records that 'Guliemus filius Johannes Shakespeare' was christened on 26 April 1564. The dates of his marriage to 'Anne Hathwey' (1582), and of the birth of his first daughter Susanna in 1583, six months later, are all on public record, as is the birth of twins Hamnet and Judith in February 1585. The marriages and burials of his two daughters, and the death of his son, Hamnet, at the age of eleven, are all on record, as is the day of his death on April 23rd 1616, though how he died is unknown.

It is also well established that he was revered, respected (and occasionally reviled) in his lifetime by many people, known and unknown, including members of his theatre company, and fellow-playwrights, such as his friend and rival Ben Jonson. Two fellow-actors, John Heminges and Henry Condell, put together a collection of his plays in the famous First Folio published seven years after his death in 1623 – a unique tribute to a dramatist. Numerous poems were written in praise of him, and to mourn his passing, including verses by Jonson and Milton: if Shakespeare was a fraud, then a gigantic far-reaching conspiracy existed to back him up.

Many of his business dealings are also well-documented: the purchase of houses, including one of the largest houses in Stratford, New Place, in May 1597, and other property. We know he became very well-off, buying a share in the premier acting company of his age – and, more mundanely, purchasing the corn tithes in local areas in Warwickshire for £440 – a huge sum in those days. Many documents provide information about sundry other business dealings and lawsuits. However, those who question Shakespeare's identity as a poet and playwright frequently refer to the dearth of information around his life in London: however, Marsh provides copious details of records of where he lived, and where he did, or did not, pay taxes.[1] Much more would no doubt have been available if the Globe had not burnt to the ground in 1613; whatever might have been saved from that disaster could have been destroyed in the Great Fire of London in 1666.

There still remain many question marks about Shakespeare's life and works. For example, when was he born? We know that he was baptised on 26 April 1564, but the actual day of his birth is a matter of conjecture. However, it was the usual custom for babies to be christened two or three days after they were born. Conveniently, there is a consensus, driven more by sentiment than evidential support, that he was born on England's national day, St George's Day, on 23 April. Most of us, then, are happy to settle for that. He was lucky to have survived: the great 18th-century researcher Edward Malone estimated that up to a seventh of the population of Stratford died that year of the plague, which hit old people and babies particularly hard.[2] Rutter notes that in the year of his birth, 'the demographics took a dive': only 39 baptisms were recorded in 1564, a reduction of some 50 per cent, and the birth rate did not recover for another three years.[3] The plague could – and did – strike at any moment, and was a persistent cause of anxiety, and often, panic: particularly serious outbreaks occurred in 1582, 1592-3, 1603-4 and 1608-9. The plague, then, is one of the reasons why this book suggests that he lived in an age of anxiety: victims died a hideous death.

There were many other health risks that gave cause for anxiety – not even the highest in the land were immune. Many children did not survive infancy, often dying of tuberculosis or dysentery. Among the afflictions, smallpox was also common: Queen Elizabeth herself contracted it in 1562, and managed to escape with minor scars, but the soldier-poet, Sir Philip Sidney, was badly scarred. Other common diseases included puerperal fever, which killed two of Henry VIII's wives, Jane Seymour and Katherine Parr, and STDs – especially syphilis, known as 'the Great Pox', which in 1630 caused the death, among others, of William Herbert, the Earl of Pembroke, one of Shakespeare's patrons; and, indeed, may have killed Shakespeare.

If there are doubts about Shakespeare's date of birth, there are also doubts about his name. Almost the only samples of his handwriting that we now have are six signatures – all spelt differently. He was baptised as William Shakspere, and that surname was the one used by his three children. But when he got married to Anne Hathaway his name was embarrassingly spelt Shagspere. The names of Shakespeare and his father are spelt differently in numerous legal documents. John Michell in his book *Who Wrote Shakespeare?* records some 57 varieties of Shakespeare's family name, rivalling Mr Heinz's 57 varieties of pickle.[4] Spelling was not standardised until the eighteenth century, when the first authoritative dictionaries emerged.

Almost nothing is known of Shakespeare's early life. But we know a lot about what was happening in Stratford-upon-Avon, and the surrounding area, while he was growing up. Indeed, we also know a great deal about what was happening in Europe, which had a great impact on England. On the continent, there was ongoing conflict, with a dangerous cocktail of political and religious issues, as Catholics and Protestants waged war. Many Protestant refugees from mainland Europe arrived in England: no visas required ... These events had an effect on a small provincial town like Stratford. For example, the sacking of Antwerp in 1576, by mutinous Spanish troops, furious at being unpaid, destroyed the Antwerp Cloth Market, and disrupted one of England's chief exports – cloth.[5] This in turn affected wool traders, and could have impacted on John Shakespeare's business acivities.[6]

The connection with Stratford-upon-Avon began when the playwright's father, John Shakespeare, moved there from nearby Snitterfield to serve an apprenticeship as a glover. The antiquarian John Leland's *Itineraries* (1540) contains this description:

> The towne of Stratford stondithe apon a playne ground upon-Avon. On the right hand or ripe of Avon, as the watar descendithe. It hathe 2. or 3. very lardge stretes, besyde bake lanes. One of the principall stretes ledithe from est to west, anothar from southe to northe. The bysshope of Worcestar is lorde of the towne. The towne is reasonably well buyldyd of tymbar. There is ones a yere a great fayre at Holy-Rode Daye [14. of Sept] The paroch church is a fayre huge piece of worke, and stondithe at the southe end of the towne ... dedicated to the Trinitie.[7]

The Shakespeare family

A great deal is known about Shakespeare's family, and neighbours, thanks largely to Edgar Fripp.[8] More recently, Edmondson and Wells (eds.) have provided more detailed information,[9] and Germaine Greer has given us an insight into the home life of the Shakespeares, in particular a portrait of Anne Hathaway, who is largely ignored in the literature.[10]

Shakespeare's father, John, became a whittawer, a leather worker, and made his living making gloves, and a number of other leather products. He also became an illicit wool trader. John Aubrey claimed that John Shakespeare was a butcher, and that his son William once served as a butcher's apprentice; this story is quite wrong. As Schoenbaum notes, there were strict regulations in Tudor England keeping the two occupations apart – glover and butcher – for health reasons.[11]

From humble beginnings, John Shakespeare became a man of property. In 1557 he married Mary Arden, who came from a prosperous Warwickshire farming family whose origins went back to Anglo-Saxon times. It would have been a Catholic wedding service, for Queen Mary was still on the throne. There were many Catholic families in Warwickshire at the time, and many, like the Ardens, remained so even under Elizabeth's rule. Old habits die hard.

Marrying into the Arden family was definitely a step up, but it was not without risks, for if John Shakespeare was a closet Catholic, the Ardens were well-known as followers of the old faith. In May 1570, one John Felton nailed to the door of the Anglican bishop of London a papal bull excommunicating the queen, and ordering all the queen's Catholic subjects

---

Was John Shakespeare a Catholic?

A number of Shakespeare's in-laws were Catholic, and it has even been claimed that John Shakespeare himself was a closet Catholic. In 1757, a document that appeared to be the last spiritual will of Shakespeare's father was found hidden among the rafters of the house in Henley Street where the Shakespeares once lived. It was signed by 'I, John Shakespeare'

The wording was that of a template will framed by Cardinal Carlo Borromeo which Jesuit priests were supposed to have distributed on visits to England in the 1580s.

Unfortunately, the document no longer exists – but Edward Malone made a copy of it. Many scholars have chosen to believe it to be genuine. Sadly for them, in 2005, Robert Bearman produced evidence that English versions of Borromeo's testament did not appear in England until the 1630s, so the will could not possibly have been that of Shakespeare's father.[12]

Even so, he was certainly baptised as a Catholic, and was brought up as a Catholic, and one does not shed one's religion as though it were an old coat. Later, this book investigates the strong probability that he remained a Catholic. As for William Shakespeare, the jury is out.

not to obey her. No one knows what Felton may or may not have revealed under the state's hideous instruments of torture, but from then on, English Catholics came under increasingly intense suspicion which in time had a direct impact on Mary Arden's family. So began what Greenblatt calls 'the Great Fear – a nightmarish sequence of conspiracy and persecution, plot and counterplot, that continued through Elizabeth's long reign.'[13]

Even so, the marriage appears to have been happy, though as was normal in Tudor times, marred by the death of several children. Their first child, Joan, born in September 1558, died while still in her infancy. A second daughter, Margaret, was born in 1562, but also sadly lived only a few months. William, as we have seen, arrived in April 1564, and survived despite a serious outbreak of the plague. He was followed by a brother, Gilbert, and a sister, also named Joan, the only girl to have survived into adulthood: another baby, Anne, arrived in 1573, and died, aged eight. There were two other younger brothers, Richard, and Edmund. William was the only one to marry and have children. At the time of Shakespeare's birth, his father was a burgess – a man of some standing in Stratford-upon-Avon. The family lived in a house in Henley Street in the centre of the town – a building that still stands today, owned by the Shakespeare Birthplace Trust. A typical late fifteenth-century house, it is constructed of wattle and daub on an oak framework.

Those early years in anyone's life leave their mark: John Shakespeare would have sent his children to elementary or 'petty' school. There, they would have learnt the rudiments of reading, thanks to a horn book: this was a reading aid consisting of a tablet made of oak, with a transparent protective sheet made of horn: on it was inscribed the alphabet, and The Lord's Prayer. From this he would have moved on to read the Ten Commandments and the Creed. All of these by this time were in English, although Queen Elizabeth did allow a Latin version of the Book of Common Prayer.

Apart from petty school, so many things would have been etched on Shakespeare's memory: sharing a bed with his brother, Gilbert, cosying up in the winter to keep warm; the arrival of other brothers, putting his nose out of joint. As the oldest boy in the family, he would have been put in charge – and blamed whenever anything went wrong. No doubt the arrival of a baby sister, Joan, would have delighted him, someone who needed looking after, an ally rather than a rival; and he must have grieved when a second sister, Anne, died far too young, at the age of eight. Perhaps Shakespeare would take Gilbert with him to do a bit of fishing in the river, and maybe develop the habit of silently philosophising as he waited for a catch. As Hamlet was to observe: 'A man may fish with the worm that hath eat of a king, and eat of the fish that hath fed of that worm ... '

What would have lingered longest perhaps were the sounds and smells of childhood: the cooking smells were best – the soups and stews flavoured with herbs from the garden, with small pieces of mutton if you were lucky, or, on a good day, a bit of tender rabbit or chicken, all served with rye bread and home-brewed ale – much safer to drink than water. Like most households, Mary Arden would have brewed up in a small malthouse adjoining the kitchen, and the smell would have been pervasive if it had not been for John Shakespeare's job as a whittawer: the stench of sheep's leather in the nearby pits, softening in a solution of dung or urine, would have overwhelmed all others. Even if the leather was finally tanned it would still have smelt – and the stink would have clung to one's clothes: in bed, even, you could not have escaped it. Very believable then, Germaine Greer's speculation that Mary Shakespeare might have tried to persuade her husband to gradually phase out the whittawing, to concentrate on dealing in wool instead.[14]

Other memories would have included the sounds of childhood – the wretched cock that woke you every morning, the hens chattering as they scratched the earth, the tittle-tattle of gossips on the street, the bellowing of cattle in the abattoir, not forgetting the deathly creaking of the wagon carrying off the bodies of plague victims and the mournful cry: 'Bring out your dead!'

Portraits of Shakespeare

Uncertainty about how to spell Shakespeare's name is compounded by question marks about what he looked like. There have been numerous attempts to put a face on our greatest playwright, and there have been many claims and counter-claims as to which likeness is the most authentic. Time to look again at that image in the National Portrait Gallery, and a

The Droeshout Engraving of Shakespeare

The Chandos portrait of Shakespeare, so-called because it formerly belonged to the 3rd Duke of Chandos; painted between 1600-1610

smaller one, a rather poor image of Shakespeare created after his death: this is the Droeshout engraving that appears in the First Folio of Shakespeare's plays published in 1623.

The First Folio was compiled by the playwright's fellow-actors John Heminges and Henry Condell, and dedicated to the 'incomparable pair of bretheren' (William Herbert, the 3rd Earl of Pembroke, and his brother, Philip, Earl of Montgomery later the 4th Earl of Pembroke). The NPG catalogue describes the image as appearing in a later issue of the First Folio and is assigned the reference number 185.

This is the image popularised by Andy Warhol, and will be familiar to most readers, appearing as it does on merchandise such as T-shirts, biscuit tins and mugs. No one could claim that it is of very high quality. There were, in fact, two Martin Droeshouts: Uncle Martin (an accomplished engraver), and his 20-year-old nephew with the same name. The whole image has the smack of a caricature done by an amateur. This engraving could be the work of the nephew, a young man who never met Shakespeare; it could well be the shoddy work of two engravers, one for the head, and an 'off-the-peg' one for the body. This would account for the asymmetrical shoulders, the ill-sorted arms, and the buttons on the doublet that seem out of alignment.[15]

Close by, there is another somewhat nondescript painting of Shakespeare, known as the Chandos portrait, so-called because it was once in the possession of Lord Chandos. Art historians are certain that it was painted in Shakespeare's life-time, probably by an amateur, a fellow-actor of Shakespeare's named Joseph Taylor. The unpretentious rough-hewn quality of this portrait gives it the smack of authenticity. It portrays a Shakespeare just out of costume, slightly dishevelled, as though posing between productions of a play; his face may still bear traces of make-up. Somewhat swarthy, perhaps: some have suggested that he may have been playing the part of Shylock. The ring in his ear, and the unlaced collar, give a slightly raffish air, appropriate, one may dare suggest, for a man of the theatre. Katherine Duncan-Jones has traced its history, and reminds us of its impressive provenance: among those who owned it was Thomas Betterton, a well-known Jacobean actor, and Sir William Davenant, who claimed Shakespeare as his godfather – indeed some have hinted that he was his natural son. The evidence that this is as close as we will ever get to a true likeness of Shakespeare is pretty compelling.[16]

These images are not the only ones on offer. Well-known is the monument to Shakespeare in Westminster Abbey unveiled in January 1741, following a fund-raising campaign by the Shakespeare Ladies Club.[17] Then there is the bust of Shakespeare in the chancel of Holy Trinity Church in Stratford-upon-Avon. Erected seven years after Shakespeare's death, it is not clear whether it is based on an actual likeness of Shakespeare made while he was still living. Indeed, at that time, accuracy was not always the most important feature of a painting or sculpture: as Duncan-Jones observes, 'Whether fashioned in late antiquity or in the Renaissance, the very earliest author portraits tend to be symbolic rather than naturalistic.'[18] Not just authors: in a king, nobility would be highlighted in any representation; in a soldier, strength; in a bishop, or a saint, piety; in a busy mercantile centre like Stratford, one's standing as a businessman. In a provincial town, financial success would have been seen as a more important attribute for Shakespeare than literary achievement, and so in the church we have an image resembling, in Dover-Wilson's words, 'an affluent and retired pork butcher' that 'does gross wrong to the dead poet.'[19] The effigy has none of the lines, generated either by laughter or pain, one could have expected on the face of a creative writer agonising over his art. The Stratford 'bust' is almost universally detested by Shakespeare lovers, though Orlin has suggested that he may well have commissioned the bust himself.[20] Does this mean she thinks Shakespeare saw himself as a pork-butcher? No, I think that the Chandos portrait wins the competition, hands down.

The Cobbe controversy could in a way be a compelling metaphor for a great deal of the writing about Shakespeare: for four hundred years, scholars have been bedevilled by the urge to define Shakespeare in the image they would like to have of him. Some have wanted him to be a genius – a view that this writer happens to share; others, more restrained, that he was a scholar if not quite perhaps a gentleman. That he was an actor, a playwright and a poet is beyond doubt, though not everyone agrees on which poems and plays he wrote; that he was the author of some of the finest works for the theatre ever written is also generally acknowledged, though this book (citing the research of many

Mystery of the Cobbe portrait

Some Bardolaters have felt that the Chandos picture hardly does justice to our greatest poet and dramatist. So the hunt has been on for more august pictures of Shakespeare, and, in 2009 'the Cobbe portrait' was triumphantly produced – so-called because it was once owned by Charles Cobbe, Anglican Archbishop of Dublin.

It is without question a fine picture and it is certainly Jacobean. The painting was 'unveiled' at the English-Speaking Union in March 2010 as the true likeness of William Shakespeare, having been exhibited first at the Shakespeare Birthplace Trust in Stratford in 2009; two years later, it went on show at the Morgan Library and Museum, New York. It can now be viewed in a National Trust property, Hatchlands Park in Surrey, but there are several copies, including one in the Bodleian Library, Oxford. The portrait is clearly that of a very well-off patrician: that skin was never sullied with greasepaint, while that beard certainly could only have been kept so trim by a personal groomer; the lace collar, the rich attire, all betoken an aristocrat of senior rank, not a man of the theatre.

The Folger library,[21] and Dr Tanya Cooper, curator of 16th-century pictures at the NPG in London, now agree that the Cobbe portrait is that of Sir Thomas Overbury. Sir Thomas was an interesting man, not least for having been murdered by his wife while he was imprisoned in the Tower of London;[22] but he was definitely not William Shakespeare.

The Cobbe portrait is sometimes claimed to be a portrait of Shakespeare, but is now widely acknowledged to be that of Sir Thomas Overbury

Shakespearian scholars) will show that a number of his plays were produced in collaboration with others.

Those of a more sceptical bent view him more prosaically: that he was a businessman, a money-lender, and an entrepreneur is also supported by the evidence of his various financial transactions. And there are also those who have formed a much less flattering view: to his critics, he has been seen as a drunken lecher, a crook, a fraudster, a plagiarist, a racist, a social climber, a misogynist and a sodomite. Some of these characteristics are given him, with affectionate humour, by comedian and writer Ben Elton in the popular – and very amusing – TV series *Upstart Crow* starring David Mitchell and Liza Tarbuck.[23] But he has also been viewed as an extraordinarily gifted observer of lover and a respecter of women – no other playwright of the time has a richer and more subtly-drawn cast of female characters. He has also been seen as an anti-racist (the noble, if tragically flawed, Othello), and a master of empathy;[24] but, also, as antisemitic (though compare his *Merchant of Venice* with Marlowe's satanic *Jew of Malta*). Some of these claims and counter-claims will be examined later in this book. However, at least one question is answered in these pages: how did Shakespeare manage to survive, and prosper, in the turbulent political and religious conflicts that dominated much of Tudor England in what we call, in this book, with some justification, an Age of Anxiety?

This book seeks to show that Shakespeare was shaped by, and helped to shape, the society in which he lived, troubled as it was by many causes of anxiety – of which the threat to health and well-being was only one. This book treats his life and work chronologically, so that his development as a person, and as a writer, is seen in the context of the time he lived in. Readers should be warned that at times, it is necessary to play detective. It is hoped that readers will enjoy joining in the investigations, and exploring the extracts from his work written during the reign of Elizabeth I. But we start with a look at his early life – how the child became father to the man – and the so-called 'lost years' of Shakespeare's life.

2

THE EARLY YEARS

Youth: the more it is wasted, the sooner it wears
– *Falstaff: Henry IV, Act II, iv*

This was a complicated time in English history, and national politics, and to understand how the whole nation was affected, including the people of Stratford-upon-Avon, it is necessary to look back briefly at preceding events. Following Henry VIII's break with Rome, radical Protestantism took over under Edward VI, and churches were vandalised, as 'idolatrous', images were destroyed.[1] Even so, much of the country remained at heart Catholic, and Queen Mary was at first welcomed; but as Protestant bishops were burnt at the stake, guilty of 'heretical beliefs', she became feared and loathed as 'Bloody Mary'. With the accession of Queen Elizabeth in 1558, the pendulum swung against both radical Protestantism and oppressive Roman Catholicism. Elizabeth inaugurated a more tolerant regime: she had no wish, in Francis Bacon's words, to 'make windows into men's hearts and secret thoughts.' For a long time, many people, including many members of the clergy, still clung to the rituals of the old faith despite the 1559 Act of Uniformity which introduced a moderate form of Protestantism.

All these conflicting events had a profound effect on society. For ten years, Elizabeth trod the path of relative moderation. Although the 1559 Act imposed various punishments – fines, property confiscation and imprisonment – for those who did not attend Church of England services, they applied to both Catholics and Puritans, and for a time a blind eye was

Engraving of a Tudor schoolroom [private collection Bridgeman Library]

turned on offenders. Elizabeth herself attended services that were more Catholic than Protestant in flavour.

At this time, Protestants and Catholics lived side by side with little animosity. Stratford was a tangled web of friendships that seem to have crossed religious lines. Although Fripp[2] describes the town as predominantly Protestant, there is some reason to doubt this. A significant number of prominent Catholic families lived in and around the town – including, as we have seen, the Ardens. The Old Faith stubbornly clung on, not least in the highest echelons of society. The historian Lawrence Stone tells us that, even after the queen's excommunication

> In 1580 there were 66 English peers: 20 of these were Catholic recusants, about 10 were of strongly Puritan sympathies, about a dozen were supporters of the Anglican settlement, and the remaining 24 were relatively indifferent to religious issues and anxious only to back the winner.[3]

If Catholicism persisted among so many members of the aristocracy,

> **The poisonous potion: Religion and Politics**
>
> National politics became more complicated after 1568, when Mary Stuart, Queen of Scots, a Catholic, fled from Scotland to seek refuge in England. There were justified fears that she might prove a rallying point for Catholic sympathisers, and she was held in protective custody for some nineteen years. There followed a series of Catholic plots against the Crown, beginning with the Rebellion of the Northern Earls in 1569, and the Ridolfi plot of 1569-1571, aimed at a coup aided by Spanish troops; this entailed a plan for Mary Stuart to marry the Duke of Norfolk, who was duly executed.
>
> As we have seen, the situation was not helped by the 1570 Papal Bull excommunicating the queen. Queen Elizabeth and her ministers now saw Catholics as threats to the state, and those who still held to the old faith – many in and around Stratford – became increasingly uneasy. Sadly, the way the law worked under the Tudors, to be a suspect often meant that you were deemed guilty.

how deeply imbued was it in the general populace? England remained in a state of flux. There were endless religious (and political) upheavals. As a result, there was a persistent sense of anxiety in the days of 'Good Queen Bess': politics and religion – who could distinguish one from the other? Many people did not know what to believe. Apart from the religious uncertainty, and the continual threat from continental Europe, there were deep concerns about the succession, too: who would succeed the queen when she died? As early as 1567, one MP observed: 'If God should take her Majestie, the succession being not established, I know not what shall become of myself, my wife, my children, lands, goods, friends or country.'

The Shakespeares could not remain unaffected by all the swings of the religious pendulum: a number of Shakespeare's in-laws were Catholic, and as we saw in Chapter 1, John Shakespeare himself was probably at least a Catholic sympathiser – his Catholic sympathies trumped for a while at least by his survival instinct. He was certainly eclectic in his friendships: the Town Clerk, Thomas Green, a Protestant, was a friend of his, as was the Catholic Reynolds family.[4] Despite the many Catholic plots, and the on-going threat from Catholic Spain, such friendships were common, though they became increasingly strained as the years passed.

From Yeoman to Bailiff

Somehow, whatever his beliefs, John Shakespeare managed to avoid controversy. In July 1559, he became one of the town's fourteen aldermen, which meant a big step up in the Tudor hierarchy: he was now to be addressed as 'Master Shakespeare'.[5] No longer a mere yeoman! Then, between 1561 and 1565 he went on to become chamberlain. This was a highly responsible position that required him to keep the town's accounts, and look after the property and revenues of Stratford Corporation.

However, even if he simply had Catholic sympathies because of his connection with the Arden family, he would have found some of his public duties hard to square with his conscience. For it fell to him to enact Queen Elizabeth's Act of Uniformity which sought to impose some kind of Protestant orthodoxy – including a requirement to attend church regularly. There was one task in particular that he had to perform as part of his civic responsibilities: the destruction of the mediaeval paintings that adorned the Guild Chapel, which were deemed reminders of the old faith.[6] This must have caused great pain not just to him, but to his extended family, as well as to many members of the town's community. To treasure such artefacts certainly did not mean that you were an ardent Papist, but these images spoke to people more loudly than words from a pulpit, and many were sad to lose them. It must have been with a heavy heart that he watched the workmen covering the beloved images of St George and the Dragon, and other saints, with whitewash.

Another of John Shakespeare's tasks was less painful: the supervision of the building of a new schoolroom above the Guildhall. When he became Bailiff of Stratford, it is virtually certain that a man in his position would have sent his son to Stratford-upon-Avon Grammar School.[7] So it is to the education of young William Shakespeare that we now turn.

William the schoolboy

The grammar school received a royal charter from Edward VI in 1553, with the name 'the Kyng's new Scole'. This was no ordinary grammar school: its teachers were highly educated Oxford graduates, and were paid more than the heads of Eton. At this school, the boys (sadly, no girls) had quite a tough regime: work started at 6.00 am, and finished at 5.00pm five-and-a-half days a week, 44 weeks a year. (Thursdays were just half a day). This meant that the boys had to attend for some 2,000 hours a year – about double of what obtains today. Not every boy would have stayed the course. As Greenblatt observes:

the instruction was not gentle: rote memorization, relentless drills, endless repetition, daily analysis of texts, elaborate exercises in imitation and rhetorical variation, all backed up by the threat of violence.[8]

They were required to speak Latin – they were punished if they spoke English. Although there was a great deal of rote learning, Rowse points out that memorizing a text every day was good practice in memory training for a future actor.[9] There were frequent tests and exams, and even small offences resulted in a whipping. This regime had to be endured up to the age of fourteen.

The curriculum was infused with the spirit of humanism that derived particularly from Erasmus, and which emphasised the teaching of virtue and wisdom found in the ancients.[10] The timetable included Latin grammar and literature, as well as rhetoric. On entering grammar school, the boys worked through Lyly's *A Short Introduction of* [Latin] *Grammar*. They moved on to Cato's *Distichs* (basically, moral precepts), and Aesop's fables – followed by Cicero's letters, Caesar, the literary dialogues of Erasmus, the plays of Plautus, and Terence, and stories from Ovid's *Metamorphoses* – all in Latin. The influence of Ovid, in particular, can be seen in many of Shakespeare's plays, as well as his poetry.[11] As well as reading such texts, students were taught the elements of composition, and translation, and in some schools enacted scenes from Plautus' plays.

Later on, students would study Virgil, Horace and Quintilian, and would be asked to translate passages from the Geneva Bible, and extracts from writers such as Ovid into English. As Wells and Taylor observe in their introduction to the 2005 Oxford edition of the *Complete Works*,[12] the young graduate from a Tudor grammar school was likely to know more Latin than the modern-day university graduate in classics. It is worth remembering that no fewer than thirteen of Shakespeare's plays – a third of his dramatic output – were based on, or derived from, classical literature.

William was clearly a star pupil at the grammar school as indicated in Sonnets 153 and 154, written while at school some time before 1582. It is thought that they were schoolboy translation exercises of a fifth-century Latin poem. (This book follows Edmondson and Wells in considering the sonnets in the order in which they were composed according to recent research – not the order in which they appeared in the 1609 collection).[13] It is amazing that a young man in his teens should have been able to produce work of this quality – probably among the first that he ever wrote. In their edition, Edmondson and Wells put Sonnet 153 in second place after Sonnet 154 on the basis that it is an improved version. Readers are invited to reach their own conclusion. To my mind, both show a very high degree of poetic intelligence. Readers may like to compare the two sonnets, and form their own judgement.

> Cupid laid by his brand, and fell asleep:
>   A maid of Dian's this advantage found,
> And his love-kindling fire did quickly steep
>   In a cold valley-fountain of that ground;
> Which borrow'd from this holy fire of Love
>   A dateless lively heat, still to endure,
> And grew a seething bath, which yet men prove
>   Against strange maladies a sovereign cure.[14]
> But at my mistress' eye Love's brand new-fired,
>   The boy for trial needs would touch my breast;
> I, sick withal, the help of bath desired,
>   And thither hied, a sad distemper'd guest,
>   But found no cure: the bath for my help lies
>   Where Cupid got new fire – my mistress' eyes.
>
>   – Sonnet 153

For those staying the course, the ethos of a good grammar school could have a dramatic impact on the students. In Robert Miola's words, most significantly, grammar school training

> fostered certain habits of reading, thinking, and writing that would have spilled over into the students' writing in English. They acquired extraordinary sensitivity to language, especially in sound[15]

As they progressed, students were also expected to give speeches, and take part in debates and act in plays, developing the rhetorical skills Shakespeare learnt, and practised – in Latin. These were not just verbal 'tricks of the trade': Rutter points out that this element of the school curriculum involved 'delivering *ethopoeia*',[16] or empathy, the ability to see the world through other people's eyes, and therefore understand their behaviour. *Ethopoeia* is exactly what is required to develop emotional literacy. Indeed, one Dr Ian Jeffrey, writing in the *The Journal of the Royal Society of Medicine*, prescribes a study of Shakespeare for doctors in training, to develop ethopoeia.[17] So it was at school that Shakespeare began to develop the sensitivity and imagination that enabled him to enter into the minds of other characters, and the language to give them voice.

The play's the thing ...

Amid all the political upheaval, it is not surprising that in Queen Elizabeth's reign, there was a concerted campaign to control theatrical performances. To start with, the campaign had a religious agenda: the traditional Mystery Plays commonly reenacted across the country were thought to foster the old religion, and over time were banned despite strong local opposition.[18] It is thought that Shakespeare probably saw one of the last performances of a Mystery Play at Coventry (only twenty miles from Stratford) before the ban finally took effect. (In Act 3 of *Hamlet*, the eponymous hero urges the actors to 'out-Herod Herod' – a favourite villain who loomed large in these plays.) One imagines a Tudor audience shouting 'Look out! Behind you!' in best pantomime tradition when he appeared ...

As these plays became a thing of the past, a secular dramatic tradition developed, involving professional actors, and venturing into new genres. Many churchmen saw this as subversive – the stage was seen as a rival to the pulpit. In their own terms, they were right to be concerned – the new drama that was emerging was probably a far greater threat to the state than the old Mystery Plays, because it focused, or enabled a focus on, not old Bible stories, but events more recent, and even current, and thus touched on the political. Accordingly, a campaign to control drama steadily gained ground. From 1579 onwards, the Master of the Revels had the power to censor plays. (The Stationers' Register which licensed new publications already had some control over printed material). The authorities also saw the need for legal instruments to keep the reins on strolling players; the 1572 Vagabonds Act, was one of a series of such measures:

> All common players ... and minstrels not belonging to any baron of this realm, or to any other honourable personage of greater degree ... shall be deemed rogues, vagabonds and sturdy beggars[19]

The penalties were severe. Actors on tour could only escape whipping if they had an insurance policy, in the form of a document showing that they were supported by a noble sponsor from members of the aristocratic establishment. Many nobles kept groups of players as part of their household, to give in-house performances (called 'closet drama'). For example, Lord Hunsdon, the queen's cousin, formed his own group in the 1560s.

In their time in the 1570s and 1580s, the Earl of Leicester's Men was the leading acting company. The company already did closet drama, and so when James Burbage asked the earl to sponsor them for public performance he was pushing at an open door; in 1574, Leicester's Men were granted the first Royal Warrant after the Act of 1572. No direct financial support from the earl was involved. The troupe performed both in the provinces, and in London, where, until custom-built theatres sprang up, they performed at inns. Other troupes followed suit. It was not until 1583 that the authorities realized that drama could be used to burnish the queen's image, and the Queen's Men also received a Royal Warrant.

In 1569, as Bailiff, John Shakespeare gave permission to two companies of professional actors from London to perform in Stratford – one was a group of doubtful provenance calling itself the Queen's Men, who were paid a very handsome nine shillings for a performance. The second group, the Earl of Worcester's Men; were rewarded with a paltry shilling.[20] Other touring companies also visited Stratford-upon-Avon. The arrival of these groups would have held a small boy like William spell-bound: the players arrived to the sound of trumpets and drums, wearing their colourful liveries. Watching these performances would certainly have played an important part of Shakespeare's education, and extended his sense of life's possibilities; they would have also given him an insight into many features of Tudor theatre: high drama, low comedy, duelling, wrestling, acrobatics, music, pageants, dumbshows[21] (as in *Hamlet*), jigs, songs. To start with, performances were often developments of old-fashioned morality plays, with characters with names like Youth, Pride, Lechery, Idleness and Iniquity, but there were also some home-spun domestic dramas frequently about clueless husbands, unfaithful wives, and lecherous priests and monks. They surely left their mark on young Shakespeare. Some of these characters were not a million miles away from Shakespeare's own creations such as Iago in *Othello*. Richard III likens himself to 'Iniquity', and Falstaff, well, he manages to embody a satisfying salad of vices. In Shakespeare's hands, they become interesting well-rounded characters, rather than cardboard caricatures.

Financial problems?

Something strange happened in the mid-seventies: John Shakespeare, who as an alderman had been a regular attender at council meetings ('the halls'), was suddenly repeatedly marked absent; he also stopped going to church on Sundays. There is also a persistent story that Shakespeare left King's New School early. According to Nicolas Rowe, his premature departure from school was due to the 'narrowness' of his father's circumstances, 'and the want of his assistance at Home, forc'd his father to withdraw him from thence ... into his own Employment.'[22]

Many authorities have followed Rowe in suggesting that the reasons for his absenteeism from church were financial. Greenblatt notes that in the closing decades of the sixteenth century there was something of a recession in the Midlands – and there was little demand for elegant gloves. It has been speculated that John Shakespeare minimized public appearances, in council meetings, and at church, in case an official, or a creditor, seized the opportunity to arraign him for debt. (A favourite time for sheriffs to seize a debtor or fine-evader was at church on Sundays.) However, there is no evidence to suggest that John Shakespeare was dodging debt-collectors. On the contrary, he was a money-lender: according to informers, he made loans of up to £100 – a huge sum, over £60,000 in today's money.[23] Fallow notes he had no difficulty in paying any fines incurred.[24]

In addition to money-lending, more seriously, John Shakespeare was for years heavily involved in illegal wool-trading. His business may have taken a hit in the mid-1570s, when there were wool shortages, and the authorities decided that that it was the fault of the illegal wool-dealers, the broggers as they were called.[25] In October 1576, wool-broggers were called in for questioning, and the following month, all wool trading was (theoretically) suspended. Worse still, in 1577, all wool-broggers had to post bonds of £100 as a surety against future illegal dealings: apparently,

John paid up. Bearman suggests that it was his dealings in wool which were the main source of any financial problems he might have had.[26]

However, there is a mystery about John Shakespeare: Fallow casts doubt on whether he in fact had serious financial problems. The man has been successful, acquiring property, and handling large sums of money. In 1575, he bought two more houses, with orchards and land attached. Are these the actions of a man running desperately short of money? Yet, according to the popular narrative, it appears that he suddenly, apparently, runs short of cash. Duncan-Jones refers to his 'declining fortunes' and 'crippling debt'.[27]

As Fallow observes, 'The years after 1576 saw a flurry of asset disposal into "friendly" hands'.[28] John started mortgaging property, and selling off land to relatives – for example, around 1578 he mortgaged the land (in Wilmcote) that his wife, Mary Arden, had brought with her to their marriage, to Mary's brother-in-law, Edmund Lambert. Later, in 1579, he sold family farmland in Snitterfield, for a mere £4.00.[29] Yet after 1576, even though he stopped attending council meetings, his fellow-townsmen kept him on as an alderman until 1586 – perhaps to afford him a degree of protection from harassment for not attending church. Indeed, he remained a person of good standing, performing jury service twice. A plausible explanation may be provided by events on the political stage.

Events both at home and abroad had repercussions for Catholics in England. The persecution of the Huguenots in France, and the extreme repressive measures against Protestants in the Low Countries, caused many to fear that similar events could occur in England – and fears too for the queen's safety. There were increased concerns about plots, real or imaginary – and a crackdown on recusancy. In 1576 the Privy Council established an ecclesiastical commission to inquire into

> singular, heretical erroneous and offensive opinions ... and to order, correct, reform and punish any persons willfully and obstinately absenting themselves from church and service

The next year, the newly-appointed Bishop of Worcester John Whitgift arrived in Stratford to root out heretics. It was noted that

Recusants convey all their lands and goods to friends, and are relieved by those which have other lands ... [or] demise their land to certain tenants[30]

Under these circumstances, for John Shakespeare to stop attending church was tempting fate, indeed. It seems more than possible that his absenteeism was for religious reasons, and that he feared that his property might be confiscated as a result. Surely this explains why he was transferring ownership of his property into friendly hands? That seems to me to be the most likely explanation. It seems very likely that he was indeed a Catholic. He had good reason to be nervous, for the whole area was becoming notorious for locals following the old faith. In 1575, one of William's teachers, Simon Hunt, who made no secret of being a Catholic, took off to the Continent to became a Jesuit – taking with him a former student at the School, Robert Debdale, whose family lived in Shottery (he was possibly a distant relation of the Shakespeares). Hunt was followed by Jenkins, a graduate of St John's College, Cambridge, well-known for its Catholic sympathies.[31] He was succeeded in 1579 by John Cottam, another Catholic, who had a younger brother, Thomas, who left to become a Jesuit. Secretly returning to England, Thomas Cottam was picked up on his way to visit the Debdale family – neighbours of the Hathaways in Shottery. Cottam was brutally tortured, and then, in 1580, hanged, drawn and quartered. Debdale was also arrested, and then freed in 1582, probably to enable the authorities to identify his contacts. These events must have caused shockwaves among the whole community in and around Stratford-upon-Avon.

So why did John Shakespeare pull his brilliant son out of school early – if he did? Did he fear that his son might become dangerously associated with his Catholic teacher? No one knows; nor is anyone certain what William might then have done. There are various possibilities. Readers may like to consider which of the following is most likely, given that very little evidence is on offer.

The first lost years

There were two periods in Shakespeare's life when we really do not know what he did, or where he went. The 'first lost years' refer to the period in his life between leaving school, and his marriage in November 1582. The 'second lost years' refers to the period following his marriage, before he arrived in London.

Although we do not know exactly when William left school, it is likely that he did so in about 1578. There are numerous theories – but no certainties, about what he did next, but no one should doubt that, for John Shakespeare, wool-brogging was more important than wool-gathering, and writing sonnets. It would certainly have been natural and normal for Shakespeare to help out his father in carrying on his business. As whittawing was not a job for a young man who could read and write, it is more likely that he helped out in the wool-brogging operation. His father would have been keen on him learning how it all worked, possibly in case William had to take over if he was arrested. The plays do show familiarity with some of the technicalities of the wool trade (e.g. the shepherd in *The Winter's Tale*).

It is less likely that, as has been suggested, Shakespeare's father may have used his influence to get his son a job in a local lawyer's office. Schoenbaum observes that a former teacher at the grammar school, Walter Roche, started a lawyer's practice in Stratford, and Shakespeare's father may have used his influence to get his son a job that used his writing skills.[32] Such theories have been questioned, on the grounds that in a lawyer's office he would have had to witness signatures on numerous documents, none of which have ever been found. Although his plays show some familiarity with some legal terminology, Shakespeare could easily have picked this up from his father's endless legal disputes – and chatting with Inns of Court students, who were eager theatre-goers.

John Aubrey has a different theory: writing in 1660, he reports that 'he had been in his younger years a Schoolmaster in the Countrey.'[33] Perhaps through the agency of one of his teachers at the grammar school – several of whom were Catholic – he was found a position as a tutor in a Catholic family in Hoghton Towers in Lancashire.[34] If his father was indeed a Catholic, he may well have encouraged his son to take up a position in that household, where he might have been employed both as a tutor and actor, for Alexander Hoghton was keen on closet drama. However, Hoghton died within a year or so of Shakespeare's arrival; in his will Hoghton singled out one 'William Shakeshafte' for special recognition. Whether Shakeshafte was another name for *Shakespeare* is much disputed. 'Shakeshafte' was a very common name in Lancashire, and it does not appear on John Michell's list of spellings of Shakespeare's name alluded to in Chapter 1. Furthermore, why a newly-recruited young tutor should have deserved special recognition among 40-odd other servants is not clear, and Schoenbaum and others give the suggestion little credence.[35]

What else might young Shakespeare in this period? In Tudor times – in any times – this was an age when a young man's fancy lightly turned to thoughts of mischief, or, as the shepherd in *The Winter's Tale* says, when there is 'nothing but getting wenches with childe, wronging the Ancientry, stealing, fighting.' The shepherd doesn't mention drinking: but we have every reason to suppose that young Will did his fair share of drinking good Warwickshire brown ale – if only because it was safer to drink than water. We do not know if he over-indulged – but what young man, throughout the ages, could ever be described as guiltless in this respect? The *British Magazine* of 1762 by 'anon' describes how the landlord of *The White Lion* recalled how young Will Shakespeare was said to have got drunk on the way to a local village, Bidford, and, overcome, had spent hours sleeping under a crab-tree. Typical pub talk, who knows. But if he did occasionally over-indulge, it would be no surprise: par for the course for any young man. If it is true, at least he had the good sense not to get drunk on his home territory, where he might have ended up in the stocks – or worse, at the Whipping-post at the High Cross in the centre of Stratford – alluded to by Grumio in *The Taming of the Shrew*. However, the favourite theory is that young William fell in love – which leads us to the next chapter: his courtship, marriage, and the impact that it had on his life.

3

THE FAMILY MAN

> The course of true love never did run smooth
> – Lysander: Act I.i Midsummer Night's Dream

Whatever else Shakespeare did as a young man, in the long summer evenings of 1582, he must at some time have made his way along the verdant lanes of Warwickshire to rendezvous with Anne Hathaway. Was she his sweetheart – or were they both just having a fling? That we shall never know – but that has not stopped endless speculation. Shottery, where Anne used to live, was little more than a small group of farmhouses, about a mile west of Stratford-upon-Avon. It was hereabouts that the young man, scarcely 18 years old, dallied with Anne Hathaway, also known as Agnes, (the names are interchangeable – the G in Agnes is silent). She was eight years his senior, and was the last remaining daughter of Richard Hathwey, a yeoman farmer. As the first-born, Anne would have been called on to help look after her younger siblings, and this may have played a part in causing her to be the last to leave home.

The Hathaway family lived in Hewlands Farm, a large timber-framed farmhouse built on stone foundations, dating probably from the late fourteenth century. Hewlands Farm was bought by Anne's grandfather in 1543; his son, Richard, Anne's father, inherited the land in 1566. Richard Hathaway died in September 1581; his second wife, Joan, who had four small children, was left to look after the farm: very handy to have Anne to

Holy Trinity Church, Stratford-upon-Avon

help out. In Richard's will he bequeathed 'unto Agnes my daughter six pounds thirteen shillings four pence to be paid unto her at the day of her marriage.'

Courtship

The Hathaways and the Shakespeares were well known to each other.[1]

Speculation abounds on how the relationship between Anne and William developed. Anthony Burgess's biographical novel *Nothing Like the Sun* constructs a whole narrative round the myth that Shakespeare was in love with a different woman.[2] A lurid story of his courtship and marriage emerges in Burgess's later biography of Shakespeare,[3] which reveals that Burgess was a better novelist than he was a historian. He takes some delight in demolishing the image that those Bernard Shaw described as 'Bardolaters' liked to have of Shakespeare, whom they tended to idealise. Certain grand literary critics of the nineteenth century chose to ignore the Anne Hathaway story (as it has largely been over the centuries), or to mention the degree to which Shakespeare's plays were sanitised in the nineteenth century ... In his poem on Shakespeare, Matthew Arnold describes him as 'the immortal spirit'; to Ruskin, Shakespeare was 'the greatest master ... whose books lay open on the table all day', and each of his plays 'had a simple and grand purpose ... '. Their view is very far removed from the raunchy version provided by Burgess who gleefully depicts the relationship between Will and Anne as one of 'wanton fornication' probably carried out in a field of rye in high summer, or, as *As You Like It* had it, of a lover and his lass:

> Between the acres of the rye
> With a hey, and a ho and a hey nonino
> Those pretty country folk would lie,
> In spring time ...

The Burgess account, then, sees the relationship starting with a quick 'roll in the hay'. He suggests that 'the lovely boy'– auburn hair, melting eyes, ready tongue with tags of Latin poetry – did not, having tasted Anne's body in the spring, go eagerly back to Shottery through the early summer to taste it again.'[4] Did not go back? This, he suggests, is because he had fallen in love with another woman, Anne Whately, and that his relationship with Hathaway was one of opportunistic lust resulting in a shotgun marriage. This story as we shall see is totally unfounded. Burgess goes on to suggest that the young man, not the first to be so ensnared, fell victim to an older woman's wiles: Anne Hathaway set her cap at William, in the hope that 'one way of finding a husband was to become impregnated by a man, who, having done the indecent thing, would then proceed perhaps with threats in his ears or a gun in his back, to do the decent.'

So, a love-match – or a shotgun job? Possibly both. It seems likely that the Shakespeare family were not overjoyed about him getting married so early in life – and under such circumstances. Nevertheless, as William was a minor, his father would have had to give his assent to the marriage. Anne's family might have hoped for a more suitable husband – and had reservations about this young man who it seemed had few prospects; on the other hand, they might have felt pleased that she had found someone at an age when most women would have been left on the shelf.

In her novel *Hamnet*, Maggie O'Farrell has an interesting take on the story, but with no evidential basis: she imagines a situation where the pair fall in love with each other, but both families oppose the marriage, and the pair decide to have a child together to force the issue.⁵ Anne's family would have been relieved that he was willing to make a respectable woman of her, once she became pregnant: for William could have bolted, run off to join a group of players in London, or off to sea. Or he could have denied that he was the father, like Bertram in *All's Well that Ends Well*. When Diana claims that he had taken her virginity, Bertram responds:

> She's impudent, my lord,
> And was a common gamester to the camp.
> – Act 5, Scene 3

Greenblatt has suggested that 'an unmarried mother in the 1580s did not, as she would in the 1880s, routinely face fierce, unrelenting social stigmatization.'⁶ Well, it is possible that an unmarried mother might go unnoticed in a busy city like London; but in small town Tudor England, where everyone knew everyone, she could not have escaped wagging tongues, and both families would have felt a sense of shame. Even so, society was generally tolerant, provided marriage preceded birth, though the authorities were concerned largely on financial grounds:

> ... the basic source of parochial concern was the fear that the bastard child, and perhaps the mother as well, would burden the poor rates.⁷

Germaine Greer cites two cases where men 'harboured' unmarried mothers; in one case, the man was excommunicated; in another, a father who supported his own pregnant daughter was dragged to the Vicar's court.⁸

Greenblatt suggests that Shakespeare was a reluctant bridegroom.⁹ All too often such theories are supported by selective quotes from Shakespeare, and might have shared the views of the Duke in *Twelfth Night*:

> Let still the woman take
> An elder than herself, so wears she to him
> So sways she level in her husband's heart
> ...
> Then let thy love be younger than thyself,
> Or thy affection cannot hold the bent;
> For women are as roses, whose fair flower
> Being once display'd, doth fall that very hour.
> – TN Act 2, Scene 4

However, it must of course be remembered that the words in Shakespeare's plays are put into the mouths of the characters – and do not necessarily indicate the views of the writer. Obvious, really. Even so, Duncan-Jones is tempted to go along with the casual dalliance with designing woman theory, with a suggestion that Anne was 'no better than she ought to have been':

> It seems more likely that her father's death left the unmarried Agnes or Anne ... without much parental care or control, and as a mature and spirited country girl she exploited her freedom to consort with the local youth. A combination of boredom with the sexual curiosity natural to his years led to Shakespeare's dalliance with her, and to what was probably his first experience of sex.[10]

Ironic, that a woman should so unkindly seek to besmirch another woman's reputation in order to defend a lusty young man! There is no question of a woman in Tudor England retaining society's respect (which Anne undoubtedly enjoyed in Stratford) if she 'consorted' with the local youth. The authorities – and the locals – would be scandalised by such behaviour and there were laws against loose women hanging around country towns. In 1592, the then Bailiff of Stratford, Richard Quiney, took measures to expel 'undesirable' women.[11]

The careless roll-in-the-hay narrative developed by Burgess, which still persists in some quarters, is challenged by Germaine Greer.[12] She points out that the two families were well-known to each other, and it is unlikely that the meeting of Anne and Will was a chance sudden surrender to a mutual bout of lust, a casual seduction, or indeed a brutal rape. Far from his being ensnared by 'a homely wench', Greer asks, in uncharacteristically romantic mode, how hard is it to believe that Shakespeare fell in love, wooed her, and ultimately won her? Or even, one wonders, whether it had been arranged?

Perhaps, Greer suggests, Anne fell in love with William. But is Greer telling a story she would like to believe? Greenblatt asserts that there is no documentary evidence that Shakespeare had any kind of close emotional relationship with Anne:[13] well of course, they certainly did not send or receive any love-letters as far as we know, letters were typically read aloud, and so intimacies were seldom expressed. All we can say is that they got married, and had three children, and stayed married as long as Shakespeare lived. Their relationship? Well, we do have Sonnet 145.

Sonnet 145

This sonnet, written in the early 1580s, sheds some light on their relationship. It is listed among Shakespeare's first poems in Edmondson and Wells' book, cited in the previous chapter.[14] It seems clear that, whether or not Anne Hathaway fell in love with Shakespeare, she seems to have been at least a willing bride. It also strongly suggests an ardent bridegroom – certainly not a resentful young man entrapped by a woman's wiles:

> Those lips that Love's own hand did make
> Breathed forth the sound that said 'I hate',
> To me that languish'd for her sake:
> But when she saw my woeful state,
> Straight in her heart did mercy come,
> Chiding that tongue that ever sweet
> Was used in giving gentle doom,
> And taught it thus anew to greet:
> 'I hate' she alter'd with an end,
> That follow'd it as gentle day
> Doth follow night, who like a fiend
> From heaven to hell is flown away;
> 'I hate' from hate away she threw,
> And saved my life, saying – 'not you'.

As Gurr has pointed out,[15] the sonnet indulges in the Tudor fashion for puns, and the pun on Anne Hathaway's name in line 13 is fairly obvious. The sonnet appears oddly in the 'Dark Lady' group, where it is surely misplaced (see Chapter 11). If Gurr is right, why is a sonnet to Shakespeare's wife mixed up with a set of poems to his mistress? The suggestion that the pun is a reference to the famous poem by Catullus – *Odi et Amo*. 'I hate, and I love' seems far-fetched.

It seems clear that Sonnet 145 is in entirely the wrong place. Because of its simplicity, it would seem to be among the first, if not the first, poem Shakespeare ever wrote. It is metrically different from all the poems in the collection: the first few lines follow a pattern associated with folk ballads –

> **Anne Shakespeare, née Hathaway**
>
> Those on the tourist trail in Stratford-upon-Avon usually head first for Holy Trinity Church, where they can view the tombstones of Shakespeare's family, and Shakespeare's monument. How often they miss that of Anne Hathaway. They then go on to see Anne Hathaway's Cottage, now beautifully preserved by the Shakespeare Birthday Trust. It was bought by the Trust in 1892.
>
> The cottage – originally a farm, known as Hewland – dates back to 1567, and descendants of the Hathaways lived there for nearly 370 years. The land surrounding it continued as a working farm until the nineteenth century. The beautifully-tended flower garden one sees today belies the fact that the cottage would have been the hub of a busy working farm: more muck than flowers, then. It was here that Anne spent the first years of her life.
>
> Anne, born in 1556, was the oldest of eight children – five boys and three girls. When still very young it is likely that she would have been given jobs around the farm – weeding, bird-scaring, milking her father's ewes. But her role may have changed as more children arrived – the oldest tends to be given the shortest straw. The first to arrive, she was probably the last to leave. It is quite likely Anne would have become an unpaid nanny to some, at least, of her younger siblings for a while, particularly, as it seems Richard's first wife died, and he remarried, and a fresh round of children arrived. So it was here that Anne learnt the skills required for being a mother.

ti TUM ti TUM ti TUM ti TUM – and was probably written in about 1582. For our money, it is less sophisticated than the other two listed by Edmondson and Wells that we discuss in Chapter 2, and has therefore, in Andrew Gurr's words, certainly some claim to be his first (known) sonnet. Readers may think that it is unlikely to be the only love poem that he wrote at the time – others he may have suppressed as being an embarrassment.

More crucially, this is a poem that could only have been written by someone who was in love; and the woman he was in love with was sweet-tongued, kind and good-natured. She was also doubtless susceptible to sweet talk. As was Shakespeare, for scenes of courtship abound in his plays. In a wonderful parody of what may or may not have been his own seduction techniques, he puts these words into Armado's mouth in *Love's Labour's Lost*, which we offer as free advice to all would-be young lovers:

> ... to jig off a tune at the tongue's end, canary to it with your feet, humour it with turning up our eyelids, sigh a note and sing a note. Sometimes through the throat as if you swallowed love with singing love, sometimes

through the nose as if you snuffed up love by smelling love, with your hat penthouse-like over the shop of your eyelids ...

– LLL ACT 3, SCENE 1

Talking of love is one thing; commitment is quite another. A deeply flawed character like Armado would have been horrified at the arrival of a child: no doubt you would not have seen him for dust. Not so, William Shakespeare.

Marriage

Burgess suggests that Shakespeare was 'two-timing' Anne with another wench called Anne Whately: the entry for 27 November 1582 in the register of the Bishop of Worcester grants a special marriage licence to be 'inter Willelmum Shaxpere et Annam Whateley de Temple Grafton'. Lapsing into the literary mode of a novelist, Burgess imagines this scenario:

> It is reasonable to suppose that Will wished to marry a girl called Anne Whately ... Sent on skin-buying errands to Temple Grafton, Will could have fallen for a comely daughter, sweet as May and shy as a fawn. He was eighteen, and highly susceptible. Knowing something about girls, he would know that this was the real thing. Something perhaps quite different from what he felt about Mistress Hathaway of Shottery.

Burgess is not the only one to swallow this story. Robin Williams suggests that a day after Shakespeare got the licence to marry Anne Whately of Temple Grafton, he is hauled off by the two older men – friends of the Hathaway family – to marry Anne, to make an honest woman of her.[16] For over 200 hundred years rigorous scholarship might have made such an assertion; but as Ian Wilson notes,[17] in 1836 Sir Thomas Philips, a book collector, came across a second document, dated 27 November 1582, which makes it clear that Shakespeare married Anne Hathaway, and not a mythical Anne Whately. The document records that two worthy Stratford farmers, John Richardson and Fulke Sandells, entered into a bond for the enormous sum of £40.00 to indemnify the bishop against any impediment to the marriage that might arise between the two – and to allow the couple to marry after just one calling of the banns, probably because the bride was heavily pregnant. The bond signed by Sandells and Richardson clearly names

'William Shagspere [sic] and Anne Hathwey of Stratford in the Diocese of Worcester, maiden'. The signatories would certainly not have risked the enormous sum of £40.00 if there had been the remotest suggestion that William Shakespeare had already been betrothed to one Anne Whately.

Stanley Wells points out that it is generally agreed by most scholars that there was a slip of a quill by a dozy clerk completing the Church register. There is no record of anyone named Whately in Temple Grafton, whether or not she was shy as a fawn; and an examination of the records in Worcester registry office reveals that a half-witted clerk often got people's names mixed up – and made many similar mistakes.[18] He (definitely not a she) writes *Baker* for *Barbar* and replaces *Bradeley* with *Derby*, and *Elcock* with *Edgecock*. On the same day as he enters Shakespeare's marriage licence, the dozy clerk records that a William Whately of Crowle was involved in an unrelated legal dispute. Most scholars now accept that the name was a clerical error: not that Whately is very similar to Hathaway.

So, happy ending: William Shagspere and Anne Hathwey got married in November 1582 – but where? Another mystery: the Holy Trinity Church in Stratford carries no record of their marriage. The wedding took place in the tiny church at Temple Grafton, off the beaten track from Stratford. As weddings usually took place in the parish where the bride was living, this suggests that Anne had moved from Shottery, perhaps to work as a domestic, or farming assistant after the death of her father. Others have suggested that they were married in this rather remote church to escape the mocking laughter of local residents in Stratford, but there is no evidence of this. Those who hope to make Shakespeare a Catholic point out that the elderly priest at Temple Grafton was known to be sympathetic to the old faith. Was that the reason why they were married there? Possible: unfortunately, the records of the church have not survived. But one should also recall that the Hathaways were strongly Protestant.

Family life

Six months after the wedding, in May 1583, their first child, a daughter, was born. As Germaine Greer points out, in Tudor times, bedding before wedding was not infrequent (though this changed within Shakespeare's life-time.)[19] Their daughter was christened with the name Susanna, unusual in Tudor times. It is an Old Testament name, (the name means 'purity') – perhaps, it has been suggested, signifying Protestant inclinations. Well, no, the opposite seems to be true: the story of Susanna and the Elders was considered apocryphal by Protestants, though it is certainly included in the King James Bible that came out in 1605. And it appears that Susanna had Catholic sympathies, even though she later married a Protestant, Dr Hall.[20]

In 1585, Susanna was joined by twins, Julia and Hamnet. After the arrival of Susanna so soon after his marriage, did Shakespeare have another child to show that he 'really meant it'? A question asked by Germaine Greer. We don't of course know. But it is likely that the arrival of twins must really have concentrated the young man's mind: with a wife and three children below the age of four, with no house, no congenial occupation, few prospects beyond working in what must have seemed an unattractive business, all still living with his younger brothers in the family house in Henley Street – how was he to sustain his family?

It was time for Shakespeare to make his own living. Perhaps, like Valentine in *The Two Gentlemen of Verona*, he went 'to seek preferment out', as so many young men were beginning to do:

> Some to the wars, to try their fortune there,
> Some to discover islands far away
> Some to the studious universities.

Of course, none of these options were open to Anne Hathaway: she was left almost literally holding the baby. Did Shakespeare have any qualms about leaving home? He could at least be fairly sure that he left his family and home in the hands of a competent housewife. He could be sure that Anne could cope, and that all the children received sufficient nourishment to survive, even in testing times, such as the winter of 1587, a time of scarcity, and high prices, and also a time when 'a burning ague' afflicted Stratford. All the evidence indicates that Anne was much more than a poor, deserted house-wife: as a farmer's eldest daughter she would have acquired many skills, from cheese-making to livestock management, to making malt.[21]

Malt-making was a complicated business, and required managing a number of employees; which made her a business woman in her own right. Greer gives a detailed account of the complicated process involved.[22] There was great demand for malt: malt was made from barley or other grain, and was used for making bread. It was also needed in brewing and distilling, for making beer, spirits or vinegar. Residues could be used to feed pigs. Only someone who was highly competent would take on such a business, and she would have had to keep accounts. Greenblatt doubts whether she could read and write: Greer suggests that it is it quite possible that she did so, for Protestants greatly valued the ability to read the Bible in pursuit of their faith. Perhaps Shakespeare taught her? She certainly needed to have at least limited writing to keep track of her business.

Greer also suggests that it is likely that she set herself up as an ale-wife, and as a market trader, because for some years at least she could not hope for any financial support from her husband. In her book she emphasizes Anne Shakespeare's life as a survivor, and a provider, even though most books on Shakespeare hardly mention Anne Hathaway. I think there is little doubt that she played a key part in holding the family together, and giving Shakespeare some peace of mind as he pursued his career. Greer draws our attention to the Latin inscription on the chancel floor beneath Shakespeare's monument.[23] The Latin was provided probably by John Hall, Susanna's husband. But the sentiment is surely Susanna's, and betokens a deep love for a mother sadly mourned:

> Mother, thou gavest me milk from thy breasts, and life, woe is me, for so great a gift must I offer only a stone? How I wish the good angel would roll away this slab and like the body of Christ, thine image could come forth! But my prayers nought availeth – come quickly, Christ, that my mother, though sealed in a tomb, may rise again and seek the stars[24]

What could a father give? What future could Shakespeare offer his young family? For a would-be writer, Stratford offered no opportunities. University was out of the question, even as a sizar (a scholarship student who repaid the university by doing odd jobs). Even if he had wanted to, not only could he not afford it, as a married man he was precluded from being either an apprentice, or a university student. But if, like Valentine, he felt the need to go and seek his fortune, at least he knew that he left his family in the safe hands of his wife. But where did he go, what did he do? This leads us to another episode in Shakespeare's life – more 'lost years'.

4

MORE LOST YEARS: LEICESTER'S MEN

' ... one man in his time plays many parts ... '
— Jacques: *As You Like It*

Jacques is right; one man in his time does indeed play many parts. How many parts Shakespeare played in the second period of lost years – from 1585 to the year of his arrival in London, both on the stage and in life, has been the subject of endless speculation. This chapter explores what might have happened, and in the total absence of hard information it must in the nature of things be highly speculative.

Previous chapters have suggested that he was a dreamer and he had already started to write; yet the opportunities, and the stimulus, for doing what was clearly in his blood were seriously constrained in backwater Warwickshire. Whatever he might have been doing in Stratford, it is likely that he became increasingly restive. The smelly life of a whittawing household was hardly compatible with creative thought. There is good reason to believe that some time after the birth of the twins Hamnet and Judith in 1585, Shakespeare left home. No one knows exactly when he left, or exactly where he went. Greenblatt[1] suggests that he left Stratford for London some time in the summer of 1586, or shortly afterwards. Rather pompously, and certainly a-historically, he talks about Shakespeare 'turning away from his domestic obligations' and suggests that the 'abandonment' of his wife and children was an ethical issue – he talks of 'their long years apart', and even compares Shakespeare with Gauguin (who famously abandoned his family and went off to Oceania ...)

Germaine Greer hotly contests the implied assumption that he was trying to get away from his wife.[2] She contends that he went away with the blessing of his wife, and his parents: they must have had some inkling where his talents lay. In Tudor times it was not uncommon for wives to be left on their own for months, if not years. A famous example is that of Margaret Paston, who stayed in rural Norfolk while her menfolk frequented the law courts, and the royal court in London. It is possible that Shakespeare was getting bored by his wife, but he must have at least respected her, for he knew he was leaving his children in her capable hands. However, questions remain: when did he move, and why? Did he jump, or was he pushed? There is a scene in *Two Gentlemen of Verona* in which there is speculation about the future of young Proteus. One man

> ... wondered that your lordship
> Would suffer him to spend his youth at home
> While other men, of slender reputation,
> Put forth their sons to seek preferment out –
> Some to the wars, to try their fortune there,
> Some to discover islands far away,
> Some to the studious universities
> For any or for all these exercises
> He said that Proteus your son was meet.
>
> – Act 1.3.4-12

In the mid-1580s, harvests were poor, grain prices were high,[3] and common land used for pasture was being enclosed by rich landowners. Many people in Stratford-upon-Avon and the surrounding area went hungry.[4] Shakespeare's father would have seen William's move as 'casting bread upon the waters.' None of his other sons were likely to obtain upward mobility in the Tudor hierarchy. As one character in *Two Gentlemen of Verona* remarks, 'Home-keeping youth have ever homely wits.' John Shakespeare probably thought there was at least an off-chance that William could somehow make the grade.

John Shakespeare would also have been aware that his friend and neighbour Henry Field, a tanner, had sent his son to London to be a printer's apprentice, and by all accounts was doing well. As a married man, William would not have been allowed to become an apprentice, nor could a married man go to university: so what were his other options? It is unlikely that he went straight from Stratford to London – the chances of becoming hugely successful in the city with very little experience must have seemed very remote. This chapter looks at some possible routes that he took that made success in London a great deal more attainable. First, a theory that Shakespeare was forced to leave.

The Poaching Theory

There is a story that he had to leave Stratford rather precipitately when accused of poaching deer on Sir Thomas Lucy's land at Charlecote Park, about four miles away. The Lucy family of Charlecote were fervent Protestants and had profited from the spoils when Henry VIII destroyed the monasteries.[5] The deer-stealing story appears in later accounts of Shakespeare's life, such as in the rough manuscript notes of a Gloucestershire clergyman, Richard Davies, who died in 1708, and a biography written by Nicholas Rowe, who died in 1718. According to Rowe:

> He had, by a Misfortune common enough to young Fellows, fallen into ill Company: and amongſt them, some that made a frequent practice of Deer-ſtealing, engag'd him with them more than once in robbing a Park that belong'd to *Sir Thomas Lucy of Cherlecot*, near *Stratford*. For this he was profecuted by that gentleman as he thought somewhat too severely ... [6]

There is no contemporary record of these events, if indeed they occurred, and the story is widely discredited, if only because Sir Thomas did not have a park in Charlecote. Rowe got his facts wrong: it was Lucy's son, another Sir Thomas Lucy, who created a deer park in the 17th Century – not as it happens at Charlecote, but in what had been the parish of Fulbrook before the villagers were dispersed by the Earl of Warwick, in an area overlooked by Daisy Hill.[7] Furthermore, there is no evidence that Sir Thomas brought an action against Shakespeare for poaching, nor could he have done so: being an injured party, the case would have been heard by some other justice of the peace. Rowe continues with the suggestion, based on hearsay evidence, that Shakespeare then wrote a scurrilous ballad about Sir Thomas, which meant he had to make a run for it to escape punishment. Part of the ballad, which refers to the luces (fish) that appeared on Sir Thomas's arms, ran as follows:

> A parliament member, a justice of peace,
> At home a poor scarecrow, at London an ass,
> If lousy is Lucy as some folks miscall it
> Then Lucy is lousy whatever befall it[8]

However, it would have been extremely foolish to make an enemy of the most influential magnate in the area, a man much respected (and feared if you were Catholic), and in good standing with the Privy Council. So I think it likely Shakespeare was neither author nor poacher: if he was, then we could say that he chose to jump – before he was pushed, or jailed. However, there are many other more plausible explanations for his departure.

Religious and political pressures

In Tudor times, it was not possible to separate religious issues from politics, and anti-Catholic measures by the authorities were increasing. One of those who led the charge in Warwickshire was none other than Sir Thomas Lucy. At Charlecote, his private tutor had been John Foxe, author of *Foxe's Book of Martyrs*, a hugely influential book that documented the victims of Catholic persecution. Sir Thomas zealously pursued those suspected of following the old faith: he was a man to be feared. Warwickshire would have kept him very busy: there were many Catholic families in the West Midlands. Some were known recusants – those who refused to attend Church of England services. Many more simply loved the rituals of the old faith, even while showing willing at church each Sunday: after all, many of the older folk in particular would have been brought up as Catholics. No one was safe: could John Shakespeare, already noted as being a recusant, also be in line for a visitation by Sir Thomas? Those who were suspected of clinging to the old faith, or failed to attend church, were fined; others, especially priests, could be picked up, tortured, and executed, like Thomas Cottam, Robert Debdale, and Edmund Campion, who was a frequent visitor to Warwickshire. Then as early as April 1583, the Queen's spy-master, Sir Francis Walsingham, got wind of the Throckmorton Plot.[9]

> **Plots against the realm**
>
> In 1583 a spy informed Walsingham that the French ambassador, Michel de Castelnau, was involved in a plot to overthrow Queen Elizabeth, and had sent 1,500 *ecus* (gold crowns) to Mary Stuart, Queen of Scots.[10] One of Castelnau's visitors was a young Catholic nobleman, Francis Throckmorton, whose family lived very near Stratford. He was arrested in November, and tortured.
>
> The authorities had every reason to be paranoid: the conspiracy involved a Spanish-backed invasion by the French, led by the Duke of Guise, head of the Catholic League, to replace Queen Elizabeth with Mary Stuart. Mary, a Catholic, had been under house arrest in England since 1568, and was the focus of several plots. Guise would have been her husband – her fourth – and the new King of England.
>
> The plot was foiled, and in July 1584 Throckmorton was executed, but the result was an increase in anti-Catholic fervour among the authorities. One of Walsingham's agents, Richard Topcliffe, ranged up and down the land arresting hundreds of suspects: innocent or guilty, male or female, it did not matter. Topcliffe took sadistic pleasure in torturing his victims to extract any information, true or false, from them.[11]

News of the Throckmorton Plot had not yet broken when another plot was uncovered much closer to home. In October 1583, the deranged son-in-law of Edward Arden, John Somerville, took it into his head to set off to London with the publicly avowed intention of shooting the queen with his pistol. Somerville was picked up by Walsingham's agents in Banbury, and on the rack he claimed he was acting under the orders of his 'allies and kin'. Across Warwickshire households known or thought to be Catholic were raided: prominent among the Catholic families was that of Edward Arden, former High Sheriff of Warwickshire, a relative of Shakespeare's mother. This made the Ardens, and the Shakespeares, uncomfortably close to the wretched Somerville.

Unluckily for Arden, he had been a ward of the Throckmortons as a child, and had married a daughter of the family, Mary. He had also affronted the Earl of Leicester, another Protestant enthusiast: in 1575, the earl had organized a massive entertainment for the queen at his castle at Kenilworth, twelve miles from Stratford, and was deeply offended when Arden refused to wear the earl's livery for the occasion.[12] The authorities also knew that he was not just a Catholic, but one who had welcomed two Jesuits, Fr Campion and Fr Persons, into his house, twenty miles north of Stratford-upon-Avon.[13] These facts, and the connection with Somerville and the Throckmortons, were enough to seal his fate: Mary Arden and other members of the family were arrested by Sir Thomas Lucy. Her husband was dragged off to be racked in the Tower. He, his wife and their daughter Margaret (who was married to Somerville) were tried, and judged guilty, even though nothing incriminating was found. His wife was sentenced to be burnt alive – the sentence was later commuted. Margaret was pardoned. Somerville allegedly hanged himself in prison.

However, there was no escape for Edward Arden, and a hideous penalty awaited. He was dragged off to Smithfield on a hurdle, half hanged, and then, while still alive, his genitals were severed, and his internal organs hauled out and burnt before his eyes; finally, he was beheaded, and his body was cut into quarters. His head ended on a spike on London Bridge, there left to rot. Shakespeare would have seen it every time he crossed that bridge.

These events created a great climate of fear as the whole area was for months combed for 'the usual suspects' by men such as Topcliffe and Lucy. The political atmosphere grew increasingly febrile: in 1585, Robert Debdale was again arrested and, the following year, executed. John Shakespeare, his family and his in-laws, were left in no doubt as to the seriousness of the situation at a very personal level. Many who had been brought up in the old faith had good reason to fear: they would have been wise to bury any potentially incriminating items – documents, crucifixes, images of favourite saints, or rosaries. Wood claims that it is quite likely that the house of John Shakespeare, a known recusant, and as we have seen related by marriage to the Arden family, was also raided.[14] All this would have made an unforgettable impression on young William Shakespeare – and would have been a source of great anxiety. He would have known that his father was baptised a Catholic. It is more than possible that Shakespeare may have felt that Warwickshire was not the safest place to be living. Perhaps he thought that leaving town was not a bad idea, under the circumstances. It is possible that his father may have thought this too.

Other reasons for his departure

There was another compelling reason why Shakespeare felt an overwhelming urge to leave home. One can readily understand how a budding playwright, with the instincts of an actor and a poet, would have found it hard to tolerate the life of small-town Stratford. After the birth of his twins, Hamnet and Judith, in February 1585, it would be understandable if he had an urge to leave earlier rather than later: a crowded household including three babies and four younger siblings would hardly have been conducive to creative thought. There were also financial pressures. How was he to support his young family?

As Greenblatt has suggested, it is likely he left home at some time after the birth of his twins, perhaps in 1585, quite possibly with the blessing of his father, who had other sons to help out. But left to do what? A number of assumptions, supported by a little detective work, are required to account for the fact within only five or six years, a country boy from rural Stratford could make his way in the highly competitive theatrical world centered on London. Many have suggested that Shakespeare somehow served an apprenticeship with a group of players, but as we have seen, anyone who was married was debarred from serving an apprenticeship. Even so, it is very unlikely that he went straight to London.

In her study *Shakespeare: An Ungentle Life*, Katherine Duncan-Jones offers a more plausible hypothesis.[15] A local grandee, Sir Fulke Greville had a keen interest in the education of boys, and was living at Beauchamps Court in Alcester, only 12 miles from Stratford, where it is recorded that he maintained 'a brave company of gentlemen'. He was a frequent visitor to the town – he was Recorder of Stratford-upon-Avon for fifteen years, and would certainly have known John Shakespeare. It was the custom at Whitsun and Christmas for boys from Stratford Grammar School to perform scenes from comedies to demonstrate their acting and oratorical skills in local exercises in 'Am-Dram'. It seems quite possible that Greville spotted Shakespeare on one of these occasions – perhaps in April 1583 when it is recorded that Greville was entertained at a local hostelry, *The Bear*.

Shakespeare's best chance of advancement at this early stage in his life would have been to take up a position in a grand house, and it seems plausible that Greville recognized his talent, and took him into his employment either as a player, or a clerk, or both. As far as John Shakespeare was concerned, with his social-climbing aspirations, his son being attached to the household of a local aristocrat might have seemed a much more acceptable option than joining a roving group of players.

Robert Dudley, 1st Earl of Leicester 1532 -1588 (unknown artist, c.1575-80). Previously strongly attributed to Steven van Meulen

Opportunity knocks: with Leicester's Men?

It is virtually certain that he was involved with at least one acting company before arriving in London; how else can one explain his amazingly high profile as both actor and playwright in the early 1590s? A young man with a Warwickshire accent, with country ways, and with (metaphorical) straw in his hair would have had no status or credibility in the cosmopolitan city of London in 1590 – unless he already had a track record.

We are still in the land of conjecture ... We now turn to another possibility suggested by Duncan-Jones.[16] She tells us that Greville was a close friend of the Dudley family, and in Chapter 2, Robert Dudley, Earl of Leicester's castle at Kenilworth was only twelve miles from Stratford. Leicester's players performed in Stratford on numerous occasions, and it is possible that Shakespeare, having demonstrated some talent, might on Greville's recommendation have been recruited as a junior member of Leicester's Men. Maybe he started as a stage-hand, and prompter. He probably played female parts – young men, not just boys, often had to do so, as no woman was allowed to perform on stage. Whatever his role, it is likely that Shakespeare made himself *persona grata* with his fellow players, not just for his acting and other skills, but because by all accounts he was personally well-liked as a courteous, well-mannered man. Schoenbaum notes that 'almost everyone seems to have thought well of "Gentle Will Shakespeare".[17] John Davies of Hereford describes 'W.S.' in positive terms:

> And though the stage doth stain pure gentle blood
> Yet generous ye are in mind and mood.

Did Shakespeare go abroad?

In December 1585, the Earl of Leicester, with an army that included his nephew, Sir Philip Sidney, went to the Low Countries to support the Dutch Protestants in their desperate war against the massive military machine of Spain, led by the Duke of Parma. The situation was dire: in 1584 William of Orange had been assassinated, and in 1585 Antwerp fell after a year-long siege. Brussels was now under threat. In England, huge events were taking place: in July 1586 Robert Debdale was rearrested as part of the Babington Plot, in which Sir Thomas Babington plotted with Mary Stuart to assassinate Queen Elizabeth. The trial of Mary Queen of Scots took place in October 1586. There was a wave of executions: Babington and his fellow conspirators met their grisly fate in September 1586, and, after endless prevarication by Elizabeth, Queen Mary was executed in February 1587.

One would think that Leicester would have had some sense of the crisis facing England and the Low Countries. Yet Leicester might have been going on a picnic as he embarked for the continent: combining work with play, Leicester took with him a large group of actors and acrobats. It is recorded that Leicester's Men gave a performance at Utrecht on St George's Day in 1586. Was Shakespeare part of the company? At this point, perhaps we may be permitted to allow our imaginations to take over. We cannot know for certain. Given a choice, any young man would have leapt at the chance of travel abroad. Circumstantial evidence here carries a heavy burden, but provides some support for this hypothesis.

A visit to a foreign country would have given Shakespeare some insight into sea-going life – as Falconer points out in his book *Shakespeare and the Sea*,[18] his plays are full of references to things maritime, and show a degree of familiarity with ships, unlikely in a total land-lubber. Secondly, it is intriguing to note that during his campaign in Europe, Leicester's Men put on a performance at the Danish castle in Helsingør (called Elsinor in *Hamlet*). Did Shakespeare take part? Perhaps, like Francisco and Bernardo, he stood on the platform before the castle, imagining the ghosts of dead soldiers and kings. Perhaps, too, he saw one of the famous tapestries that King Frederick II commissioned in 1581 – ideal for a Polonius to hide behind ...

But let us keep our boots on the ground: travelling with the military would also have given Shakespeare an insight into what it was like to be a soldier. One thinks of Jacques' speech in *As You Like It* on the seven ages of man, one of which is that of the soldier: the lines combine bravado and aggression:

> Full of strange oaths, and bearded like the pard,
> Jealous in honour, sudden and quick in quarrel,
> Seeking the bubble reputation
> Even in the cannon's mouth.
>
> – AYLI Act 2, Scene 7

Shakespeare paints vivid pictures of scenes of military life, so much so that Duff Cooper, the British soldier and diplomat, was convinced that Shakespeare did some military service.[19] One day during the First World War, Duff Cooper heard a sergeant warning his men against firing a rifle with the sun in their eyes. Later, as he sat in the trenches reading *Love's Labour's Lost*, he was amazed to see these lines from Berowne, which showed that Shakespeare had some knowledge of military tactics:

> Advance your standards, and, upon them, lords!
> Pell-mell, down with them; but be first advised –
> In conflict that you get the sun of them.
>
> – LLL Act 4, Scene 3

Particularly memorable is the way Shakespeare covers the recruitment of soldiers. In 2 *Henry IV* there is a very funny scene where all the able-bodied recruits are weeded out, leaving just three 'scarecrows' – Shadow, Feeble and Wart – reminding us of the Duke of Wellington's comment about his soldiers: 'I don't know what effect these men will have upon the enemy, but, by God, they frighten me.' One thinks on the one hand of the skivers and chancers such as Falstaff and Bardolph you find in any army – the barrack-room jocularity of Shakespeare's soldiers has the ring of authenticity, and would speak to any of today's squaddies.

There is a tiny fragment of documentary evidence that Shakespeare was a member of Leicester's Men: in 1586 Sir Philip Sidney called on one of Leicester's players to take a message back to England to give to his wife. The letter did not arrive. Sidney wrote again

> I wrote to you a letter carried by William my lord of Leicester's jesting player, enclosed in a letter to my wife and I never had answer thereof ...

The term 'jesting player' does not necessarily mean that the messenger was a comedian – and in any case the word 'comedian' is often used in Tudor English to refer to any actor. Some scholars have suggested that 'William' is Will Kempe, a leading comic actor of the day, but he was almost invariably referred to as Kempe or Will Kempe. As Duncan-Jones indicates, it is far more likely that Sidney would have used a junior but quick-witted young man like Shakespeare 'meet to be sent on errands' than a key player like Kempe, who was a star attraction.[20] In Kronborg Castle in Helsingør, there is a record of a payment to William Kempe in 1586.[21]

Whoever the messenger was, he was in serious trouble: Sidney was furious, because the letter was delivered to the wrong person – namely Lady Leicester. This was very embarrassing, as it contained disparaging comments about her hopes of joining her husband to join in the fun and games that Leicester saw as an essential part of his military campaign.

The whole story could have featured as a sub-plot in one of Shakespeare's plays. Clearly, this *faux pas* was a good time for Shakespeare to make an excuse and leave Leicester's Men rather than return to brave Sir Philip Sidney's wrath.

As it turned out, there was in any case no future with Leicester's Men. In 1588, Leicester was put in command of an army of conscripts ('trained bands'), based at Tilbury, ready to resist any invasion mounted by the Spanish Armada. It is possible that had he remained with the earl, Shakespeare would have been recruited along with the other players as part of this army. It was probably in the marshes around Tilbury that Leicester caught 'tertian fever' (malaria) which killed him in September, causing Elizabeth much grief; his death also marked the end of Leicester's Men.

'Resting'

Perhaps Shakespeare decided to lie low for a while. In the language of actors, 'resting' is of course a euphemism for 'unemployment' – giving him time to catch up with family life in Stratford. Perhaps, too, he needed time for reflection – the fate of Robert Debdale, Anne Hathaway's former neighbour in Shottery, must have been a shock to the whole family, already severely shaken by the execution of Edward Arden. It is also possible that he took refuge from these dramatic events in writing: Shakespeare may have started to write *Arden of Faversham* around this time, to be completed later.[22]

However, there was little opportunity for anyone to rest in the Shakespeare household. It is quite likely that William was once again required to help out in the family business. As Fallow notes, the Elizabethan father 'had total sway over his family', and would certainly have set all his sons to work. Indeed, Fallow even suggests that it is probable that his talented son 'first went to London as a businessman rather than as an impoverished poet.'[23] However, it is doubtful if he could ever have achieved what he did in London, in such a short time, without more experience of theatre life, and the arrival in Stratford of the Queen's Men in 1587 must have presented an unmissable opportunity: perhaps the Queen's scarlet livery sported by the company may have carried some weight in causing Shakespeare's father to let his son join them?

5

THE QUEEN'S MEN

> 'Love all; trust a few.
> Do wrong to none: be able to thine enemy
> Rather in power than use; and keep thy friend
> Under thy own life's key: be chequed for silence
> But never taxed for speech.'
>
> – *All's Well that Ends Well*

The Queen's Men were granted the official Royal Warrant in March 1583. The close knowledge that Shakespeare had of the plays enacted by the troupe make it very likely that he worked with them for a period. At this time, the Queen's Men were the best-known professional company in the kingdom – and also the most widely-traveled.[1] Initially, the company were formed to keep the queen and her court entertained, and it was under the control of the Master of the Revels, Sir Edmund Tilney.

Sir Edmund also had responsibility to ensure that no play was ever performed with any inflammatory content. Thus a play about Sir Thomas More was heavily censured – there is no certainty when it first appeared on the stage. It is not surprising that the authorities were almost paranoid about subversion. With the Reformation and the Counter-Reformation in full swing, England was under constant threat by the Catholic powers of France and Spain. The danger was enhanced by the knowledge that there was what we have come to call (ever since the Spanish Civil War) a fifth column at work in England – an underground ready to reinstate a Catholic monarchy. There is little doubt that the queen's life was frequently in real danger from a minority of Catholic fanatics. Two years after Pope Pius V excommunicated Elizabeth, the next pope, Gregory XIII, celebrated the St Bartholomew's Day Massacre of Huguenots in France with a Te Deum Mass, and uttered these very threatening words:

> ... whosoever sends her out of the world with the pious intention of doing God's service, not only does not sin but gains merit.[2]

Walsingham set up a huge network of spies to counteract these threats, and was highly successful in uncovering numerous plots against the crown, such as the Throckmorton Plot. Operating out of his house in Seething Lane, near the Tower of London (today, an office block still bears his name), Walsingham recruited secret agents both in England and abroad, including the Vatican and the Low Countries, and many of Europe's capitals – in Spain, Paris and elsewhere, as well as other provincial cities.[3] His spies identified threats from abroad, and at home. In addition, we have seen how local Protestant worthies such as Sir Thomas Lucy mounted their own campaigns to track down the Catholic threat. The arrest and execution of a relative of his, Edward Arden, would have given Shakespeare a sharp reminder of how dangerous any association with Catholics could be.

So, how did theatre fit into the plot of this huge political drama? Queen Elizabeth's court with all its glamour was in itself theatre: but the authorities also saw the potential for live theatre to send out pro-regime messages. Queen Elizabeth was involved in a battle for the hearts and minds, if not the souls, of the people. Accordingly, the Queen's Men were not formed just to entertain: they also served as a Tudor propaganda organ. Dressed in the royal livery, the arrival of the Queen's Men in towns and villages across the country carried this strong message: the paramount importance of loyalty to the Queen, and the Protestant faith, the only defence against chaos, anarchy – and invasion by the military might of Catholic Spain. Many of the plays enacted contained obsequious references to the queen, which made her almost god-like. As Duncan-Jones points out, *The True Tragedy of King Richard the Third* (rewritten subsequently by Shakespeare), refers to 'Worthy Elizabeth' and her mission 'to put anti-Christ to flight', and warns

> For if her Grace's reign be brought to end
> Your hope is gone, on whom did peace depend[4]

William Cecil, 1st Baron Burghley; Queen Elizabeth I; Sir Francis Walsingham; Line engraving by William Faithorne, 1655

Crude, perhaps, but at its time, seemingly effective. As Lake comprehensively documents, the world of 'Good Queen Bess' was characterized by an almost perpetual and pervasive anxiety, caused initially because of the queen's refusal to marry, and serious worries about the succession. As early as 1566, a remarkable tract warned that it was

> most certain that unless the succession ... be ... in time appointed and ordered, England runneth to most certain ruin and destruction[5]

as competing interests within the realm would wage war.

The political motivation for setting up the Queen's Men may have come from Walsingham. Given Walsingham's obsession with security there can be little surprise that the object was to extend the reach of royal – and Protestant – influence into the provinces. Positive messages were definitely needed to shore up the power of the Tudor monarchy: for years Queen

Sir Francis Walsingham (attributed to Hieronymous Custodis)

Elizabeth hardly ventured beyond her royal palaces, and in view of the lingering influence of the old faith 'it was all the more important for her performers to concentrate on extending the royal outreach to Dorset and Devon in the southwest and the north beyond Coventry where their patron did not go.'[6]

The Queen's Men, then, was founded for largely political reasons: twelve leading actors from other troupes – including the Earl of Leicester's – were headhunted ruthlessly by Sir Francis Walsingham.

Sir Francis Walsingham (1532-1590)

Visitors to see the collection of Tudor and Stuart portraits in London's National Portrait Gallery might easily overlook a picture of a solemn man in a large white ruff gazing out, like Cassius, with a lean and hungry look. His dark clothes look like those of a sinister undertaker merging as they do with a dark and murky background. The dark background suits him, for from 1573 to 1590, Sir Francis Walsingham was best known as the queen's master-spy.

Walsingham was one of the most important figures in Elizabeth's England. As a committed Protestant, like many others, he had gone into exile on the continent during the reign of Mary I ('Bloody Mary') and was well aware of the blood-letting during her reign. Later, under Elizabeth, he served for a time as ambassador in Paris; there he personally witnessed the horrors of the St Bartholomew's Day massacre of Protestants in 1572.[7] He also knew about the extreme brutality of the Spanish campaign in the Low Countries – not just the massacre at Maastricht, but the cruelties of the Inquisition.

It is not surprising then that the Tudor establishment was deeply concerned above all with avoiding a repetition of Bloody Mary's Catholic regime: paranoia was justified by the several plots, of which the Babington Plot was but one example. Walsingham was determined to protect England, and Queen Elizabeth, and was prepared to use all means – bribery, blackmail, forgery, torture, even assassination, to do so. This meant recognizing that Catholics, any Catholics, could represent a danger to the state.

Among those so recruited (from Sussex's Men) was the comedian Richard Tarlton, believed to be the Yorick over whose skull Hamlet broods.[8] It is believed that Shakespeare may have played the part of Dericke with Tarlton in *The Famous Victories of Henry V*.

It is not clear how widely the Queen's Men were seen as organs of propaganda for a benign – and Protestant – queen. Audiences in the provinces would probably have taken them at face value, as entertainment, and it was in the provinces that they mainly performed. Many of the plays were comedies, but it was the history plays that Walsingham was really concerned with: as Lake observes, he regarded the history play as the best way for the company to spread his version of history, 'virtually inventing the history play in the process'. Lake observes that the history plays

> operate *both* as works of history, attempts to revive the past, to bring the dead to life before the audiences' very eyes, *and* as political and moral commentaries of immediately contemporary resonance.[9]

And so we have plays, such as an early version of *King Leir*, (in this case, fake history) in which Shakespeare is said to have acted, with the message of horrors of a divided kingdom (Shapiro suggests that he may have seen a revival of the play put on by the Queen's Men working with Sussex's Men at the Rose Theatre in 1594 – and seen how poor it was).[10] *The true Tragedy of Richard III*, *King John*, and of course *The Famous Victories of Henry V* (all forerunners of Shakespeare's own plays) were written and performed to demonstrate how the Tudors were a legitimate bulwark against popery, and foreign invasion, and would have conveyed a very patriotic message.[11]

Why do most authorities believe that Shakespeare worked for a while with the Queen's Men? James Shapiro insists that we just don't know what Shakespeare did in these 'lost years', and claims that there is no evidence that he wrote or acted in any of the Queens Men's plays. However, he agrees that Shakespeare was 'deeply familiar' with their repertoire.[12] For that reason, most authorities, like Duncan-Jones, believe that he must have worked closely with the troupe, very probably, initially, as a junior member.[13] How else can one explain Shakespeare's familiarity with their plays? He was certainly aware of the plays' short-comings, and it is clear that he set about rewriting them in the years to come, turning them into great drama.

The Queen's Men come to Stratford

Shakespeare, we have suggested, was 'resting' when the Queen's Men arrived in Stratford-upon-Avon in the summer of 1587, and he would have welcomed them with open arms. Having worked with Leicester's Men, he must surely have missed the life of an actor, working with professionals, and so his blood would have been stirred when he heard the sound of their trumpets and drums signaling their arrival. He would have rushed out on to the street to join the other excited townsfolk to view the actors, dressed in scarlet, marching, dancing, even juggling, as they made their way through the town to the bailiff's house. So how was it that he managed to join them?

The records show that in 1587, the Stratford corporation paid the Queen's Men twenty shillings – more than anywhere else on their travels. They played to packed houses: in Stratford a bench was broken during their performance – it is said by an actor playing the part of Henry V who over-exuberantly leapt on it to rally his troops. Shakespeare was undoubtedly among the onlookers. His Muse may have been fighting for him, because their arrival, looking for new talent, presented a huge opportunity.

Yes, new talent they desperately needed. In June, while on tour, there was an incident in Thame when two actors from the company came to blows. According to contemporary accounts, one actor, William Knell chased another, John Towne, and cornered him. Towne, in desperation drew his sword in self-defence – and fatally wounded Knell, who died within thirty minutes. With one actor in his grave, and another under arrest, at a stroke, or perhaps one should say, at a thrust, the Queen's Men lost two key actors. Towne's claim that he acted in self-defence was eventually accepted, but, pending the outcome of his trial, the show had to go on.

This incident left the Queen's Men seriously short of two key actors. Under these circumstances, the company may well have been pleased to recruit Shakespeare. With his literacy skills, and the experience of working in Leicester's Men under his belt, Shakespeare would have seemed an attractive proposition. This was a route well trod: when the Queen's Men first formed, in 1583, three of its actors – Laneham, Wilson and Johns had been head-hunted from Leicester's Men. What is certain is that if Shakespeare did join the Queen's Men, this was an extraordinarily good piece of luck. Service with the troupe would have been a very positive experience: the players were very popular, and quite well paid. They also had the cachet of the Queen's livery.

Duncan-Jones' suggestion that John Heminges also joined at this time seems possible given that the next year he married Knell's widow, with whom he subsequently had some fourteen children – although a marriage contract with Mrs Knell did not necessarily involve a contract with the Queen's Men. Heminges was a near contemporary of Shakespeare's at the King's School, and became one of Shakespeare's closest friends – he played the part of Falstaff for over twenty years. The evidence regarding Heminges is still strong. Along with Henry Condell he became a close associate of Shakespeare, who remembered both of them in his will. Condell and Heminges went on to produce the First Folio of Shakespeare's plays, which lists the names of all the principal actors in the plays. (Apart from Heminges and Condell, the list includes Richard Burbage, Augustine Phillips, and William Kempe, George Bryan and many others, most of whom had been Queen's Men). What is odd about this is that Heminges had been a grocer's apprentice, and only became a Freeman in the Grocer's Company in April of that year; it seems likely that in his years as an apprentice he had become a keen theatre-goer in London, and had become stage-struck.

How certain can we be that Shakespeare joined the Queen's Men? It must be admitted there is no absolutely conclusive evidence. But after he left Leicester's Men he must have done something to ease his way into acceptance in London, and work with the Queen's Men would have helped to give him an entree. So, if the Queen's Men could recruit a grocer while on tour, why not a former whittawer and wool-broker: especially one who had some experience of working in theatre, and was generally well-liked? For 'Gentle Shakespeare' was, by all accounts, in Ben Jonson's words, 'honest, and of a free and generous nature.'[14]

Shakespeare, the emergent writer

Joining the Queen's Men, then, would have been a huge slice of luck: it enabled Shakespeare to learn more about the tools of the trade of the professional theatre, and to gain experience in a relatively non-threatening arena, while on tour: for London audiences were likely to be much more difficult to please than audiences in the provinces. Going on tour would have greatly widened his knowledge of England, though whether he also visited Edinburgh and Dublin is doubtful.[15] Without this experience, it is unlikely he would fall on his feet in the competitive world of London's theatre-land: thus the arrival of the Queen's Men in need of extra hands would have been a godsend.

For the troupe, he would have been a godsend, too: the fact that Shakespeare had been to grammar school meant he was well ahead of most actors in terms of education. For the skills he had in reading and especially writing would have been invaluable – there was a constant need for play scripts to be copied out and amended and updated for actors to memorise their lines. Duncan-Jones claims that it is likely he would not just have copied some of the language used in them.[16] As he wrote out the scripts, his creative instincts doubtless came into play, and he would become an active, interventionist editor, and would rewrite them. There can be no doubt that the Queen's Men would have been very pleased with the result, and this would have gradually led to his role being redefined as 'overseer': which is what happened.

As evidence for this claim, Duncan-Jones cites as an example a play called *Locrine*, an early revenge tragedy in the Senecan tradition possibly written by George Peele, though another candidate has been suggested, Charles Tilney, who was executed in 1586 for his part in the Babington Plot. Like another old play, *Gorbuduc*, the play draws on Geoffrey of Monmouth's fantasy history of ancient Britain, which among other things suggests that the kingdom was founded by Trojans who escaped Troy, a myth much favoured by the Tudors. The play was part of the repertoire of the Queen's Men; some years later, in July 1594 it was entered in the Stationers' Register, and printed – and there, on the title page are the words

> Newly fet foorth, oueerfeene and corrected,
> – By *W.S.*

Does W.S. stand for our favourite playwright? Duncan-Jones thinks so even though several other lesser-known writers share these initials. It is possible of course that these initials could have been a marketing ploy by the publisher, for by 1594, Shakespeare had published his best-selling poems *Venus and Adonis*, and *The Rape of Lucrece*, so adding *W.S* to the title page would certainly have boosted sales. There would have been no commercial mileage in a publisher attributing a play to someone who was lesser-known.

Bate notes that Shakespeare had something of a reputation for being a 'fixer-upper' of other people's plays.[17] I think the probability is that Shakespeare did indeed have a role in writing *Locrine*. However, there is also a question mark as to when exactly Shakespeare rewrote or 'oversaw' it. Bate and Rasmussen claim that the play must have been revised after the publication of Spenser's *Complaints* in 1591,[18] by which time Shakespeare had ceased to work with the Queen's Men. What is certain is that *Locrine* was written some years before it was finally published. The earliest extant printed version ('newly set forth') is a quarto dated 1595. The date of publication is not necessarily crucial: acting companies were reluctant to print the plays they performed, because once in print, any other company could then perform them. This was, of course, centuries before performing rights, and laws of copyright had to wait until 1709 to be enacted. Publications often appeared in plague years when theatres were closed, and money was short. In the early 1590s, the plague had caused public performances of plays to be banned for two years or more, and actors were having a hard time to make ends meet. (What's new ...)

Locrine was not the only play that Shakespeare reworked:, a number of the Queen's Men's plays whose original authorship is unknown were at some point rewritten by Shakespeare. They include *The Famous Victories of Henry V*, *The Troublesome Reign of King John*, and *The True Tragedie of Richard III*, *King Leir*, and an early version of *Hamlet* often called *ur-Hamlet*.

While the Queen's Men played an important part in Shakespeare's development, he soon realised that this was not where his future lay. The Queen's Men became complacent – and their repertoire gradually became somewhat tired (the comedies often degenerated into buffoonery). Thomas Kyd's *Spanish Tragedy*, which took London by storm in 1587, and Marlowe's *Tamburlaine* plays (1587?). showed what could be done. Nothing in the Queens Men's repertoire could equal Marlowe's other plays, which demonstrated the dramatic power of the use of blank verse.[19] By 1591, the Queen's Men were overtaken by Lord Strange's Men and Philip Henslowe's Admiral's Men, and their popularity faded away. Shapiro notes that in 1594 the Queen's Men sold off their most valuable play scripts to a publisher, and 'took to the road'.[20] From that time they were a spent force, and finally dissolved with the queen's death in 1603.

Summing up

Have we at times strayed too far from the known facts of Shakespeare's life? Perhaps, but before we proceed, it should be emphasized here that it is certain that Shakespeare was a member, in one capacity or another, of at least one professional acting company before he went to London. There is strong evidence that he became closely involved with the Queen's Men, and it is unlikely, though possible, that that company would have taken him on if he had had no previous acting experience; so a period with Leicester's Men seems more than plausible.

However, it is absolutely not necessary to assume that Shakespeare ever went to war, or ever went to sea, to explain the many references to both these areas of activity in his plays. There is a widespread belief, with some justification, that he was a genius, which this author believes is a question-begging term. It is evident that the man who wrote these plays had an outstandingly creative imagination, and exceptional empathy; furthermore, the plays he wrote display a superb command not just of stage-craft, and poetry, but also the language of the common man – the language of the ale-house and the street. He also quite clearly had a very good ear. His skill in listening, and his prodigious memory, meant that almost every day he would have heard others speak of their experiences, and this would certainly have fed into his writing; and if he didn't hear the language of the court in the exchanges between the Earl of Leicester and Sir Philip Sidney on their campaign in the Low Countries, he would have picked it up from the same ale-houses and inns, which were frequented by young nobles 'slumming it'. This extraordinary combination of attributes is a more than adequate explanation for the successes that awaited him, in his lifetime; and for the accolade the world has since bestowed on him.

Certainly, it is hard to believe that he did odd jobs, including a bit of whittawing, and a bit of am-dram, in Stratford throughout the eighties. If that is what happened, how could he have managed to emerge from his thespian chrysalis in the early 1590s (or even earlier) as the talk of the town – and an object of envy by other dramatists? But that is for a later chapter. First, an overview of the city where Shakespeare was to spend so much of the rest of his life.

6

LONDON

'Gilded tombs do worms enfold.'

— The Merchant of Venice II.vii

Observant visitors to Tudor London would have noted that grand buildings rubbed shoulders with squalor and filth;[1] they would have admired the royal palaces, and the grand houses of the nobility, but even these places were not totally clear of pollution, lacking plumbing as they did. It was not until 1599 that the queen's 'saucy cousin' Sir John Harington invented the first flushing lavatory he named 'Ajax', which duly received royal approval.[2] For most people, the chamber pot was the weapon of choice, and the street was the sewer.

Of the Tudor royal residences, only three have survived: St James' Palace, Hampton Court, and Eltham Palace. The other palace in Greenwich – Placentia – was replaced with the elegant buildings we see today by Charles II. In all of them, random deposits of filth would have been an ever-present hazard. A German visitor to Greenwich, Paul Hentzner, provides us with a striking description of Placentia in 1598:

> We were admitted into the presence chamber, hung with rich tapestry, and the floor, after the Tudor fashion, strewed with hay, through which the Queen passes on her way to chapel. At the door stood a gentleman, dressed in velvet, with a gold chain, whose office was to introduce persons of distinction. It was Sunday, when there is the greatest attendance of nobility ... [3]

John Norden's map of London in 1593, engraved by Pieter van den Keere. Parts of Southwark on the south bank of the river have been developed.

By *hay* he probably means *straw*, or *reeds*. One has visions of the palace having to be mucked out almost daily, as if it were one of the queen's stables ...

Also notable were the Guildhall, (destroyed in World War II and since rebuilt), and the Royal Exchange, modelled on the Great Bourse at Antwerp; it was opened by the queen in 1573, but was destroyed by the Great Fire in 1666. To these should be added the houses of the great nobility – such as Crosby Hall, where Richard III lived, which was moved to Cheyne Walk in Chelsea in 1910, where it still stands, not far from the house of Sir Thomas More. However, dominating all others in the city was St Paul's Cathedral, even though its wooden spire was destroyed by lightning in 1561. The only other building that could rival it was Westminster Abbey – named by Elizabeth the Collegiate Church of St Peter. (Its two western towers were not built until the eighteenth century).[4]

St Paul's was vast – about as long as 13 double-decker buses (585 feet). Started under the Normans, it was still impressive, despite the fact that all traces of 'Popery' were removed or destroyed by Edward VI. By Shakespeare's time, its function as a place of worship had to compete with a very different secular role. The whole world gathered in a social melée: here foregathered traders, tailors displaying the most recent fashions (pointed shoes out, high heels in – hence 'well-heeled') coney-catchers (conmen), stall-holders, lawyers and their clients, people looking for work, swaggering gallants, and wenches of easy virtue. Delivery men, and members of the public, used it as a short cut. In the cathedral close, booksellers plied their trade: sermons, prayer books, satires, pamphlets, gossip-sheets, poetry and plays were all on sale. Most of Shakespeare's works published in his lifetime bore the imprint of stationers in St Paul's Churchyard.

No doubt it was the areas where these buildings existed that impressed Paul Hentzner:

> The streets in this city are very handsome and clean but that which is named from the goldsmiths who inhabit it, surpasses all the rest: there is in it a gilt tower, with a fountain that plays.

So we turn to the poorer areas, many of which sat side by side with those inhabited by the rich. Writing in about 1600, John Stowe reports that the Council complained to the Middlesex magistrates about

> multitudes of base tenements and houses of unlawful and disorderly resort ... and the great number of dissolute loose and insolent people harboured in such and the like noisome and disorderly houses, as namely poor cottages, and habitations of beggars and people without trade, stables, inns, alehouses, taverns, garden houses converted to dwellings, ordinaries, dicing houses, bowling alleys, and brothel houses.[5]

Brothels were required by law to display a prominent sign. The Bishop of Winchester owned the land south of the river where many of the 'stews' plied their trade. A famous establishment was called the 'Cardinal's Hat' in

The Armada Portrait of Queen Elizabeth, 1588, formerly attributed to George Gower Collection Woburn Abbey (The naval scenes depicted were added much later)

honour of the bishop, and London's prostitutes were known as 'Winchester geese'. Sexually transmitted diseases were very common.

Then there was the plague. What was known as the 'Great Poxe', the plague was a recurring problem in London – and indeed in England. It was a horror story: no one knew what caused it, and it seemed to strike randomly. A whole family might have to be carted off; in other households, all might seem well – and then someone might suddenly keel over. In most cases, the victim knew what was coming: the symptoms started with a headache, which developed into a fever; the lymphatic glands would start to swell, often in the groin, then pustules would grow, and explode. A high temperature would develop, then delirium, then either death, or a coma preceding death. The public were terrified, and saw it as God's judgement on wickedness and vice. Houses where cases were identified were boarded up, and the suffering was unimaginable. In one year, twenty per cent of the population died of the plague: the 'Great Poxe' was never far away. For many people living in London, then, life was in the words of Hobbes, 'nasty, brutish and short.' Not just the common folk: life could be pretty short for the nobility too – if syphilis, typhus or the plague didn't get you, the axeman might. In the Tudor age, 'one in five peerages' families continued to die out in the male line in every generation.'[6]

To seek momentary relief from the pressures of everyday life, city-dwellers could go to see a play, or a bit of bear-baiting, or visit a brothel. Or they could resort to ale-houses – or inns or taverns, for there wine and spirits were also served, as well as food.[7] Some might choose to witness a grisly public execution. Such events always attracted huge crowds, perhaps, faced with the hardships and dangers of city life, thinking that at least someone was worse off ... It is difficult to contemplate how *schadenfreude* might have played such a major part in daily life in Tudor times.

The authorities were also greatly concerned about the streets which were often clogged up with rubbish, human excrement, and dead animals. There were many complaints that householders kept too many dogs which 'unsweetened their keepers' houses'. In 1584-5 the London corporation hired men to have over 1800 dogs killed (they were thought to be a cause of the plague).[8] Many of their bodies were hurled over the city wall at Houndsditch over the years. Clearly, no one thought that dogs might have been part of the solution because of the rats they killed. Other livestock – horses, mules, cows, sheep, and even pigs, would certainly have caused the streets to be pretty unsweetened, too. And where there were slaughter-houses, congealed blood festered in the street, and kites, ravens and vermin had a field day. No wonder the plague was so virulent.

Despite the squalor and disease, the city was beginning to act as a social magnet. In the last four decades of the sixteenth century, London's population increased from 160,000 to around 200,000. Stowe reports that much of the housing was 'sore decayed'. Numerous laws sought to limit the population, but there were problems of enforcement, and attempts to limit new developments were largely ignored. None of the problems deterred newcomers from far and wide – a variety of dialects from across the British Isles could be heard on every street, for any notion of Standard English was yet to come. Writing in the mid 17th century, the lexicographer Thomas

Blount observed that the 'Babel' of the vernacular made England what he called 'a self-stranger' nation, and in the dictionary he compiled in 1656 he attempted to make 'English Englished'.[9] At some time in 1589 or 1590, William Shakespeare added a voice from Warwickshire to add to the mix.

Polyglot London

Among those who arrived in London were foreign merchants – and foreign refugees escaping persecution for religious reasons, particularly from Flanders, France and Germany. It is estimated that during this period about 5 or 6 per cent of London's population were foreigners.[10] Many languages could be heard on the streets of London, for the city was both the commercial and political capital of the country. It was thus frequented not just by merchants and refugees, but also sailors, ambassadors, spies – and even tourists. Musicians, too: the court employed several generations of Italian Jews who spoke Hebrew, Italian – and Ladino.[11]

Attitudes to foreigners varied. In the 1570s there was a great deal of sympathy for Huguenots escaping massacre, and the first generation were broadly welcomed. They usually paid their way, were not a charge to the public purse, and gave employment to locals. However, the welcome mat was not always on offer. In 1593, someone pinned a note to the door of the Dutch Church urging the strangers to 'fly, fly and never return.'[12] There is speculation that this emanated from Christopher Marlowe: 'the Dutch Church libel' was written in iambic pentameters, alluded to his plays, and was signed *Tamburlaine*. There were complaints that the queen permitted refugees from the Low Countries to be 'in better case and more freedom than her own people',[13] and there were anti-refugee riots from time to time. Contrary to his folk-hero image, Sir Walter Raleigh had a ruthless streak.[14] He did not throw down his cloak for the refugees (as reputedly he once did for the queen as she walked from Placentia to Greenwich Park) – he thought they should be sent home. It is noteworthy that Shakespeare eloquently spoke up for the foreigners in 'The Strangers' speech in *Sir Thomas More*.

However, Raleigh would have appreciated the Italian fencing instructors – there was a small but influential Italian community. Italians brought banking, trading and architectural skills, and, then as now, the hospitality sector. Schoenbaum notes that The Oliphant, an Inn on Bankside, was a favourite watering hole for the Italian community – called in *Twelfth Night* 'The Elephant' where it is 'best to lodge'. In *Othello*, the Duke asks 'Marcius Luchese, is he not in town?' a reference to Sr Lucchese, from Lucca, who ran a restaurant in Hart Street, in the parish of St Olave's.[15]

Queen Elizabeth herself was fluent in six languages by the age of eleven: apart from English, she learnt Latin, Greek, French, Spanish, and even Welsh. Later she picked up Italian. Not all educated English people were as scholarly, but it was rare to find any educated man or woman who was monolingual. And not just the educated: Gallagher describes how many different people – soldiers, servants, prisoners, students, tourists, even diplomats – learnt foreign languages, usually orally, largely outside educational institutions.[16]

Living as we do in an age when English has become a world language it is easy to forget that at this time, English was still very marginal: internationally, French, Italian and Spanish, in particular, had far greater cachet – Italian, for example, was the *lingua franca* across the Mediterranean for commercial purposes, largely due to the influence of Venice; French was widely used by the international aristocracy, as well as being the language of diplomacy. On mainland Europe, English was virtually useless: anyone who sought to travel or trade in Europe had to have at least a working knowledge of one or more of these languages – though, in extremis, Latin could sometimes be relied on. So unlike today, (sadly) at that time there was in England a great deal of interest in at least 'getting by' in a foreign language. Gallagher points out that with the development of printing technology, between 1480 and 1715 at least 294 editions of conversational manuals for teaching other European languages were produced.

As for literature, if a book wasn't written in Latin, then it was more likely to be written in French or Italian. And Shakespeare? Of course, he wrote in English – though he liked to include dialect words, occasionally, from Warwickshire. His plays do include fragments of other languages: French, of course, particularly in *Henry V*. In several plays, one can find Italian and other languages, including even Hebrew.[17]

'Baggage books'

Printed versions of popular plays were eagerly sought after, but most plays never appeared in print. It is possible that a number of Shakespeare's plays have disappeared forever. *Twelfth Night* only survived because the King's Men retained a manuscript copy. It was not printed until 1623, when it appeared in the first edition of Shakespeare's collected plays, the First Folio. Publishing a 'play-book' was not straightforward: as early as 1557 the Stationers' Company had been set up by Royal Charter. The company was a trade guild regulating printing, publishing and bookselling – the differentiation had yet to evolve. All publications had to be licensed by the company in their record book, the Stationers' Register. To sell or publish a book or other publication, a bookseller had to pay a small fee. The authorities kept a sharp look out for any kind of publication that could have an impact on law, order or the authority of the government or the church.[18]

The attitude among the literati to these 'playbooks', and indeed to drama, was one that can only be described as 'literary snobbery'. Sir Thomas Bodley,

The Tudor Palace of Placentia in Greenwich

founder of the famous library in Oxford, put 'playbooks' in the same ephemeral category as almanacs and proclamations and 'other idle books'. He would not permit such 'riff-raffs' into his library – its reputation would suffer if 'we stuff it full of baggage-books'.[19] Bodley assumed that most books, if they were worthy of attention, were in Latin and Greek: Wells notes that in 1605, only thirty-six books of the 6,000 books in his library were in English.[20] In Bodley's defence, it has to be said that many of the books were poorly printed, and because of the price of paper, were as small as possible. They came in three formats – folio, quarto and octavo. A folio was a book made from sheets of paper folded once: these books would be around 38 cms tall. Only books that were regarded as important, such as Shakespeare's collected plays, the First Folio, were printed in this size.[21] A Quarto was a book made from sheets of paper folded twice, so the book would only be half the size of a folio. Plays were not regarded as serious literature, so they were printed in the quarto format. In Shakespeare's lifetimes, some eighteen of his plays, the sonnets, and both his long poems, came out in print as quartos, except *3 Henry VI*, which came out as an octavo. Books printed in the octavo format were tiny, being printed on paper folded three times – half the size of a quarto. So one sheet of paper could yield sixteen pages.

Bodley showed little awareness of the emergence of vernacular literature on his doorstep, as it were – and indeed on the stage. Awareness that literature could be written in English was raised of course by Chaucer and

The First Folio of Shakespeare's plays

The publication of the present book celebrates the 400th anniversary of the publication, in 1623, of the First Folio, seven years after Shakespeare's death. The First Folio contains 36 of his plays compiled by two of his colleagues/friends, John Heminges and Henry Condell – a unique tribute to a playwright. Those who think Shakespeare was a fraud must consider why two of his friends went to the trouble to produce such a collection – and why his friend and rival Ben Jonson wrote a dedicatory poem on the first page opening.

Heminges and Condell used as sources 'foul papers' – Shakespeare's own early drafts, 'prompt copies' used by actors in the theatre, and where possible printed versions that typically appeared as quartos. (Only seventeen of his plays were printed in his lifetime). Without the First Folio, we would have lost about half of his plays – including *Twelfth Night*, *Antony and Cleopatra* and *Macbeth*.

Piers Ploughman, but was reinforced by Sir Thomas Wyatt and Henry Howard, the Earl of Surrey, who introduced the Petrarchan sonnet into the English language; and it was Surrey who also achieved an important breakthrough with his translation of Vergil's *Aeneid* into English. Published in 1557, Surrey's work is one of the earliest examples of English blank verse. It took dramatists like Marlowe, Kyd and Shakespeare to realise the potential of using blank verse on the stage to achieve a truly dramatic impact, but with accompanying action, rather than mere oral performance. It is doubtful whether they thought they were thereby turning a form of public entertainment into a major art form, but they certainly saw that enriching the language with poetic diction could give drama a new powerful dimension – and a big step up from the crudeness of the morality plays.

London's Theatre-land

During Elizabeth's reign, theatre became an important cultural influence: a number of foreigners commented on the liveliness of the London theatre in London. According to the playwright, Thomas Heywood,

> playing is an ornament to the city, which strangers of all nations, repairing hither, report of in their countries, beholding them here with some admiration: for what variety of entertainment can there be in any city of Christendom, more than in London? [22]

A Dutch visitor to England, Johannis de Witt, writing in about 1596, was so impressed that he was even moved to make a sketch of the Swan Theatre labelling its various features:

> There are four ampitheatres in London of notable beauty, which from their diverse signs bear diverse names. In each of them a different play is daily exhibited to the populace. The two more magnificent of these are situated to the southward beyond the Thames, and from the signs suspended before them are called the Rose, and the Swan. There are two others outside the city towards the north on the highway ... There is also a fifth, but of dissimilar structure, devoted to the baiting of beasts.[23]

Shakespeare benefitted greatly from the existence of these custom-designed theatres, which had none of the constraints that courtyard theatre in pubs imposed, including limited acting space and smaller audiences.

> **James Burbage: theatre pioneer**
>
> It has been claimed that Burbage was the founder of the modern professional theatre, and certainly he was among those who engineered a radical departure from the mediaeval morality plays. A builder and carpenter by trade, he saw the potential for making a living from drama, but realised that only a hand-to-mouth living could be made by theatre groups on tour: one needed a permanent place where performances could attract regular audiences.
>
> His first attempt to achieve this was a pub called the *Red Lion*, but this did not last long. The courtyards of pubs were a poor substitute for custom-built theatres. James Burbage's *Theatre* was built in 1576 in Shoreditch, where he obtained a 21-year lease from one Giles Allen. In a precursor to IKEA, it was a timber-framed construction that could be taken apart and reassembled on another site. This was a wise precaution, because the time would come when he would have to do just that. (See Chapter 21).

Shakespeare thus came onto the scene at a remarkable time in the development both of the professional theatre, and drama was slowly coming to be seen as a genre of literature. However, the authorities saw drama as having a political rather than a literary significance. Thus, the Master of the Revels closely scrutinised each playscript, and once it was duly approved and signed off, it became the 'prompt copy' used during rehearsals and performances.[24] The Master of the Revels could stop a performance in its tracks if it was seen to be subversive in any way. Those who offended – actors and playwrights – could end up in jail.

Burbage's Theatre was followed shortly after by other theatres: the *Curtain* was built nearby in 1577, but it was not until 1587-8 that Philip Henslowe's *Rose*, the home for a time of the Admiral's Men, was built. Edward Alleyne's *Swan*, which housed the Earl of Pembroke's Men, was built in 1595, four years before *The Globe*. Another theatre, at Newington Butts (near today's Elephant and Castle) never achieved the popularity of other theatres nearer the city. It is clear that Londoners were avid theatre-goers. There were also special performances sponsored by the court, by noblemen in their great houses, and corporate bodies such as the Inns of Court.

The pioneers of the modern theatre did not have it easy. Finding sites for a theatre was far from straight-forward: there was likely to be strong opposition from anyone of influence, noble nimbies one could call them – who did not want a theatre on their doorstep. For theatres had a bad reputation, especially among Puritans, who regarded them as 'Devil's work'; no doubt too, they thought they also lowered property values. This complaint came in a letter from the Bishop of Worcester to the Archbishop of Canterbury:

> To which places also do usually resort great numbers of light and lewd disposed persons, as harlots, cutpurses, cozeners, pilferers, and suchlike ungodly[25]

There is no reason to suppose that Shakespeare behaved like a saint at this time. In Sonnet 31 he speaks of 'the trophies of my lovers gone', and if this anecdote, written by diarist John Manningham in 1601, is to be believed, Shakespeare had something of a reputation as a ladies' man. Seeing Burbage playing Richard III, a woman watching the play suggested he came round to her house that night, calling himself Richard III. Shakespeare overheard this conversation, and 'was entertained and at his game' before Burbadge appeared. When it was announced that Richard III was at the door, Shakespeare sent back the messenger, stating William the Conqueror came before Richard III.[26] This story reminds us that women as well as men enjoyed the theatre: those who have accused Shakespeare of misogyny should remember that women too frequented playhouses, and his plays 'have always appealed to women'[27] as well as men.

Theatres depended wholly on attracting an audience, for there was no accompanying 'merchandise' – souvenir mugs, theatre programmes and the like. Play scripts belonged to the acting companies, which tried to avoid printing copies for sale, for rival companies could then add them to their repertoire. A play script might be published simply to make up for a shortfall in income, for example when theatres were closed because of the plague.

What is astonishing to us, in a world largely dominated by visual imagery – film, TV, books, advertisements – is that the world of make-believe created in these theatres was conjured up almost entirely through words. The actors' words were assisted by glamorous costumes (often the discarded clothing of aristocrats) – very important in an age when 'the apparel doth oft proclaim the man.' Costumes consumed much of a theatre's expenses, for example, Edward Alleyn reportedly spent £16.0 – a huge sum – on one cloak of velvet with a cape embroidered with gold, pearls and red stones, and one robe of cloth of gold.' The gorgeous, elaborate costumes were the second biggest cost of a major production after the cost of the building itself.[28]

The stages on which plays were performed imposed heavy constraints on what different locations could be depicted. Music helped; and the beating of drums could certainly help to create a martial atmosphere. A cannon ball rolling down a wooden track concealed in an exterior wall could create the illusion of thunder – indeed, with a 3-D effect. (Today's Globe Theatre in London still boasts this special effect.) However, it was words, clothed in the language of poetry, that had to create the scene, in the mind's eye of the spectators – of the forest of Arden, the field of Agincourt, the Rialto in Venice, a tropical island, the edge of a cliff near Dover, or a Scottish castle. The point is, of course, made eloquently in the Prologue to *Henry V*:

> O for a Muse of fire, that would ascend
> The brightest heaven of invention,
> A kingdom for a stage, princes to act
> And monarchs to behold the swelling scene!

It was almost as if the players were inviting the audience to enter into a contract of make-believe, almost entirely through the power of words. In no other forum has the power of poetry been more clearly demonstrated: and no wonder then, that most plays were written as poems. That said, Shakespeare writes in both poetry and prose – the latter mainly but not exclusively for comedic scenes, where he honours the discourse of ordinary folk. The words had to be delivered by actors who had to perform prodigious acts of memory, not just of one play, but of up to six plays a week – for the appetites of audiences were not easily satisfied, the desire for novelty pressing, and the competition keen. One actor often had to play several different parts, and since most acting companies had no more than a dozen or so actors, they might have to change roles – and costumes – several times in a play. This meant that plays had to be written in such a way that allowed for costume changes. For example, in *Hamlet*, one actor might be a soldier on the battlements of Elsinore at the start of the play; then Laertes; a quick change to become Rosencrantz (or Guildenstern); and then, back to Laertes again, at the end.

With this burgeoning of the popularity of drama, Shakespeare's arrival in London could not have been better timed: the huge upsurge in interest in drama must have pump-primed his creative juices.

7

ENTER, SHAKESPEARE

We know what we are
But know not what we may be

– *Hamlet*, Act 4, Scene 5

It was into the social and political morass of London that Shakespeare entered, probably in 1589. At the time it was said that 'some players have gone to London very meanly and have come in time to be exceedingly wealthy.' Fallow suggests that he arrived in London to pursue his father's business interests in the wool trade,[1] but though that is possible, I think it is more likely that he had already become hooked on the theatre. Shakespeare was not the first Stratfordian to move to London: Richard Field, three years older than Shakespeare, took up an apprenticeship as a printer there in 1579. The Fields were close friends and neighbours to the Shakespeare family. Field's employer in London was French-born Thomas Vautrollier, who ran a flourishing business in the old Blackfriars monastery situated between St Paul's and the river. In 1588, Field took over both the business – and his employer's widow. He printed Shakespeare's first best-selling poem.

Arriving in the city, Shakespeare may well have sought the company of fellow actors from the Queen's Men, or Leicester's Men. If so, he would probably have found lodgings in Shoreditch where many of them lived: the Burbage brothers lived in Holywell Street; the Beeston family lived in Hog Lane. Playwrights, too, lived close by, including Christopher Marlowe and

Robert Greene. It was here, too, that the two custom-built theatres were situated – the Curtain, and the Theatre, both of which had been there since the 1570s.

Shoreditch was a very insalubrious area of London, full of hastily improvised rat-infested dwellings, cheap alehouses and brothels. According to Thomas Nashe, it was an area frequented by 'the outshiftes of the City with never a rag to their backs' and prostitutes 'sodden & perboyled with French surfers.'[2] Among their number were penniless and often limbless discharged soldiers, desperate refugees, and coney catchers on the lookout to empty the purses of young men fresh from the country – making William with his Warwickshire accent a prime target. Violence was never far away: it was definitely best not to venture out after dark on one's own. To quote Nashe again:

> wee scoffe and are iocund, when the sword is ready to goe through us; on our wine benches we bid a Fico for ten thousand plagues.

It was while lodging in Shoreditch that he gained an insight into the low-life that features in so many of his plays. John Aubrey, who interviewed William Beeston, the son of an actor who worked with Shakespeare, noted that 'he was the more to be admired because he was not a company keeper, lived in Shoreditch; wouldn't be debauched, and if invited to, writ that he was in pain.'[3]

However, there is another theory about where he might have lodged: there is in the Folger Library in Washington DC a copy of a law book called *Archaionomia*, acquired by the library in 1938.[4] It was published in 1568, and edited by an antiquarian, William Lambarde. Opening the Folger Library's copy of Lambarde's book one reads what purports to be Shakespeare's signature. A handwritten note claims that 'Mr Wm Shakespeare lived at No 1, Little Crown, Westminster NB near Dorset Steps, St James's Park.'

However, there must be a question mark over both the address and the signature in this book. The Library of the University of Toronto houses the Wenceslaus Hollar Collection.[5] Hollar was a Czech engraver born in 1607, and among his etchings is a detailed map of London. There is no mention of 'Dorset Steps': the address provided does appear suspect. What about

> **William Lambarde (1536-1601)**
>
> Lambarde, the son of a draper, was educated at Jesus College, Cambridge and Lincoln's Inn. For a time, he was an MP, and in 1566 he braved the Queen's displeasure by taking part in a debate in Parliament about the royal succession. He was Lord of the Manor of Westcombe in Greenwich. In 1575 Lambarde founded some alms houses, named Queen Elizabeth's College. These were rebuilt in 1819, and are situated directly opposite Greenwich railway station.
>
> Lambarde's most famous work was *A Perambulation of Kent*. He entered the service of Burghley, and was highly prized for the clarity of his writing: he drafted or amended a number of Parliamentary bills – one of them 'to restrain the printing of hurtful books.'[6] Lambarde's skills in drafting bills were clearly much needed, as indeed they still are in Westminster. William Fleetwood commented in 1585: 'All our bills are long bills, full of tautology and *cakaphonia*, penned in barbarous English ... '[7] It is debatable how much has changed ...

the signature?[8] Strangely, it is buried amid a decorative border on the title page and requires spectral imaging to make it legible.[9] That is a very odd place to write one's name. These scrawled words are unlikely to be those of William Lambarde. There must be considerable doubts about their authenticity – and this could well be just one among a number of Shakespearian frauds.[10]

When did Shakespeare start writing?

The contentious question arises – when exactly did Shakespeare start writing his own plays as opposed to 'overseeing' other people's scripts? What work had he already done that gave him an entrée into the highly competitive world of London theatre? We know he saw and probably acted in plays in the Queen's Men's repertoire, some of which were later rewritten by Shakespeare; and as already noted he was acknowledged, in print, for 'overseeing' the script of the play *Locrine*, performed by the Queen's Men (whatever 'overseeing' meant).

It is time to look at the first three plays we know of that Shakespeare wrote, or had a serious hand in. Here one should thank Rory Loughnane for drawing our attention to the fact that of the hundreds of plays written in the 1580s, only 32 have survived.[11] Almost a third of those that survived are by Marlowe and Lyly; one of them, *Two Gentlemen of Verona*, is wholly by Shakespeare; two others are by Shakespeare and others – *Arden of*

Faversham (with Anon, 1588), and *Titus Andronicus* (with Peele, 1589); so Shakespeare was already beginning to make his mark. No one can say whether he wrote other plays that have disappeared, but Loughnane claims that the attrition rate is so high it is very plausible that others may have been lost.[12]

It is not our intention to blind the reader with science. There is a danger of one's enjoyment of Shakespeare's works being blighted with linguistic analysis: in Wordsworth's words, 'we murder to dissect.'[13] This book offers an attempt to summarise the current state of knowledge unearthed by this invaluable research, and, crucially, offers an appreciation of each one of

> **Literary studies: an art, or a science?**
>
> Modern research utilizes the computer for linguistic analysis to try to establish the chronology and authorship of the plays, a methodology known as stylometrics, a growing area in Shakespeare studies. This has shown beyond doubt that many, if not most, plays of the late Tudor and Jacobean age involved collaboration by two or more writers, not necessarily writing contemporaneously. One of the pioneers of this approach was MacDonald P. Jackson who has contributed dozens of books and articles to this area of study, (eg, Jackson 2002).[14]
>
> Scholars such as Jackson have sought to determine authorship by identifying verbal parallels using the database built up by the Chadwyck-Healey Literature Collections, ProQuest, and LION – *Literature Online*, The University of London's Online Library (the world's largest cross-searchable data base of literature and criticism). LION contains more than 350,000 works of poetry, prose and drama in the English language from the 8th century to the present day. The search engine enables the researcher to compare different works of literature to provide co-occurrences of rare phrases, collocations, lexical choice, and variant spellings. For a case-study in the methodology used, see Jackson pp182-193 in Taylor and Egan, *op cit*.[15] There are also other techniques. Literary studies are, for good or ill, being turned into a science by this group of scholars. However, the bathwater of linguistic analysis should not be allowed to drown the baby: aesthetic judgement and appreciation remain vital. (See for example the article by Jackson in Loughnane and Power 2020).[16]
>
> Computer analyses rest on the principle that 'an individual writer's word-choices form a unique pattern that can be distinguished from those of other writers.' (Pruitt 2017)[17] In effect, stylistic features are being viewed as a kind of linguistic fingerprint: each writer has his (or her) own idiolect. What facilitates the idea is the fact that the norms of Standard English were still being evolved during Shakespeare's lifetime, and grammar, punctuation, imagery, idiom and spelling – especially in Tudor times – were idiosyncratic, so that signature language patterns can be identified. However, it must be admitted that, to continue with the fingerprint analogy, in practice, the prints are at times smudged, and murky, and continue to keep the scholars busy.

the works considered. For a look at the minutiae of the research methods used, and to get a measure of the degree to which scholars at times differ, the interested reader is referred to Taylor and Egan's *The New Oxford Shakespeare Authorship Companion* (OUP, 2017) to which this author is deeply indebted.[18]

Dating Shakespeare's plays is a matter of on-going controversy. What were the first plays that Shakespeare is known to have written? In recent decades, computer-based research methods have replaced the sometimes acrimonious guess-work that flourished in past centuries on the chronology (and authorship) of Shakespeare's plays. The result one has to admit, is not decisive, for Taylor and Loughnane in the aforementioned *Authorship Companion* admit that they are often reduced to a 'Best Guess'. The conclusions are still not set in stone. On the whole, we follow the course plotted by this work. *Two Gentlemen of Verona* wins the race to be first by a short head.[19]

Two Gentlemen of Verona

Professor Stanley Wells[20] has long taken the view that this play is Shakespeare's earliest, on the basis that it includes basic dramatic techniques that are much less sophisticated than Shakespeare's later work. Warren clinches the argument: the character of Lance (with his dog) was almost certainly written for the famous comic actor Richard Tarlton, who regularly performed with the Queen's Men on stage with his dog, and who died in September 1588. Warren even suggests that this play could have been written as early as 1583, probably for amateur performance in Stratford-upon-Avon; this suggestion is borne out by its primitive plot, its brevity – and the unusually small cast.[21] There is certainly a home-grown feel about the play: there is no record of it being performed, and the text as printed in the First Folio is muddled, and lacks stage directions, and confuses Verona with Milan and Padua.

This is definitely a young man's play, in all senses: indeed, the opening almost reads like a dialogue between the young Will Shakespeare and himself: one half of him (Proteus), is passionately in love with Julia, and wants to stay at home. The other half, (Valentine), longs to leave Verona to seek 'the wonders of the world' (as one of the servants, Panthino, puts it, 'to seek preferment out') – or as others might put it

Some to the wars, to try their fortune there
Some to discover islands far away
Some to the studious universities.

– Act 1, Scene 3

The play does exhibit some of the characteristic features of immature young men, including self-absorption – and gormlessness. The two young men imagine women to be fickle, and cruel, and fail to register the positive signals they get. What conflict there is is between the young men, who fight over the same woman. Meanwhile the young women seem to queue up to gain their affection – no accounting for taste ... Julia (disguised as a boy) pursues Proteus, while Silvia falls for Valentine. She tries to convey her feelings for him by asking him to write a love letter to 'a secret, nameless friend' and then tells Valentine to give it to himself:

> SILVIA: Well, I guess the sequel.
> And yet I will not name it, and yet I care not
> And yet, take this again
> (*She offers him the letter*)
> And yet I thank you
> Meaning, henceforth, to trouble you no more.
> SPEED (*aside*): And yet you will, and yet another yet.
> VALENTINE: What means your ladyship? Do you not like it?
> SILVIA: Yes, yes, the lines are very quaintly writ,
> But since unwillingly take them again.
>
> – Act 2, Scene 1

Speed, the servant, is much quicker on the uptake than the witless Valentine, and only at the end of the scene does the latter realise that Silvia's letter is intended for him. However, the women in the play have their own fair share of foolishness: seriously, what sensible woman would have anything to do with either Proteus or Valentine, whose affections almost depend on which way the wind blows?

More amusing perhaps is the relationship between Lance and his dog, Crab: Lance is totally out of control of his pet – and Crab doesn't know how to behave. He steals the leg of a chicken from Silvia's table, makes himself very unpopular with his smell, and, in answer to a call of nature, inflicts the final insult, as described by Lance:

> LANCE (to Crab): Nay, I remember the trick you served me when I took my leave of Madam Silvia: did not I bid thee still mark me and do as I do? When didst thou see me heave up my leg and make water against a gentlewoman's farthingale? Dids't thou ever see me do such a trick?
>
> – Act 4, Scene 4

Perhaps Silvia felt better when she heard the song 'Who is Silvia?' that appears in many anthologies. The song, and the fun and games with Lance and his dog, sit uneasily beside Act 5, Scene 4. where Proteus threatens to rape Silvia. Valentine intervenes to save her, and what happens next passes belief: Proteus asks for forgiveness – not from Silvia, but from his friend. Neither of them asks if Silvia is all right after the attempted rape, and Valentine then blithely offers to hand her over to Proteus – who then decides that after all Julia has the fairer face, and hands her back to Valentine. The women get the men they wanted, but should definitely be warned to be careful what they wish for ... The women are passed like parcels. No wonder George Eliot was disgusted by this play, the main point of which is really about male friendship: in the words of Valentine: ''Twere pity two such friends should be long foes.' There is serious doubt as to whether the title of this play is meant to be ironic. These two rakes should not count as gentlemen in anyone's book ...

Arden of Faversham

Competing with *Two Gentlemen* to be the first by Shakespeare is *Arden of Faversham*. This play was entered in the Stationer's Register in April 1592,[22] and printed in the same year, but, as we have seen, most plays were performed often years before they went into print. In the Tudor way of doing things, the title page, without any attempt at a 'spoiler alert', summarises the plot:

> THE LAMENTABLE AND
> TRUE TRAGEDY OF MASTER
> ARDEN OF FAVERSHAM IN KENT.
> Who was most wickedly murdered, by
> the Means of his Disloyal and Wanton
> Wife, Who for the Love She Bare to One

> Mosby, Hired Two Desperate Ruffians,
> Black Will and Shakebag, to Kill Him.
> Wherein is Showed the Great Malice and
> Dissimilation of a Wicked Woman, the
> Insatiable Desire of Filthy Lust and the
> Shameful End of All Murderers.

This title page suggests it is a secular morality play; sometimes described as a domestic tragedy, it is best seen as a crime drama – and helped to popularise this as a recognised genre. (The Lord Chamberlain's Men – to become Shakespeare's company – performed four crime dramas, the first *A Warning for Fair Women*, possibly by Heywood, featured a murder near Shooters Hill in Greenwich.) *Arden* might also be seen as a forerunner of Agatha Christie or Simenon – or any detective procedural. However, it is not a 'Whodunnit', because very early on the identity of both victim and criminals is made obvious. At the time, this sensational murder (which occurred in 1551) was the subject of numerous pamphlets and ballads. Bate and Rasmussen suggest that it was almost immediately re-enacted on London stages.[23] It derives much of its content from Holinshed's *Chronicles of England, Scotland and Ireland*, which came out in 1577. Taylor and Loughnane suggest the probable date of the version we now have is late 1588 (just after *Two Gentlemen*) – but hedge their bets by saying the date range could be as early as 1587 or as late as 1592.[24]

The authorship of *Arden of Faversham* remains a somewhat contentious issue: many editions of his Collected Works have ignored it. But it is now definitely recognised as part of the canon, albeit, like most plays of the time, as a collaborative work. Jackson adduces strong evidence to show that the middle section of the play – Scenes 2-8 and possibly Scene 9, are by Shakespeare.[25] The imagery at times reflects the experience of a man who has lived close to nature and the countryside. The name of any collaborator remains a matter of guess-work – Kyd, Nashe, Peele and Marlowe have all been ruled out by most authorities. Thomas Watson is a possibility, but none of his plays have survived, and therefore it has proved impossible to carry out comparative stylometric analysis.[26]

Shakespeare's creative imagination goes into overdrive in Scene 8. Mosby is given a soliloquy indicating a character of some complexity: contemplating the murderous plot that he and Alice have hatched, he has taken to the bottle (unlike Macbeth, who takes to the sword). His troubled mind is 'stuffed with discontent/My golden time was when I had no gold.' (Scene 8). But he realises that he cannot turn back – and knows too that to escape punishment he will need to finish off his accomplices and even his lover, Alice, Arden's wife. She then appears, prayer-book in hand, tormented by conscience as she, in turn, contemplates the murder of her husband:

> I pray thee, Mosby, let our springtime whither
> Our harvest else will yield but loathsome weeds
> Forget, I pray thee, what has pass'd betwixt us
> For now I blush and tremble at the thought
>
> – Scene 8

When Mosby angrily responds, she does a *volte face*, suddenly terrified at the prospect of losing him, and starts to tear out pages from her prayer book to signify her devotion to him, showing that low life can still be the stuff of high drama.

However, the play is not only high emotional drama. The play includes a number of other characters, almost all of whom have reasons to hate Arden. So, as Poirot might observe, they all had motive; but opportunity? The plot thickens: Alice hires two murderous ruffians, Black Will and Shakebag, to murder her husband; but there is high comedy when they turn out to be serially incompetent. In the end they complete their bloody task – in precisely the most compromising place of all – in Arden's own home. His body is bundled out in the snow, just before retribution knocks on the door with the arrival of Franklin, who smells a rat: he swiftly discovers the corpse by following the bloody footsteps in the snow.

There is now general agreement among scholars that Shakespeare had a hand in the play, but some still have doubts. For example, Martin Wiggins, a much-respected Shakespearian scholar, said he was certain that it was not written by a professional dramatist, but was the work of a gifted amateur. For example, he argues that there was no way an actor playing Shakebag could fall into a ditch and emerge covered in mud, given the constraints of a Tudor stage.[27] How certain can we be? Time to consult Terri Bourus, an academic and theatre practitioner in Florida: having directed a production of *Arden* in 2014, Bourus says that actors found no problem in acting it even without a muddy ditch to hand. Audiences, then and now, are entirely capable of imagining a muddy ditch without having to manufacture a trap door that was rarely available in Tudor drama.[28] Bourus is sure that the play was never written by an amateur.

Before we move on to the next play, many readers may share the niggling doubts about the dating of *Arden*. Sharpe's suggestion that *Arden* came first is fairly compelling.[29] Think about it: if you were a country boy from Warwickshire making perhaps a first stab at writing a play, would it not be more likely that you would set it in familiar territory – a small town in England – rather than a city in far-away Italy? I think it is more than possible, likely even, that Shakespeare wrote his parts of *Arden* (Scenes 4-8, and possibly, 9), perhaps in draft form, much earlier, and it was completed later. A thought to conjure with.

Titus Andronicus

Perhaps Shakespeare felt it was time to show his mettle with a real blockbusting tragedy, one to rival the drama and cruelty of Marlowe's *Tamburlaine*, at the time a huge success. Vickers provides compelling evidence that George Peele was a co-author of *Titus Andronicus*, probably

Peacham Drawing of a scene from *Titus Andronicus* (reproduced by permission of the Marquis of Bath, Longleat House, Warminster, Wiltshire)

contributing Act 1, Scene 1, and possibly Scene 2.[30] To make the authorship even muddier, there is evidence that the 'Fly' scene (when a mad Titus accuses his brother Marcus of murder when he kills a fly) was added much later by Middleton, possibly around 1608.

Titus Andronicus is, in Wilson's words, 'a work of brilliantly engineered dramatic force.'[31] The play is strongly influenced by Senecan revenge tragedies:[32] for example, Seneca's *Thyestes*, like *Titus*, includes mayhem, murder and cannibalism. Taylor and Loughnane's best guess for the writing of *Titus* is late 1589.[33] It would have appealed to those who enjoyed extreme violence on the stage. However, those of a more serious bent would immediately have their attention grabbed in the very first scene, when

Shakespeare and Race

There is increasing interest in this area of study. The Arizona Center for Mediaeval and Renaissance Studies has an on-going conference 'by and for scholars of color' called RaceB4Race; in 2020 Shakespeare's Globe in London ran a conference on Shakespeare and race. Those interested are referred to the work of Ayanna Thompson, editor, of *The Cambridge Companion to Shakespeare and Race.*[34]

Clearly, no one expects Shakespeare to have an enlightened 21st-century view on race. For example, he could be forgiven for thinking that 'race' is something that exists in nature, despite the findings of modern anthropology and genetics.

One cannot really expect him to do much more than reflect the 'spirit of his age'. There is no question that he knew black people in London – Queen Elizabeth's government attempted (unsuccessfully) to deport them in 1596.[35] So, in the plays there are references to 'blackamoores,' the term was more descriptive than pejorative, for the status of 'blackamoores' in Tudor England varied: some had important positions in England – it is not the case that they were all enslaved people or menials.[36]

It could be said Shakespeare is ahead of the curve on the issue of race and 'race-making'. The play questions any ideological assumptions that black men are somehow inferior. For example, in *Titus Andronicus*, Aaron the Moor is an evil villain: but as a literate, classically educated African he challenges any racial stereotypes that his audience might have had, and he compares favourably in several respects with Titus.

Aaron also speaks up for blackness. In Act IV Scene 2 he asks 'Is black so base a hue?', and later comments 'Coal-black is better than another hue'. Then, again, Othello the noble Moor, is black (and clearly a victim of racism). Cleopatra, too, is black, as is the Dark Lady of the sonnets – either a Sephardic Jew or a woman of colour, we cannot say. But both the Dark Lady, and Cleopatra, are seen as figures that can be, are, loved.

Marcus Andronicus produces a speech that could have been potential dynamite in Tudor England:

> Princes, that strive by factions and by friends
> Ambitiously for rule and empery,
> Know that the people of Rome, for whom we stand
> A special party, have, by common voice,
> In election for the Roman empery,
> Chosen Andronicus
>
> – Scene 1

The Tudor establishment, and those in the know (most of London) knew all about 'factions and friends' in the corridors of power – who then (as now?) jockey for position in pursuit of influence if not power. Indeed, 'Friends and factions' acting as 'evil advisers' to the crown were a standard feature of English politics for centuries, and useful scapegoats for those who were reluctant to criticise the monarch directly. However, the E-word was politically loaded – *election*. Before the execution of Mary, Queen of Scots in 1587, the idea of elective monarchy had been canvassed by Protestants anxious to avoid the Crown being inherited by a Catholic; after her execution, the same idea was being canvassed by Catholics, anxious to avoid the accession of Mary Stuart's son, the Protestant James VI of Scotland. Shakespeare managed to get away with using the E-word by safely embodying it in what was touted as a 'noble Roman history'. However, it is hard to credit him with a political motive: it is inescapable that he was trying to beat Marlowe and Kyd at their own game by producing a crowd-pleasing, block-busting, gory tragedy. Some of the speeches in the play have great poetic power, such as this soliloquy from Titus, agonising over what has happened to his daughter Lavinia:

> When heaven doth weep, doth not the earth o'er flow?
> If the winds rage, doth not the sea wax mad?
>
> – Scene 5

Titus Andronicus is a hard play to like. It is obscenely violent. The ending of *Hamlet* seems like a picnic in comparison. Yet *Titus Andronicus* was a triumph, and saw frequent revivals – and Shakespeare was now seen as a significant player on the London scene: doors opened that otherwise might have remained closed. Unusually, two editions of *Titus Andronicus* were published by 1594, indicating its immediate popularity: Shakespeare had definitely arrived. However, it was really necessary for his survival to find a patron. Enter the future Earl of Derby, Lord Strange.[37]

8

LORD STRANGE'S MEN

reputation is an idle and most false imposition;
oft got without merit, and lost without deserving
— Iago to Cassio, *Othello*

After the death of the Earl of Leicester in September 1588, Leicester's Men, including Burbage, Kempe and Pope moved to London to become members of Lord Strange's Men. Their new patron was Ferdinando Stanley, Lord Strange, soon to become the Fifth Earl of Derby. Shakespeare followed suit: he would have been a welcome addition to this group, for by now he was known not merely as a 'fixer-up' of other men's plays, (in Jonathan Bate's words),[1] but as a capable playwright, with *Two Gentlemen of Verona*, *Arden of Faversham*, and *Titus Andronicus* to his name.

In his portrait, Ferdinando, Lord Strange, appears a louche playboy: his hat is askew, and there is a twinkle in his eye, and a slight smile; his jaunty stance suggests fun and laughter. He carries a lance, and one hand rests on a helmet, though he was a habitué of the tiltyard rather than the battlefield. His main interest lay in the arts: he enjoyed music, dance and poetry – and, above all, the theatre. Ferdinando and his brother, William, welcomed different groups of players to the family house in Lathom. Among the writers the family had dealings with were Robert Greene, Christopher Marlowe, possibly Thomas Kyd, and Edmund Spenser. To this list must be added the name of William Shakespeare, as writer, and maybe bit player, if not a full member of Lord Strange's Men. To be settled in London, no longer on tour, performing in plays at Burbage's Theatre, and working with England's top playwrights, Shakespeare was in his element.

This period played an important part in his development as a playwright. The huge successes of *Titus*, and the Henry plays discussed in this chapter, marked him out as a key player in London's theatre land – and a member of Lord Strange's Men, the top troupe. Between 27 December 1591 to 8 February 1592, 'the Seruants of our verie good lord Strange', as they were called by the Privy Council, played no fewer than six times at court. Over the same period, there were single performances by the Queen's Men, Sussex's Men, and Hertford's Men.²

Shakespeare also benefitted a great deal by working, in particular, with Christopher Marlowe: he was still on a learning-curve. He learnt a great deal, I think, about the craft of writing, and the crafts of play-making and staging. This is not to diminish him: as Grayson Perry observed, 'Craft is what you learn, art is about self-realisation.' If his involvement in the *Henry VI* plays might be seen as a kind of apprenticeship, his play, *Richard III*, which shows total, and inspired, mastery of the craft of play-writing indicates that he had successfully graduated – and had come into his own. However, it was during his involvement in what came to be called *Henry VI* Parts 2 and 3 that, for the first time, perhaps, he was also made aware that drama was not just a form of entertainment – it could have political significance.

The Stanley family

Ferdinando came from an immensely powerful Catholic family – his father Henry Stanley, the 4th Earl of Derby, was Lord Lieutenant of both Lancashire and Cheshire, and owned vast estates. He was also Lord of the Isle of Man. Henry Stanley had been an adviser to Catholic Queen Mary, and his marriage to Lady Margaret Clifford, a descendant of Henry VII, meant that he had a distant claim to the throne.

Even so, Starkey reminds us that Elizabeth shrewdly retained Henry Stanley among her close coterie of advisers along with several others she inherited from Mary.³ His Catholic sympathies must have been tested almost beyond endurance when he was ordered to preside over the trial of Mary, Queen of Scots, in 1586.

With their royal pedigree and Catholic faith, the Stanleys were regarded as a potential threat by Lord Burghley, the Queen's principal adviser. After the execution of Mary, Burghley knew that English Catholics in exile were seeking a new figurehead – and the Earl of Derby was in their sights.

Ferdinando Stanley, Lord Strange (1559-1594), and 5th Earl of Derby

He was also to discover, in time, that historical drama was also fraught with potential danger, for any depiction of historical events based on English history could so easily be interpreted in unforeseen and unwelcome ways, and attract the heavy hand of authority. How could this happen? Surely, he must have thought, having a patron like Lord

Strange, the future Earl of Derby, would offer protection from any danger? Things did not turn out that way.

Ferdinando Stanley, even today, remains something of an enigma. In exile in Antwerp, the Jesuit, Father Robert Persons, wrote that 'the Earl of Derby's religion is held to be doubtful, as some do think him to be of all three religions [ie Roman Catholic; Church of England; Puritan] and others of none.'[4] So Ferdinando was distrusted on all sides. It seems he attempted to show as little interest in politics as possible, instead focusing on his favourite pursuits, which included hunting, falconry, and the arts. However, Burghley's agents had intercepted two incriminating letters, carried by Catholic priests, naming Ferdinando as a successor to Elizabeth after she had been assassinated; but they also cast doubt on his reliability.[5] It is not possible now to say how sympathetic he was to the Catholic cause. It is likely that in both politics and religion, he saw caution as the better part of valour – especially after his cousin, Sir William Stanley, serving under Leicester in the war in the Low Countries, defected to join Parma's army. That certainly did not help his position – and the execution of Mary, Queen of Scots, placed Ferdinando one step closer to the throne – and one step nearer the scaffold …

Ferdinando was fully conscious of these lurking suspicions, and in the febrile atmosphere following the Spanish Armada, he saw the need to demonstrate that he had no political ambitions.[6] In 1591, he conspicuously demonstrated loyalty by taking part in the court's annual Accession Day's tilts, celebrating the day the Queen came to the throne. Burbage and Shakespeare may have acted as one of his squires on the occasion. This may have been the first time that Shakespeare saw his future patron the Earl of Southampton, who also took part in the tilts.

His bid for innocence – on the stage

With their interest in drama, it was perhaps only natural for Ferdinando and his brother William Stanley, to think that it could be used to demonstrate their loyalty to the Crown: their weapon of choice was the history play. Many authorities have noticed that the plays depart from the historical record to give the Stanley and Clifford families undue prominence as loyal servants of the Crown.

> **The Tudor History play**
>
> During the Tudor period history plays (including fake history such as *King Lear* and its predecessor *King Leir*) were becoming the vogue; they were to become a standard genre, and their role in shedding light on contemporary politics was already recognised, at least among those in the know. An early example is *Magnyfycence* by John Skelton (1519). Henry VIII was 'Magnyfycence', sabotaged by 'Folly' (Wolsey), and was, clearly, an overt piece of political propaganda. *Kynge Johan* (1538) by John Bale, gave the characters real names.
>
> The four plays that Shakespeare wrote, or helped to write, in the early 1590s are set in the reigns of Henry VI and Richard III. They depict a turbulent time in English history: between 1455 and 1485 England saw a civil war between two competing royal families – the House of Lancaster, and the House of York, known to contemporaries as 'the Cousins' War'. It later came to be known as the Wars of the Roses – the white rose of York and the red rose of Lancaster. The name derives from the scene of *1 Henry VI* (Act 2, Scene 4) when the two competing factions meet in the Temple Gardens in London and pick roses to show their affiliation – an example of 'fake history' created by Shakespeare in an inspired piece of theatre.[7]
>
> When Henry VI came to the throne, he was king of both England and part of France. The plays show the loss of France, the loss of Henry's crown – and the virtual extinction of both competing houses, along with thousands of nobles and foot soldiers, so demonstrating the horrors of a civil war. The three Henry VI plays end with *Richard III* whose death at the battle of Bosworth saw the coronation of Henry VII, a *deus ex machina*, the first of the Tudors, providing at last a haven of security.

There is some doubt about the genesis of the *Henry VI* plays, although it seems likely that it was Ferdinando or his brother who initiated them. They may have been influenced by Sir Philip Sidney's *An Apology for Poetry*, also known as *The Defence of Poesy*, written and privately circulated in the early 1580s. Sidney argued that both philosophy and history were important, and combining them with poetry could move men to virtuous action. I think that Shakespeare certainly subscribed to this view, even though he would no doubt be the first to admit that he himself was not the embodiment of virtue.[8] Commissioning the plays, Ferdinando could have given the writers access to Raphael Holinshed's *Chronicles* (originally published in 1577, republished in 1587), to ensure a degree of historical authenticity. They also seem to have had access to Edward Halle's *The Union of the two noble and illustre famelies of Lancastre and Yorke*. Access to these books was important, for it is unlikely that any of the writers could have afforded to buy them. It is unlikely that Ferdinando or William were involved in the writing process – though there is evidence that William Stanley was a writer of in-house plays, for private performance only.[9] They certainly must have had some influence over the writing, because the plays depart from the narratives of Holinshed and Halle, to raise the profile of the Stanley and Clifford families, emphasising, across the generations, their proven track-record of loyalty to the Crown. This was Ferdinando's hidden agenda.

The plays were performed by several different companies. (The going rate for a company to perform a play was about £6.00). So, although it is likely that Shakespeare had a role as an actor in Lord Strange's Men, these plays were also performed by other acting groups. including the Earl of Pembroke's Men.[10] It certainly suited Ferdinando's purpose to have the plays performed by other acting companies, to spread the word more widely. The linguistic and computer-assisted evidence adduced by scholars shows that several writers were involved initially in the *Henry VI* cycle.[11] It is possible that Shakespeare had a relatively minor role in writing these plays, it was not until some years later that he left his mark on the plays in a rewrite. Confusingly, Part 1 was written after Parts 2 and 3.

Henry VI, Part 2

For Ferdinando, the reign of Henry VI had the advantages of demonstrating both patriotism (at the expense of the French), and the loyal track record of the Clifford and Stanley families. The first of the Henry plays to be written – the one we now know as 2 *Henry VI* – had a completely different name when it was first published. Its title is a virtual summary of the play: *The First Part of the Contention betwixt the two famous houses of York and Lancaster, with the death of the good Duke Humphrey: And the banishment and death of the Duke of Suffolk, and the Tragical end of the proud Cardinal of Winchester, with the notable rebellion of Jack Cade. And the Duke of York's first claim unto the Crown.* Not exactly a pithy title: seemingly Tudor audiences were not troubled by 'spoiler-alerts'. The play is attributed to William Shakespeare, Christopher Marlowe, and (possibly) another. It was probably written about 1590, and later revised and added to by Shakespeare after he joined the Lord Chamberlain's Men. The first version was entered on the Stationers' Register in March 1594. The version in the 1623 Folio of Shakespeare's works is about a third longer, indicating his later additions.[12]

The absence of the king's name from the title reflects how ineffectual he was. At the start of the play, the English nobles are furious that in signing a treaty with France, Henry has renounced historic claims to French land, and is to marry Margaret of Anjou – without a dowry. His feisty French wife makes up for what King Henry lacks. It is she who turns against him at the battle of St Albans, and exclaims in exasperation 'What are you made of? You'll not fight nor flee ... ' Not that the king is wicked, indeed, he is well-meaning. He longs for a country where all could live in harmony with each other – but his hopes are dashed by the nobles scheming around him:

> HENRY: The winds grow high, so do your stomachs, lords.
> How irksome is this music to my heart?
> When such strings jar, what hope for harmony?
>
> – Act 2. Scene 1

Unfortunately, Henry does not live in an ideal world, where politics are as harmonious as music: for harmony does not sit well with the Machiavellian world of *Realpolitik* – the world inhabited by the poisonous Duke of York. These are York's thoughts after he learns that his fellow-courtiers have put him in charge of an army to deal with Ireland:

> YORK: My brain, more busy than the labouring spider,
> Weaves tedious snares to trap mine enemies
> Well, nobles, well: 'tis politely done
> To send me packing with a host of men
> I fear me you but warm the starved snake
> Who, cherished in your breasts, will sting your hearts
> 'Twas men I lacked, and you will give them me
> I take it kindly. Yet be well assured
> You put sharp weapons in a madman's hands
>
> – Act 3, Scene 1

The imagery strongly resembles that which appears in *Richard III* – like father, like son. York was not the only scheming courtier: the concept of evil, corrupt courtiers misleading the monarch is a leitmotif of mediaeval and early modern politics in England – the good Duke Humphrey (Gloucester) is the exception who proves the rule, and it is he who his rivals, including Suffolk and the Bishop of Winchester, seek to destroy. Their problem is that he is the Lord Protector of the young king, and he is too honest, and powerful, for their liking.

Gloucester's Achilles heel is his wife, Eleanor Cobham, who suffers from 'the canker of ambitious thoughts'. She dreams of her husband supplanting the king, and is encouraged by Sir John Hume, an *agent provocateur*, to consult a witch. She does not realise that Hume has been hired to 'undermine' her (and thus her husband.) She is subsequently accused of witchcraft and treason; a witch she consulted is sentenced to be burnt to death, and three others are executed. The duchess is forced to do a humiliating public penance, and her husband loses his position as Lord Protector. When the king then banishes the duchess to the Isle of Man, the gaoler is none other than the loyal Sir John Stanley – the lord of the Isle of Man.

The Cliffords have a higher profile than the Stanleys in 2 *Henry VI*. The role that Lord Clifford plays is important for Ferdinando's reputation: an ancestor of his, Sir Robert Clifford, was involved in the Perkin Warbeck plot against Henry VII – possibly as an *agent provocateur*, (or possibly turning King's Evidence); for both he and his father-in-law, William Barley, were not just pardoned, but rewarded. In this play Lord Clifford remains determinedly loyal to the king, despite the latter's shortcomings. Together with Buckingham, he fearlessly confronts the rebel Jack Cade and his mob in the 1350 rebellion:

> CLIFFORD: What say ye, countrymen? will ye relent,
> And yield to mercy whilst 'tis offer'd you;
> Or let a rebel lead you to your deaths?
> Who loves the king and will embrace his pardon,
> Fling up his cap, and say 'God save his majesty!'
> Who hateth him and honours not his father,
> Henry the Fifth, that made all France to quake,
> Shake he his weapon at us and pass by.
> ALL: God save the king! God save the king!
>
> – 20.10-18

Cade fights back, and the fickle crowd turn against Lord Clifford; but he wins the war of words, and Cade takes to his heels. Clifford captures many of the rebels and brings them to the king with halters round their necks.

The treatment of Cade's rebellion is interesting: Cade and his supporters camped out on Blackheath in 1450 and presented *The Complaint of the Poor Commons of Kent*, sometimes called 'the Blackheath Petition'. Its object was to 'punish evil ministers and procure a redress of grievance' – the latter related to excessive taxation and extortion.[13] These demands received widespread support – indeed, the campaign might have been viewed sympathetically by many in a Tudor audience, who had very similar complaints. Peter Lake suggests that the Jack Cade scenes, where the rioters commit acts of astonishing brutality, reflected the social unrest in 1591.[14] However, their demands would have horrified most people: they included the arbitrary killing of any nobleman they found, and the destruction of London Bridge and the Tower of London. More popular, perhaps, would have been the demand by a butcher: 'Let's kill all the lawyers!' This vivid treatment of the horrors of civil unrest might be compared today with the accounts of those who stormed the Capitol in Washington in 2021.[15]

In the Jack Cade scenes, the playwrights were skating on very thin ice as far as the authorities were concerned. In 1591, a fanatical Puritan, William Hackett, called for revolt in terms that echoed those of Jack Cade – and was duly executed.[16] The playwrights chose to play safe, departing from Holinshed, and calling Cade's and his followers a 'rabblement'. Cade's rhetoric becomes wilder and wilder – they included abolishing money, claiming the maidenhead of all brides for himself, and killing anyone who could read or speak a foreign language.[17] However, ridicule turns to horror when Lord Saye and Sir James Cromer, who have been captured, are dragged off to be beheaded: their heads are subsequently brought in, and made to kiss each other.

Shakespeare would have been well aware that Cade's *Complaints* echoed the current situation in Tudor England. News from Stratford made it clear how tough life was for people at the bottom of the pile, despite a series of laws passed in Elizabeth's reign designed to relieve poverty.[18] The early 1590s saw a succession of poor harvests, and wages plummeted as food prices rose, and exorbitant taxes were collected by ruthless tax-collectors. There was an influx of what the authorities called 'sturdy beggars' into

London: poor people thrown off the land. In the summers of 1592 and 1593 riots took place, involving apprentices, the unemployed, and war veterans, returning unpaid.[19] The authorities panicked.

Shapiro suggests that Shakespeare was familiar with *The Art of Poesie* by George Puttenham, who coined the word *Amphibologia* – 'when we speak or write doubtfully and that the sense may be taken two ways.'[20] So in these scenes we can detect the element of creative ambiguity in his plays – what he called equivocation. Creative ambiguity was to become the hallmark of Shakespeare's plays: perhaps this was the time when, perhaps unconsciously, perhaps instinctively, he began to see the need for plays to be ambiguous – to be capable of different interpretations, so one always has a let-out clause if confronted with an accusation. Ambiguity also has an aesthetic function: there is pleasure to be found in seeking different interpretations.[21] In this case, for example, Shakespeare could not appear to side with the rioters, but it is likely that he had some sympathy with their concerns: and so, while there is humour in these scenes, it is gallows humour of the grimmest kind, and it is possible that Shakespeare is laughing with Cade's men as well as laughing at them. Skating on thin ice, indeed.

The Jack Cade episode showed the folly of popular rebellion – but folly was not the preserve of the Poor Commons of Kent. As the play draws to its unsatisfactory end – clearly requiring a sequel – England degenerates into civil war initiated not by social concerns, but by the pride, ambition and lust for power by a small group of the nobility who embark on a course of mutual slaughter. Here again Lord Clifford has a high profile, coming out strongly in support of King Henry, and dying on the battlefield, at the hands of the treacherous Duke of York. It is left for Young Clifford to carry off his father's corpse, swearing revenge. We shall see how this works out in *3 Henry VI*.

Henry VI, Part 3

The Third Part of Henry the Sixth or *The Tragedy of Richard, Duke of York* is attributed to William Shakespeare, Christopher Marlowe, and possibly another. It was probably written in late 1590, and again revised by Shakespeare a few years later. It was entered on the Stationers' Register in May 1594 (as was *Shrew*).[22] It begins with a confrontation between the rebels led by York, and the king and his retinue, including Clifford. York arrogantly sits in the 'the chair of state', and when King Henry is surrounded by Warwick's soldiers threatening him with violence, the king weakly suggests that he should remain on the throne, to be succeeded by York. It is obvious that this shameful compromise cannot hold. An argument follows as to whether Henry has a right to the throne, and Clifford swears his loyalty to the King, declaring:

> King Henry, be thy title right or wrong,
> Lord Clifford vows to fight in thy defence:
> May that ground gape and swallow me alive,
> Where I shall kneel to him that slew my father!
>
> – 1.159 – 163

Henry's wife is furious that her son Edward should be disinherited, and vows to fight on. York is as bad as his word, and the civil war starts up again. In this play, the Stanley family has a somewhat lower profile, but in Scene V, Lord Stanley helps to rescue the king from Middleham Castle: the king personally thanks Stanley. We must wait until *Richard III* to see how Stanley leaves his mark on Tudor history.

3 *Henry VI* is a hard play to like: it features almost a revolving door of would-be monarchs, and a great deal of violence – with no fewer than four battles. The first of these takes place in Wakefield, when Clifford demonstrates his ruthlessness in the service of the Crown by killing Rutland, the young son of the Duke of York. Then York himself is captured. He is brought before Queen Margaret, whom he describes as having 'a tiger's heart wrapped in a woman's hide'. The prisoner is made to stand on a mole hill, a paper crown on his head, as Margaret offers to wipe his tears with a handkerchief stained with the blood of his dead son. Clifford and Queen Margaret then stab him to death.

There follows another battle, the Battle of Towton, the bloodiest ever fought on British soil, with at least 30,000 men slaughtered, more were killed, per capita than died on the Somme.[23] In one heart-rending scene, a son discovers he has killed his father – in another, a father realises he has killed his only son. More battles follow, as we watch the English aristocracy at war with itself, egged on by Margaret, the 'she-wolf of France'.

Henry VI, Part 1

The First Part of King Henry the Sixth; or, *Harry the Sixth* is attributed to Marlowe, Thomas Nashe and Anonymous. It was probably written in 1592, (after Parts 2 and 3) and later heavily adapted by Shakespeare, after he left Lord Strange's orbit, probably in 1595, when he turned the plays into a unified tetralogy for the Lord Chamberlain's Men. How far Shakespeare was involved with writing *1 Henry VI* still remains controversial. Most authorities agree that it is likely that he wrote Act 2, Scene 4, Act 4, Scene 2, and parts of Act 4 Scenes 3-5.[24]

The play was a sell-out when it was first performed in 1592: its focus on the wars in France would have resonated with a Tudor audience, for the Earl of Essex was involved in a French campaign at the time. The depiction of La Pucelle – Joan of Arc – as a witch would have also appealed to the audiences, and the scene when she is surrounded by dancing fiends was almost certainly by Marlowe. She is a more sympathetic figure elsewhere in the play, however, where a very different Joan of Arc emerges. Given the contrast in tone and style with the witches' scene, I think it likely that these lines, addressed to the Duke of Burgundy, who has defected to the English, are by Shakespeare. Burgundy is persuaded by these lines, not bewitched:

> JOAN: Look on thy country, look on fertile France
> As looks the mother on her lowly babe
> When death doth close his tender-dying eyes
> And see the cities and the towns defaced
> By wasting ruin of the cruel foe.
> See, see the pining malady of France!
> Behold the wounds, the most unnatural wounds
> Which thou thyself hast given her woeful breast.

– Act 3, Scene 7

The first scene that most authorities agree was written by Shakespeare is Act 2, Scene 4, one of the most inspired pieces of theatre set in the Temple Rose Garden. Here the nobles compete in their desire to control the crown, held by the weak Henry VI, and signal their allegiance by selecting the red rose of Lancaster, or the white rose of York. Tragically, while English blood is shed in a civil war in England, English (and of course French) blood is wasted in France. For the next scenes assigned to Shakespeare are in Act 4, in which Talbot reaches his tragic end when he and his son are surrounded by the French, and die in battle. Realising that there is no hope of survival, Lord Talbot urges his son John to escape while he can in a highly dramatic scene:

> JOHN: Is my name Talbot? And am I your son?
> And shall I fly? O, if you love my mother.
> Dishonour not her honourable name
> To make a bastard and a slave of me!
> The world will say 'He is not of Talbot's blood
> that basely fled when noble Talbot stood!
> TALBOT: Fly to revenge my death if I am slain!
>
> – Act 3, Scene 4

But John remains adamant. It was George Talbot, 6th Earl of Shrewsbury, who was appointed a custodian of Mary Queen of Scots by Elizabeth, and who had been, according to Guy, one of the few nobles whom the queen unreservedly trusted. The Shrewsbury and Stanley families were very close, and one could say that therefore the Stanleys come out well if only by association.

Civil dissension – the viperous worm

Why did Ferdinando choose for his plays the reign of Henry VI, one of the feeblest monarchs, in English history? Noted so far is Ferdinando's agenda. However, these plays are full of *Amphibologia*, and can be seen as an example of Shakespeare's creative ambiguity – and not just in the Jack Cade scenes. The message to any Tudor audience would have been that the monarchy, if properly conducted, was a major source of stability. Henry VI's rule could be seen as an awful warning of the chaos that results from a feeble monarchy. However, there is a much subtler agenda for those who want to see it: they could be seen as expressing moral convictions about right and wrong, and the abuse of power (and thus critical of both monarch and nobles). Then there is the role of women in politics (Margaret of Anjou, Lady Gloucester) – the plays do not show them in a very favourable light, either: Tudor audiences might have detected an echo of Elizabeth's England. What might the more politically-minded have seen? They would perhaps have noted that Elizabeth was indecisive, and was surrounded by courtiers vying for power, just like King Henry. This might well have been seen as an echo of the well-known rivalry between Essex and Sir Walter Ralegh.[25] As always, one sees what one wants to see ...

However, there are no exact parallels between the reign of Henry VI, and Elizabeth's rule, and the plays would have worked well as good theatre, and still do so in the hands of skilful directors. Amid the litany of death and disaster, the *Henry VI* plays had all the elements that make for exciting drama – conflict between scheming courtiers, conspiracy, violence, murder and witchcraft, all relevant to Elizabethan England. For most playgoers, the plays could be seen as just a rollicking story with lots of battles and sword-play. Perhaps the moral of all three plays is best summed up in these lines from *1 Henry VI*:

> Civil dissension is a viperous worm
> That gnaws the bowels of the commonwealth
>
> – Act 2, Scene 1

What is certain is that Ferdinando would not have countenanced his actors performing anything that was remotely subversive, and the playwrights must have felt secure in the patronage of one of the most powerful earls in the country. What could possibly go wrong?

9

THE BATTLE OF THE SEXES

Who taught thee how to make me love thee more,
The more I hear and see just cause of hate?

– Sonnet 150

As we have seen, both Shakespeare and Christopher Marlowe (and 'another') worked together on the *Henry VI* plays. There is no doubt that Kit Marlowe had a big influence on Shakespeare, showing him how well-honed blank verse could have a huge impact on the stage. During his brief life, Marlowe was unquestionably the top playwright. However, it is questionable whether Shakespeare was entirely happy with the company he was keeping in Shoreditch. Although the contact he had with Kit Marlowe was stimulating, as Kyd observed, Kit was given to 'rashness in attempting sodden pryvie injuries to men'. Brawling, or being jailed for debt or affray, seemed to be par for the course for Shakespeare's fellow-playwrights. Marlowe and Tom Watson[1] had already spent time in a stinking hole called Limbo in Newgate prison, accused of affray in Hog Lane. In another incident in May 1592, Kit was bound over to keep the peace.

It was as if time in jail was for them a necessary rite of passage. As Nashe observed in *The Unfortunate Traveller*, only a spell in jail could make a man wise.[2] The likes of Kit Marlowe, Tom Nashe, and Robert Greene were wild spirits that Shakespeare might have found uncomfortable to be around socially, even if he worked with several of them on different plays. For these 'university wits' seemed half-witted.

Shakespeare avoided involvement with the adventures of these 'roaring boys' of the 1590s, as they became known in Elizabethan England: as we have seen, he was 'not a company keeper', and was content to be a bystander as he got on with his next play.

The Taming of the Shrew

If Shakespeare was looking for a Tudor crowd-pleaser, *The Taming of the Shrew* might have seemed to be a likely candidate – though Phyllis Rackin observes that there is no evidence that it was particularly popular at the time, perhaps because it was slightly 'old hat'.[3] In England, and across Europe, there was a folklore tradition featuring many jokes, ballads and plays about shrew- taming. Not just a feature of oral culture, either: ducking-stools and similar ways of dealing with 'scolds' were common. Today, of course, this goes down like a lead balloon: the best that can be said is that in this play, Petruchio never physically beats his wife – nor she him. Even so, there is no doubt that Petruchio's campaign to dominate Katherine is in today's terms a serious case of attempted control and coercion. It is likely that Tudor theatre-goers – many of whom were women – would see it as so absurd that it could not be taken seriously.[4]

There has been some confusion about the play, because another version – called *The Tamynge of A Shrewe* – was put on by the impresario Philip Henslowe at Newington Butts on 11 June 1594, and was entered in the Stationers' Register in May 1594. *A Shrew* is now seen as 'a memorial reconstruction' (polite term for pirated copy based on someone's memory – or possibly a corrupt prompt copy) of Shakespeare's *The Shrew*, which did not appear in print until the First Folio in 1623.

The dating of *The Taming of the Shrew* may be seen as something of a case-study in scholastic sleuthing.[5] Different authorities have suggested dates when it was written any time between 1582 and 1593. Because the play contains a number of references to Warwickshire, Brian Morris has suggested that Shakespeare wrote *The Shrew* in 1589, when home still loomed large in Shakespeare's mental landscape.[6] However, it must have been written after Marlowe's *Dr Faustus* (1591) because it contains quotations from Marlowe's play. Taylor's and Loughnane's 'best guess' is late 1591.[7]

There have also been questions over the authorship of *Shrew*. After detailed linguistic research, Dr Nance has concluded that Marlowe co-wrote the play with Shakespeare.[8] Using a new computer program, he looks at Act 1, Scene 1, where Lucentio and Tranio arrive in Padua. Analysis reveals that Marlowe has ten times more unique lexical parallels in this scene than Shakespeare. For example, the only playwright to use the word *metaphysics*, or variants thereof, is Marlowe. Furthermore, when Lucentio arrives in Padua to 'haply institute/A course of learning and ingenious studies', he goes on to say:

> And therefore, Tranio, for the time I study,
> Virtue and that part of philosophy
> Will I apply that treats of happiness
> By virtue specially to be achieved.

This seems much more the voice of a Cambridge University man than that of a jobbing playwright from the provinces, writing a comedy.

The opening scene – the so-called Induction – features a drunken tinker named Christopher Sly, the name of one of Shakespeare's fellow actors, and thus an in-joke. After he wakes up, he is duped into thinking he is a lord, and is then provided with a play to watch. Is Shakespeare implying that shrew-taming is a fit subject for dim-witted drunken tinkers? Rackin observes that 'Framed by the Induction, the taming plot comes to the audience as a farcical theatrical performance rather than a representation

Will Kempe danced a jig from London to Norwich in 1600 in nine days

of actual life.'[9] However, Tina Packer, artistic director of Shakespeare and Company in Lennox, Massachusetts, claims that 'the sexism is completely accepted ... Nowhere is it questioned.'[10]

In the play there are two sisters – no, the tinker isn't seeing double. The beautiful Bianca has no shortage of suitors, but her father insists that she cannot marry before her older sister, the tough and strong-willed Katherine, whom no one is queuing up to court; so she is a problem for her younger sister. Bianca's suitors pay a fortune-seeker, Petruchio, to court Katherine, and, as expected, she proves a handful. Nevertheless, he woos and marries her, and then sets out to 'tame her' by any means possible: this includes denying her food and rest, and insisting that she has to agree with whatever he says no matter how ridiculous.

Much of the dialogue echoes the sparring between Benedick and Beatrice in *Much Ado About Nothing*. In Act 2, Scene 1, Katherine's spirited repartee matches that of Petruchio. Wells notes its sexual sub-text and sees it as courtship ritual,[11] but her spirited responses earlier in the play are in stark contrast with her demeanour at the end, which is ludicrous, and could only have been seen as a joke to a Tudor audience:

> PETRUCHIO: Come on, i' God's name; once more toward our father's.
>   Good Lord, how bright and goodly shines the moon!
> KATHERINE: The moon! The sun: it is not moonlight now.
> PETRUCHIO: I say it is the moon that shines so bright.
> KATHERINE: I know it is the sun that shines so bright.
> PETRUCHIO: Now, by my mother's son, and that's myself,
>   It shall be moon, or star, or what I list,
>   Or ere I journey to your father's house.
>   Go on, and fetch our horses back again.
>   Evermore cross'd and cross'd; nothing but cross'd!
> HORTENSIO: Say as he says, or we shall never go.
> KATHERINE: Forward, I pray, since we have come so far,
>   And be it moon, or sun, or what you please:
>   An if you please to call it a rush-candle,
>   Henceforth I vow it shall be so for me.
>
>   – Act 4, Scene 1

There is a serious question, *pace* Tina Packer, as to whether Shakespeare really believes that Petruchio's approach is just and reasonable – any more than he really believes that Katherine is really tamed. I don't think so. In the exchange above, Hortensio clearly rolls his eyes to heaven ('Give me strength ... '), and Petruchio comes over as a somewhat crazed bully, a role that perhaps the drunken tinker aspires to, but is never likely to achieve. Katherine is the rational one. It is almost as if in her mind's eye Petruchio is a candidate for a care home, and she seems to be saying:

'There, there. A moon: of *course* it is, dear. Where's matron?'

And Shakespeare concludes by leaving the question open:

He that knows better how to tame a shrew
Now let him speak.

– Act 4, Scene 1

The play, of course, remains controversial today, in the so-called Me-Too age of the early 21st century,[12] and is best described perhaps as 'challenging'. A production at the Everyman Theatre in Liverpool set the play in North Africa, enabling or encouraging a predominantly white audience to indulge in a spurious sense of racial and cultural superiority. A 2012 RSC production by Lucy Bailey saw it as a tinker's sexual fantasy, and the stage was turned into a gigantic bed. The great American actress Meryl Streep, who played Katherine in Joseph Papp's Delacorte Theater production of *Shrew* in New York's Central Park in 1978, has a different take: 'Really what matters is that they have an incredible passion and love; it's not something that Katherine admits to right away but it does provide the source for her change.' Reviews at the time noted the electric sexuality of the performance.[13] In Justin Audibert's RSC production of the play in 2019, the roles are reversed: the shrew is a man, and the tamer a woman.[14] For all its vitality, the production is so far removed from Shakespeare that one might as well have written a different play.

Although the play is supposed to be a comedy, that's not always how it comes over to a modern audience. Some of us have an ahistorical urge to call the police and have Petruchio jailed for coercive and controlling behaviour. There is an understandable tendency in some quarters to see the play as misogynistic,[15] but one wonders whether perceptions are becoming distorted by 21st-century agendas. If one seeks an example of Shakespeare's creative ambiguity, look no further. Phyllis Rackin shrewdly comments that seeing the play as a 'crudely misogynist story tells us more about our biases than about those of Shakespeare's original audience.'[16] Why has it become oddly popular in modern times, both on screen and stage? Surely, because the issues raised are as relevant today as they have ever been.

Personally, I find it hard to view a man who can create the characters of Portia, Rosalind, or Cleopatra, as a misogynist. However, I think there is a strong possibility that *Shrew*, and the Dark Lady sonnets, discussed below, were produced at a time of emotional crisis in Shakespeare's personal life. I have a lurking suspicion about what I think might be the origin of this play – a reason for writing it other than just a wish to create a crowd-pleaser. There is no evidence for what follows, and readers may think too much psychological guesswork is involved: is it possible that while at Stratford, with Shakespeare being so much younger than Anne Hathaway, she tended to take control in various ways, no doubt with the best of intentions? If so, Shakespeare may well have found it difficult to avoid feeling slightly resentful. In that case, this could explain why he might want to write a play that enables him to fantasise about a man being 'in control.' He might not even have been aware of this hidden motivation. Perhaps we should not call it either a rom-com or a farce, but a fantasy. As a footnote, we need to recognise that in the 21st century, violence against women – including domestic violence – remains a serious ongoing problem. It all goes to show how Shakespeare still speaks to us today.

Back in Stratford-upon-Avon, there were other pressing, personal reasons why Shakespeare at this time may have felt anxious. First, in 1592, the news from home was bad – the West Midlands, like much of the rest of the country, was undergoing an economic recession. To make matters worse, his father was again listed with eight others as a suspected recusant by the local Protestant activist, Sir Thomas Lucy.[17] In addition, at this time Shakespeare became involved in a destructive affair of the heart.

Obsession: the Dark Lady sonnets

How can we explain the comparatively lean years 1591-1592? What was he doing over this period? Writer's block? Possibly. However, we suggest that this was a time when he had a brief but all-consuming affair, during and after which he wrote 26 sonnets about his tortured relationship with the so-called 'Dark Lady'. These are sonnets 127-144, and 146-152.

During the 1590s, the writing of sonnets was still very much in fashion: poets, and everyone at court, were heavily into them, vying with each other in their output. Sonnets were circulated in manuscript among friends in a sort of Tudor form of samizdat,[18] seeing who could write the wittiest and most elegant works. They were usually fairly conventional literary exercises. Conforming to the standard Petrarchan model in subject matter, they featured an adored but cruelly chaste and unattainable mistress with conventional features of beauty – golden hair, lily-white skin, and lips and (on a good day), fragrance like a red rose. Apart from several notable sonnet sequences, echoing Sidney's *Astrophil and Stella*, they were seldom intended for publication.

In Chapter 2 we referred to the ground-breaking book by Edmondson and Wells, setting out Shakespeare's sonnets in chronological order – in the order in which they were written.[19] Scholars such as Jackson have concluded that the Dark Lady sonnets were written between 1590 and 1595 – even though they come at the end of the 1609 publication.[20] These sonnets are often cited to support theories about Shakespeare's sex life. The fact that the poems were not published until 1609 suggests that Shakespeare wrote them in the first instance for himself. He did however share at least some of them with his close friends. So it was that in 1598 Frances Meres was able to praise honey 'tounged' Shakespeare whose 'sugared' sonnets were circulated, he said, among his 'priuate friends'. Perhaps we may be permitted to imagine

Allegedly a portrait of Emilia Lanier, née Bassano – Nicholas Hilliard miniature

ourselves, along with Francis Meres, as being among his 'priuate friends' as we read them.

In the past, Shakespeare's sonnets have been interpreted in two ways: there were those like Sidney Lee who argue that the poems have no provable connection with real life, and therefore should be regarded merely as literary stand-alone texts: definitely not autobiographical.[21] Nevertheless, many readers find it almost impossible to read the sonnets without thinking that some of them at least are expressions of personal feelings that are compellingly real,[22] and many scholars have seen them as reflecting Shakespeare's experience in real life. It is hard not to agree with Stephen Greenblatt that

> the sonnets are a thrilling, deeply convincing staging of the poet's inner life, an intimate performance of Shakespeare's response to the tangled emotional relationships with a young man, a rival poet, and a dark lady ... [23]

James Shapiro questions this approach: he points out that there is virtually no text written in Tudor times, other than perhaps devotional religious works, that are remotely autobiographical. He argues that Shakespeare could easily construct poems using his imagination.[24] It is certainly true that there are several references in his plays to poems expressing 'fake' emotions – for example in *Twelfth Night*, Touchstone suggests that 'the truest poetry is the most feigning.' (Act III,1)

In my view Shapiro's comment certainly applies to the plays. But the sonnets? Here I must differ from Shapiro. I think Shakespeare takes seriously Sir Philip Sidney's dictum 'to look in your heart and write.' It is difficult to see these lines as being a mere literary exercise:

> My love is as a fever, longing still
>   For that which longer nurses the disease.
>   Feeding on that which doth preserve the ill
>   Th' uncertain sickly appetite to please ...
>
> – Sonnet 147

They are so personal, so graphic, so visceral in some of the emotions expressed, that they have to be at least partly autobiographical. And this Dark Lady comes over as a real person, for 'My mistress eyes are raven black', the poet says in Sonnet 127, and we learn

> In the old age black was not counted fair,
>   Or if it were, it bore not beauty's name;
> But now is black beauty's successive heir,
>   And beauty slandered with a bastard shame;
>
> – Sonnet 127
>
> My mistress' eyes are nothing like the sun;
>   Coral is far more red, than her lips' red:
> If snow be white, why then her breasts are dun;
>   If hairs be wires, black wires grow on her head.
> I have seen roses damasked, red and white,
>   But no such roses see I in her cheeks;
>
> – Sonnet 130

It has been claimed that these sonnets were perhaps written as a satirical dig at the clichés of the Petrarchan sonnet tradition – and certainly, as Bate observes, there came, a decade or so later, a vogue for satirical sonnets.[25] Even so, I think, with Bate, that they surely have to reflect Shakespeare's emotional experience. The Dark Lady is flesh and blood, certainly not a Petrarchan stereotype. As Wordsworth observed,

> ... with this key
> Shakespeare unlocked his heart.[26]

So who was this mysterious lady who kissed but, as far as we know, never told? It is very hard to resist going on a literary wild goose chase. A.L. Rowse argued strongly that the Dark Lady was probably Emilia Lanier née Bassano.[27] She is certainly a possible candidate; she was too well-educated to marry a commoner, but not blue-blooded enough to marry a lord. So she might well have dallied with a gifted poet and playwright.

These sonnets are such a break with tradition that they could read like an elaborate literary joke, where the lily-white skin of the ideal lady is replaced by one of darker hue. (Emilia Lanier?) But I don't think Shakespeare is laughing. I think that he has really fallen in love with this woman, and sadly, it has not turned out well. As the sonnets develop, the relationship seems to have become akin to a nightmare. The poet feels shackled in a destructive relationship from which he cannot escape:

> Prison my heart in thy steel bosom's ward
> for I being pent in thee
> Perforce am thine and all that is in me
>
> – Sonnet 133

It's an emotional morass, a place of torment and torture, an addiction that feeds on itself. His relationship is like a fever that has left him deracinated, and the images of sickness are really quite sinister. Nothing is 'sugar'd' in these sonnets:

> Past cure I am, now reason is past cure
>
> My love is as a fever, longing still
> For that which longer nurseth the disease
> Feeding on that which doth preserve the ill
> Th'uncertain sickly appetite to please.
>
> – Sonnet 147

She appears to be a cultured woman, for like Emilia Lanier, she could play a virginal, and he appears to be enchanted by her. When he hears her play, he envies

> those jacks that nimble leap,
> To kiss the tender inward of thy hand
>
> – Sonnet 128

Such tender moments do not seem to last long, for soon the poet is overtaken by guilt, shame, and self-disgust – and love has turned to obsession:

> The expense of spirit in a waste of shame
> Is lust in action: and till action, lust
> Is perjured, murderous, bloody, full of blame,
> Savage, extreme, rude, cruel, not to trust;
> Enjoyed no sooner but despised straight;
> Past reason hunted; and no sooner had,
> Past reason hated, as a swallowed bait,
> On purpose laid to make the taker mad.
> Mad in pursuit and in possession so;
> Had, having, and in quest to have extreme;

> A bliss in proof, and proved, a very woe;
>   Before, a joy proposed; behind a dream.
>   All this the world well knows; yet none knows well
>   To shun the heaven that leads men to this hell.
>
> – Sonnet 129

The word *hell* is often used in Tudor England to refer to a woman's sexual organs: as the sonnet sequence continues, obsession turns to ambivalence. In Sonnet 131, his mistress is 'tyrannous', and 'cruel', even though she is his 'fairest and most precious jewel'. She is also promiscuous, and he is appalled that she has also enslaved his (male) friend:

> Beshrew that heart that makes my heart to groan
>   For that deep wound it gives my friend and me!
> Is't not enough to torture me alone,
>   But slave to slavery my sweet'st friend must be?
>
> – Sonnet 133

Not just a friend: he is also emotionally involved with the man:

Emilia Lanier 1569-1645

Emilia Lanier (also Lanyer), has become something of a feminist icon. She also features in the play *Emilia*, by Morgan Lloyd Malcolm, about her life and her alleged relationship with Shakespeare. The play was a sell-out success at London's Globe Theatre in 2018.

Emilia Lanier was the daughter of a court musician, Baptista Bassano, of Venetian and Jewish origin, a member of a large Sephardic family: this would explain her dark colouring.[28] Orphaned at the age of six, Emilia was informally adopted by Susan Bertie, Dowager Countess of Kent. In one of her poems, Emilia describes her as 'the Mistress of my Youth/The noble guide of my ungoverned days'.[29] The countess gave her a good, if courtly, education. According to the diarist and quack Simon Forman, 'she had been favoured much of Her Majesty and of many noblemen and has had great gifts and been made much of.'[30]

Forman records that Emilia 'was paramour to my old Lord Hunsdon that was Lord Chamberlain, and was maintained in great pride.' It was too good to last: in October 1592, falling pregnant, to avoid scandal ('for colour') she was married off to a court minstrel of Huguenot stock, Alphonso Lanier. Not surprisingly, this marriage of inconvenience was not a happy one.

> Two loves I have of comfort and despair,
> Which like two spirits do suggest me still:
> The better angel is a man right fair,
> The worser spirit a woman coloured ill.
> To win me soon to hell, my female evil
> Tempteth my better angel from my side,
> And would corrupt my saint to be a devil,
> Wooing his purity with her foul pride.
> And, whether that my angel be turn'd fiend,
> Suspect I may, yet not directly tell,
> But being both from me both to each friend,
> I guess one angel in another's hell.
>   Yet this shall I ne'er know, but live in doubt,
>   Till my bad angel fire my good one out.
>
> – Sonnet 144

Comfort and despair compete with each other, and perhaps change to a kind of acceptance, in one of Shakespeare's best, and most subtle poems – an unromantic, pragmatic recognition that love has to be negotiated with reason and either honesty, or self deception, rather than passion alone.

> When my love sweares that she is made of truth,
>   I do believe her though I know she lyes,
> That she might thinke me some untutord youth,
>   Unlearned in the worlds false subtleties.
> Thus vainly thinking that she thinks me young,
>   Although she knowes my dayes are past the best,
> Simply I credit her false-speaking tongue:
>   On both sides thus is simple truth supprest:
> But wherefore sayes she not she is unjust?
>   And wherefore say not I that I am old?
> O loves best habit is in seeming trust,
>   And age in love, loves not t'have yeares told
> Therefore I lye with her, and she with me,
>   And in our faults by lyes we flattered be.
>
> – Sonnet 138

Resignation to a sad and failing love affair does not prevent the poet from a pun in the last two lines, creating a witty ambiguity: what great punch lines to end the sonnet! This is closer to Larkin than Petrarch. As

Bate observes, the conventions of Courtly Love 'dictate that love is true, the lady is pure, the poet is young and full of desire, and sex does not take place.'[31] Every one of these rules is broken. Even so, Shakespeare shows complete mastery of the sonnet form, and many of us think that this group of poems, so painful, yet so eloquent, are among the best he ever wrote.

It was too bad to last: in his heart, the poet knows that 'she who made me sin awards me pain.' There is a hint in sonnets 144 and 147 that she left him with a nasty souvenir – an STD.[32] What is clear, though, is that for a time, Shakespeare was obsessed with the Dark Lady; and so it is that his next plays feature men who are obsessed.

10

POWER PLAY

I'll have her, but I will not keep her long.

– *Richard III*

Shakespeare's experience of working with other writers on the history plays taught him a great deal about how he was to survive in the highly competitive (and political) world in which he found himself. By now, Shakespeare must have felt strongly the desire to cut loose, and write his own plays. However, it may well be that he was for a time too distracted by his unhappy love affair to write his first solo play – *Richard III*. Thus it is possible that he was quite glad to be asked to collaborate on another play, *Edward III*, especially if Marlowe was involved. This was the last of these earlier plays that Shakespeare wrote collaboratively.

Edward III

There is no certainty about when this play was written, but Taylor and Loughnane's best guess is early 1592.[1] Little is known about its performance history. For a long time *Edward III* was not thought to be by Shakespeare: it is not mentioned in Frances Meres' 1598 list of Shakespeare's plays. Most scholars now agree that Shakespeare had a hand in it, although there is no consensus on who the other writer, or writers, may have been.

Reading *Edward III*, one is struck by the fact that two extremely long scenes – attributed to Shakespeare – are devoted to the attempted seduction of the Countess of Salisbury – these in a history play that deals with events that cover a period of some fifty years: Edward was England's second longest reigning mediaeval monarch. Why are these scenes disproportionately long? It is as if Shakespeare could not leave the scenes alone, and a plausible reason can be found in the sonnets considered in the last chapter. For it is clear that for a time Shakespeare was obsessed with the Dark Lady: he knew about obsession. It was perhaps for him a new dimension of human experience: he may not have consciously decided to write about it, but he may well have come to realise how it could be explored, and exploited, for dramatic purposes. Conscious, or otherwise, his next two plays featured two monarchs who were obsessed – *Edward III* with a woman, *Richard III* with power. Perhaps Shakespeare himself was, for a time, obsessed with obsession.

Edward III's first appearance in print was in 1596. The title page of *The Reigne of King Edward the Third* states that the play 'hath bin sundrie times plaied about the Citie of London', but does not name the author. There has been some doubt about Shakespeare's role in writing *Edward III* because it is not included in the First Folio in 1623. This could have been because the Scots do not come out well in it. In 1598, George Nicholson, the queen's agent (and Cecil's spy) in Edinburgh, wrote a letter complaining about the negative portrayal of Scots by a visiting group of players from England, (whom one thinks may have had suicidal tendencies).[2]

Christopher Marlowe 1564-1593

There is no doubt that Kit Marlowe had a big influence on Shakespeare, showing him how well-honed blank verse could have a huge impact on the stage. As we have seen, both he and Shakespeare worked on the *Henry VI* plays.

Born in Canterbury, the son of a shoe-maker, Kit Marlowe went as a scholar to King's School in Canterbury and from there went on to Corpus Christi College Cambridge. After graduating, he stayed on to do a Masters, but frequent extended absences caused the university authorities to hesitate about giving him a degree. There is some evidence to suggest that he went abroad on various spying missions for Burghley, who may have persuaded the authorities to grant him his degree.

The dating of his plays can only be approximate. They were *Dido Queen of Carthage* (1585-7, with Nashe), *Tamberlaine* 1 and 2 (1587), *The Jew of Malta* (1589), *The Tragicall History of Dr Faustus* (1591), *Edward II* (1592), *The Massacre at Paris* (1590-93). His great unfinished poem *Hero and Leander* was published posthumously in 1598.

Probable portrait of Christopher Marlowe, 1585, by an unknown artist (Corpus Christi College, Cambridge)

It is possible the play was omitted from the First Folio in order to avoid offending James I, who was of course also James VI of Scotland.

Most scholars agree that Shakespeare had a hand in the play, although no one knows who else may have been involved. Other contributors have been suggested, including George Peele, and Thomas Kyd. The graphic description of the Battle of Sluys, in the mouth of a French mariner, could well have been written by Marlowe. The consensus is that Shakespeare wrote Scenes 2 and 3 dealing with the Countess of Salisbury, and perhaps some of the battle scenes later in the play.

Much of *Edward III* consists of dialogue full of bluster and bravado. It is hard to avoid the feeling that Shakespeare is growing weary of the procession of kings and queens, and of battles lost and won between nobles who have little to offer except ambition. So it is likely that he was glad to concentrate on the scenes of attempted seduction, leaving most of the rest to his collaborators. In Scene 2, the Countess of Salisbury is in Roxborough Castle, besieged by a Scottish army. King David of Scotland and his crony Douglas play the pantomime villains, as they squabble over who should have the beautiful countess, and who her jewels, when they capture the castle. However, Edward III's army sends the Scottish army packing, and the king rescues the countess.

An unedifying episode now follows when the king becomes besotted with the countess: one catches glimpses of the later Shakespeare beginning to emerge. He clearly takes pleasure in verbal wit and poetic experimentation – together with a healthy dose of humour. He even gives the king, who is better with swords than with words, a satirical half-baked attempt at a love poem: in one memorable phrase, Harriet Archer describes the king in this scene as 'a Pantomime Petrarchan',[3] and one sees what she means by these lines, the king's clumsy attempt at a sonnet, which runs out of juice after eleven lines:

> And let me have her likened to the sun
> Say she hath thrice more splendour than the sun
> That her perfections emulate the sun
> That she breeds sweets as plenteous as the sun
> That she doth thaw cold winter like the sun
> That she doth cheer fresh summer like the sun
> That she doth dazzle gazers like the sun
> And in this application to the sun
> Bid her be free and general as the sun
> Who smiles upon the basest weed that grows
> As lovingly as the fragrant rose.
>
> – Scene 2

There is a definite touch of playfulness in these scenes with the countess, in which perhaps the lady 'doth protest too much': for she is so grateful to be rescued, and so keen that the king should stay awhile with her in her castle, that he may have misinterpreted the signals, and falls for her. Suddenly, from blank verse, king and countess find themselves talking in rhyming couplets that clearly come over as slightly flirtatious. Shakespeare turns the countess into something of a coquette.

The king misinterprets what he takes to be the countess's 'signals', but even so, nothing excuses what transpires, as he presses his suit on a clearly unwilling woman. It is Edward's turn to play the pantomime villain. In one very comic scene, he summons a minion, Ludovic, known for his 'poet's wit', to pen a love letter to persuade the countess into an adulterous liaison. Ludovic, said to be 'a fellow ... well-read in poetry' asks who he is writing to, and the king answers one who is 'better than beautiful'. Puzzled, Ludovic answers:

> LUDOVIC: Write I to a woman?
> KING: What beauty else could triumph on me
>   Or who but women do our love-lays greet?
>   What, thinks thou I did bid thee praise a horse?
>
> – Scene 2

This never fails to raise a laugh in the theatre. Ludovic seems to be slightly dim, for he must surely be aware that the king is smitten by the countess's charms. When asked to read out what he has written so far, he responds with this totally inappropriate first line, which presumably refers to Diana, goddess of the moon, traditionally associated with chastity:

> LUDOVIC: 'More fair and chaste than is the queen of shades –

The king grows desperate with irritation, for only a half-wit would attempt an adulterous liaison by using the word *chaste*; he exclaims:

> I did not bid thee talk of chastity
> To ransack so the treasure of her mind
> For I had rather have her chased than chaste!
> Out with the moon line, I will none of it
>
> – Scene 2

Almost a laugh a line! The play briefly attempts to turn from the risible to the lyrical: Harriet Archer suggests that *Edward III* is unique among these early history plays in 'its staging of a self-conscious act of poetic invention'.[4] The play does indeed include at least one memorable line – so memorable, that Shakespeare recycles it in Sonnet 94: 'Lilies that fester smell far worse than weeds'. Clearly, the countess's beauty has finally begun to elicit an uncharacteristic burst of lyricism as his passion becomes obsessive:

> Whether is her beauty by her words divine
> Or are her words sweet chaplains to her beauty?
> Like as the wind doth beautify a sail
> And as a sail becomes an unseen wind
> So do her words, her beauty, her beauty, words
> O, that I were a honey-gathering bee
> To bear the comb of virtue from this flower
> And not a poison-sucking envious spider!
> To turn the juice I take to be a deadly venom!
>
> – Scene 2

The king's maladroit attempts to seduce the countess turn ugly. He even tricks the countess's father, the Earl of Warwick, into swearing an oath without specifying what it will involve – it amounts to a blank cheque. Warwick is then given the grotesque task of persuading his daughter to accede to the king's demands. Can this man, King Edward, really be the would-be reviver of Arthurian chivalry, the noble founder of the Order of the Garter?[5] At last comes the denouement. The countess, appalled by his approaches, finally agrees on conditions that she knows neither of them can accept: she will succumb provided that they both agree to murder their consorts. She offers him a knife to dispatch his wife. If he does not agree, she will use the other knife, not on her husband, but on herself. The king is finally brought to his senses – he is 'awaked from his idle dream'; to everyone's relief, his moments of madness are over. Overwhelmed by guilt he exclaims

> Even by that power I swear, that give me now
> The power to be ashamed of myself
> I never mean to part my lips again

> In any words that tend to such a suit
> Arise, true English lady, whom our isle
> May better boast of than ever Roman might
> Of her, whose ransacked beauty hath tasked
> The vain endeavor of so many pens
>
> – Scene 3

These two scenes owe much to myth, and heavily draw on William Painter's *Palace of Pleasure* Novel 6, an example of Tudor pulp fiction. If Shakespeare had access to Ferdinando's library, he might also have consulted Froissant's French *Chronicles*, translated by Lord Berners in 1535, and Holinshed's *Chronicles* 1587.[6] Shakespeare allows imagination to trump history in these scenes, for it is widely reported that Edward was a very devoted husband to his wife, Philippa, by whom he had thirteen children: but even though these events almost certainly never took place, they do make compelling theatre, and have often been performed as stand-alone scenes.

As has been noted, humour rubs shoulders uneasily with incipient violence. King Edward III, seen a national hero at the time, is shown in a less than perfect light, and the episode could perhaps be seen as an act of healthy lèse-majesté, showing that even kings are not spared physical, or in this case moral, weakness. Edward is later mortified when the French king mocks him for being

> a belly god
> A tender and lascivious wantonness
> That th'other day was almost dead for love
>
> – Scene 6

The shaft hits home: how can Edward redeem his honour – and prove his strength and ruthlessness? Perhaps this explains why he felt it necessary to send his son, Prince Edward to 'win his spurs' by engaging in his first battle at Crécy, at the age of sixteen. The young man is ritually invested in his famous black armour, and is then let loose on the enemy, to sink or swim. There follows a harrowing scene: first the renegade Artois arrives, stating the Prince is surrounded, and needs to be rescued: ''tis impossible he should escape,' he exclaims. The king replies

> Tut! let him fight! We gave him arms today,
> And he is laboring for a knighthood, man!

Then a breathless Derby arrives to tell the king that the Prince is 'close compassed with a world of odds.' Edward again refuses to go to his son's aid: it is almost as if he sees his son as a surrogate to redeem his honour. He tells Derby

> Then will he win a world of honour too
> If he by valour can redeem him hence
> If not, what remedy? We have more sons
> Than one to comfort our declining age.
>
> – Scene 8, 21- 24

When Audley arrives, with the dire news that the prince is 'in danger to be slain', the king coolly responds: 'Why then his epitaph is lasting praise.' It seems he is a man who values 'honour' above the life of his son. When Prince Edward finally arrives, triumphantly bearing his lance, now in splinters, accompanied by the body of the King of Bohemia he has slain, he is knighted by his own sword 'yet reeking warm' with the blood of Frenchmen. However, the word *honour* seems heavily compromised – especially when the French refer to the English invaders as *ravens* – birds of prey that feed on dead bodies, and thus seen as symbols of death.[7]

The play also features the siege of Calais, when King Edward, angered by the resistance he encounters, threatens to hang the famous six burghers of Calais – he only spares them after the intercession of the queen. Visitors to Calais can still see them, commemorated in Rodin's famous sculpture. Also notable is the Battle of Sluys, which destroyed the French fleet and killed upwards of 18,000 Frenchmen.[8] Of course, impossible to stage, so the words carry a heavy burden, having to create a sea battle in the minds of the audience through this account by one of the few surviving French sailors:

> Purple the sea whose channel filled as fast
> With streaming gore that from the maimèd fell
> As did her gushing moisture break into
> The cranny cleftures of the through-shot planks ...
> Here fled a head dissevered from the trunk;
> There mangled arms and legs were tossed aloft

> As when a whirlwind takes the summer dust
> And scatters it in middle of the air
>
> – Scene 4 161-168

It is reported that Froissart, the French chronicler, actually met Edward III, and likens him to that embodiment of chivalry, King Arthur. Both Froissart and le Bel found it hard to explain how Edward III managed to conquer France: he explains it by the chivalrous qualities and high reputation of Edward.[9] It is hard to square that judgment with the ruthless brutality with which he savaged France: perhaps Shakespeare is hinting that so-called chivalry is a chimera?

Richard III

At least Richard III does not claim to be chivalrous. As far as we know, *Richard III* was the first play that was written exclusively by Shakespeare – and it is one of his finest. There still remains some doubt as to the date when it was written. Taylor and Loughnane's best guess of mid- to late 1592 seems about right.[10] It represents a huge step up in terms of quality and dramatic appeal. The use of wit, word play and irony is particularly noticeable – memories of the best scenes in *Edward III*.

Over time, most critics have seen the three *Henry VI* plays, as political, pro-Tudor propaganda,[11] but this view might be said to be more applicable to their sequel, *Richard III*. Also notable is the enhanced role of the Earl of Derby in *Richard III*: it is in this play that the Stanley family really comes to the fore. His character is variously referred to in the stage directions as *Stanley* or *Derby*. (He only became the Earl of Derby after Henry VII became king). John Jowett in his superb edition of the Oxford Shakespeare's *Richard III* solves the inconsistency by anachronistically making him Earl of Derby throughout.[12] The earl plays a significant part throughout the play: he is courteous to the womenfolk, and warns Dorset to escape while he can. Notwithstanding the fact that his son is held hostage by Richard, Stanley plays kingmaker at the Battle of Bosworth in 1485 when he mobilises his men at a key moment in the battle on the side of Henry Tudor (memorably depicted in Lawrence Olivier's film of *Richard III*). In addition, according to Shakespeare (who relied on Holinshed and Halle) it was Lord Stanley who found the crown under a thorn bush, and places it on Henry's head, though this is disputed by some historians. But it makes good drama. If in *2 Henry VI*, we had Warwick the Kingmaker, in *Richard III*, that role is thus played by Stanley. This would certainly have been grist to Ferdinando's mill. Would it be enough to remove the shadow of suspicion cast over the earl?

Richard III could be seen as showing that the commonwealth of England did have the legitimate right to depose a monarch if he proved tyrannical, or murdered the rightful claimant. That the *deus ex machina* was the first Tudor monarch, Henry VII, who replaced Richard III, meant that this idea would certainly have been deemed acceptable to the authorities. But even Henry Tudor appears to have only a minor role in the play: the dominant figure throughout is, overwhelmingly, Richard: his character – 'the bottled spider' and 'poisonous hunchbacked toad' – is so odious that no one could but welcome his replacement, whoever he was. Many of us will recall in particular Lawrence Olivier's self-confession to the audience – he gives us forewarning in *3 Henry VI* Scene 4 in this soliloquy:

> Why, I can smile, and murder whiles I smile
> And cry 'Consent!' to that which grieves my heart,
> And wet my cheeks with artificial tears
> And frame my face to all occasions ...
> I can add colours to the chameleon
> Change shapes with Proteus for advantages
> And set the murderous Machiavel to school
> Can I do this, and cannot get a crown?
> Tut, were it further off, I'll pluck it down

It is possible that these lines were written when Shakespeare was revising the *Henry VI* trilogy to build a connection between *3 Henry VI* and *Richard III*. Reading these lines, it is no wonder that even today Lawrence Olivier as Richard still gets thousands of hits every year on Youtube.

Since the play was written, hardly a year has passed when there has not been a performance of *Richard III* somewhere in the world. It is without doubt Shakespeare's first truly great play. Jowett's description of him reminds one of certain modern political leaders, and deserves quoting:

> Nothing is more typical of Richard than his puncturing of ceremony, his distortion of formal rhetoric, his disrespect for convention, and his attrition

of order in all its aspects. His entrances are violent; he interrupts speakers with deflating irony.[13]

We should also perhaps hear what Stephen Greenblatt has to say about King Richard in his book *Tyrant: Shakespeare on Power*. Who might he have been thinking of?

> ... limitless self-regard, the law-breaking, the pleasure in inflicting pain, the compulsive desire to dominate. He is pathologically narcissistic and supremely arrogant. He has a grotesque sense of entitlement, never doubting he can do whatever he chooses. He loves to bark orders and to watch underlings scurry to carry them out. He expects absolute loyalty but is incapable of gratitude. The feelings of others mean nothing to him, He has no natural grace, no sense of humanity, no decency.

Greenblatt continues:

> He is not merely indifferent to the law, he hates it and takes pleasure in breaking it. He hates it because it gets in his way and because it stands for a notion of the public good that he holds in contempt. He divides the world into winners and losers.[14]

Typical of Richard's duplicity is the very first scene, where he embraces the brother he is about to murder – the first of a series of victims. The way he sets Tyrrell on to murder the princes in the tower is particularly chilling. Why do we find such scenes so compelling? Shakespeare had watched how the clowns Tarlton, and Kempe, engage with the audience. King Richard does the same – he confides in us as we watch. He turns soliloquys into a secret-sharing process, nudging our elbows as it were as he shares his villainous plans, almost seducing us into becoming accomplices, as though trying to give us a vicarious thrill. As the list of his victims grows longer, initial amusement turns to horror. Among them is Lady Anne, whose husband and father-in-law (Henry VI) he has murdered. In a grotesque scene, he interrupts the latter's funeral, and courts her over the coffin. Lady Anne is appalled by this 'dreadful minister of hell', but Richard woos her with his words – and indeed his sword, with which he invites her to kill him. She is somehow paralysed with fear, or hypnotized, into agreeing to marry him – thereby turning her marriage contract into a death warrant. For Richard then, again, treats his audience as accomplices as he casually shares with us his plan:

> Was ever woman in this humour woo'd?
> Was ever women in this humour won?
> I'll have her, but I will not keep her long ...
>
> – Act 1, Scene 2

Particularly compelling is the scene where Richard 'plays the crowd': rather than trying to persuade them to accept him as king, he manipulates the crowd into doing the persuading. With an apparent show of reluctance, he agrees to accept the crown that he has spent his whole life scheming for:

> RICHARD: Would you force me to a world of care?
>   Well, call them again [*Exit Catesby*]
>   I am not made of stones.
>   But penetrable to your kind: entreats,
>   Albeit against my conscience and my soul ...
>
> – Act 3, Scene 7

It all goes to show that one should be careful of what one wishes for.

Returning to the view that *Richard III* was a piece of Tudor propaganda: it is true that in defeating and killing Richard at the Battle of Bosworth (with the help again of Lord Stanley) Henry VII and the Tudor monarchy are seen as bringing a new dawn of peace and prosperity to England; but was this Shakespeare's purpose? Possible. It is perhaps just as likely that Shakespeare saw the chance of cashing in on the popularity of the *Henry VI* plays by writing a sequel. Or he may have been asked to do so to depict Lord Stanley in a good light. (Though he also refers to 'redoubted Pembroke', perhaps hedging his bets.)

However, Shakespeare did assist the consolidation of the Tudor dynasty in this tetralogy in another way. Shakespeare's dramatic rose garden scene in the Temple Gardens in *1 Henry VI*, where the two groups of nobles picked red or white roses, which in fact never occurred, helped to reinforce the Tudor myth. Henry VII claimed to bring the two Houses, Lancaster and York, together by his marriage to Elizabeth of York, the eldest daughter of Edward IV, thereby ending the Wars of the Roses. The Tudor rose, the five red petals of the House of Lancaster surrounding the five white petals of the House of York, became a central motif of the Tudor dynasty.

However, there is a lingering suspicion that the Tudor myth really is a myth: many readers will know Josephine Tay's *The Daughter of Time*, in which Inspector Alan Grant and his assistant turn the history into a police investigation – and exculpate Richard,[15] despite the fact that historians, from Polydor Virgil and Sir Thomas More to Halle and Holinshed, all depict Richard as a villain. But many members of the Richard III Society – and its American branch – claim that the real villain was Henry VII, who, in order to win popularity, certainly had Empson and Dudley executed, simply for obeying his instructions; and Henry might well have ordered the murder of the two princes in the Tower. Even so, people were desperate to put an end to the strife that had torn the country apart for a generation – and were glad to accept the myth of Henry the peace-bringer.

11

FRIENDS, AND ENEMIES

' ... an upstart crow, beautified with our feathers ... '

– Robert Greene

It was becoming apparent that there were great uncertainties working in the theatre world: success was determined by the box-office. It seems likely that *Shrew*, while not exactly a failure, did not do as well financially as the Henry plays. Perhaps this explains why Shakespeare reverted to history, or his version of it, with *Edward III* and *Richard III*. To add to the uncertainty, every time there was an outbreak of the plague, theatres were closed down, though in the summer of 1592, it was riots that shut down the theatres. The plague followed immediately after, and kept them closed for months. Reluctantly, Lord Strange's Men went on tour in the provinces: this meant a lot of hard work for only meagre returns.

Meanwhile, there were serious political worries. With the continuing threat of Spain, the authorities became increasingly paranoid. In 1591, the Privy Council had issued two very harsh anti-Catholic proclamations. Anyone who sheltered or protected Jesuits or seminary priests were to be locked up as 'venomous vipers', 'the abettors and maintainers of Traitors'.[1] The proclamations initiated a surge in the activities of informers, and a huge purge, spearheaded by the odious Richard Topcliffe: nobleman or commoner, male or female, it mattered not. One of the first to be informed on was Anthony Browne, 1st Lord Montague, who, though a well-known Catholic, was a loyal and trusted supporter of the crown. That very summer he spent a huge sum on entertaining the queen and her retinue at his family home, Cowdray House near Midhurst in Sussex.[2] This did not protect him from a hostile investigation – he was known to harbour Catholic dissenters, and indeed his brother served on a ship in the Spanish Armada (where he was killed.) He was only spared imprisonment or worse by dying, allegedly, 'of natural causes' in October 1592.[3]

In this fraught political atmosphere, for much of the year Shakespeare's family must have lived in a state of anxiety: as mentioned in Chapter 9, John Shakespeare, among nine others, had been reported for failing to attend church, and there was a serious danger of him falling foul of the authorities. If Montague could be investigated, who was safe? Memories were still fresh of what happened to Edward Arden and his family. Fortunately for him, it seems that Sir Thomas Lucy had added a note to his report on the recusants on his list, stating 'We suspect these nine persons

John Rogers Burnt at the Stake. John Rogers (circa 1505-4 February 1555) was an English clergyman, Bible translator and commentator. He guided the development of the Matthew Bible in vernacular English during the reign of Henry VIII and was the first English Protestant executed as a heretic under Mary I of England, who was determined to restore Roman Catholicism.

next ensuing absent themselves for fear of process' – in other words, to avoid debt collectors, who frequently swooped at a time when church services were being held.[4]

However, in June 1592, the Jesuit Father Robert Southwell, a distant relative, again through the Arden connection, was arrested by Topcliffe.[5] Living on the continent, Southwell had responded to Elizabeth's proclamation with a rebuttal entitled 'A Humble Supplication to Her Majesty', making a strong case for the legitimacy of a loyalist and non-political version of Catholicism. He argued that the queen's subjects were bound in conscience 'to obey the just laws of their princes'. He also claimed that the real threat to the monarchy were not Catholics, but Calvinists who believed that monarchs could be deposed on religious grounds – a shaft aimed at Protestant Lord Burghley.[6] In captivity, Southwell was for years subject to the most appalling torture at the hands of Topcliffe.[7] For three years a dark cloud hung over the Shakespeare family, for it was not unknown for relatives of 'traitors' to be picked up as 'the usual suspects'. What Shakespeare knew was that Edward Arden's remains still hung on London Bridge as an awful warning. What he did not know was that intercepted correspondence from Southwell implicated Ferdinando, Lord Strange. It is probable that Ferdinando did not know, either – but he must have slept uneasily, knowing what happened to Lord Montague.

Under attack

Meanwhile, Shakespeare had to contend with the internal politics of the theatre world, and this may well have provided a welcome distraction. Playwrights, and the playing companies they wrote for, were highly competitive, so it is not surprising that anyone on the road to success should have to face rivals. However, one man became outright hostile, even venomous: and this man was one of his neighbours in Shoreditch – Robert Greene.

Robert Greene was one of the 'University wits', along with Marlowe, Nashe and others, who chose (in Tudor terms) to slum it by writing plays. At the time, as we have seen, plays were not regarded as serious literature at all, and those who wrote them were only one step up from actors. In 1592, Greene wrote a pamphlet attacking Shakespeare, calling him 'an upstart crow'. This pamphlet, allegedly written on his death-bed, was 'the first unmistakeable reference to Shakespeare in London'[8]. Greene's parting shot – he died on 3 September 1592 – was called *A Groatsworth of Witte Bought with a Million of Repentance*. It was an exercise in self-pity, and an attack on several of his fellow dramatists – 'Base-minded men all three of you'; his targets were Marlowe, Nashe – and Shakespeare. Shakespeare was especially singled out:

> 'there is an upstart crow, beautified with our feathers, that with his tiger's heart wrapped in a player's hide supposes he is as well able to bombast out a blank verse as the best of you; and being an absolute Johannes Factotum, is in his owne conceit the only Shake-scene in the country'.

The reference to Shakespeare is inescapable: the pun on his name is obvious enough. Readers will also have noticed that his comments refer to *3 Henry VI*, quoted in Chapter 8, in which the Duke of York, before he is done to death, calls Queen Margaret 'a she-wolf of France', vilifying her with the words 'O tiger's heart wrapped in a woman's hide!'

Greene is accusing Shakespeare of being a mere jumped-up actor aping the language of his betters. Was he attacking Shakespeare, the actor, or Shakespeare, the playwright? Or, indeed, both? Was he also accusing Shakespeare of plagiarism? That is possible, although most Elizabethan playwrights paid each other the compliment of borrowing from, or adapting, other plays. Elizabethans did not see this as plagiarism.[9]

So why did Greene single out Shakespeare as an object of odium? He appears to have been angered by the unexpected success of a country bumpkin, Shakespeare, with his Warwickshire accent, who didn't even have a university degree. The success of *Titus* was

Woodcut of Robert Greene in his shroud by John Dickenson, in a pamphlet *Greene in Conceipt* (1598).

> **Robert Greene 1558-1592**
>
> Robert Greene, born in Norwich, probably attended Norwich Grammar School. His father was either a sadler, or an inn-keeper and so was, himself, a parvenu. Greene was a sizar at St John's College, Cambridge – a *sizar* was a student who worked his way through college, undertaking sometimes quite menial tasks in exchange for free meals, lower fees, and subsidised or free lodgings.
>
> The degree he attained at Cambridge was not brilliant, but it did enable him to play the gentleman. He wrote numerous prose works, but he never managed to obtain the sponsorship that he sought. He had some success for a while with the plays he started to write from 1590. However, he was no gentleman: he ditched his wife and child, having spent her dowry, frequented the brothels of the South Bank, and ended up with a prostitute known as Em. He died in September 1592, allegedly from 'a surfeit of Rhenish wine and pickled herring'.[10] The scholar and erstwhile Professor of Rhetoric at Cambridge, Gabriel Harvey, had this to say about Robert Greene:
>
> 'Who in London hath not heard of his dissolute and licentious living ... his unseemly apparel and more unseemly company ... ' and ' ... his scandalous and blasphemous raving?'[11]

bad enough, but the knife was twisted when *Henry VI* played packed houses, generating good ticket sales; the first recorded performance of a *Henry* play (according to Henslowe's diary) broke all records, yielding almost four pounds. Greene's own plays did not perform nearly as well: for example, a performance of *Friar Bacon and Friar Bungay* amounted to a measly seventeen shillings and three pence.[12] Hardly surprising, in view of the fact that the play features two friars trying to get a brass head to speak with the help of the devil. Hmm, unlikely to be a hit, one would think.

It may have been galling, too, to learn that Shakespeare was a member of writing teams working for Lord Strange that variously involved Nash, Kyd and Marlowe, but gave Greene only a marginal role, if any at all. Was he not a university wit, too? No wonder Greene was jealous. His venomous pamphlet *Groatsworth of Wit* was printed posthumously, and entered on the Stationers' Register in September 1592 'at the peril of Henry Chettle' the publisher. There is, however, a dispute as to whether Greene really was the author of the pamphlet: in 1969 Warren B. Austen carried out a computer-based study which he claimed yielded stylometric evidence showing that Chettle wrote *Groatsworth*. This is contested by Richard Westley, who argued that Austen's study is marred by flawed sampling.[13]

Aftermath

On the basis that there is no such thing as bad publicity, Shakespeare may not have been too upset by the pamphlet. Tudor language was famously extravagant, whether it was the language of flattery or of bitter vitriol: halcyon days, perhaps, when you could say or write what you meant without being sued, or 'cancelled' to use that ugly 21st century euphemism (though of course you might be murdered or challenged to a duel). No 'safe spaces' then, and so, no doubt, hurt feelings abounded. But Shakespeare probably took the comments in the pamphlet in his stride, for it paid him the ultimate compliment: he was too good to be ignored. Even so, both Shakespeare and Marlowe felt bound to complain to the publisher, Henry Chettle, who many suspected, even without any computer-based analysis, had written *Groatsworth* himself. In his response, Chettle offered Shakespeare a handsome apology, (but not Marlowe, who by now had an unsavoury reputation); he praised Shakespeare's civil demeanour, observing that he was

> excellent in the quality he professes. Besides, divers of worship have reported his uprightness of dealing, which argues his honesty, and his facetious grace in writing that approves his art.[14]

The phrase 'divers of worship' is also interesting: it may refer to Lord Strange, but as we saw in Chapter 10, there are reasons to think that Shakespeare was beginning to disengage from the earl. Kit Marlowe, who seemed to be very much in the know about political developments, may have indicated to him that the future did not lie with Lord Strange. Whether Shakespeare knew Marlowe was a spy for the government is not known, but it is possible that Marlowe gave Shakespeare some hint about the spider's web of politics in which Ferdinando was becoming enmeshed. However, this is speculation: with theatres closed, Shakespeare may have felt an urge to write poetry – and the need to find another patron.

Shakespeare's new patron

Enter Henry Wriothesley (pronounced *Risley*), Third Earl of Southampton, Shakespeare's next patron: it seems more than likely that Shakespeare felt drawn towards this glamorous young man, who was the ward of Lord Burghley himself. We do not know how they first met, but it was noted that Southampton, 'did pass the time in London merely in going to plays every day', and perhaps went backstage on one occasion, and struck up an acquaintance with Shakespeare. Anthony Burgess suggests that John Florio, Southampton's secretary, a keen theatre-goer, may have introduced him to the earl.[15] It is likely they were at the theatre when they caught one another's eye. Shakespeare would have certainly been impressed by the young earl, so cultured, so witty, so sophisticated. However, it was no use whatsoever dedicating a play to him – he did not have a group called 'Southampton's Men', and plays as literature were, as we have seen, definitely *infra dig*: no, only a poem – an epic poem – would do.

Thus it was to Southampton that Shakespeare dedicated his first long poem, *Venus and Adonis*, which was inspired perhaps by the publication of Sir Philip Sidney's *Astrophel and Stella* in 1591. Shakespeare had other reasons for turning from drama to poetry. It is likely that he had an urge to prove that Greene's attack on him was unjustified by demonstrating that he was *au fait* with the classics, and that he was as accomplished as any university wit.

The Third Earl of Southampton: Henry Wriothesley, 1573-1624

Born into a Catholic family, the young earl became the ward of Lord Burghley, Queen Elizabeth's First Minister after he was orphaned at the age of eight. Sent at the age of twelve to St John's College, Cambridge, he went on to Gray's Inn to study law. In his teens, he was persuaded to agree to marry Burghley's granddaughter, Lady Elizabeth Vere, daughter of the Earl of Oxford – possibly to influence him away from his Catholic sympathies. However, he then refused to carry out his promise, thereby, according to the pernicious rules of Tudor wardship, incurring a fine of £5,000.[16]

Earlier in 1591, he had slipped away from his studies at Gray's Inn to follow the Earl of Essex in a campaign in Normandy, and he seems to have fallen under Essex's spell. Both Southampton and the young Earl of Essex (also a ward of Burghley) were, in the words of Duncan-Jones 'strongly inclined to same-sex relationships.'[17]

Portraits of him show that he was as beautiful as a woman, and, as such, represented a Renaissance ideal of male youth and beauty. Yet in spite of the long tresses of hair he sported over his left shoulder, and his fair complexion, his eyes convey something of a masculine stare. In 1595, he jousted in the Queen's Accession Day tournament, when George Peele described him as 'gentle and debonair'. Yet he acquitted himself well in battle on several occasions – and was not reluctant to draw a rapier in a quarrel.

So, time for a poem – not just any old poem, but an epic, *Venus and Adonis*, possibly written in early 1593,[18] and published in the same year. Such a poem would have greatly appealed to this young earl. The poem opens with the dedication below – historic, because this was the first time Shakespeare's full name appeared in printed form:

> To the Right Honourable
> Henry Wriothesley, Earl of Southampton
> and Baron of Titchfield
>
> Right Honourable, I know not how I shall offend in dedicating my unpolished lines to your Lordship, nor how the world will censure me for choosing so strong a prop to support so weak a burden. Only if your Honour seem but pleased [will] I account myself highly praised. And vow to take advantage of all idle hours, till I have honoured you with one graver labour. But if the first heir of my invention prove deformed, I shall be sorry it had so noble a godfather: and never after e'ar so barren a land for fear it yield me still so bad a harvest. I leave it to your Honourable survey, and your Honour to your heart's content which I wish may always answer your own wish, and the world's hopeful expectation.
>
> Your Honour's in all duty
William Shakespeare

To the modern reader, this will appear almost embarrassingly servile, as if it had been written by a Uriah Heap figure (whom readers will recall grovelling in *David Copperfield*). In Tudor times such dedications were par for the course: they were formulated to elicit a financial gift; ideally, they might also secure the support of a rich patron who wielded some influence at court. A forlorn hope, in Southampton's case, for although he was a ward of Lord Burghley, the young earl's word would have carried little weight in court circles. Whether Shakespeare was aware of this is not clear, but there is little doubt that he felt attached to the young man, and thought that dedicating a poem to him would strengthen their relationship, as well as reap a financial reward. How much he was paid we do not know, but given the flamboyant character of the Earl of Southampton, who was known for his profligacy, and given the huge success of the poem (thus giving maximum publicity to the young earl) it probably earned Shakespeare a substantial sum – maybe ten pounds or more.

Venus and Adonis

The poem Shakespeare dedicated to the earl is based on a story in Ovid's *Metamorphoses*. Venus, the Goddess of Love, falls in love with a beautiful young man, still a boy, really, and makes desperate attempts to seduce him. But he resists all her charms: he is far more interested in hunting. Her attempts to dissuade him from hunting fail, and he is eventually killed by a wild boar. Venus sadly turns him into a flower. The poem is highly erotic, yet is also light-hearted, with touches of comedy. Readers may recall Bette Davis's remark: 'Sex is God's joke on human beings.' The poem is also extremely well-crafted – lines like those below do not roll off the quill pen with ease. How many young men would be likely to succumb to blandishments such as these, addressed by Venus to Adonis?

> Torches are made to light, jewels to wear,
> Dainties to taste, fresh beauty for the use,
> Herbs for their smell, and sappy plants to bear
> Things growing to themselves are growth's abuse
> Seeds spring from seeds, and beauty breedeth beauty;
> Thou was't begot, to get it is thy duty ...

Surely Shakespeare was writing this with his tongue in his cheek. It is certain that lines like these would have appealed to the young earl – and the young men at the Inns of Court, or at University, would have been delighted with them, too. The words roll off the tongue with their smooth rhythm and evocative imagery, and the reference to 'things' is joyfully ambiguous – 'thing' often referred to the genital organ in Tudor times. In addition, the *double entendre* at the end (*to get it* – to get what?) is amusingly enhanced by the rhyming pattern of the last two lines.

They would have been even more delighted by the way in which Venus offers Adonis all her delights:

> 'Fondling,' she said, 'since I have hemmed thee here
> With the circuit of this ivory pale
> 'I'll be a park, and thou shall be my deer:
> Feed where thou wilt, on mountain or on dale;
> Graze on my lips, and if those hills be dry,
> Stray lower where the pleasant fountains lie.
> Within this limit is relief enough

> Sweet bottom grass and high delightful plain,
> Round rising hillocks, brakes obscure and rough
> To shelter thee from tempest and from rain:
> Then be my deer, since I am such a park
> No dog shall rouse thee, though a thousand bark.'

No wonder the poem was printed at least nine times in Shakespeare's lifetime – twenty times before the Civil War. The first edition of the poem was printed by Richard Field, Shakespeare's Stratford friend, in April 1593, 'to be sold at the sign of the White Greyhound in Paul's Churchyard', and was an instant success. In Osric's words 'a palpable hit' – especially 'among the younger sort'. And no wonder the young men of Cambridge in their student skit, the *Parnassus* plays, exclaim 'O sweet Master Shakespeare, I'll have his picture in my study at the Court', and continue:

> 'Let this duncified world esteem of Spenser and Chaucer,
> I'll worship sweet Master Shakespeare, and to honour him
> will lay his Venus and Adonis under my pillow.'[19]

Venus and Adonis was the best possible response to Robert Greene's attack, for it established beyond doubt that Shakespeare was a great poet, rather than a 'mere' dramatist. A first edition of the poem even found its way into the Bodleian library. There is no doubt that the young earl would have been delighted to have this great poem dedicated to him.

How wise was Shakespeare in choosing Southampton as his patron? That he was seen as something of a playboy was bad enough; more seriously, he was suspected of having Catholic sympathies – his father had been involved in the rebellion of the Northern Earls. In addition, he was very friendly with the ambitious Earl of Essex, who was viewed with suspicion by powerful people at court. However, it is likely Shakespeare was both attracted to the earl, and impressed by his expensive life-style.

Bad News

Shakespeare's Muse was rudely interrupted. In April and May 1593 when there was a repetition of the 1592 riots, this time aimed mainly at foreigners: gangs of unemployed youth roamed the streets, and widespread disorder threatened. The queen retreated to the safety of Windsor Castle,[20] and the authorities were taking no chances. A violently xenophobic pamphlet allegedly written by the playwright Thomas Kyd was seen to fan the flames and resulted in his arrest on 12 May. A search of the lodgings he shared with Marlowe found what was claimed to be heretical literature. Savagely tortured on the rack, he implicated Marlowe. Kyd was finally released, but he was a broken man (he died the following year). These events were shocking enough – but then even worse was to follow.

Accused of heresy, Marlowe was hauled in for questioning on 20 May. Momentarily freed, he left plague-stricken London to the nearby town of Deptford, where on 30 May he met up with some of his cronies in a local inn. These were not just ordinary cronies – they were all secret agents working for the government. There was, allegedly, an argument about the bill, which led to a fight, and he was killed, allegedly in self-defence, stabbed through the eye by Ingram Frizer, the cousin of Sir Francis Walsingham. This event has produced endless conspiracy theories. In the first place, why was Marlowe not already in prison? Charles Nicholl, playing detective, among others, has drawn attention to many irregularities surrounding the murder – among them, a hushed-up coroner's report, the pardon given within a month to Frizer, and the hasty burial. Was he assassinated because he knew too much about Burghley's spying activities? Or was it a personal vendetta? Surely not just a pub brawl? [21]

Others have suggested that Marlowe was not killed at all: in plague-ridden London there were plenty of unclaimed corpses. A stranger's body could have been hastily buried, while Marlowe escaped to the continent (where some claim he wrote Shakespeare's plays). No doubt many theories about his death abounded in Shakespeare's time: not surprising that 'Rumour, painted full of tongues' is a character in *2 Henry VI*. Rumour still lives on, among some members of the Marlowe Society. All one can say is that Shakespeare must have been deeply shocked by these events. If all the world was indeed a stage, it was not clear who wrote the script – or how it would end.

Meanwhile, the plague still raged – it is estimated that a tenth of London's population died in that hot, dry summer of 1593.[22] Those who could fled the city: there was a mighty exodus of queen and court, and all who could afford to leave, or had somewhere to go to, left the city. Nashe sought sanctuary in one of Lord Strange's great houses in the north. And Shakespeare? Stanley Wells suggests that Shakespeare may have been given access to Southampton House, the young earl's London home in Holborn, 'a centre of literary and intellectual patronage'.[23] With the plague raging in London, this seems unlikely. A number of authorities including Duncan-Jones have suggested that it is probable that Shakespeare was given a safe bolt-hole from the plague in Southampton's house at Titchfield in Hampshire.[24] If so, no doubt he felt he had to earn his keep by writing a second poem dedicated to the earl.

William Cecil, 1st Baron Burghley, 1520-1598 (Workshop of Nicholas Hilliard)

12

UNTO SOUTHAMPTON DO WE SHIFT OUR SCENE

This above all: to thine own self be true,
And it must follow, as the night the day,
Thou canst not then be false to any man.

– *Hamlet*, Act 3, Scene 1

As mentioned in the last chapter, it was during the months of the plague that Shakespeare may have weathered the storm by spending some time as a guest of the young Earl of Southampton. His poem *Venus and Adonis* and the dedication to the earl was his entry ticket to Titchfield, and the time he spent there, away from the hurly-burly of theatre life, saw his second great poem, *The Rape of Lucrece*, written at about the same time as more of his sonnets.

The Rape of Lucrece

In his Dedication to *Venus and Adonis*, he had promised his patron 'one graver labour'. The result is *The Rape of Lucrece*. As the title implies, it is an ugly story. The poem was entered on the Stationers' Register in May 1594 – about a year after *Venus*. The Dedication of the first poem talked of honour and deference; a year later, that of *Lucrece* speaks of love, indicating a possible shift in the relationship between Shakespeare and the earl:

> The loue I dedicate to your Lordship is without end: whereof this Pamphlet without beginning is but a fuperfluous Moity. The warrant I haue of your

Henry Wriothesley, 3rd Earl of Southampton, as a teenager (1593). Attributed to John de Critz the elder (National Trust, Hatchlands Park)

Honourable difpofition, not the worth of my vntutord Lines makes it affured of acceptance. What I haue done is yours, what I haue to doe is yours, being part in all I haue, deuoted yours. Were my worth greater, my duety would fhew greater, meantime, as it is, it is bound to our Lordfhip; To whom I wifh long life ftill lengthned with all happineffe.

Your Lordships in all duety
William Shakefpeare.

Should we see this as a routine form of words, or something that betokens something else? It is easy for us to look at this through the lens of a modern reader, and jump to conclusions; but as Burrow observes, 'men embraced and kissed each other with far greater freedom than most Anglo-Saxon males do now.'[1] Burrow also points out that at that time, the fact that men shared books and bed did not indicate a homosexual relationship. Hyperbolic words of praise and expressions of love are common in Tudor dedications – and Southampton was showered with similar words of devotion. For example, Nashe dedicated his novel *The Unfortunate Traveller* to Southampton, describing him as 'a dere lover and cherisher ... as well of the lovers of Poets, as of Poets themselves.'[2]

In his biography of Shakespeare in 1709, Nicholas Rowe attributes to the actor Sir William D'Avenant the remark that Southampton once gave Shakespeare a thousand pounds. 'A bounty very great, and rare at the time.' Most commentators cast doubt on this story: Schoenbaum reminds us that Southampton was in serious financial difficulties in the nineties, and was forced to lease out the porter's lodge, and rooms in his house.[3] Even so it is quite likely that Southampton gave Shakespeare a handsome reward

'Young man among the roses', Nicholas Hilliard circa 1587. Possibly Robert Devereux, 2nd Earl of Essex, who became Queen Elizabeth's favourite

for *Venus*, and Shakespeare, no doubt, hoped for the same for his next poem dedicated to the young earl.

The poem retells the legend recounted by both Livy and Ovid, and repeated by Chaucer. In summary, *Lucrece* is the anguished story of Lucretia, the beautiful and chaste wife of a Roman general, Collatinus. While Collatinus is away from home, Tarquin, the son of the Etruscan King of Rome, approaches Lucretia's bed-chamber, intent on rape; he has a lengthy struggle with his conscience, but once inside her bedroom, his pulse quickens as he regards the sleeping woman, where even the pillows seem to invite her kisses. Lucretia is naturally horrified to find Tarquin standing over her bed, and realising what he intends, eloquently speaks in her defence. Tarquin reposts that 'my uncontrolled tide turns not' and she in turn replies:

> 'Thou art,' quoth she, 'a sea, a sovereign king
> And lo, there falls into thy boundless flood
> Black lust, dishonour, shame, misgoverning,
> Who seek to stain the ocean of thy blood.'

Heedless, Tarquin stamps out the light, and then gags Lucretia. The actual rape is not described, but the poem makes very ugly reading: this outline hardly does justice to the drama and psychological insights embodied in the poem's 1800 lines. Lucretia is clearly entirely blameless, yet nonetheless feels an overwhelming sense of guilt and shame, a feeling all-too-common among rape survivors. She can hardly bear to think of the dawn, when the world will reveal what has happened during the night, and her eyes weep as she laments:

> 'They think not but that every eye can see
> The same disgrace which they themselves behold
> And therefore would they still in darkness be,
> To have their unseen sin remain untold.
> For they their guilt with weeping will unfold
> And grave, like water that doth eat in steel
> Upon my cheeks what helpless shame I feel.'

On her husband's return, she denounces Tarquin, calls for revenge – and stabs herself to death. The response of her husband and his men is brutally inappropriate. They show no understanding at all of the depth of Lucretia's feelings. They decide to depose the king, and exile his family – offering a political response that hardly does justice to the violence inflicted on Lucretia. It is as if the rape provides a convenient excuse for carrying out a political coup. Lucretia herself is subjected to the final humiliation. Her bleeding body is carried through the streets of Rome 'so to publish Tarquin's foul offence ... '

Shakespeare displays a remarkable insight into the mind of a woman in distress in an age where such sensitivity was extremely rare – it is most unusual for its time. Indeed, it is likely that many people at that time would see a woman's suicide in these circumstances as a sign of guilt. The poem has none of the light-heartedness of *Venus and Adonis*, and was not nearly as popular; however, a copy of this poem, too, ended up in the Bodleian library, so perhaps Sir Thomas Bodley approved, anyway.

It has been claimed that *Lucrece* may have been influenced by Shakespeare's cousin, the Jesuit Robert Southwell, who had been arrested in 1592. In the same year Southwell's didactic poem *Saint Peter's Complaint* was published anonymously, and was so popular that it was reprinted many times.[4] But it had circulated in manuscript form for some years before; it is very likely that Shakespeare – Southwell's cousin – read it. The opening lines give some indication of its content:

> Launch forth, my soul, into a main of tears,
> Full fraught with grief, the traffic of thy mind;
> Torn sails will serve thoughts rent with guilty fears,
> Give care the stern, use sighs instead of wind:
> Remorse thy pilot, thy misdeed thy card,
> Torment thy haven, shipwreck thy best reward.

The title page of the 1616 edition of Southwell's poems, with Shakespeare safely dead, contains this preface: *To my worthy good cosen Maister W.S.* No other relations had these initials. Southwell observes that most poets 'have wedded their wills' to 'unworthy affections' – his term for worldly love. The publication of this letter to 'W.S.' would have been unwelcome in Shakespeare's life-time, for it would certainly have attracted the attention of the odious Richard Topcliffe (if he had been alive – he died in 1604). As Devlin notes, Southwell wrote in his preface:

> Worthy cosen, Poets, by abusing their talent, and making the follies, and faygnings of love the customary subject of their base endeavours, have so discredited this facultie, that a Poet, a Lover and a Lyar, are by many reckoned but three words of one signification

It seems certain that, more in sorrow than in anger, this was addressed to Shakespeare. It is a moot question whether Shakespeare received it – and whether he took on board the criticism of the levity and prurience of *Venus and Adonis*? Perhaps so – and if so, it could have had an effect: *The Rape of Lucrece* is a sea-change from *Venus and Adonis*. There is no clever word-play, no subtle innuendo, no titillation, no female lechery. Instead, we have a sober depiction of courage, integrity, chastity and righteous anger, directed at lust and the abuse of power. It is interesting to compare and contrast this poem, designed for public consumption, with the sonnets, which are highly personal, written only for himself, or perhaps his private friends, and which clearly at times strike a different note, in that they involve 'worldly affections'.

More sonnets, 1594-1595

The sonnets are an extraordinary – unique – contribution to the canon of English literature. Yet what some of them mean, when, why and for whom they were written – who wrote them, even – these are questions the answers to which are even today hotly disputed by scholars. What can be agreed is that they do not merely show a total mastery of the poetic form, but they also display subtle psychological insights that place Shakespeare way ahead of his time. The 34 sonnets he wrote at this time were, like all the others, first published in the collection of 154 sonnets that came out in 1609 with the title *Shake-Speares Sonnets Never Before Imprinted*. The sonnets are an awkward piece of the chronological jigsaw, because as we have seen, the order they were written in was not the order in which they appear in the 1609 publication.[5] In their book *All the Sonnets of Shakespeare*, Edmondson and Wells assign the group of 34 sonnets discussed here – numbers 61 – 77, and 87 – 103 to the years 1594-5 (all dates slightly subject to correction). Only four of them – sonnets 63, 67, 68 and 101, are addressed unequivocally to, or are about, a male. For example, Sonnet 63 meditates on how time competes with beauty, but claims that 'age's cruel knife'

> ... shall never cut from memory
> My sweet love's beauty, though my lover's life.
> His beauty shall in these black lines be seen
> And they shall live, and he in them still green.
>
> – Sonnet 63

Apart from these four, the other sonnets could be addressed to, or are about, a male or a female, so they are somewhat ambiguous. To my mind, however, it seems convincing that it is to his relationship with Southampton that these sonnets refer. While none of the sonnets in this chapter imply the degree of intimacy seen in the Dark Lady sonnets, they do express love for a young man. I think the gender of his lover is almost irrelevant: the sonnets are above all about that most vital of all human emotions, love. The publisher John Benson seems to have had a problem with this, and consequently in his 1640 edition all (or, in fact, nearly all ...) the male pronouns were changed to female (*he* to *she*, etc.) and phrases like 'sweet boy' were changed to 'sweet love'.[6] Again, one can't help wondering whether these sonnets are autobiographical. Edmondson and Wells are cautious on the issue:

> We believe that many of Shakespeare's Sonnets are deeply personal poems, written out of Shakespeare's own experience. This does not mean that we should seek to tell a coherent biographical narrative through them, nor should we impose one upon them.'[7]

Perhaps the existence of these 34 sonnets, and others like them written later on, by a man about his male lover, is one reason why some readers, even today, prefer to believe that they are not autobiographical, and that they were written merely as a literary exercise, as Sidney Lee suggested.[8] The other strategy that has been adopted for dealing with these sonnets is to downplay – even ignore – them: Duncan-Jones suggests scholars and anthologists, particularly men, have been reluctant to face the issue of whether Shakespeare was gay or bi-sexual, and accordingly pay relatively little attention to those that are either to, or about, a beautiful young man.[9] She suggests that, lured perhaps by what Mario Praz called 'The Beauty of Medusa'[10], many have felt that no great writer is complete without a *femme fatale*. So Petrarch had Laura, and Dante had Beatrice. Nearer home, Keats had Fanny Brawne (*La Belle Dame Sans Merci*) and Yeats had Maude Gonne. Less romantically, perhaps, James Joyce had his Nora Barnacle. Accordingly, Shakespeare was assigned his Dark Lady.

Now many readers may find it hard to reconcile a collection of poems that address a beautiful young man in such affectionate terms conjoined with other poems depicting an agonized obsession with a woman. It is hard to avoid the obvious conclusion that he was bisexual.[11] We live in an era when awareness of bisexuality is increasing, and characters like the late musician and cultural icon David Bowie became – remain – much admired not just for their art, but for their courage and honesty in 'coming out'. In an interview in *Playboy* magazine, Bowie stated: 'It's true – I am a bisexual. But I can't deny that I've used that fact very well. I suppose it's the best thing that ever happened to me'[12] Shakespeare would probably never have made a similar statement, even if the word *bisexual* had been known in Tudor times. Shapiro notes that in Shakespeare's time 'People didn't think in terms of "heterosexuality" or "homosexuality" either'.[13]

With the publication of the sonnets in 1609, it would seem that, in modern parlance, he 'came out'; alternatively, if he did not authorize the publication, he was 'outed'. Either way, it seems that in Tudor times, this was not an issue; still less in the reign of James I. It became an issue in subsequent centuries, but today, the past is another country. The great Shakespearian actor Sir Ian McKellen has claimed that there was no doubt that Shakespeare slept with men.[14] Professor Stanley Wells, President of the Shakespeare Birthplace Trust commented: 'Of course Sir Ian is not the first to say so. It goes back centuries, especially because some of Shakespeare's sonnets are unquestionably addressed to a male ... As the T-shirt that Sir Ian sometimes wears, says "Some people are gay. Get over it!"'[15] It's not just the evidence of the sonnets: Polly Findlay's RSC production of *The Merchant of Venice* (2015) makes it clear that Antonio and Bassanio are lovers, and it seems that no eyelids were batted among the Tudor audience. Nor should our eyelids bat, either: for these sonnets are not about sexuality – they are about love.

The sonnets have attracted myth-makers like moths to a flame: one claim, that these were mere literary exercises, can be discounted; another is that the Earl of Southampton remains a central figure throughout all of them; a

> **The traditional story**
>
> Many books on Shakespeare envisage the following narrative – impossible because the relationship with the Earl of Southampton ended in 1594, and many of the sonnets were written years earlier – and later – and according to Edmondson and Wells do not fit in with this story-line:
>
> 'Following the two great poems that Shakespeare wrote, the Countess of Southampton, asked Shakespeare to write 17 sonnets (*the Procreation Sonnets*) to persuade her effete son to marry and have children. Shakespeare formed a deep attachment to the young man, and wrote a long sequence of sonnets, many of which were about him, but some of which addressed more philosophical issues. He often addressed the earl with words like *sweet boy* when he was well into his twenties. At some time or other, Shakespeare also had an intense affair with a Dark Lady, and was deeply wounded when the Earl of Southampton took her over. Later, Shakespeare had to contend with a rival poet.'

third, that they were written in sequence, as printed. As we have seen, they were not. So many stories have been built around what is still often called 'Shakespeare's sonnet sequence'. If one thinks in those terms, those in the 1609 volume do indeed seem to be telling a story – the traditional story outlined above. But the story falls apart if the sonnets are considered in the order in which they were written, rather than the order in which they were printed.

Apart from the likelihood that the Dark Lady sonnets were written years earlier (See chapter 11), there are, in my view, many things unconvincing, indeed, wrong, about this story. For example, let us just look at the so-called 'Procreation Sonnets' (1-17), which urge a beautiful young man to marry and have children. Unfortunately for the traditional story, the Procreation Sonnets were not written until 1595-7 when Southampton (born 1573) was well into his twenties, no longer the young seventeen-year-old young man envisaged in the 17 Procreation Sonnets. Along with many other scholars, I believe that the Procreation Sonnets were not addressed to Southampton but to someone quite different, as we shall see in Chapter 20.

Time to look at this group of sonnets in more detail. No clear narrative appears: what does emerge is emotional turmoil. While some of the sonnets in this group struggle with philosophical issues such as the passing of time, many are addressed to a lover:

> Against my love shall be as I am now,
> With time's injurious hand crushed and o'erworn;
> When hours have drained his blood and filled his brow
> With lines and wrinkles ...
>
> – Sonnet 63

'Against' is glossed by Colin Burrow 'To secure me against the time when ... ' as meaning 'in preparation for the time when'.[16] It is noticeable that a number of sonnets in this group shows a morbid preoccupation with death and tend to exaggerate the effects of 'time's injurious hand' on Shakespeare and/or his lover.' (Shakespeare was only about 30 when these sonnets were written.) The examples multiply: Sonnet 64 refers to 'time's fell hand'; in Sonnet 65, we have 'sad mortality', Sonnet 66 talks of 'restful death', Sonnet 74 talks of 'the prey of worms'. We even have 'widowed womb' in Sonnet 97. So many of these poems show a preoccupation with death – both mortality and the slow death of a relationship.

I think we can also detect the influence of the saintly Robert Southwell, Shakespeare's 'cousin' who was, after years of torture, executed in February 1595.[17] It is very possible that Shakespeare saw *St Peter's Complaint*, which was widely circulated in manuscript before the execution. Knowing this

---

Lord Strange – the final curtain

Ferdinando's story now moves away from the stage to the real-life drama of Tudor politics. On the very day that he became the Fifth Earl of Derby on the death of his father, in September 1593, a local Catholic named Richard Hesketh delivered a letter inviting him to become Queen Elizabeth's successor. Ferdinando was horrified. He knew well that any talk of the succession was regarded as high treason. Was the letter genuine? If so, it was like a death warrant. Could it be a trap, engineered by Lord Burghley? Either way, Ferdinando was a dead man walking: mere suspicion was enough to send a man to the scaffold.

In a desperate attempt to prove his innocence, he rode to London with Hesketh, and then vehemently denounced him to the authorities. If Ferdinando had hoped to be rewarded for his loyalty, he was quickly disabused. He was kept away from the enquiry, and shunned by the court. Complaining bitterly that he was 'crossed in court, and crossed in the country', he returned to the family home in Lathom.

Within a few months, Ferdinando fell seriously ill: within a week, on 16 April 1594, he was dead. It was generally believed that he had been poisoned with arsenic – but by whom? By Catholics, who saw him as having betrayed Hesketh – and their cause? Or by agents of Burghley, who decided he presented a serious danger to the state? To this day, nobody can be sure.[18]

poem, and hearing of Southwell's dreadful end, could partly account for the many sombre references in these sonnets. Several other deaths over this period would also have had an effect, including those of Marlowe (murdered May 1593), and Thomas Kyd (destroyed by torture December 1594) – and the probable murder in April 1594 of Lord Strange, now the fifth Earl of Derby, under very mysterious circumstances.

End of an Affair

Whatever the cause, these sonnets are not exactly filled with joy and clearly signal the end of an affair: the relationship appears to have been one-sided if Sonnet 61 is to be believed, in which the poet sleeps alone. The sonnet asks

> Is it thy will thy image should keep open
> My heavy eyelids to the weary night?
> ...
> It is my love that keeps mine eye awake
> Mine own true love that doth my rest defeat
> To play the watchman ever for thy sake
> For thee watch I whilst thou doth wake elsewhere,
> From me far off, while others all too near
>
> – Sonnet 61

Sonnets 67 and 68 clearly signal doubt and disillusionment.

> Ah wherefore with infection should he live
> And with his presence grace impiety.
> That sin by him advantage should achieve
> And lace itself with his society?
>
> – Sonnet 67

In Sonnet 68, images of death prevail over those of love and beauty:

> Thus is his cheek the map of days outworn
> When beauty lived and died as flowers do now
> Before these bastard signs of fair were borne
> Or durst inhabit on a living brow;
> Before the golden tresses of the dead
> The right of sepulchres were shorn away

> To live a second life on second head;
> Ere beauty's dead fleece made another gay.
>
> — Sonnet 68

To my mind, one cannot help feeling that 'dead fleece' is an error of taste, as is the suggestion that his lover's golden tresses may also one day inhabit someone else's head (Queen Elizabeth habitually wore a wig made of human hair.) Altogether, this is a pretty grotesque way of praising his lover's looks. Furthermore, who conjoins a love poem with references to infections, and the tresses of corpses? There are strong indications that all is not well: Sonnet 70 hints at *blame* and *slander*; In Sonnet 71 a fine line is drawn between sorrow and self-pity: 'No longer mourn for me when I am dead ... ' Shakespeare was far too young to think of dying. These excerpts indicate increasing unhappiness:

> Farewell – thou art too dear for my possessing'
>
> — Sonnet 87
>
> Then hate me when thou wilt, if ever, now
>
> — Sonnet 90
>
> But do thy worst to steal thyself away
>
> — Sonnet 92

In the last sonnets in this sequence the poet cannot forget the beauty of the person addressed, but Sonnet 95 refers to *a canker in the fragrant rose*: realization finally dawns that there is no future in this relationship.

Exit Southampton

It is easy to see why this relationship was going nowhere. For a start, one of Southampton's cronies – and, according to Duncan-Jones, lovers – was the young Robert Devereux, Earl of Essex, who combined superficial charm with a ruthless ambition, and a strong streak of cruelty. Essex, arrogant and unpredictable, was a narcissist, easily given to both anger and jealousy: he would have had little time for anyone such as Shakespeare who had any close relationship with Southampton.[19]

In early 1594, Essex was growing increasingly involved in rivalry with Burghley and his son, Robert Cecil, for influence over Queen Elizabeth. In an attempt to gain favour with the queen, he claimed to have evidence that

Dr Lopez, Elizabeth's trusted physician, a man of Jewish heritage,[20] was involved in a plot against her life. Lopez, who had been acting for Burghley in his secret and politically dubious peace negotiations with Spain, insisted he was innocent, but Essex managed to get him convicted of treason in a grossly unfair trial; Burghley did nothing to protect him.[21] Despite the queen's doubts about his guilt, in June 1594 Lopez was given the brutal ending meted out to traitors, pleading his innocence to the end. The sight of Essex and Southampton in their cups, gloating over the poor man's hideous death, must have stuck in Shakespeare's craw; even if he did not witness this scene, he would have known about it.

The whole episode smacked heavily of antisemitism. Is it fanciful to suggest that Shakespeare found these events repellent? Perhaps they explain *The Merchant of Venice*. Perhaps, too, they have reverberations in Sonnet 94 – the last line appeared in *Edward III*:

> They that have power to hurt and will do none,
> That do not do the thing they most do show
> Who, moving others, are themselves as stone –
> Unmoved, cold, and to temptation slow ...
> ...
> For sweetest things turn sourest by their deeds
> Lilies that fester smell far worse than weeds
>
> – Sonnet 94

Finally, in October 1594 two of Southampton's retainers, the Danvers brothers, arrived, seeking refuge after committing murder. Amid the hue and cry, Southampton gave them shelter, and then smuggled them out of the country to France. It was becoming increasingly apparent that the company Southampton was keeping would not have endeared him to Shakespeare. It was a case of a poet meets the Bullingdon Club.[22] Meanwhile, there was wild talk of Essex seeking fame and fortune in a raid on Cadiz in 1596 to clock up credit with the queen and do a bit of looting. Southampton planned to join him though the queen forbade his participation.[23] However, looting was definitely needed, for the young earl was living way beyond his means.

It is obvious, too, that this relationship was doomed from the start, really. The poet and the Southampton set were poles apart: Southampton was part of an aristocratic coterie, and Shakespeare could never have wanted to be a member of it. Distaste with the company Southampton kept morphed into final disillusionment, and Shakespeare wrote this valedictory sonnet, which, with its legal and financial imagery sounds more like a negative auditor's report than a 'Dear John'. This should surely have been the last in this sequence:

> Farewell, thou art too dear for my possessing,
>   And like enough thou know'st thy estimate
> The charter of thy worth gives thee releasing;
>   My bonds in thee are all determinate.
> For how do I hold thee but by thy granting
>   And for that riches where is my deserving?
> The cause of this fair gift in me is wanting
>   And so my patent back again is swerving
> Thyself thou gave'st, thy own worth then not knowing
>   Or me to whom thou gav'st it else mistaking
> So thy great gift, upon misprision growing
>   Comes home again, on better judgment making
>   Thus have I had thee as a dream doth flatter
>   In sleep a king, but waking no such matter.
>
> – Sonnet 87

13

A LITTLE LIGHT RELIEF

'We are wise girls to mock our lovers so.'
– The Princess in *Love's Labours Lost*, Act 5, Scene 1

During his stay in the Earl of Southampton's household, Shakespeare would have met the Anglo-Italian John Florio, who was living in Titchfield at the time. It is just possible that they had met before, because Florio was very familiar with the theatre. Some have even suggested that he *was* Shakespeare, mainly because Shakespeare's plays contain so many references to Italy, and so many Italian names.[1] However, of course, Florio was a scholar, not a playwright. No one seriously believes that Florio was Shakespeare: Michell, in his authorship survey, does not even mention him as a contender.[2] That is not to say that Florio, and Italian residents in London, weren't a strong influence, as we shall see.

So, what was this Anglo-Italian scholar doing in a remote country house in Hampshire? Florio was well-known to the young earl's guardian, Lord Burghley, and had even done a little spying for him – he had played a part in uncovering the Babington Plot. It is possible that Burghley had infiltrated Florio into the household as a tutor, to keep an eye on the young earl, and keep him out of trouble: for Southampton was thought to nurture Catholic sympathies. (It was known that Fr Campion had been one of his confessors.)

So why was it significant that John Florio and Shakespeare were known to each other? It has often been commented that Shakespeare's knowledge of Italy is difficult to explain. Hudson notes some remarkable coincidences

A LITTLE LIGHT RELIEF

John Florio (1552 – 1625) by William Hole, engraving, 1611

involving Italian references to *Othello* – and vice versa.³ Some have argued that he must have travelled there during his lost years. Others have argued that the author of the plays was someone else who had travelled in Italy (such as Edward de Vere, Earl of Oxford).⁴ However, I think that Shakespeare's familiarity with Florio explains a great deal: much could have been gleaned from him. It should also be remembered that apart from the conversation manuals we mentioned in Chapter 8, there were enough Italian speakers in London to act as informants. For example, there were refugees, court musicians and entertainers from Venice, and a number of Italian fencing teachers, as well, of course, as merchants and seamen passing through. The knowledge of Italian topography displayed in Shakespeare's plays (not always accurate) could just as easily have been acquired from them. Schoenbaum notes that the *Oliphant*, an Inn on Bankside, was a favourite watering hole for the Italian community⁵ – there is a reference

---

John Florio: the Italian connection?

John Florio (1552-1625) has been described as the most important humanist in Renaissance England.⁶ His father had been a Franciscan Friar, and, having converted to Protestantism, took refuge in London to avoid the Inquisition. Florio described himself as *Italus ore, Anglus pectore* – 'An Englishman in Italian'. Fluent in both Italian and English, he had a huge impact on multilingual London as a lexicographer, author and translator.

He published several language manuals, and a book listing around six thousand Italian proverbs; he also produced an influential Italian-English dictionary. His acclaimed translation of Montaigne's essays was finally published in 1603 – these were much used by Shakespeare. At some point he became attached to the Earl of Southampton's household, and he dedicated to the earl his pamphlet, *The World of Words*.⁷

in *Twelfth Night* to 'The Elephant' where it is 'best to lodge'. In *Othello*, the Duke asks 'Marcius Luchese, is he not in town?' a reference to Sr Lucchese, from Lucca, who ran a restaurant in Hart Street, in the parish of St Olave's.

In the 1590s, Florio was heavily involved in compiling his 46,000-word Italian-English dictionary, finally published in 1598. To assist his studies, Florio had an extensive library of Italian books that Shakespeare could have had access to; Shakespeare might also have had access to Florio's wife. Florio had earlier written about his ideal of feminine beauty: 'to be accounted fair', a woman had to have 'black eyes, black brows, black hairs' (*sic*): a sharp reminder of the Dark Lady sonnets. This presumably described his first wife, a young Italian woman, Anna Soresollo whom he married in 1574.[8]

Jonathan Bate came up with an intriguing theory: with her husband engrossed in his work, Anna may well have felt neglected; and when Shakespeare arrived, she may have succumbed to what might be called bored housewife syndrome.[9] It is easy to imagine how Shakespeare, in turn, may have succumbed to her Mediterranean charm. How long their dalliance may have lasted we can only guess, but according to Bate's theory, she soon found other offers more tempting – we need look no further than Shakespeare's friend, the Earl of Southampton. As Bate suggests, the young earl might have resented Florio as both a teacher and as a spy – and exacted revenge by sleeping with his wife: between aging actor and glamorous young earl there could be no contest. There is, however, one insuperable objection: Anna Soresollo died of the plague in 1593. While the story gets some support from some of the sonnets, I think 'not proven' is the verdict; but if she was having an affair, it would have occurred in, or before, 1593.

While at Titchfield, or shortly after he left, Shakespeare found time to write two plays. Given the morbidity of some of the sonnets reviewed in the last chapter, one wonders whether Shakespeare was not just bisexual, but slightly bipolar – for the two plays he wrote during or after composing those brooding, introverted sonnets, with their numerous references to death, were both comedies. Perhaps writing comedy was a form of therapy, or a form of escape.

The Comedy of Errors

The Comedy of Errors is often seen as a surrealistic farce, best watched after a drink or two. It is tempting to place the play very early, if only because it was inspired by two comedies set in Syracuse by Plautus, whose work Shakespeare learnt about at Stratford Grammar School.[10] For this reason, it was often assumed to be among the first he wrote. Taylor and Loughnane[11] argue convincingly for a later date, mid- to late 1594, on numerous grounds; they also point out that 'the play's Plautine plot seems particularly suitable for the learned audience at Gray's Inn' where it was first performed on 28 December 1594 at the Yuletide revels. In observing the classical ideals of unity of place and time – all the events in the play occur in one place, Ephesus, and in one day – Shakespeare may have wanted to counter Greene's accusations that he was somehow 'unlearned' in the classics. With its zany humour, it was almost literally a howling success with the classically educated audience at Gray's Inn.[12]

Shakespeare updated Plautus by making ambitious changes, including moving the action from Syracuse to Ephesus. It features two identical twin brothers who were separated, years before the play starts, in a shipwreck, and who were given the same name – Antipholus. The running (some would say limping) joke is the confusion that occurs when Antipholus of Syracuse arrives in Ephesus, where his twin lives. As they are identical, everyone muddles them up in a comical series of misunderstandings: so far, so Plautus. However, Shakespeare, with great skill, and a good deal of impudent hubris, has added two servants who are also twins, and who also share the same name, Dromio, thus doubling the possibility of confused identities. The more one reads this play, the more cleverly plotted and scripted it becomes. And the more daft, really. The plot is handled so deftly, that despite the ludicrous storyline, it is hard to recognise it as a first attempt at comedy, as some have suggested.[13] For these and other reasons, most authorities now accept the later date of 1594.

The length of the play – by far Shakespeare's shortest – suggests that it was written quickly for an occasion such as a Christmas festivity. The play combines farce with classical references, and bawdiness – for example, this exchange about a 'kitchen wench' by the pair from Syracuse, the sort of dialogue that smacks of the Music Hall circa 1910:

> DROMIO: ... she is spherical, like a globe;
>   I could find out countries in her.
> ANTIPHOLUS: In what part of her body stands Ireland?
> DROMIO: Marry, sir, in her buttocks: I found it out by the bogs ...
> ANTIPHOLUS: Where stood Belgia, the Netherlands?
> DROMIO: O sir, I did not look so low
>
> – Act 3, Scene 2

Putting aside its offensiveness, this exchange also helps to date the play, because the first ever globes, made by Molyneux, came onto the market in London in 1592, and were very popular.[14]

However, the play also has hidden depths, and touches on serious issues, such as the treatment of people who have mental health problems. For example, why has Shakespeare moved the location of the play from 'Epidamnum' to Ephesus? According to the Bible, Ephesus was frequented by exorcists specialising in 'casting out demons' or, in modern parlance, sorting out people with mental health issues.[15] Arriving in the city a stranger, Antipholus 2 obviously has no knowledge at all of the life, activities – or even the wife – of his lost twin brother, and behaves accordingly. Everyone thinks he is Antipholus 1, and decide that the latter must have gone mad. And so they bring in an exorcist, Dr Pinch:

> PINCH: I charge thee, Satan, housed within this man
>   To yield possession to my holy prayers,
>   And to thy state of darkness hie thee straight
>   I conjure thee by all the saints in heaven.
> ANTIPHOLUS OF EPHESUS: Peace, doting wizard, peace! I am not mad.
> ADRIANA: O that thou wert not, poor distressed soul

What helps us to date this play is the fact that one R. Phinch wrote a book denouncing exorcism as 'false miracles' and 'popish jugglings' and in 1590 wrote a book on the subject.[16] Turning anti-Catholic anti-exorcist Puritan R. Phinch into a slightly dotty exorcist, Dr Pinch, in his play, Shakespeare is without any doubt having a joke at R. Phinch's expense, showing himself thereby to be no friend to Puritans.[17] And a friend of the Catholics?

Perhaps so, for the abbess who helps to resolve the problems at the end of the play is a figure of authority and gravitas. Abbess Aemilia undertakes to deal calmly and rationally with the man the others think is mad.[18] This betokens a more humane understanding of mental health problems than was common in an age when people paid to watch the poor souls locked up in Bedlam as a form of entertainment. This is not the last time an abbess, or a friar, plays a key role in a Shakespeare play: does this make him a closet Catholic? If so he was running a bit of a risk.

Love's Labour's Lost

Perhaps Shakespeare thought it time for something more sophisticated than *The Comedy of Errors* to appeal to the Royal Court. And so we come to *Love's Labour's Lost*. The play is set in the Court of Navarre: there, the king and three of his nobles have vowed to abjure the company of women, and to refrain from wine and luxury, in order to concentrate on philosophy. *Quelle bonne idée!* One of the courtiers reads out one of the clauses in the agreement:

> BIRON: 'Item; if any man be seen to talk with a woman within the term of three years, he shall endure such public shame as the rest of the court can possibly devise.'

Hélas! Their plan is wrecked almost immediately:

> This article, my liege, yourself must break;
> For well you know here comes an embassy
> The French King's daughter with yourself to speak –
> A maid of grace and complete majesty –
> About surrender-up of Aquitaine
> To her decrepit, sick and berid father
> Therefore this article is made in vain ...
>
> – I.i

So, thankfully for the audience, the plan to abjure female company is ruined almost immediately by the arrival of the princess on a goodwill mission, named in some versions of the play as a queen (as indeed in real life she was, Marguerite de Valois) – possibly renamed a princess for diplomatic reasons. She is accompanied by a bevy of beautiful and high-spirited maids of honour. One by one, the men succumb to their charms, though, as sadly so often happens, there are serious doubts about the honesty of their intentions. Needless to say, the women all come out on top. It is extremely funny. The play was a huge hit with everyone except one Robert Tofte, a poet and gifted translator, who took his girlfriend to see it in 1598. His 'forward dame', as he describes her, did not enjoy the performance, and the date was not a success.[19]

The play may not have been a success for Tofte and his dame, but it went down well with both the court, and the public. *A Pleasant Conceited Comedie called Loues labors loft as it was performed before her Highness this laft Chriftmas Newley corrected and augmented by W. fhakefpeare* appeared in a Quarto version in 1598. According to Taylor and Loughnane,[20] it was written in late 1594 or early 1595; however, there are reasons to believe the play may have been started several years earlier. The play has no obvious source.[21] All we can be certain of is that it was performed at court during the Christmas season of either 1594 or 1595. There have been suggestions that the play was originally written for a performance in the 'play room' at the Earl of Southampton's house at Titchfield. That may be so; but I think that William Stanley, Ferdinando's younger brother, had more to do with the play than Southampton. The pageants that take place in the play – the Muscovites, the Nine Worthies, the Owl and the Cuckoo – have their origin in the tradition of royal entertainments of the time, more like an early modern cabaret: enter, William Stanley.

It is likely that after Ferdinando's death, Shakespeare allowed a decent – and politic – interval to pass before continuing any connection with William Stanley. There is an unproven claim by 'the Derbyists' that Shakespeare was the pen name of William Stanley (well, they do share the same initials). What is certain is that Stanley wrote plays. In 1891 the American scholar James Greenstreet discovered in London's Public Record Office a letter written in 1599 by one George Fenner, a Catholic secret agent.[22] The letter speculates on how William Stanley might take part in establishing a Catholic monarchy. However, doubt is cast on William's reliability: Fenner laments that William was 'busy in penning comedies for the common players.' So, William Stanley wrote plays, did he? The 'Derbyists' who have theorised that Shakespeare was the *nom de plume* of William Stanley, begin to scent blood.

Although there is no evidence that Stanley wrote any of the plays so far considered in this book, it is more than possible that William Stanley wrote an early draft of this 'closet drama'. I think it very much looks as though this play was originally written for the Stanley's family house at Lathom for in-house performance, even if it was rewritten by Shakespeare at Titchfield later on. Of course, am-dram is a very different kettle of fish from professional performance in a theatre. Is it possible that Stanley had one of his efforts rewritten by a professional – indeed, by Shakespeare?

The original idea for the play could easily have come from Stanley: the play is set in the court of Henri de Bourbon, at a time when he was King of Navarre at Nerac in south-west France: this was off the beaten track for most visitors to France. Stanley knew France well, and had probably visited Nerac on his way to and from Spain. The insight into the court of Navarre and its free-thinking and amorous atmosphere could well have come from him. He even knew the names of courtiers present at the court of the King of Navarre in Nerac – slightly renamed in the play: Biron, Longaville and Dumaine. Stanley could well have written an entertainment based on his experiences in Nerac for performances in the family home at Lathom. Subsequently, as indicated by the title page, Shakespeare could have been involved in rewriting it.

As we saw, the play was 'Newly corrected and augmented by W. Shakespeare'. Yes, W. Shakespeare, not W.S. It is the first play that was published with his name writ large on the front cover. Obviously, correction and rewriting is a normal part of the creative process, as every writer knows; but *augmentation*? That Shakespeare augmented the text certainly implies that he added material to something already written. Is there a clue in this comment from the critic and historian John Pendergast?

> Perhaps more than any other Shakespearean play, it explores the power and limitations of language, and this blatant concern for language led many early critics to believe that it was the work of a playwright just learning his art.[23]

'Just learning his art?' That could hardly describe William Shakespeare in 1594. However, we suggest here that the play contains some crude elements, written by another hand perhaps earlier than 1594, that would justify Pendergast's observation. His comment does suggest to me that

William Stanley, the 6th Earl of Derby, 1561-1642

Shakespeare was perhaps 'augmenting' material from someone else, an amateur writer, perhaps, such as William Stanley. Let's look at what other evidence we have.

It is striking that the king is named, not Henri, but – Ferdinand! Almost Ferdinando, William's brother, no less! Could he have been persuaded, after a drink or two, to take part in a bit of closet drama? Quite possibly. But the name is certainly significant: it seems certain that this play came out of the Derby stable. Unfortunately, we cannot explore the dual authorship theory by reading any of William Stanley's comedies and comparing them with Shakespeare's. The beautiful buildings at Lathom, were razed to the ground by Oliver Cromwell, and the contents destroyed. (Lathom House today is a Georgian building.)

However, a close look at the text does seem to indicate there are at least two hands on the wheel. Some lines are almost doggerel; others show Shakespeare's iambic pentameter at its best. These lines read like pantomime:

> LONGAVILLE: I beseech you, a word. What is she in the white?
> BOYET: A woman sometimes, an you saw her in the light.
> LONG: Perchance light in the light. I desire her name.
> BOYET: She hath but one for herself: to desire that were a shame.
> – Act 2, Scene 1

Or this:

> KING: This child of fancy, that Armado hight,
>   For interim to our studies shall relate
>   In high-born words the worth of many a knight
>   From tawny Spain lost in the world's debate.
>   How you delight, my lords, I know not, I;
>   But, I protest, I love to hear him lie
>   And I will use him for my minstrelsy.
> BIRON: Armado is a most illustrious wight,
>   A man of fire-new words, fashion's own knight.
> LONG: Costard the swain and he shall be our sport;
>   And so to study, three years is but short.
> – Act 1, Scene 1

The tortured phrasing, mangled syntax, mechanical rhythm, forced or false rhymes, the somewhat archaic words (eg *hight, wight, swain*) –

these all offer stylistic clues indicating an amateur writer 'still learning his art'. One hears the same sort of stuff today at any Christmas pantomime in Britain. The evidence is mounting that it was a 'comedie' written by an amateur. Compare these exchanges with this, from Biron. Its elegant rhythm is in stark contrast to the mechanical drumbeats of the pantomime patter:

> Learning is but an adjunct to ourself
> And where we are our learning likewise is:
> Then when ourselves we see in ladies' eyes,
> Do we not likewise see our learning there?
> O, we have made a vow to study, lords,
> And in that vow we have forsworn our books.
> For when would you, my liege, or you, or you,
> In leaden contemplation have found out
> Such fiery numbers as the prompting eyes
> Of beauty's tutors have enrich'd you with?
>
> – LLL Act 4, Scene 3

There is much in the same vein. However, the play is not just marked by stylistic unevenness – it also contains other oddities. At two points in the play there are two different versions of more or less the same speech – in each case the first is marked 'deleted' by editors. (Was this Shakespeare accommodating William Stanley's original version, and then adding his own?) It does seem, at the very least, possible that William Stanley suggested that Shakespeare should rewrite for the public an entertainment he had written for a private audience.

I think that the evidence for Stanley's involvement is quite compelling. However, there are also lingering doubts. First, the names of three of the young nobles would have been quite well known from pamphlets circulating at the time about the French civil wars. In addition, Anthony Bacon spent six years in Nerac in the 1590s, and wrote letters about his time there to his brother, Francis Bacon, whom Shakespeare knew. It is possible that he obtained some of the information included in the play from this source. Nevertheless, readers may find that the evidence presented here for William Stanley's involvement in this play convincing. Further research may cast more light on the question.

Time to explore the play in more detail. As the men in turn succumb to female charm, they attempt to keep their loves secret from one another. It is Biron who leads the charge, as he approaches Rosalinde with arguably the best chat-up line in history:

> BIRON: Did not I dance with you at Brabant once?

The reply, and exchanges that follow, are a delight:

> ROS: Did not I dance with *you* at Brabant once?
> BIR: I know you did.
> ROS: How needless was it then to ask the question.
> BIR: You must not be so quick.
> ROS: 'Tis long of you to spur me with such questions.
> BIR: Your wit's too hot, it speeds too fast, 'twill tire.
> ROS: Not till it leaves the rider in the mire.
> BIR: What time o' day?
> ROS: The hour that fools should ask.
> BIR: Now fair befall your mask!
> ROS: Fair fall the face it covers!
> BIR: And send you many lovers.
> ROS: Amen, so you be none.
> BIR: Nay, then I shall be gone.
>
> – Act 2, Scene 1

Not just the best chat-up line in history, perhaps the best put-down, too! And those who recall Katherine falling in the mire in *Shrew*, will note that this time, it is the man who ends up in the mire.

Anyone who has seen this play will be aware that it is a joyous comedy involving the battle of the sexes. With its very funny scenes, it is surprising *Love's Labour's Lost* was not popular in the eighteenth and nineteenth centuries; but since 1946, with Peter Brook's production at Stratford, it has become a favourite with both actors and audiences.[24] The play ends when the young men are sentenced to wait another year before their approaches can be considered:

> BIRON: Our wooing doth not end like an old play
>   Jack hath not Jill. These ladies courtesy
>   Might well have made our sport a comedy
> KING: Come, sir, it wants a twelvemonth and a day

> And then t'will end.
> BIRON: That's too long for a play
>
> – Act 5, Scene 2

This play was performed at court to the queen's evident enjoyment. As a footnote it is noteworthy that John Florio also left his mark on the play. Folio's work *First Fruits* published in 1578 includes a proverb that reappears in Act I of *Love's Labour's Lost* in a speech by Holofernes:

> Venetia, Venetia,
> Chi non ti verde, non ti pretia

Indeed, the title of the play may also derive from these lines in John Florio's *First Fruits* and its sequel *Second Fruits*:

> We need not speak so much of love, all books are full of love
> With so many authors, that it were labour lost to speak of love[25]

Do we detect here a certain sense of disillusionment in these lines? Or perhaps this is Shakespeare the anguished sonneteer, speaking – in an attempt to persuade himself that love, like chivalry, is also a chimera, and thus is an illusion one should not take seriously. A strategy not unknown among disappointed lovers.

14

THE LORD CHAMBERLAIN'S MEN

Let's talk of graves, and worms, and epitaphs
– *Richard II*, Act 2, Scene 1

It is likely that Shakespeare returned to London some time in 1594, once the worst of the plague was over. Marsh suggests he took up residence in the Parish of St Helen's, Bishopsgate.[1] St Helen's was a much more salubrious area than Shoreditch, though not far away from it. It is also possible that he found lodgings for a time with his old friend and fellow-Stratfordian, the printer Richard Field. Field had printed *Venus and Adonis*, and the first two editions sold well.[2] Unfortunately for Field, he then sold the title, along with the rights for *The Rape of Lucrece*, to his friend the bookseller, John Harrison. Suggestions that he did so because the eroticism of *Venus and Adonis* offended his Protestant conscience are unlikely, given that he also went on, with Harrison, to publish an unexpurgated version of Ovid's extremely racy *The Art of Love* (*De Arte Amandi*).[3] Field was well-known to be a fine printer. He had printed George Puttenham's *The Arte of English Poesie*, Sir John Harington's translation of *Ariosto's Orlando Furioso*, and Sir Thomas North's *Plutarch*, all dedicated to the queen.[4] Shakespeare referred to many such books in his plays, causing some to doubt whether he really was the author of his plays: how did he have access to these expensive books?[5] It is possible Shakespeare read them in Field's printing house in Blackfriars. Shapiro suggests that he 'probably worked from a copy of Plutarch given, or lent him, by Field, an expensive and

Henry Carey, 1st Baron Hunsdon (1526-1596). Steven van Herwijck. (Private collection on loan to the Globe Theatre)

beautiful folio that cost a couple of pounds.'[6] Duncan-Jones thinks it is quite possible that he did not just his reading, but some of his writing, at Field's printing works.[7]

In London he was glad to pursue his first love: the theatre. A shadow had fallen over Lord Strange's Men following Ferdinando's mysterious death in April. William Stanley, the sixth earl, became embroiled in a ruinous dispute with Ferdinando's widow, Lady Alice Spencer, over land and property. Alice was determined not to allow the acting troupe to fall into the hands of William – once described by George Carey as a 'nidicock'.[8] However, in any case, William was busy with his new responsibilities as the sixth earl.

Dispiritedly, the actors soldiered on for a few weeks, weathering the plague, and eking out a living on tour under the name of Lady Alice. In May they performed in Winchester – their last recorded performance. Sadly, it earned a paltry 6s 8d reward for their pains.[9] The prolonged months of plague were a disaster for actors, and many acting companies ceased to exist. Some actors joined up with one of the two remaining major companies, the Lord Chamberlain's Men and the Lord Admiral's Men. These two companies became dominant, both in public theatres, and at court. The Lord Admiral's Men performed in Philip Henslowe's Rose Theatre on the south bank, under the leadership of Edward Alleyn; The Lord Chamberlain's Men performed in Burbage's Theatre in Shoreditch.[10]

Lady Alice decided that her troupe needed a new home. It so happened

> **Lord Hunsdon**
>
> Henry Carey was a political heavyweight; born in 1526, it is believed that he was the natural son of Henry VIII and Mary Boleyn, Anne Boleyn's sister, and was thus the queen's cousin – and one of her most trusted confidantes. Elizabeth showered honours on him, including the Baronial estate of Hunsdon, which had belonged to Mary I.
>
> He put down the rebellion of the Northern Earls in 1569, and became head of Elizabeth's bodyguard. He was made Lord Chamberlain in 1588. You could say he was a man of action, rather than of the theatre. Readers may recall that until she became pregnant, his mistress was Emilia Bassano.

that her sister, Elizabeth, was the wife of George Carey, the son of Henry Carey, Lord Hunsdon, the Lord Chamberlain, and it was possibly through the agency of the two sisters that the troupe transferred their allegiance, to become the Lord Chamberlain's Men: and so in May 1594, they exchanged the Stanley eagle for the Lord Chamberlain's swan. Shakespeare moved on, too. It is likely that any money he received from Southampton went into buying a share in the Lord Chamberlain's Men – their patron, Lord Hunsdon. For a playwright to become a shareholder in an acting troupe was actually unprecedented. In the words of Bart van Es, 'No other English literary playwright had ever held such a position.'[11] However, Shakespeare was in good company: his fellow share-holders were his old acting colleagues Richard Burbage, Will Kempe, John Heminges, George Bryan, Augustine Philips and Thomas Pope. It was to this group (which later became the King's Men after James I came to the throne) that Shakespeare remained professionally attached for the rest of his career.

Audiences were now becoming increasingly demanding, and productions correspondingly more lavish – and the plays more ambitious, with a much larger cast. In effect, they were the Hollywood spectaculars of the age, and small companies did not have the resources to put them on. (The Queen's Men once performed a version of *Richard III* with only four actors, each of whom had to play up to seven different parts; 'spear carriers' were acted by children. The production was not a success.)[12]

Although the troupe was called the Lord Chamberlain's Men, it was Lord Hunsdon's son, George Carey, a keen theatre-goer, who kept a watchful eye on their activities, and they soon became the premier acting company in the country, sporting the Lord Chamberlain's livery. Many of the actors had been among Leicester's Men, and then Lord Strange's Men: Shakespeare must have been delighted to join up again with his old friends. As part of his duties as Lord Chamberlain, Hunsdon was in charge of the queen's household, including state visits, meetings and entertainments. The queen had an insatiable appetite for new plays, and the records show that Shakespeare's plays became part of the repertoire. That summer, they performed two of Shakespeare's comedies, for which they were paid £20;[13] they were at court again in December 1594 (possibly with *The Comedy of Errors*), and again before the queen at Greenwich in January 1595. *Love's Labour's Lost* was also so successful that it was selected for a royal performance at court in 1595 or 1596. *Richard III*, too, was extremely popular.

With Marlowe dead, Shakespeare would certainly have been welcomed by the Lord Chamberlain's Men as their top playwright: it was at this time, perhaps at the request of George Cary, Shakespeare revised the *Henry VI* plays.[14] However, there were potential political problems inherent in these plays. For trouble awaited just around the corner in Elizabeth's England: there was growing anxiety about the succession issue: what was to happen to the monarchy when the queen died? Elizabeth was now visibly aging, and there were persistent rumours that she was mortally ill, and even dead. Yet any talk of her succession was taboo: she worried that if she named a successor she might be forced to abdicate – or that it would quicken her own end. 'Think you that I could love my own winding sheet?' she once famously said. Anyone who raised the issue was in trouble – yet so they did, and even conspired with King James in Scotland behind her back.[15] Yet nothing could stop the rumour-mongering: and the history plays with their endless battles for power seemed to act as an echo-chamber. For they raised questions about kingship, and how it was ordained, whether by God's command, or *Realpolitik*; and in what circumstances the Crown could be transferred from one person to another. The *Henry VI* plays raised questions about such problems, even if they didn't clarify them. Lack of clarification was an essential component of these plays, to avoid running foul of the authorities. No surprise then that ambiguity played a key role in his next play, *Richard II*.

Richard II

Shakespeare turned his attention to *Richard II* probably in the middle months of 1595.[16] With *Richard II*, Shakespeare was on dangerous ground: was it not dicing with death to write a play about a monarch who has favourites, and who is rebelled against, deposed, and subsequently murdered? It could easily be seen as deeply subversive. The patronage of the Lord Chamberlain surely must have seemed like a solid insurance policy: if anyone could keep Shakespeare out of political trouble, he definitely could. Even so, Shakespeare also took out his own insurance policy: he manages to get us to empathise with Richard by beguiling us with the poetry of his words, especially in the later scenes. He even manages to persuade some of us that Richard isn't really a tyrant at all. Thus, E.M.W. Tillyard, for example, claims that 'Shakespeare knows that Richard's crimes never amounted to tyranny and hence that outright rebellion against him was a crime.'[17] He also ensures that Richard eloquently asserts his divine right to be king. This is how he addresses the rebel Northumberland:

> Because we thought ourself to be thy lawful king
> And if we be, how dare thy joints forget
> To pay their awful duty to our presence?
> If we be not, show us the hand of God
> That hath dismissed us from our stewardship;
>
> – Act 3, Scene 3

He also warns that Bolingbroke's treason can cause the loss of many innocent English lives – a powerful argument for a Tudor audience. He points out that 'bleeding war' can bedew England's 'pastures grass with faithful English blood.' (Act 3, Scene 3)

The play begins very oddly: it alludes to the so-far unexplained death of Thomas of Woodstock, the Duke of Gloucester, and seems to assume the audience already knows about this. It has been suggested that the audience must have been familiar with another play, *Woodstock* (1592), or Samuel Daniel's epic poem in *The First Four Books of the Civil Wars* (1595).[18] The first scene features an angry spat between Bolingbroke, the Earl of Hertford, and Mowbray, the Duke of Norfolk. Bolingbroke accuses Mowbray of treason and plotting Gloucester's murder, which Mowbray angrily denies.

Attempts to defuse the quarrel fail, but the two are adamant, and are determined to fight a duel, and King Richard sets the date. So far, so regal: at this point, Richard appears to be a plausible intercessor.

However, in the next scene there is a hint that the king himself is responsible for the murder, not Bolingbroke or Mowbray.[19] The plot thickens: why did the king have Gloucester murdered? The play gives no clear answer. But this information provides a quite different perspective on Richard. Gloucester's widow urges John of Gaunt (Richard's old uncle) to avenge the murder of his brother, but, Gaunt says his duty to the Crown, God's anointed, is higher than that to his murdered brother:

> God's is the quarrel, for God's substitute
> His deputy anointed in His sight
> Hath caused his death, the which if wrongfully
> Let heaven avenge for I may never lift
> An angry arm against his minister.
>
> – *Richard II*, Act 1, Scene 2

Time for the duel: Bolingbroke and Mowbray arrive 'in arms' intent on fighting it out, and one envisages a Tudor audience waiting in eager anticipation for a wonderful display of swordsmanship – only to be disappointed: the king intervenes, giving the judgement of Solomon, and banishes them both. John of Gaunt, convinced that at his great age he is unlikely ever again to see his banished son, Bolingbroke, bids him a sorrowful farewell. Bolingbroke's last words in this scene sums up the sad words of exile:

> Where'er I wander, boast of this I can,
> Though banish'd, yet a trueborn Englishman.[20]
>
> – Act 1, Scene 3

It becomes evident that Richard has his own reasons for banishing Bolingbroke: he has his eye on his inheritance, for Gaunt is one of the richest lords in the country. He also fears Bolingbroke, for he knows how powerful the Dukedom of Lancaster is: he has 'observed his courtship to the common people'. This would have reminded a Tudor audience of Essex, who had challenged Raleigh to a duel some years earlier, and who was cultivating his popular image as a national hero. In a sinister aside, Richard hints that if Bolingbroke does return, he won't have long to live.

Richard turns to the situation in Ireland, where he faces rebellion. He has spent so lavishly on the luxuries of court life and his coterie, Bushy, Bagot and Green, 'the caterpillars of the commonwealth', that he needs 'large sums of gold' to fund the war in Ireland. Hearing that Gaunt is dying, Richard can hardly wait, and hurries round with his sycophantic courtiers, seeing a way to augment his finances by confiscating Gaunt's 'coffers of gold' – and Bolingbroke's inheritance:

> RICHARD: Now put it, God, in the physician's mind
>   To help him to his grave immediately
>   The lining of his coffers shall make coats
>   To deck our soldiers in these Irish wars
>   Come gentlemen, let's all go visit him
>   Pray God we may make haste and come too late
>   – Act 1, Scene 3

Unfortunately, Richard arrives too soon, and is forced to hear his uncle 'speak truth to power' as he lies on his deathbed. Richard does not like what he hears. Gaunt talks of an ill-ruled England, and a king misled by his sycophantic cronies: he foresees that Richard's 'rash fierce blaze of riot cannot last'. Gaunt's famous paean of patriotism is followed by bitter words of lamentation:

> This royal throne of kings, this scepter'd isle,
> This earth of majesty, this seat of Mars,
> This other Eden, demi-paradise,
> This fortress built by Nature for herself
> Against infection and the hand of war,
> This happy breed of men, this little world,
> This precious stone set in the silver sea,
> Which serves it in the office of a wall,
> Or as a moat defensive to a house,
> Against the envy of less happier lands,
> This blessed plot, this earth, this realm, this England,

But:

> .... England is now leased out – I die pronouncing it
> Like to a tenement or pelting farm

> England, bound in with the triumphant sea
> Whose rocky shore beats back the envious siege
> Of wat'ry Neptune, is now bound in with shame
> With inky blots and rotten parchment bonds
> The England that was wont to conquer others
> Hath made a conquest of itself.
>
> – Act 2, Scene 1

Gaunt's long speech still has an uncanny resonance in today's England after the country at last parted company with the European Union following the 2016 British Brexit referendum.[21] Would Gaunt have been a 'Remainer' or a 'Leaver'? See how easy it is to choose what Shakespeare's lines mean to you, in any way you want!

With Gaunt's death, and his son Bolingbroke banished, the king is now free to disinherit him by seizing

> The plate, corn, revenues and moveables,
> Whereof our uncle Gaunt did stand possess'd
>
> – Act 2, Scene 1

Richard goes on to alienate the most powerful families in the land by imposing an unpopular tax burden to fund his war in Ireland – and makes the mistake of going in person to Ireland to fight the rebels. In his absence, Bolingbroke returns to England with an army to reclaim his Dukedom, and Richard hastens back. However, his forces melt away, and the king now stands powerless in his own kingdom. The shock is palpable:

> RICHARD: What must the king do now? must he submit?
>   The king shall do it: must he be deposed?
>   The king shall be contented: must he lose
>   The name of king? o' God's name, let it go:
>   I'll give my jewels for a set of beads,
>   My gorgeous palace for a hermitage,
>
> – Act 3, Scene 3

A different Richard now emerges: he has become a tragic victim. *Richard II* is a revelation – if not a revolution, for in contrast to the bombast of the *Henry VI* plays, we have a monarch tortured by self-doubt – nearer to a Hamlet than a Bolingbroke. At one point, (in Act IV, Scene 1) Richard sees himself as a 'sun-king of fire to Bolingbroke's flood'; later he wonders if he is 'a glistering Phaeton' who drove his father's chariot too close to the sun. Or perhaps, he broods, he is

> a mockery king of snow
> Standing before the sun of Bolingbroke.

The imagery thus reflects a dramatic role-reversal. It is clear that Richard can't last as a monarch: and the moment comes when he is required to hand over his crown 'in common view'. It is so ironic that the final denouement takes place in Westminster Hall. For it was Richard who had remodelled the hall with its amazing hammer-beams, a building that remains breathtaking to this day.

Bolingbroke's fellow nobles start bickering – before hurling down their gloves to challenge one another, until the stage is almost comically littered with gloves. One of them even has to borrow a glove to join in. It is now Bolingbroke's turn to act as peace-maker. When the news came that Richard has finally abdicated, the Duke of York proclaims 'Long live Henry, the fourth of that name', and Bolingbroke is presented with a *fait accompli*. 'In God's name, I'll ascend the regal throne,' he declares. Unlike Richard III, he shows no sign of reluctance in doing so.

To a modern eye, applying the principles of Realpolitik, he has little choice but to accept: the king is clearly a spent force, and an empty throne is a recipe for anarchy. The Bishop of Carlisle's protest is quickly silenced and Richard is now brought in, to hand over the crown in a kind of improvised ritual that is a parody of a formal coronation:[22]

> RICHARD: Give me the crown. Here, cousin, seize the crown;
> Here cousin:
> On this side my hand, and on that side yours.
> Now is this golden crown like a deep well
> That owes two buckets, filling one another,
> The emptier ever dancing in the air,
> The other down, unseen and full of water:
> That bucket down and full of tears am I,
> Drinking my griefs, whilst you mount up on high.
>
> – Richard II, Act 4, Scene 1

As though to find out who he is, a beggar or a king, Richard calls for a mirror 'to show me what a face I have'. The poignant scene that follows would have had a telling effect on a Tudor audience. He asks:

> Was this the face that faced so many follies,
> And was at last out-faced by Bolingbroke?
> A brittle glory shineth in this face:
> As brittle as the glory is the face
> *Dashes the glass against the ground*
> For there it is, crack'd in a hundred shivers.
> Mark, silent king, the moral of this sport,
> How soon my sorrow hath destroy'd my face.
>
> – *Richard II*, Act 4, Scene 1

The cracked mirror has a huge dramatic impact – and this abdication still has the power to move:

> BOLINGBROKE: Are you contented to resign the crown?
> RICHARD: Ay, no; no, ay; for I must nothing be;
> Therefore no no, for I resign to thee.
> Now mark me, how I will undo myself;
> I give this heavy weight from off my head
> And this unwieldy sceptre from my hand,
> The pride of kingly sway from out my heart;
> With mine own tears I wash away my balm,
> With mine own hands I give away my crown,
> With mine own tongue deny my sacred state,
> With mine own breath release all duty's rites:
> All pomp and majesty I do forswear ...
>
> – *Richard II*, Act 4, Scene 1

These are among the finest lines that Shakespeare ever wrote, certainly in his history plays, and he exploits the inverted ritual to maximum theatrical effect. Shakespeare might have had in mind *Samuel* in the 1539 Great Bible: 'Oh howe are the myghtie ouer throwen.'

Richard II in context

Shakespeare must have known he was skating on thin ice: in September 1595, a month or so after he had completed *Richard II*, a tract was being widely circulated in London written by Father Parsons, one of the Catholic plotters in Antwerp who had contacted Ferdinando in 1593. This document, entitled *A Conference about the Next Succession of the Crown* caused a furore: it raised the question whether 'princes for good cause can be deposed.' It suggested that Richard deserved to be deposed, for, like Elizabeth, he was a tyrant who allowed favourites to sway his judgement, and was thus guilty of misrule: a shaft aimed at Cecil. The tract argued for an elective rather than a hereditary monarchy, and suggested that the 'Commonwealth' (ie Parliament) had the right to determine the succession on its own.[23]

This does not happen in the play. The lords are shown to be going 'as to Parliament', but get no further than Westminster Hall. Shakespeare was certainly not going to write a scene in which Parliament overthrows a monarch – that would have been madness – suicide, in fact. York says, very ambiguously 'I am in parliament to pledge for his truth', but the deposition is forced through by a cabal of nobles, not parliament. Richard refuses to read the list of Bolingbroke's accusations, and Northumberland remarks, the 'commons will not then be satisfied.' Commons? Does this refer to the House of Commons, or to the general public? It is very ambiguous: basically, the play very cannily skirts round any hint that parliament had a role in deposing a monarch, as Lake observes. Lake suggests that Shakespeare may have written *Richard II* after reading Parson's *Succession*,[24] but I think this unlikely. More likely, if he had read Parson's document, he probably would not have dared to write the play – it would have been too dangerous.

Parsons' tract was maliciously dedicated to the Earl of Essex, whose hawkish views on combatting Catholic Spain were anathema to English Catholics in exile. In envisaging him as a successor to Queen Elizabeth, it deliberately sought to implicate him in treason, and thus to destroy him, claiming

> No man is in more high and eminent place or dignity
> at this day in our realm than yourself

The queen was furious, and in November 1595 she summoned him to her Privy Chamber at Richmond. The earl was ashen faced; according to an eye witness, he 'was exceedingly troubled at this great piece of villainy done to him: he is sick and continues very ill.' Nevertheless, the first performance of *Richard II* took place the next month, and was enormously successful. Six editions of it were printed before Shakespeare's death – some of them omitting the potentially highly seditious scenes in which Richard was deposed, and later murdered. How did Shakespeare get away with this highly controversial play? Playwrights were jailed for far less. There is no doubt that Shakespeare escaped punishment partly because he was under the protection of the Lord Chamberlain. The fact that the play was about events that had occurred over 200 years before was an ameliorating factor, as was also, perhaps, the fact that Shakespeare was earning increasing respect as a writer.

Richard II would not have been written or performed without the approval of either Lord Hunsdon or his son George Cary – but why did they think it a good idea? Possibly they – and particularly George – just wanted to repeat the success of the *Henry VI* series, with a new play, to 'put bums on seats' in the ugly phrase favoured today. Peter Lake suggests that Shakespeare may by this time have developed a political agenda: he claims that 'The play is very careful to demonstrate with forensic clarity just how and why Richard is guilty of tyranny.'[25] Is that true? In fact, punches are pulled: for example, it is never made absolutely clear that he had Gloucester murdered, his profligacy at court is hardly mentioned, and never really demonstrated. Moreover, his wife, the queen, remains loving and loyal to 'sweet Richard'. There is no doubt that a Tudor audience was meant to feel sorry for him at the end of the play, even though also aware of his faults.

No, it is much more likely that the political agenda emanated not from Shakespeare, but from Lord Hunsdon or his son George. The play was not meant to suggest that Elizabeth was a tyrant: it was about the possibility of an impending tyranny – they were worried that Elizabeth's successor might be a tyrant like Bloody Mary – or Bolingbroke. Note how many heads rolled after he became king. Fears that a tyrant could succeed the queen were fuelled by the fact that Philip of Spain had been the husband of Mary I – Bloody Mary. If one of his generals managed to land an army on England's shores, and recruited powerful English allies, as Bolingbroke did, who could predict the outcome? So perhaps the play was intended to be a warning.

It may also have offered a hint about the ambitions of Essex. Many authorities are convinced that in the character of Bolingbroke, Lord Hunsdon or his son had Essex in mind;[26] could it be part of their plans to discredit the ambitious earl? A warning to the queen, and all her subjects, of the dangers of overweening lords? This description of Bolingbroke riding through the streets of London was highly suggestive:

> YORK: Then, as I said, the duke, great Bolingbroke,
> Mounted upon a hot and fiery steed
> Which his aspiring rider seem'd to know,
> With slow but stately pace kept on his course,
> Whilst all tongues cried 'God save thee,
> Bolingbroke!'
>
> – *Richard II*, Act 5, Scene 2

Did they see Bolingbroke as Essex? Certainly, Essex did: sure enough, the time came when Essex attempted to emulate Bolingbroke. But that is another story.[27]

If Essex saw himself in Bolingbroke, Queen Elizabeth certainly saw herself in Richard. In August 1601, six months after Essex was executed after his abortive rebellion, William Lambarde, Keeper of the Rolls and Records in the Tower of London, was summoned to Greenwich Palace to go through his records with the queen. When he reached the reign of Richard II, she burst out 'I am Richard II, know ye not that?' Elizabeth certainly saw warnings in history – and in drama: 'this tragedy was forty times played in open streets and houses,' she exclaimed.[28]

Perhaps it was about this time that George Carey realised that it was sensible to steer Shakespeare towards safer ground, away from the political minefield of the history play. So it was that Shakespeare turned to less dangerous territory in Verona, and Athens, as we shall see in Chapter 15.

15

WHAT FOOLS THESE MORTALS BE

And when love speaks, the voice of all the gods
Make heaven drowsy with the harmony.
– *Love's Labours Lost*, Act 4, Scene 3

Despite his successes, Shakespeare may have had serious financial pressures. New lodgings did not come cheap, and he had spent a lot of money on the shares he bought in the Lord Chamberlain's Men. Did he meanwhile also have to send remittances to his wife and family? Duncan-Jones adduces evidence that his record here is not that great: it is more than possible he had a cash-flow problem. In 1601, Thomas Whittington, a shepherd who had worked for Shakespeare's father, made a will in which he made bequests to 'the poor people of Stratford' – including Shakespeare's wife, Anne, and a number of Hathaways.[1] Was his father meanwhile selling off small plots of land to pay recusancy fines – or to avoid confiscation by the authorities? It was probably not until 1596 that Shakespeare would have had a regular income of several hundred pounds – Schoenbaum suggests that his income then was a handsome £250.[2]

If his family was having financial difficulties, Shakespeare was probably not fully aware of them. Anyone who has worked in theatre knows how easily it can come to seem like the whole world, dominated by the actors, the characters that they portray, and the current (and next) production. Nick de Somogyi gives a very good idea of what life was like for actors in London at the time, and their 'exhausting schedule'.[3] Audiences had an insatiable demand for new plays, and also loved seeing repeated performances of old favourites: so a typical day would have meant rehearsing a new production in the morning, performing another play in the afternoon, and learning lines for another in the evening. If, like Shakespeare, you were a playwright and play-director, as well as an actor, and a share-holder (with other responsibilities), theatre work must have been totally absorbing: and for the time being, Shakespeare was fully occupied by the lives of two star-cross'd lovers in Verona.

Romeo and Juliet

According to the Folger Library[4] website, the word 'love' appears 2,146 times in Shakespeare's collected works (including a handful of 'loves' and 'loved'). Add to that 59 uses of 'beloved' and 133 instances of 'lov*ing*' and that's an awful lot of love. It was to love that Shakespeare turned, away from the political minefield of *Richard II*, even though some might say that love could be as dangerous as politics. So indeed Romeo and Juliet found, for their love was blighted and their lives needlessly lost, by the unexplained feud between the Montagues and the Capulets.

Although scholars have assigned dates of the play variously to any time between 1593 and 1596, Taylor and Loughnane's best guess for the writing of *Romeo and Juliet* is late 1595.[5] It was in 1595 that a fencing manual by Vincentio Saviolo was published, from which Shakespeare may have learnt some recherché fencing terms (such as *punto reverso*, and *alla stoccata*) used in his play.[6] Unusually, the play appeared in print four times within

---

Burbage's new theatre project

At this time, there was still some uncertainty about where the Lord Chamberlain's Men could put on their public performances. Their lease on the theatre at Shoreditch was due to expire in the following year, and it was thought that Giles Allen, the owner, was unlikely to renew it.

It was Burbage who offered a solution. In early 1596 James Burbage negotiated the purchase of part of the old Blackfriars Priory at a cost of £600. His plan was to convert it to an all-weather indoor theatre which would attract a more select clientele ready to pay extra for protection from the elements. Burbage could only have afforded the huge outlay involved with financial assistance from Shakespeare and his other investors.

two years, possibly to generate an income that was difficult to obtain from performances because of theatre closures.

Several possible sources of the play have been suggested, but the most likely is a long poem by Arthur Brooke, *The Tragicall Historye of Romeus and Juliet*.[7] However, Brooke's poem and Shakespeare's play are so different that it is likely that Shakespeare kept (almost) the same title deliberately, to invite comparisons. The message of Arthur Brooke was highly judgemental: he blames the lovers for their 'unhonest desire': the lovers are vilified, the apothecary is hanged, the nurse banished, and the friar is malign, not benign.

In contrast, Shakespeare's storyline and characterisation is almost completely different from the poem. He blames the feuding parents: his moral perhaps could be 'Love may not conquer all, but can heal.' Shakespeare's play, like Brooke's poem, begins with a sonnet, but with a very different message:

> Two households, both alike in dignity,
> In fair Verona, where we lay our scene,
> From ancient grudge break to new mutiny,
> Where civil blood makes civil hands unclean.
> From forth the fatal loins of these two foes
> A pair of star-cross'd lovers take their life;
> Whose misadventured piteous overthrows
> Do with their death bury their parents' strife.
> The fearful passage of their death-mark'd love,
> And the continuance of their parents' rage,
> Which, but their children's end, nought could remove,
> Is now the two hours' traffic of our stage;
>   The which if you with patient ears attend,
>   What here shall miss, our toil shall strive to mend.

Above all, Brooke's verse can in no way match the quality of Shakespeare's poetry. For example, one cannot avoid being profoundly moved – enchanted, really, by this wonderful dialogue in sonnet form between the two young lovers, which depicts their relationship not as lust, but as a sacrament:

> ROMEO (*To JULIET*): If I profane with my unworthiest hand
>   This holy shrine, the gentle fine is this:
>   My lips, two blushing pilgrims, ready stand

> To smooth that rough touch with a tender kiss.
> JULIET: Good pilgrim, you do wrong your hand too much,
>   Which mannerly devotion shows in this;
>   For saints have hands that pilgrims' hands do touch,
>   And palm to palm is holy palmers' kiss.
> ROMEO: Have not saints lips, and holy palmers too?
> JULIET: Ay, pilgrim, lips that they must use in prayer.
> ROMEO: O, then, dear saint, let lips do what hands do;
>   They pray, grant thou, lest faith turn to despair.
> JULIET: Saints do not move, though grant for prayers' sake.
> ROMEO: Then move not, while my prayer's effect I take.

Now comes what everyone has been waiting for: the kiss

> Thus from my lips, by yours, my sin is purged.
> JULIET: Then have my lips the sin that they have took.
> ROMEO: Sin from thy lips? O trespass sweetly urged!
>   Give me my sin again.
> JULIET: You kiss by the book.
>
> – *Romeo & Juliet*, Act 1, Scene 5

A scene from Zeffirelli's film of *Romeo and Juliet* (1968) with Olivia Hussey as Juliet and Leonard Whiting as Romeo

Their union is sealed in poetry when Juliet completes Romeo's half-completed line. Their love is not just a sacrament, a sign of spiritual reality: it becomes sacrificial (in Capulet's words, 'Poor sacrifices to our enmity') and even though we know the story, and may have seen the play many times, the ending never fails to move, as the two warring families stand united in grief over the bodies of the two dead lovers in the crypt of the Capulets. Shakespeare's play is above all about love, the power of love, both to destroy, but also crucially as a positive force in human lives. We can only hope that the Montagues and the Capulets, once bound together by anger, remained bound together in the end by grief at the loss of their young – and a recognition of the power and importance of love.

Was Shakespeare a plagiarist?

In the amusing TV series *Upstart Crow*, the inkeeper's daughter accuses Shakespeare of plagiarism – stealing Brooke's poem. Whether Shakespeare was a plagiarist is a question that is often asked, and there are those who think that Ben Elton's innkeeper's daughter has a point. However, the very fact that this question is asked implies that the questioner has a modern perspective of what plagiarism means: today, of course, it is highly pejorative.

But in Shakespeare's day? Elizabethans highly valued learning, and scholars, and that meant those who doffed their hats to sources both classical and near-contemporary, by quoting from them, using them, and creatively recycling them, were much respected. Knowledge was meant to be flaunted.[8] Some have suggested that in accusing Shakespeare of 'borrowed plumes beautified in our feathers' Robert Greene in his *Groatsworth of Wit* is accusing the playwright of plagiarism. (In fact, Greene himself could be said to be plagiarising Horace, who uses the self-same phrase.)[9] I think it possible that he was referring to Shakespeare's acting ability, but there is no doubt that the vitriol was fuelled by jealousy. Jonathan Bate explores the issue of Shakespeare's so-called plagiarism in his book *How the Classics Made Shakespeare*. He points out that

> since antiquity, discourses on poetry had used the figure of the bee to represent not only verbal sweetness and flowing felicity, but also the successful art of assimilation. As a bee gathers pollen from many flowers, and transforms them into its own honey, so the best writers emulate their sources but create works that are not servile to their origins.[10]

Does anyone think that the musical *My Fair Lady* plagiarises Bernard Shaw's *Pygmalion*? Or *West Side Story* plagiarises *Romeo and Juliet*? As Bate points out, in Shakespeare's two long poems, and indeed his plays, it is likely that his desire to acquire literary respectability, and to hold his own with the 'University wits', may have been one of his motivations, and 'Elizabethan ideas about novelty and indebtedness were very different from ours.'[11] Playwrights frequently borrowed words and ideas from the classics, and each other. Like much of Chinese traditional art, '*imitatio* of the acknowledged classics was a cardinal virtue.'[12]

A Tudor literary critic

A contemporary perspective is provided by a cranky old pedant named Francis Meres (1564-1647) – the first ever Shakespeare critic. Meres matriculated at Cambridge in 1591, and obtained an MA at Oxford in 1593. We should give him some credit for helping us to date some of Shakespeare's plays.

Meres' commonplace book called *Palladis Tamia* was published in 1598. A copy is held in the Bodleian Library in Oxford, with the sub-title *A Wit's Treasury*. The book is a very odd collection of quotations, aphorisms, maxims and random observations. As Jason Scott-Warren has indicated, his observations seem today quite quirky, if not actually almost deranged.[13] Here are some examples from hundreds of pages of contorted comparisons:

> 'As a cock croweth in the darkness of the night, so a preacher croweth in the darkness of this world.'
> 'As the beautie of a whore doth allure: so the garishnesse of the world, doth entice.'
> 'Flies feed upon ulcers: so Lawyers upon discord.'

There are almost endless pages of similar comparisons – what Scott-Warren calls a 'Sargasso Sea of similitude'. The book contains a 'Comparative Discourse of our English poets with the Greek, Latin, and Italian poets. If you persist long enough through what he calls Meres' 'spray-gun of classical references', you come across these laudatory comments about Shakespeare:

> As the soul of Euphorbus was thought to live in Pythagorus, so the sweet, witty soul of Ovid lives in mellifluous & honey-tongued Shakespeare, witness his *Venus and Adonis*, his *Lucrece*, his sugar'd sonnets among his private friends, &c.
>
> As Plautus and Seneca are accounted the best for comedy and tragedy among the Latins, so Shakespeare among the English is the most excellent in both kinds for the stage; for comedy, witness his *Gentlemen of Verona*, his *Errors*, his *Love Labours Lost*, his *Love Labours Wonn*, his *Midsummer's Night Dream*, & his *Merchant of Venice*; for tragedy, his *Richard the 2*, *Richard the 3*, *Henry the 4*, *King John*, *Titus Andronicus*, and his *Romeo and Juliet*.
>
> As Epius Stolo said that the muses would speak with Plautus' tongue if they would speak Latin, so I say that the muses would speak with Shakespeare's fine-filed phrase, if they would speak English.

Francis Mere's list of plays is the first documentary evidence we have of some of these plays, and makes it quite clear that they were all written before 1598. The list is not comprehensive – he has omitted '*Henry the 6*', but intriguingly has included *Love's Labours Wonn* (which ironically has been lost). His literary tastes seem to be rather random – he praises many other Elizabethan writers who are either very marginal, or unknown. Even so, credit is due to him for doing his best to 'big up' the English language when it was still fighting a battle for respectability with those like Sir Thomas Bodley who thought that really the only texts of any literary merit were in ancient Greek or Latin.

A Midsummer Night's Dream

While Burbage dreamed of his new theatre, Shakespeare busied himself with his own dream – his next play, written probably in early 1596.[14] The first printed edition of *A Midsummer Night's Dream* came out in 1600, with Shakespeare's name on the title page. The play has numerous sources including Arthur Golding's translation of *Ovid's Metamorphoses* (1595), *The Golden Ass* by Lucius Apuleius, and Chaucer's *Knight's Tale*. Perhaps the main theme of the play is best summed up by these two lines, from Puck:

> Shall we their fond pageant see?
> Lord, what fools these mortals be!

There has been speculation that it might have been written specially for performance at a wedding: in the opening scene, Theseus, the Duke of Athens, is about to wed the Amazon queen, Hippolyta. What better time to perform a celebratory romantic comedy, as part of the festivities celebrating marriage nuptials? Duncan-Jones suggests that *Dream* was put on as a 'command performance' for the wedding of Sir Thomas Berkeley and Elizabeth Carey, Lord Hunsdon's grand-daughter in February 1596 – a time when Shakespeare had become associated with Lord Hunsdon and the Carey family.[15] Shakespeare certainly rose to the occasion. In *Midsummer Night's Dream*, Shakespeare returns to the theme of star-crossed lovers. This time, there are four of them: the lovers Hermia and Lysander, Demetrius, in love with Hermia, and Helena in love with Demetrius.

The play is often billed as a romp in the forest, a 'rom-com', and it can certainly be enjoyed as such. There are, however, some dark elements in the play that are frequently overlooked, even in the very first scene:

'My mistress with a monster is in love' A Drawing of Puck, Titania and Bottom by Charles Buchel (1872-1950)

> THESEUS: Hippolyta, I woo'd thee with my sword,
> And won thy love, doing thee injuries;
> But I will wed thee in another key,
> With pomp, with triumph and with revelling.

I recall an excellent open-air production of *A Midsummer Night's Dream* in Regent's Park in London: as the Duke reminiscences how he 'woo'd' the Amazonian queen with his sword, as he says, doing her injuries, the queen's body language quite clearly indicates that she cannot stand him. Not many women like being wooed with a sword ... In the same scene, the extremely patriarchal structure of society is immediately underlined by the arrival of Egeus and his daughter Hermia, accompanied by Demetrius and Lysander. Egeus insists that Hermia should marry the man of his choice, Demetrius – threatening to kill her if she disobeys him. Hermia is adamant that she wants to marry Lysander. Egeus accuses Lysander of bewitching his daughter:

> ... Lysander, thou hast given her rhymes,
> And interchanged love-tokens with my child:
> Thou hast by moonlight at her window sung,
> With feigning voice verses of feigning love ...
>
> – Act 1, Scene 1

Strong echoes of *Romeo and Juliet*. The story line is dramatic, indeed, melodramatic: every melodrama has an archvillain such as Egeus. At this stage, the play is more of a nightmare than a dream: women, it seems, are there to be woo'd with a sword, forced into marriage, and threatened with death if they are disobedient – what has curiously come to be called 'An honour killing' in some societies. I think this play makes it clear where Shakespeare stands on these issues. What is not clear is why Egeus favours Demetrius over Lysander: as Lysander points out, he himself is 'as well derived as he/As well possess'd'. Moreover, there is a question mark over Demetrius's character, which any reasonable father should surely be concerned about:

> LYSANDER: Demetrius, I'll avouch it to his head,
> Made love to Nedar's daughter, Helena,
> And won her soul; and she, sweet lady, dotes,

Devoutly dotes, dotes in idolatry,
Upon this spotted and inconstant man.

– Act 1, Scene 1

Egeus it seems is impervious: no doubt he does not want to lose face – weak men mistake obduracy for strength. From his point of view, his daughter must at all costs obey him – and the duke backs him up. Hermia will have none of it: Lysander comes up with a solution. He suggests that they elope, escape into the forest, and make their way to the house of his devoted aunt, where they can marry. Hermia is delighted at this proposal, and clearly has a very romantic view of the woods:

HERMIA: And in the wood, where often you and I
Upon faint primrose-beds were wont to lie,
Emptying our bosoms of their counsel sweet,
There my Lysander and myself shall meet

– Act 1, Scene 1

Poor deluded maid, she has a shock in store ... There is something of a pantomime about this play: this is reflected in some of the dialogue – the rhyming couplets are reminiscent of lines in another pantomime, *Love's Labour's Lost*, as they exchange their views about Demetrius:

Oberon, Titania and Puck with Fairies Dancing. From William Shakespeare's *A Midsummer Night's Dream* by William Blake

> HERMIA: I frown upon him, yet he loves me still.
> HELENA: O that your frowns would teach my smiles such skill!
> HERMIA: I give him curses, yet he gives me love.
> HELENA: O that my prayers could such affection move!
> HERMIA: The more I hate, the more he follows me.
> HELENA: The more I love, the more he hateth me.
>
> – Act 1, Scene 1

Hearing of Hermia's plan, Helena persuades Demetrius to join her in following the lovers to the forest: she nurses the desperate hope that she can somehow win him away from Hermia. What the four young runaways don't seem to realise is that the forest is not full of primrose paths – as any Elizabethan member of the audience could tell them, the woods are something else. To most people, the forest was a place of danger: in the vast acres of trees that still covered much of England, there lurked outlaws, bandits, wild beasts and a spirit world of fairies, and goblins. In Ann Barton's words, 'the forest was viewed as a sentient being, capable of listening and even responding to things humans do and say in it.'[16] In a brilliant Glyndebourne production of Benjamin Britten's *A Midsummer Night's Dream*, the trees on stage are almost members of the cast: they move about, their boughs lower to listen, and in Britten's score, you can detect the branches sharing secrets with the leaves, in competition with the other spirits of the wood.

Shakespeare's forest has fairies, and a Hobgoblin, Puck ('Robin Goodfellow'). Puck is mischievous, but not a villain – Oberon has some claim to this role. Oberon, King of the Fairies, is in the midst of a quarrel with his wife, Titania, over who should have a page, an Indian boy they both lay claim to. (One fears he may be regarded as a fashion-accessory ... post-colonial consciences were yet to come.) Furious at her disobedience, Oberon decides to punish his wife by getting Puck to drop magic juice over her eyes while she is sleeping: when she awakes, she will immediately fall in love with the first person she sees.

> OBERON: Having once this juice,
>   I'll watch Titania when she is asleep,
>   And drop the liquor of it in her eyes.
>   The next thing then she waking looks upon,

> Be it on lion, bear, or wolf, or bull,
> On meddling monkey, or on busy ape,
> She shall pursue it with the soul of love:
> And ere I take this charm from off her sight,
> As I can take it with another herb,
> I'll make her render up her page to me.
>
> – Act 1, Scene 3

Titania wakes up, and is duly bewitched: enter, Bottom, equipped for the occasion with the head of an ass, thanks to another of Puck's tricks. Bottom, of course, is bemused to be showered with love from this beautiful stranger. He is totally unself-aware ... just as well for his mental health. But what of Titania's mental health? Oberon is in a sense gaslighting her.[17] Bruce Boehrer only slightly overstates his case: '*A Midsummer Night's Dream* ... is patently about bestiality ... ' Oberon turns his wife 'into an erotic bond-slave of an ass ... '[18] Today, he could be locked up for mental cruelty, coercive behavior, and perpetrating and condoning bestiality. Even in Shakespeare's day, 'love magic', which was frequently practised, was seen as dangerously capable of abuse, and the 1542 Conjuration Act made it a criminal offence to provoke 'any person of unlawful love'. An act of 1604 act imposed the death penalty for second offenders.[19]

Women really do not come out well in this play. It's not just Hippolyta and Titania, who are seen as victims: we are supposed to find amusing the sad attempts of Hermia and Helena to hold on to their men at all costs, as they are manipulated by Puck's magic tricks. The plot-line has the effect of turning the romantic love in *Romeo and Juliet* into a foolish farce. No doubt a Tudor audience were hooting with laughter at these shenanigans: one may be forgiven for not caring a hoot. We can only agree with Puck: 'What fools these mortals be.'

The play does touch one last dark note: Demetrius at one point shows his true colours by speaking most cruelly to Helena, undermining her, destroying her self-esteem – 'I am as ugly as a bear,' she muses, and he brutally threatens to leave her at the mercy of wild beasts – and even threatens to rape her if she does not leave him alone.

The play does have some very good one-liners – and bursts of real poetry:

> OBERON: I know a bank where the wild thyme blows,
>   Where oxlips and the nodding violet grows,
>   Quite over-canopied with luscious woodbine,
>   With sweet musk-roses and with eglantine:
>   There sleeps Titania sometime of the night,
>   Lull'd in these flowers with dances and delight;
>
> – Act 1, Scene 3

However, for many of us, the real show-stopper, and scene-stealer, is Bottom, along with his team of actors, both in rehearsal, and in a performance that is a parody of a play: these scenes are the funniest in the whole of Shakespeare. Bottom, the incompetent theatre director, is something of an actor's in-joke: perhaps Shakespeare was having a good laugh at his own expense.

Somehow, like all pantomimes, all is well in the end. The fairies have worked their magic: everyone realizes that it was all but a dream, and all greatly enjoy the mechanicals' performance of *Pyramus and Thisbe*, Bottom's crowning moment. The right people are married off to each other, and even the Queen of the Amazons appears to have come around. Puck gets the last word:

> If we shadows have offended,
> Think but this, and all is mended,
> That you have but slumber'd here
> While these visions did appear.
> And this weak and idle theme,
> No more yielding but a dream.
>
> – Act 5, Scene 8

As Prospero remarks in *The Tempest*, 'We are such stuff as dreams are made on, and our little life is rounded with a sleep.' There have been dozens – hundreds – of productions of *A Midsummer Night's Dream* in the last fifty years, and everyone has their own favourite. Mine was the Canadian Robert Lepage's 1992 production at London's National Theatre, where the actors gradually woke up in a large bed that was like a raft, being punted across the stage on a large pool of water. They entered the play almost as though sleep-walking.

This was a much more conventional production, however, than Russell

T. Davies' controversial gay BBC version (2016), which began with Theseus appearing as a fascist dictator, having his captured bride wheeled on, strapped to a cart, and wearing a straitjacket: she read out the lines assigned to her on an iPad held in front of her by a courtier. Maxine Peake played a butch Titania who exchanged a lesbian kiss with Hippolyta at the end of the play. For some, a step too far from Shakespeare's play; for others, a performance that captured the creative ambiguity that had become Shakespeare's hallmark.

16

COURTING CONTROVERSY

It is apparent foul play; and 'tis shame
That greatness should so grossly offer it

– *Salisbury KJ IV.ii*

By this time, Lord Hunsdon was reaching his end, and it was certainly his son, George Carey, who had the closest dealings with the troupe. It was probably George who proposed another history play: always good box office, he may have thought. Perhaps it could be used to launch Burbage's new theatre in Blackfriars. A play called *The Troublesome Raigne of King John* had enjoyed a brief success in the late 1580s: why not create another new improved version?

King John was possibly even more controversial than *Richard II*. Maybe George thought all the better; or maybe he was not as attuned to political dangers as his father. One senses that Shakespeare may have been reluctant, on several grounds: after *Richard II*, was it not tempting fate to write another history play? Besides, reworking a second-rate play might well have had little appeal: it may have seemed a job for a hack rather than a well-established playwright. Moreover, Richard II was, for all his faults, a sympathetic character, and much more rewarding to write about; the same could not be said of King John. Certainly, in the canon, *King John* seems anomalous: *Richard II* is a far better play. I don't think that Shakespeare's heart was in it, and this shows, I think, in the quality of the writing. Perhaps he was just trying to please George Carey.

What Lord Hunsdon might have thought is anyone's guess, but we shall never know, for halfway through the writing of the play, on 22 July, he died: overnight, the Lord Chamberlain's Men became Lord Hunsdon's Men, no longer with quite the same cachet. This was a blow, but there was hope that George would become the next Lord Chamberlain, in which case the troupe would regain its prestigious title, so the project went forward.

Magna Carta

The reign of King John is remembered by us today mainly because it saw the emergence of *Magna Carta*. John was forced to sign *Magna Carta* at Runnymede on 15 June 1215 – but within months he reneged on it, and it was reissued in 1217. Fifty years later the first national parliament in England took place, and in 1297, *Magna Carta* was written into the laws of the land. It is significant, though hardly surprising, that Shakespeare ignored it, even though it was a standard text studied at the Inns of Court.[1] Clause 39 in particular was way ahead of its time:

> 'No free man is to be arrested, or imprisoned, or disseised, or outlawed, or exiled, or in any other way ruined, nor will we go against him or send against him, except by the lawful judgment of his peers or by the law of the land.'[2]

This clause was honoured more in the breach than in the observance, but *Magna Carta* remained alive in the law of the land, if for the time being semi-dormant. It first appeared in print in the early years of the reign of Henry VII. It became weaponised in the Tudor era not so much to defend the rights of 'free-born Englishmen' (*sic*), as was to occur in the seventeenth century, but to defend the church. Clause 1 stated that 'The English church shall be free and shall have all its rights undiminished and its liberties unimpaired.' This was used to claim that the English church needed to be protected against the Papacy. Opponents of Henry VIII cited this clause to protest against his seizure of church property, and the dissolution of the monasteries. Thomas More also referred to *Magna Carta* to defend both himself, and the established Catholic Church; but citing the document failed to prevent his execution in 1535.[3] Robert Aske, the leader of the Pilgrimage of Grace in 1536 also cited *Magna Carta* to protest against the dissolution of the monasteries – and was hanged for his pains.[4]

Successive Archbishops of Canterbury cited *Magna Carta* to argue against proposed reforms to the church.[5] Under Elizabeth, the Court of High Commission was set up to deal with those suspected of heresy, and was empowered to incarcerate offenders without bail,[6] but *Magna Carta* was cited to oppose the actions of this court by two Puritans in the early 1590s.[7]

Shakespeare had no wish to end up like Thomas More or Robert Aske, and I think that if he was aware of Magna Carta, he was very well-advised not even to mention it in *King John*. In his play, the rebel barons who forced King John's hand at Runneymede are not seen as legal innovators, indeed they are not seen at all. The Earls of Essex, Pembroke, Salisbury and Lord Bagot stand in, as it were, for the 25 barons who brought John to book. Far from these lords being seen as champions of the law, they come over as a threat to the realm, first by kowtowing to King John, and then by treacherously supporting a French invasion.

That said, Peter Lake's comment that 'Writing a play about King John in the early or middle 1590s was not an ideologically neutral act',[8] is something of an understatement. So why did Shakespeare choose to write this play – if indeed it was his choice, and not the suggestion of George Carey?

George Carey, 2nd Lord Hunsdon, 1547-1603

George Carey matriculated at Trinity College Cambridge at the age of thirteen. In 1569 George accompanied his father to take part in quelling the Northern Earls' rebellion, and was knighted in the field for bravery.

He served as a Member of Parliament for several years, and in 1583 he became 'Captain of the Isle of Wight, and Admiral of the County of Southampton'. With the threat of the Spanish Armada looming, he strengthened the fortifications of Carisbrooke Castle.

George Carey was an enthusiastic theatre-goer, and by all accounts was a generous patron of actors and playwrights, though, like most people, he had reservations about Nashe.[9]

King John

There is no doubt that this play, *The Life and Death of King John*, could be as politically risky as *Richard II*, even if there was no mention at all of *Magna Carta*: after all, a play in which the king goes mad and loses his crown hardly enhances the institution of monarchy. The defects of the king are compounded by nobles who treacherously ally themselves with an invasion army from France. This could well remind a theatre audience that similar events could occur in Elizabeth's England, though the main threat came from Spain, not France. A message from the play might well have been that only the strength of the monarch, and the strong support of her servants and her people, could save the country from a similar fate. The problem was that John's claim to the throne was illegitimate.

In the Tudor era, not surprisingly, King John was generally viewed from a Protestant perspective: the king's conflict with the Pope over the appointment of Stephen Langton as Archbishop of Canterbury, and John's raid on the wealth of the church, were seen as precursors to Henry VIII's own break with Rome and the founding of the Church of England. This is the narrative of the Protestant martyrologist John Foxe in his *Actes and Monumentes* (commonly referred to as *Foxe's Book of Martyrs*).

There were at least three different plays about King John in the sixteenth century. A play by Bishop Bale, *Kynge Johan*, written in the time of Henry VIII, was virulently anti-Papal. A second play, also anonymous, but probably written by George Peele[10], *The Troublesome Raigne of John King of England*, was also clearly a piece of anti-Catholic propaganda; this play was published in 1591. Most authorities believe that Shakespeare used *The Troublesome Raigne* as a major source, along with Holinshed's *Chronicles*. However, there are only two lines that the plays have in common, and Shakespeare develops a slightly different perspective, though he still manages to stay just this side of causing controversy. According to Taylor and Loughnane it was probably written in mid-1596.[11] There is no record of it being performed, although it must have been, because it appears on Francis Meres' 1598 list; as far as we know, it did not appear in print until the 1623 Folio edition.[12] The play is far from being one of Shakespeare's best, and perhaps there was no demand for a published version.[13]

In the opening scenes of the play, on the instructions of the king of

France, the French ambassador Chatillon challenges John's right to the English throne, claiming that the rightful king is Arthur, the son of John's deceased older brother Geoffrey. King John is adamant that he is in the right, citing his 'strong possession' – a phrase known by the authorities to be used by Queen Elizabeth's enemies: according to them, the sole justification for her claim to the throne is that she was 'in possession'.[14] John's mother Eleanor leans over to whisper in his ear

> Your strong possession much more than your right,
> Or else it must go wrong with you and me:
> So much my conscience whispers in your ear,
> Which none but heaven and you and I shall hear.
>
> – Act 1, Scene 1

This tells the audience that both the king and his mother are aware that Arthur indeed is the rightful king. Thus the succession issue comes to the fore yet again – an issue that casts a shadow over many of the history plays. John does not hesitate: he angrily decides to settle the issue on the battlefield: so far, so heroic. A canny hero, too, perhaps, as he follows in Henry VIII's footsteps:

> Our abbeys and our priories shall pay
> This expedition's charge
>
> – Act 1, Scene 1

However, before the king dons his armour to go to war, another succession issue is brought before the court: the dispute between the two Falconbridge brothers. The younger claims his father's inheritance, on the grounds that his older brother, Philip, is the bastard son of Richard Coeur de Lion (Richard I): same mother, different fathers. The dispute is resolved when Philip proudly agrees to accept his position as the son of a king, rather than the lord of Falconbridge, and offers his allegiance to Queen Eleanor, his grandmother. The character of 'The Bastard' is thus in stark contrast with that of the king: he places honesty and integrity before any claim to title or land – and King John, impressed, knights him on the spot: the bastard becomes Sir Philip Plantagenet. In the rest of the play, he acts as a kind of cynical chorus or commentator on the action.

The scene changes to the European mainland: at this time, the king of

England owns more of France than the King of France. The French and English armies join battle at Angers: the French claim the city for Arthur – King John insists that it is his. King John demands that the citizens open the city gates:

> KING JOHN: Acknowledge then the King, and let him in
> CITIZEN: That can we not: but he that proves the king
>   To him will we prove loyal; till that time
>   Have we rammed up our gates against the world
> – Act 2, Scene 1

Naturally, the residents wait to see who will win the battle before surrendering the keys, tacitly implying that 'Might is right'. But the conflict has become a stalemate: still the burghers of Angers refuse to open the gates, and angrily, both kings threaten to join forces to storm the city. The citizens shrewdly suggest a diversion: why not unite the warring sides by the marriage between King John's niece Blanche to Louis, the Dauphin? Evidently, John has no stomach for a continuing war, and accepts the counsel of his mother, Eleanor:

> Son, list to this conjunction make this match
> Give with our niece a dowry large enough
> For by this knot thou shalt so surely tie
> Thy now unsured assurance to the crown
> – Act 2, Scene 1

In effect, her plan is to buy off the French: however, in a grotesque failure of judgement, as Blanche's dowry, John hands over five provinces of France, and 30,000 marks. John is effectively bribing the French to abandon Arthur's cause, thus securing his position on the English throne. Plainly he is putting his own self-interests above those of his realm; the audience is left in no doubt that anyone who does such a deal – especially with 'the perfidious French' – betrays his country. For King Louis, it's a bargain – and he conveniently forgets that his original aim was to fight for Arthur's right to the English throne. In this way, a war of principle is settled with a sordid deal that will sicken Arthur's mother, the Lady Constance. The agreement angers the English nobles, and the Bastard denounces it, citing 'That smooth-faced gentleman, tickling Commodity' – his word for self-interest:

> Mad world! mad kings! mad composition!
> John, to stop Arthur's title in the whole,
> Hath willingly departed with a part,
> And France, whose armour conscience buckled on,
> Whom zeal and charity brought to the field
> As God's own soldier, rounded in the ear
> With that same purpose-changer, that sly devil,
>
> ...
>
> And this same bias, this Commodity,
> This bawd, this broker, this all-changing word,
> Clapp'd on the outward eye of fickle France,
> Hath drawn him from his own determined aid,
> From a resolved and honourable war,
> To a most base and vile-concluded peace.
>
> – Act 2, Scene 1

Back in England, Cardinal Pandolf tries to impose the Pope's authority over the king, demanding that the Pope's nominee, Stephen Langton, be accepted as the next Archbishop of Canterbury, John is at first defiant:

> Tell him this tale; no Italian priest
> Shall tithe or toll in our dominions;
> But as we, under heaven, are supreme head
>
> – Act 3, Scene 1

Pandolph responds by threatening the king with 'the curse of Rome' – excommunication. John remains adamant. In words that closely echo the Pope's Excommunication of Queen Elizabeth in 1570, Pandolf then excommunicates King John. At this point in the play, King John would have been seen as a Protestant hero by many in the audience.

There has been some speculation as to what Shakespeare's private religious beliefs may have been, given that John ends up very far from being any kind of hero. Of course, he has the king fulminating against the 'usurp'd authority of the Pope, and that 'meddling priest', but this play is more nuanced than the source play. The Papal Legate, Pandolph, appears in both plays. In Shakespeare's play, he comes over as a dignified figure who provides good advice, and at one point helps to save England from a French invasion. Does that make Shakespeare a closet Catholic, or at least a Catholic sympathiser? Opinion is divided on this issue: another example of Shakespeare's creative ambiguity.

There is no ambiguity in the *The Troublesome Raigne:* Pandolph is depicted as obsequious and manipulative and the older play is much more hostile to the Vatican than Shakespeare's play. For example, the *Troublesome Raigne* highlights the greed of the Roman church, and unsavoury relationships between monks and nuns. In one comic scene a friar is forced to reveal where the Abbot keeps his gold. The friar takes him to the Abbot's chest, which, broken open, reveals an attractive nun. At which the friar exclaims

> O, I am undone! Fair Alice the nun
> Hath took up her rest in the Abbot's chest.
> Sancte benedicite, pardon my simplicity!
> Fie, Alice, confession will not salve this transgression.

The droll use of internal rhymes plainly indicates that the text here is meant to mock rather than shock. However, there is no mistaking the underlying message: monks hoarded gold, and were depraved hypocrites and fornicators. Worse still, monks are shown to be poisoners and regicides sanctified by the Church: when a monk tells the Abbott of his plan to poison the king, he is given blessing and absolution. There is none of this in Shakespeare's play: true, in the end, it is a monk who poisons the king, but there is no indication that the monk had any official support.

Even so, in Shakespeare's play, Pandolf threatens to excommunicate the French King Philip unless he 'becomes champion of our church' and resumes his war against John: the king reluctantly agrees to do so. Thus the deal he struck with John is not worth the parchment it was written on. To start with, the war goes John's way: the Duke of Austria is killed by the Bastard, and Arthur is captured and imprisoned.

At this point, John emerges in his true colours as a monarch ruthless in his exercise of power. He recruits a minion to murder young Prince Arthur

> HUBERT: So well, that what you bid me undertake
> Though that my death were adjunct to my act,
> By heaven, I would do it.
> KING JOHN: Do not I know thou wouldst?

> Good Hubert, Hubert, Hubert, throw thine eye
> On yon young boy: I'll tell thee what, my friend,
> He is a very serpent in my way;
> And whereso'er this foot of mine doth tread,
> He lies before me: dost thou understand me?
> Thou art his keeper.
> HUBERT: And I'll keep him so,
> That he shall not offend your majesty.
> KING JOHN: Death.
> HUBERT: My lord?
> KING JOHN: A grave.
> HUBERT: He shall not live.
> KING JOHN: Enough.
> I could be merry now. Hubert, I love thee;
> Well, I'll not say what I intend for thee ...
>
> – Act 3, Scene 3

No, the king doesn't actually command Hubert, but hints strongly that his servant's advancement depends on his reading his murderous mind. In the event, Hubert cannot bring himself to kill the young man. Tragically, Arthur does subsequently die, but in an accident, when he jumps from a wall. Hearing of his death, everyone assumes that John had him murdered. John tries to blame Hubert for his death, but this thin attempt at deniability can't really succeed, as Hubert has the king's warrant. In Elizabeth's England, this episode is possibly the most dangerous moment, politically, in the play: for there is a strong echo of Elizabeth's own attempt to blame Davison for the execution of Mary, Queen of Scots.[15] As Guy comments, Davison was lucky not to be hanged.[16] This scene from *King John* would make uncomfortable viewing for the queen, and it is thus unlikely that the play was ever performed at court.

End game

For John's erstwhile supporters,[17] the discovery of Arthur's body is the last straw: they are certain that the young prince was murdered on his orders. Their revulsion is such that they join forces with the French invaders. As disaffection grows across the country, the rebels and their French allies take over almost the whole of Kent. Commodity strikes again: to try to strengthen his weakening position, John gives into the Papacy's demands, and appoints their nominee, Stephen Langton, as Archbishop of Canterbury. John's action would probably have been seen as a total betrayal by a Tudor audience, most of whom would recall that Henry VIII and Queen Elizabeth would never have dreamed of giving in to the Vatican.

In this play, then, we have a king for whom 'Commodity' rules. King John is totally lacking in scruple or judgement: he is a king who does sordid deals with France, vacillates according to the way the wind blows, reneges on his commitments, and deals with the devil, or at least the Papacy, in order to shore up his rule. He is, in short, a king who puts his own self-interest ahead of the good of the country. He pays a heavy price, as the whole country rises against him. A beaten man, John starts to lose his mind, retires to Swineshead Abbey, where he dies, poisoned by a monk.

Meanwhile, fortunately for England, the French invasion has ground to a halt, as massive reinforcements were lost at sea: the French ships run aground on the Goodwin Sands.[18] Pandolf secures a peace agreement, and a withdrawal of remaining French forces. Just as well, for half the English army has been lost, drowned in the wash in East Anglia while trying to quell a rebellion. The play ends on a note of hope: Prince Henry is thankfully accepted as the next king, Henry III.

So what is the message of this play? Perhaps George Carey saw it as a warning: events like these can occur unless competence, integrity, principle, and determination are embodied in the persona of a strong monarch committed to the good of the realm, rather than self-interest, or *commodity*, to use the word favoured by the Bastard. In this play, there is only one man who somewhat ironically shows any integrity, or any sense of idealism: the Bastard. It is he who delivers the final encomium:

> O, let us pay the time but needful woe,
> Since it hath been beforehand with our griefs.
> This England never did, nor never shall,
> Lie at the proud foot of a conqueror,
> But when it first did help to wound itself.
> Now these her princes are come home again,
> Come the three corners of the world in arms,
> And we shall shock them. Nought shall make us rue,
> If England to itself do rest but true.
>
> – Act 5, Scene 7

I think it was while writing this play that Shakespeare came at last, fully, to see that self-interest, rather than idealism, or the welfare of the populace, was a major factor in the political life of the country. Oh, and forget chivalry. One final comment: perhaps the ambiguity with which he depicts the king's relationship with the Vatican, and the character of Pandolf, means that Shakespeare was himself guilty of commodity – but the extent to which he was aware of this we shall never know.

From drama to tragedy

In July 1596 there was another outbreak of plague and all the theatres were closed until late October. Once again, the players had to go on tour, and Shakespeare went with them, for he was still active as a player as well as a playwright and shareholder. On 1 August they played at the Market Hall in Faversham: probably from there they went deeper into Kent.

It was while Shakespeare was on tour that the tragic death of his son Hamnet occurred. The boy was eleven and a half years old. In the burial register of Holy Trinity Church, the entry for 11 August reads: 'Hamnet filius William Shakspere'. There is no record of the cause of death. Germaine Greer thinks it is unlikely Shakespeare attended the funeral: once players were on tour, no one knew exactly where they were.[19] However, we have good reason to suppose that it would have been a bitter blow to lose his only son, especially as his wife was now past child-bearing age. According to Maggie O'Farrell's novel *Hamnet*, he and Anne were both overcome with grief, and *Hamnet*, recreated in the character of Hamlet, is a sensitive reimagination of their grief-stricken response.[20] I think it is certain that both of them must have been almost inconsolable: to lose a child, any child, is desperately sad for any parent, even when infant mortality is a frequent occurrence; to lose an only son doubly so. Shakespeare must have felt terrible that it happened in his absence; and must have deeply reproached himself for all the times that he should have had with Hamnet, the opportunities lost forever.

Where might Shakespeare have left a written record of his grief? It is hard to find any one of the sonnets that could be so interpreted, though Sonnet 33 could be so interpreted, with a pun on sun/son:

> Even so my sun one early morn did shine
> With all triumphant splendour on my brow;
> But out, alack, he was but one hour mine,
> The region cloud hath mask'd him from me now

In James Joyce's *Ulysses* Stephen Dedalus suggests at a literary meeting in Dublin's National Library that Shakespeare's 'boyson's death is the death scene of young Arthur in *King John*'.[21] There is a theory that this poignant speech by Lady Constance in *King John* might have been inspired by Hamnet's death:[22]

> Grief fills the room up of my absent child,
> Lies in his bed, walks up and down with me,
> Puts on his pretty looks, repeats his words,
> Remembers me of all his gracious parts,
> Stuffs out his vacant garments with his form;
> Then, have I reason to be fond of grief?
> Fare you well: had you such a loss as I,
> I could give better comfort than you do.
> I will not keep this form upon my head,
> When there is such disorder in my wit.
> O Lord! my boy, my Arthur, my fair son!
> My life, my joy, my food, my all the world!
> My widow-comfort, and my sorrows' cure!
>
> – Act 3, Scene 4

I think it is quite possible that following Hamnet's death, Shakespeare later inserted the above speech by Lady Constance into the script of *King John*. Strangely, this speech in the play occurs after her death has been announced – and before Arthur dies, so that suggestion is plausible. What also seems plausible is the imagined reconstruction in Kenneth Branagh's film *All is True*, of Shakespeare's last years in retirement. In this film, in which Judi Dench plays the part of Anne Hathaway, and Sir Ian McKellen stars as the Earl of Southampton, Shakespeare is haunted by the death of his only son twenty years earlier.[23] It also seems quite possible that after hearing of the death of his son, Shakespeare coped with grief perhaps in the only way he knew how: by immersing himself in his work. *The Merchant of Venice* emerged in early 1597.[24] Grief affects people in different ways.

17

BAD NEWS

I hold the world but as the world, Gratiano;
A stage where every man must play a part,
And mine a sad one.
– The Merchant of Venice, Act 1, Scene 1

The cheerful, patriotic words of the Bastard, Sir Richard Plantagenet, at the end of *King John*, would have sounded somewhat hollow in 1596, for there was, in truth, little reason for England to be cheerful. The wars in the Low Countries and Ireland were not going well. In May, the crack troops of Spain's mighty army captured Calais: the queen could hear the sound of Spanish heavy artillery from her barge in Greenwich,[1] a sharp reminder that the enemy were only twenty miles or so from the English coast. Meanwhile, an expedition in May, led by Francis Drake and John Hawkins, to conquer Las Palmas, and attempts to seize possessions in Spanish America, ended in an expensive fiasco. Less than half the English fleet returned to Plymouth in January 1596, the crews decimated by a virulent form of dysentery, lootless and leaderless, for both Hawkins and Drake died during the expedition.

Another expedition led by Lord Howard and the Earl of Essex mounted an attack on the Spanish mainland, and successfully seized Cadiz. The operation was successful but the patient died: against the queen's instructions, Essex sacked the city, forgetting the merchant ships with their rich cargoes. The Spanish set fire to the ships, and 12 million ducats went up in smoke. This may have helped to bankrupt the Spanish state, but did nothing to fill the queen's straitened coffers. The queen had an accountant's view of military adventures, and the Cadiz expedition cost more than it gained.[2] Very little of the loot from the city ended up with the Crown. Elizabeth was furious – and Essex was assigned most of the blame. To England, Essex may have appeared a hero – but to the queen, he was a frustrating disappointment.

King Philip II of Spain was so incensed that he prepared a second *Gran Armada* to mount an invasion in 1596; with England's fleet of warships depleted, and other ships under repair in Chatham's dockyard, and with her two greatest seamen dead, England was in greater peril than in 1588. Walsingham's spies kept him fully informed of the impending threat, and frantic attempts were made to strengthen England's defences. Then, unbelievably, history repeated itself: half of Philip's warships sank, battered by October gales.[3]

Throughout the summer of 1596, then, the court, facing threats of Titanic proportions, set about rearranging the deckchairs, as courtiers jockeyed for position and influence. Burghley was now a sick old man, and Essex, who had hoped to replace him when he died, went into a sulk when Burghley's son, Robert Cecil, was appointed Secretary on 5 July instead. Essex's position was becoming increasingly problematic.[4] The queen was angered by rumours that he was engaging in liaisons with some of the ladies at court.[5] Interestingly, an Earl of Essex appears briefly only in Act 1, Scene 1 of *King John*. Shakespeare may have tactfully erased him from the cast list.

England's future lay on a knife edge – her army was grossly underfunded,[6] was pitifully understrength in comparison with Spain's, and as the (very funny) recruitment scene in *Henry IV* indicates, there were fatal flaws in the military recruitment system.[7] In London, the city was a gossip factory. In *Henry IV*, there is a character named Rumour, 'painted full of tongues', who

> ... doth double, like the voice and echo
> The numbers of the feared.
>
> – HIV Scene 1

Stage fright

While these momentous events were a cause of great anxiety to the whole country, Shakespeare and his fellow thespians had more immediate causes for concern, for following the death of Lord Hunsdon in July, Elizabeth's court held their breath as they wondered who would replace him as Lord Chamberlain. His son George Carey hoped that he would be appointed in his father's place. For a few weeks George and his players were in limbo: they could no longer call themselves the Lord Chamberlain's Men, and had to be called Lord Hunsdon's Men. And so they remained: for disappointment awaited George Carey. On 8 August, the queen appointed William Brooke, the 10th Baron Cobham to be the new Lord Chamberlain. Lord Cobham was very much an establishment figure: he was a Knight of the Garter, and a Privy Councillor – and Robert Cecil's brother-in-law. So in reality there was little contest: it seems that George spent more time in his family home on the Isle of Wight than at court,[8] and it is possible too that he showed more interest in the theatre than was thought healthy. He should not have been too surprised at Lord Cobham's appointment.

As the new Lord Chamberlain, Cobham had little reason to take over as patron of the players, and so Lord Hunsdon's Men remained unchanged: the patronage of the Lord Chamberlain was no longer on offer. The change in status could have been cause for concern, but at least Cobham did not interfere with the troupe, as he might have done. It seems that he left court entertainment issues to the Master of the Revels, Sir Edmund Tilney, and Shakespeare's company had little reason to complain: in the 1596-7 festive season, the company performed at court six times between 26 December and 8 February. In the same season, Henslowe's Admiral's Men gave none.[9]

The real problem was that the new Lord Chamberlain showed no interest in protecting the players from the hostility of the City of London authorities, and the actors feared the worst. With theatres closed from June to October because of the plague, Lord Hunsdon's Men depended on the Cross Keys in Gracious Street, and Nashe reported that the players

> are piteously persecuted by the Lord Mayor and aldermen, and however in their old lord's time they thought their state settled, it is now so uncertain they cannot build upon it.[10]

With all these worries to occupy his mind, Shakespeare would have had little time indeed to brood on the death of his son: indeed he might have been thankful to immerse himself in his work. On top of everything else, there was pressure on him to produce another play: time to play safe, perhaps, to move the locus away from England, and power politics, to somewhere far away from English history: Venice, for example. This was perhaps the rationale behind *The Merchant of Venice*: this play would not have been seen as controversial. There was a long folk tradition of plays depicting Jews as villains, indeed as grotesque caricatures, as in Marlowe's very popular *The Jew of Malta*. With the execution of the unfortunate Dr Lopez, the queen's physician, a Jewish exile from Portugal, still in his memory, no doubt Shakespeare decided to provide a somewhat nuanced depiction of the character of Shylock. It will be recalled Essex claimed to have unearthed this alleged plot to poison the queen in a desperate attempt to curry favour.

The Merchant of Venice

Taylor and Loughnane give early 1597 as the most likely date for the writing of the play,[11] and perhaps he threw himself into writing it to try to avoid his thoughts dwelling on the death of his son. As Antonio says in the opening scene of the play:

> ... such a want-wit sadness makes of me,
> That I have much ado to know myself
>
> – Act 1, Scene 1

Francis Meres' 1598 list of Shakespeare's plays describes *The Merchant of Venice* as 'a comedie'. There is a Jewish proverb: 'As soap is to the body, so laughter is to the soul.' Tell that to Shylock. Few see the play as a comedy, and many people find it hard to appreciate: there have been attempts to play down the racist elements in the play. Harley Granville-Barker famously labelled it a 'fairy tale', almost a pantomime, in fact: 'there is no more reality in Shylock's bond, and the Lord of Belmont's will, than in *Jack and the Beanstalk*.'[12] Certainly the three caskets sub-plot has a folk origin, and would not be out of place in a pantomime, but looking at the main plot, Harold Bloom, that great fan of Shakespeare, faces reality with a paradox that many of us find puzzling. He accepts that the play is 'profoundly anti-Semitic', but adds, however, 'That Shakespeare himself was personally anti-Semitic we can reasonably doubt.'[13] As the Americans say, go figure. But we are with Bloom in not shrinking from considering this play, for it tells us a lot not just about the time it was written, but also about the times we live in.

How many of us join Francis Meres in seeing the play as a comedy? If that was so intended, then the pound of flesh demanded of Antonio would have been a pretty sick joke. It is nearer a tragedy than a comedy, despite the attempt to turn the ending into a jolly jape. Though *The Merchant of Venice* was probably written in early 1597, it was not published until 1600. The 'Andrew docked in sand' alluded to in Act 1, Scene 1 is a reference to a Spanish ship, the *St Andrew*, which was captured in the Cadiz expedition of 1596, but was still in the news a year later, so this helps to date it. The play had immediate public appeal: the trial and public execution of Roderigo Lopez, would still have been fresh in the public memory as well as his own.

Shakespeare and the Jews

We cannot be certain what Shakespeare thought of Jews – nor can we be certain how much he knew about their history and culture. But there were Jews living in London, including the court musicians of the Bassano family (we met Emilia in Chapter 9).[14] Shylock's family, like the families of many other Sephardic Jews scattered around Europe and the Mediterranean, would have suffered persecution before being expelled from Spain and Portugal where they had lived for generations,[15] and of course faced more of the same in many of the areas they settled.

Shakespeare would have been subjected in his youth to a great deal of anti-Jewish propaganda in the folk morality plays that used to be performed, and the myths spread by word of mouth about their villainy. It should however be noted that Shakespeare's Jew is nowhere near as bad as Barabbas, the bloodthirsty stage villain in Marlowe's *Jew of Malta*, who declares

As for myself, I walk abroad a-nights
And kill sick people groaning under walls
Sometimes, I go about and poison wells

However, we have several indications of Shakespeare's cast of mind, for he gives Shylock a common humanity with Christians. So this play is a great deal less anti-Semitic than other plays featuring Jews, who were frequently caricatured as monsters. One could also add that Christians do not come out well in the play, either.

In 1946 the New Yiddish Theatre Company staged *The Merchant of Venice* at the Adler Hall, Whitechapel in the heart of London's East End. Here, Meier Tzelniker (as Shylock) and his daughter Anna Tzelniker (as Portia), with director Robert Atkins in their dressing room. (Courtesy of The Jewish Museum, London)

The play begins with Antonio (the merchant of Venice) feeling 'aweary of this great world'. All his money is tied up in trading ventures, and three argosies are missing on the high seas. It should be noted that this was a time when fortunes could be won, and lost, on the high seas: Drake's voyage to the Spice Islands (the Moluccas) resulted in a 5000 per cent profit.[16] Not every such venture was successful: in 1596, three English ships set out for the Indies and were lost at sea.[17] No wonder that Antonio's mind 'was tossing on the ocean', as Saliero suggests.

Meanwhile, Antonio's friend Bassanio, a fortune-hunter, also has a problem: he has his eyes on Portia, a beautiful and very rich heiress. To be accepted as her suitor he needs money which he does not have, and requests a loan of 3,000 ducats from Antonio. Not having received the benefit of advice from a Polonius, who in *Hamlet* urges his son to 'Neither a borrower nor a lender be', Antonio commits the folly of being both: borrowing from Shylock to lend to Bassanio. Shylock, who has been regularly insulted by Antonio and his cronies, suggests this 'merrie jest':

> Go with me to a notary, seal me there
> Your single bond; and, in a merry sport,
> If you repay me not on such a day,
> In such a place, such sum or sums as are
> Express'd in the condition, let the forfeit
> Be nominated for an equal pound
> Of your fair flesh, to be cut off and taken
> In what part of your body pleaseth me.
>
> – Act 1, Scene 1

What could possibly go wrong? The agreement is sealed: Antonio agrees to pay back the money within three months, by which time he is sure the safe return of his argosies will make him a rich man. Meanwhile, the scene shifts from Venice to Belmont.

The Three Caskets

With the money borrowed from Antonio, Bassanio kits himself out as a plausible suitor, and heads for Belmont to try his luck with Portia. Under the terms of her father's will, Portia is in limbo: she is required to make all her suitors choose between the three caskets of gold, silver and lead. The man who chooses the right casket is to become her husband. What sort of a father would subject his daughter to this kind of lottery? One would think that someone with the legal skills of a Portia would find her way out of this problem. But she complains:

> I may
> neither choose whom I would nor refuse whom I
> dislike; so is the will of a living daughter curbed
> by the will of a dead father. Is it not hard,
> Nerissa, that I cannot choose one nor refuse none?
>
> – Act 1, Scene 2

Nevertheless, the scenes in which various suitors are either summarily turned down, or choose the wrong casket, give Shakespeare the opportunity to create great moments of both comedy and drama. Of course, the man lined up to choose the right casket (the one made of lead) is Bassanio, the fortune hunter, who while acknowledging Portia's beauty, is quite clearly after her money: Portia is as much an investment as a person. Indeed, she is treated, by father and suitor alike, as a commodity, as Lucy Irigaray has noted:[18] in effect, Bassanio invests to acquire her, like any capitalist seeking a return on his investment.

Portia is not the first nor last woman to fall for a handsome cad. How did he know which casket to choose? That we shall never know. One would think that a fortune-hunter like Bassanio would go for the gold casket. In some productions, Portia gives a subtle hint: definitely cheating. Some see a rhyming clue in the words of the song Portia calls for (*bred, head, lead*). Anyway, for better or worse, choose the right casket he did, and his undeserved reward is the hand of Portia, who declares him to be her lord, her governor, her king:

> Myself and what is mine to you and yours
> Is now converted: but now I was the lord
> Of this fair mansion, master of my servants,
> Queen o'er myself: and even now, but now,
> This house, these servants and this same myself
> Are yours, my lord: I give them with this ring;
> Which when you part from, lose, or give away,
> Let it presage the ruin of your love
> And be my vantage to exclaim on you.
>
> – Act 3, Scene 2

While Portia provides us with a fair summary of the legal position of a married woman in Tudor times, this speech certainly raises modern eyebrows, especially as this is not the woman we all remember as *avocate extraordinaire*. Nevertheless, Portia seals the contract by giving Bassanio a ring, with a verbal clause that gives her a potential legal loophole – an opt-out from the verbal marriage contract. To which Bassanio produces, on cue, a bland reply, no doubt with his (ring finger) crossed behind his back:

> But when this ring
> Parts from this finger, then parts life from hence:
> O, then be bold to say Bassanio's dead!

The contrast between Portia, the dutiful daughter obeying her father's instructions, even after he has died, and Shylock's daughter Jessica, who defies (and robs) her father, and runs off with Lorenzo, is stark. Portia is seemingly rewarded with a stable relationship with a husband, who, however unworthy, at least makes her, in Tudor eyes, respectable. Whereas Jessica, in following her own desires in defiance of her father, ends up with Lorenzo, who simply wants the loot she brings with her. Too late she discovers his true nature:

> JESSICA: In such a night
> Did young Lorenzo swear he loved her well,
> Stealing her soul with many vows of faith
> And ne'er a true one.

The Pound of Flesh

When the three months are up, Antonio's argosies are missing, believed lost, and he cannot repay the three thousand ducats on the day specified. Shylock obstinately insists on his murderous bond, his 'pound of flesh'. At this point, Shakespeare does risk losing his audience with Shylock's famous speech, claiming joint humanity with Christians – warts and all:

> SALARINO: Why, I am sure, if he forfeit, thou wilt not take his flesh: what's that good for?
> SHYLOCK: To bait fish withal: if it will feed nothing else, it will feed my revenge. He hath disgraced me, and hindered me half a million; laughed at my losses, mocked at my gains, scorned my nation, thwarted my bargains, cooled my friends, heated mine enemies; and what's his reason? I am a Jew. Hath not a Jew eyes? hath not a Jew hands, organs, dimensions, senses, affections, passions? fed with the same food, hurt with the same weapons, subject to the same diseases, healed by the same means, warmed and cooled by the same winter and summer, as a Christian is? If you prick us, do we not bleed? if you tickle us, do we not laugh? if you poison us, do we not die? and if you wrong us, shall we not revenge? If we are like you in the rest, we will resemble you in that.
>
> – Act 3, Scene 1

This sounds like a *cri de coeur* at a time when the situation of the Jewish community in Venice was subject to a whole range of humiliating restrictions, including being confined to a ghetto and subject to a curfew. They were forbidden certain occupations, and Venetian law required them to maintain charitable banks with controlled rates of interest from which

Christians might borrow.[19] So Shylock had every reason to be bitter, especially when exposed to the racist insults of those claiming to be Christians such as Antonio and his friends. Nor should we ignore the closing lines of the speech above, continued below, which underline the fact that Shylock is no worse than Antonio and his fellow Christians: their religion preaches love and forgiveness – but they do not eschew revenge, thus making them worse than Shylock for being hypocrites:

> SHYLOCK: If a Jew wrong a Christian, what is his humility? Revenge. If a Christian wrong a Jew, what should his suffrance be by Christian example? Why, revenge. The villainy you teach me I will execute, and it shall go hard but I will better my instruction.

Revenge is ugly – but it is also understandable. In Shylock's case, the last straw would have been when his daughter steals his money and jewellery and elopes with a Christian, the aforesaid Lorenzo. And so Shylock starts to sharpen his knife. In the nick of time, Portia arrives, acting as a *deus*, or one should say a *dea, ex machina*, 'dressed as a doctor of laws'. She is accompanied by her maid Nerissa, also in disguise. Portia urges Shylock to 'render the deeds of mercy':

> The quality of mercy is not strain'd,
> It droppeth as the gentle rain from heaven
> Upon the place beneath: it is twice blest;
> It blesseth him that gives and him that takes: ...
>
> – Act 5, Scene 1

The scene is one of the most dramatic in Shakespeare. The tension builds up, until Portia traps Shylock with a legal technicality: he may have the flesh as long as he does not shed blood. She then points out that dire penalties await any 'alien' who plots against the life of a citizen of Venice. The tables are turned, and, deprived of his wealth, his house, his daughter (who eloped with a Christian) and even his religion, Shylock departs, now, a tragic figure, no doubt accompanied by the jeers of a Tudor audience. Underlying the whole play is the mutual hatred of Christian and Jew, and, in truth, all of them should be in the dock: Shylock for his murderous intention, and the Christians, for their greed, hatred, hypocrisy and intolerance.

The Merchant of Venice is one of Shakespeare's most troubling plays, and actors and directors have tried various ways of depicting Shylock on stage – as hero, victim, comic-villain, stage villain – or just villain. Arnold Wesker was moved to write his own version of the play in a dramatic example of wishful thinking.[20] In Wesker's version Antonio and Shylock are old friends, and the bond is intended to be a joke. It is the inflexible Law of Venice, not Shylock, that is on trial, and it is the law that insists on the pound of flesh being extracted: for the letter of the law is sacrosanct.

However much we may try to twist and turn, the thought is unavoidable that Shakespeare was a prisoner of his culture in meeting his audience at least halfway in his depiction of Shylock as the malevolent Jew: that was the stereotype in Tudor times, and the play does not do much to change it. The best that can be said is that it avoids grotesque caricature. It should also be noted that the Christians also come out badly in the play. Bassanio is a sordid fortune-hunter. Their friend, Lorenzo, is an unprincipled seducer and greedy receiver of stolen goods. Antonio's cronies are pretty poor specimens of humanity, and Antonio himself calls Shylock 'a cutthroat dog'. Shylock also claims that he had 'spit upon my Jewish gabardine' and

> ... did void your rheum upon my beard
> And foot me as you spurn a stranger cur

It is tempting to see this play as primarily about anti-Semitism; a feminist reading would also emphasise the gender issues we have touched on. There is a third dimension that we should note: whether or not Shakespeare had

Shakespeare's play on trial

As a footnote to the play, a mock appeal by Shylock to the US Supreme Court of Justice was launched in Venice.[21] In charge of the proceedings was Justice Ruth Bader Ginsburg, the iconic 'RBG', who sadly died in 2019. (She was replaced by an ultra-conservative judge a month before Donald Trump lost the US presidential election.)

The appeal saw a battle of wits between Shakespeare scholars Stephen Greenblatt and James Shapiro. The outcome: the court decided that Portia was an imposter, and should go to law school; Shylock's forced conversion to Christianity was overturned, and his loan to Antonio repaid. As James Shapiro commented: 'it was hard to ignore the messages of gender equality and religious tolerance implicit in her (RBG's) rulings ... Supreme Court Justices weren't supposed to go around promoting their ideological views ... '[22]

this in mind, the play does represent a contrast in value systems. Antonio and his cronies are heavily embedded in the culture emerging of early capitalism. Compare the Rialto in Venice, with all its greed and materialistic wheeling and dealing, not to say stealing, and its financial obsessions, with the almost idyllic ambience of Belmont: Portia lives in a different world, with her capacity for genuine love, generosity, mercy, loyalty, and her disregard for mere money. The three caskets are a kind of physical metaphor: lead has none of the meretricious attractions of gold and silver. In choosing the lead casket, Bassanio, by some miracle shows a capacity to eschew the meretricious: one senses that this flawed individual may not be totally beyond hope.

If there is comedy, we have to wait for it long, for, apart from several racist jokes about the nationality of Portia's various suitors, humour only really occurs at the end of the play, in scenes that many productions omit. The Globe Theatre's production in the Sam Wanamaker indoor theatre in

Judi Dench as Portia and Polly James as Nerissa in the Royal Shakespeare Company production of the play, 1971

London in 2022 ends the play in Act IV. The ending provided by Shakespeare is something of an anti-climax: Bassanio and Graziano are, with extreme difficulty, persuaded to show their appreciation by giving their rings to 'the lawyers' Portia and Nerissa. On the men's arrival in Belmont after the trial, Portia simulates anger over the loss of the ring she gave him, and Bassanio tries desperately to exculpate himself:

> BASSANIO: Sweet Portia,
> If you did know to whom I gave the ring,
> If you did know for whom I gave the ring
> And would conceive for what I gave the ring
> And how unwillingly I left the ring,
> When nought would be accepted but the ring,
> You would abate the strength of your displeasure.
>
> – Act 5, Scene 1

To which Portia responds:

> If you had known the virtue of the ring,
> Or half her worthiness that gave the ring,
> Or your own honour to contain the ring,
> You would not then have parted with the ring.
>
> – Act 5, Scene 1

Similar exchanges take place between Nerissa and Graziano. Shakespeare turns this whole episode into a 'merrie jeste', and the men are forgiven.

Does Portia really forgive Bassanio? In some productions, the relationship between Antonio and Bassanio is depicted as homosexual. When Antonio is finally saved from Shylock's knife, the two embrace each other so warmly that Portia looks shocked. Possibly with a bit of wishful thinking, M. Lindsay Kaplan suggests that in handing over her ring, Bassanio has broken their marriage contract, and Portia could thus regain all she has signed over to him as her husband.[23]

In *The Merchant of Venice* there are elements that are seldom remarked on, including the role played by Portia – not as the talented lawyer who saves the day, but as the victim (or if you prefer a survivor) of male-dominated society. In the words of M. Lindsay Kaplan, 'one strand of the play's Christian ideology attempts to subsume and incorporate Jews and women into a social hierarchy'[24] in which both are victims. If Shylock's legal rights are seriously circumscribed, so are Portia's: legally bound by her father's will, she cannot choose her own husband. However, it is clear that Portia is no mere victim: she has agency, both as mistress in her house, and as an (unlicensed) legal practitioner.

No, *The Merchant of Venice* is not really a bag of laughs, and discussions of the play have tended to focus on racial, not gender, issues. In his book *Shakespeare and the Jews*, James Shapiro gives a nuanced view:

> I am not proposing that Shakespeare was antisemitic (or, for that matter, philosemitic). *The Merchant of Venice* is a play, a work of fiction, not a diary or polygraph test; since no one knows what Shakespeare personally thought about Jews ... [25]

As Shapiro remarks, 'the words may be Shakespeare's, but the destructive prejudices are our own.' What we can say, though, is that whether he was conscious of this or not, Shakespeare depicts a society in Venice whose values have been warped by money, materialism, greed and prejudice; in short, a society not a million miles away from our own. I think the play has the great merit of forcing us to look in a mirror. How far has society really moved on?

18

PRIDE COMES BEFORE A FALL

'Pride [goeth] before destruction, and an high minde before the fall.'
– Geneva Bible: *Proverbs* 16: 18

It wasn't just working on a new play that helped Shakespeare cope with the death of his son. There was another irksome matter he had to put his mind to: a coat of arms for his father. John Shakespeare was no longer the important local figure in Stratford that he used to be, and it seems he wanted to raise his standing in society. A coat of arms would permit him to prefix his name with *Mr.* or add *gent.* after his name. In status conscious Tudor England, having a heraldic device mattered to a degree that today we cannot imagine. In *Richard II*, returning from exile, Bolingbroke is incensed by the assault on his honour by the king – and in particular the king's confidants, Bagot, Bushy and Green, the 'caterpillars of the commonwealth':

> From my own windows torn from my household coat
> Razed out my imprese[1], leaving me no sign
> Save men's opinions and my living blood
> To show the world I am a gentleman
>
> – *Richard II*, Act 3, Scene 1

Yes: John Shakespeare had an urge to show the world that he was indeed a gentleman. In October 1568, London's College of Arms records an application for a coat of arms for him, but it was not pursued, probably because the cost was too high. A second application is dated October 1596.

It was not a simple process: it fell to his son to negotiate his way through the red tape, paying the necessary fees, as well as the necessary sweeteners, 'brown envelopes', for the notoriously corrupt Garter King of Arms, Sir William Dethick.[2] Final approval was obtained in the autumn. It cited the grandfather's 'valiant and faithful service' to Henry VII and notes that John 'hath been Justice of the Peace ... and Bailiff officer and chief of Stratford upon Avon fifteen or sixteen years past.' For good measure he also 'hath land and tenements of good William Dethick'.[3] Moreover, he also 'hath land and tenements of good wealth and substance, £500'. The coat of arms awarded is described

> Gold, on a Bend Sable, a spear of the first steeled argent.
> And for his crest or cognisance a falcon his wings displaying
> argent standing on a wreath of colours: sup. a spear gold
> steeled as aforesaid upon a helmet with mantles and tassels.

The motto was *Non Sanz Droiet* – Old French for 'Not without Right'. Awarded to the oldest male member of the family, this honour meant that his male issue could assume the title of gentleman, and sport the coat of arms on 'shields, seals, rings, buildings, utensils, liveries, tombs and monuments.' So, John Shakespeare was awarded this title, 'Gent'. This meant that his son could inherit the same title, even though he would never have obtained it if he had applied in his own name, as a player. An ex-JP and ex-Bailiff had much more clout than a mere actor and playwright – though it is almost certain it was the player who stumped up the cash.

I think the impetus for this application would have come from Shakespeare's father, not the son, for Shakespeare never seems to have used the title. It may well be that he feared mockery: Ben Jonson has a character named Sogliado in his play *Every Man out of his Humour* who is mocked for paying £30 for his coat of arms, with the motto *Not Without Mustard*. ('Gold' becomes yellow in print.) Jonson turned Shakespeare's aspiration to be a gentleman into a long-standing joke even after he died.[3] It is also possible that Shakespeare found that

> New honours come upon him
> Like our strange garments, cleave not to their mould
> But with the aid of use
>
> *– Macbeth*

Or perhaps the death of his only son gave him a sense of futility. In Macbeth's words:

> ... all our yesterdays have lighted fools
> The way to dusty death. Out, out, brief candle!
> Life's but a walking shadow, a poor player
> That struts and frets his hour upon the stage
> And then is heard no more: it is a tale
> Told by an idiot, full of sound and fury,
> Signifying nothing.
>
> – *Macbeth*, Act 5, Scene 5

So it was that Shakespeare could, if he so wished, call himself 'Gent'. when in May 1597 he bought a 'pretty house of brick and timber', the second largest in Stratford. Standing directly opposite his old school, it was originally built by Hugh Clopton in 1483 – the same man who paid for the fine bridge across the River Avon, which still exists today, with its fourteen arches, a Grade 1 listed structure. Sadly, the house itself was demolished in 1759, and where it stood is now a lovely memorial garden, maintained by the Shakespeare Birthplace Trust, with specially commissioned artworks inspired by Shakespeare's writing.

The house was an impressive three-story building with five gables, ornamental beams and no fewer than ten fireplaces. It also had an extensive back garden. Shakespeare named his new acquisition 'New Place', and he paid William Underhill the low price of 60 pounds, in silver.[4] The low price was almost certainly a tax dodge – but also reflected its poor state of repair. With New Place needing attention, Shakespeare probably now spent some time in Stratford, particularly as theatres were closed again that summer because of the plague and social unrest; thereafter, London called, and it was left to his wife Anne to complete the refurbishments.

Drama Off-Stage

We saw in the last chapter some of the reasons why 1596 was an *annus horribilis*, during which England narrowly escaped invasion. The Earl of Essex compounded his failure at Cadiz by failing yet again the following year – this time in his attempt to seize Spanish treasure ships, off the Azores.

At that very moment, a third *Gran Armada* approached the shores of England. Yet again, it was incredibly, strong gales – 'God's wind' – that scattered the Spanish ships.[5]

As if this existential threat were not enough, the world of theatre was itself becoming an off-stage drama. For Shakespeare and his troupe, 1597 saw a worsening situation: it looked as though they faced expulsion from the theatre where they had performed for so many years. It will be recalled that this had been built by James Burbage in 1576 on land owned by their aged landlord, Giles Allen. The puritanical Allen was increasingly unhappy about the players occupying his land, and he showed marked unwillingness to extend the lease beyond its expiry in April 1597. The only current alternative was the Curtain Theatre in Shoreditch, where the troupe sometimes performed, but it was showing signs of age, and was an unattractive venue. The players' best hope then lay with the new venture by James Burbage: since February 1596, he had spent huge sums on converting the former Dominican Priory into an indoor theatre, all the more urgent, given the excessive rains that summer. The project involved converting seven 'vpper Roomes' into the original hall, and the construction of a stage, and side galleries.[6]

However, there was a serious problem: the scheme was faced with mounting opposition. In July, local residents of the Blackfriars precinct – and powerful friends – had petitioned the Privy Council to stop Burbage's development. The petition advised that

> one Burbage hath lately bought certain rooms in the same precinct near adjoining unto the dwelling houses of the right honourable Lord Chamberlain and the Lord of Hunsdon, which the said Burbage is now altering and meaneth very shortly to convert and turn the same into a common playouse.[7]

Yes: Nimbyism was alive and well in 1596. The petitioners pointed out that if the theatre were allowed, it would

> grow to be a very great annoyance and trouble, not only to all the noblemen and gentlemen thereabout inhabiting, but also a general inconvenience to all the inhabitants of the same precinct, both by reason of the great resort and gathering together of all manner of vagrants and lewd persons that

under colour of resorting to the plays, will come thither and work all manner of mischief[8]

The petition had been skilfully drawn up by the Dowager Countess of Bedford, Elizabeth Russell, a formidable woman in her late sixties. The Countess was not one to be trifled with. The portrait of her, with her staring eyes, pursed lips and white starched headdress made her look uncannily like a cobra about to strike. She was known to lock up anyone who crossed her in her own personal dungeon in her country manse, Bisham Abbey in Berkshire. The Countess, a devout Puritan, was outraged at the development of Burbage's theatre almost on her doorstep, and pursued a relentless campaign to close it down. Anyone who refused to sign her petition did so at their peril.

The petition subtly implied that the theatre might be a place for subversive activities involving 'masterless men': the Elizabethan establishment was paranoid about public disorder, which broke out several times in the 1590s. There had been a particularly violent outburst of unrest in 1595, provoked by years of excessive heat, plague, floods and four years of ruinous harvests.[9] A large crowd of rioters gathered outside the house of the Lord Mayor of London: and threatened to 'hang him if he durst come out'. Another three thousand men gathered outside the city armed with clubs and poles. The

---

Elizabeth Russell (1528-1609)

Elizabeth Cooke Hoby Russell, self-styled 'Countess', had very powerful connections, including the queen (godmother to one of her sons), and Lord Burghley. Her first husband was Sir Thomas Hoby, first cousin of Robert Cecil, and translator of Castiglione's *Il Cortegiano* (The Courtier) – the Bible of the English aristocracy. Widowed in 1566, her second husband was 21-year-old John Russell, 2nd Earl of Bedford – unusually, thirteen years her junior. The Russell family and the Brooke family were very close – the Dowager Elizabeth tried to marry off her daughter Bess to Henry Brooke, the new Lord Cobham.

Lady Elizabeth was part of a Puritanical mafia who loathed theatres and all they stood for. A proto-feminist, in 1605 she published under her own name her own translation of *A Way of Reconciliation,* written by a Huguenot seeking to resolve disputes among Protestants. At the time, this was almost unheard of for a woman.

Owning much of Berkshire, she pursued endless property disputes with powerful local landowners. There was violence on both sides. Shakespeare didn't stand a chance in any conflict with this relentlessly ruthless woman.

Portrait of Elizabeth (Cooke Hoby) Russell – Dowager Countess of Bedford

panic-stricken authorities decided that the theatres were to blame, and closed them down.[10]

Lady Russell had the ear of many members of the Privy Council – and they were all-too-ready to listen; indeed, this tough woman gave them no choice. Among the signatories to her petition were not just local residents, but powerful friends – and some less powerful. Shakespeare would have been shocked to see the name of his friend Richard Field on the list: Field was obviously unable to withstand the forceful Lady Russell. He was even more shocked to see the name of George Carey, sponsor of Shakespeare's troupe, on the list! Carey's action has been described as 'one of the most astounding acts of betrayal in theatre history.'[11] Not so astounding, I think: George Carey was hoping to become the new Lord Chamberlain when the elderly Lord Cobham died, and needed to make friends at court. In addition, his sister Margaret was married to the Lady Russell's son, Edward Hoby, and the Countess would have played the family loyalty card.

The outcome was a foregone conclusion: the project was closed down by the Privy Council. It was a disaster: James Burbage lost a great deal of money – by some estimates, up to £1,000. A disappointed man, he died in January 1597. His funeral took place in St Leonards' Church on 2 February 1597, when he was laid to rest very near the grave of Richard Tarlton, the comic actor. The funeral would have been attended by large numbers of the theatre fraternity. Many saw him as a victim of Puritanism.

There was one glimmer of good news: the elderly Lord Chamberlain, Lord Cobham, died in March, just over a month later: would the new Lord Cobham, the son, Henry Brooke, be appointed? However, he was a man of poor judgement, neither liked nor respected,[12] and to the relief of Shakespeare's troupe, George Carey was appointed the new Lord Chamberlain.[13] Lord Hunsdon's Men became the Lord Chamberlain's Men again! Resentment over Carey's betrayal gave way to relief, as the Lord Chamberlain's men could now regain their status – and the protection that came with it. The Lord Chamberlain's Men remained the leading theatre company for many years to come, so much so that under James I, they became the King's Men.

However, the immediate problem was that the failure of Burbage's project spelt financial ruin. How long would the troupe have a stage to perform on? More in hope than expectation, James Burbage's son, Richard, carried on negotiations with the landlord of the Theatre in Shoreditch, Giles Allen, to extend the lease. However, Allen clearly wanted the actors out, insisting on financially impossible demands, and the negotiations ground to a halt.

Another crisis

In the summer, another crisis developed that affected not just the Lord Chamberlain's men, but the whole future of professional theatre. In July, Pembroke's Men put on a play called *The Isle of Dogs* by the satirist Thomas Nashe and Ben Jonson, a newcomer on the theatre scene. Frustratingly, no one knows what it was about, or why it caused deep offence, though it is surmised that the authorities were being lampooned as lap-dogs.

On 28 July, London's Lord Mayor and fellow alderman declared that they were outraged by the play's 'profane fables, lascivious, matters cozening devices, and scurrilous behaviours' and demanded that the Privy Council should suppress the play, and for good measure close down all the theatres. They also attacked the audience as

> vagrant persons, masterless men, thieves, horse stealers, whore mongerers, cozeners, coney-catchers, contrivers of treason, and other idle and dangerous persons.[14]

All copies of the play were destroyed by the authorities; Nashe escaped to Great Yarmouth, but Jonson and two of his fellow actors ended up in the Marshalsea prison. Their incarceration was supervised by none other than Richard Topcliffe, who smelt a seditious rat. At the end of July, the Privy Council took further steps, ordering

> that no plays shall be used within London or about the city or in any public place during this time of summer, but also those playhouses that are erected and built only for such purposes shall be plucked down, namely the Curtain and the Theatre near Shoreditch.[15]

Surrey's justices including one William Gardiner, who had a personal vendetta against Shakespeare, also acted similarly against theatres in the Bankside and Southwark or anywhere within three miles of London. Thus, a key part of London's theatre season was shut down, and actors and theatre owners were deprived of an income. The acting troupes were reduced to the hardship of going on tour – the Lord Chamberlain's Men travelled round Kent in August, followed by Bristol and Bath in September.[16]

It is unlikely that Shakespeare went with them. Shakespeare had his own financial pressures, for he needed money to spend on the house he had bought in Stratford. Thus he turned his mind to publishing some of his more popular plays. starting with *Richard II* and *Richard III*. They were followed later in the year by *Romeo and Juliet*. However, there was no question of resting on his laurels, for George Carey was eager for new plays with which to entertain the court. And so it was likely that Anne Hathaway was left to supervise the work of restoration of New Place, while Shakespeare took up his quill pen again, this time, to write a history play with a difference: indeed, two plays, *1 Henry IV* and *2 Henry IV*. These plays resulted in yet another huge off-stage drama.

The Hand of the Censor

It may seem strange that Shakespeare decided to take as his starting point an old play, *The Famous Victories of Henry V*, which had certainly been performed in 1587 or even earlier.[17] It is likely that Shakespeare saw the play being performed, and may even have played a part in it. It was first published in 1598, where the title page notes 'As it was plaide by the Queens Majesties Players'. No one knows the author.

It should not be too difficult to run up a decent version of an off-the-peg old play from the 1580s like *The Famous Victories*. So what persuaded Shakespeare to do so? There are several possible explanations. One is that after being busy with his property development project in Stratford, he was pushed for time. It is likely too that the old play appealed to him, because it conflated two genres, history and comedy. Much better, he may have thought, than just another boring procession of kings and barons jockeying for power and influence: comedy could breathe new life into the history play.

There is another reason why Shakespeare may have embraced the idea of writing a play that combined history with comedy: he saw an opportunity to have a laugh at Puritanism. He had seen actors harassed by an intolerant and oppressive city corporation, dominated by Puritans; he had also seen the puritanical Giles Allen refusing to extend the lease for the theatre, thereby threatening the livelihood of his actor friends – and indeed his own. Above all, he had seen his friend James Burbage's brilliant idea for an indoor theatre killed at birth by a puritanical old harridan, Lady Russell, and her coterie of puritanical friends. To cap it all, he had seen his old and respected friend, James Burbage die, perhaps from a broken heart, as a result.

Shakespeare decided to give top-billing to the comedic elements in the play, and retain one of the characters who lived during the reign of Henry IV – Sir John Oldcastle. To the present-day inhabitants of Farringdon in London, Sir John Oldcastle is the name of a Wetherspoon pub. But the gentleman was a real person – and his descendants still lived and were at court. Historically, Oldcastle had had a dissolute youth, when he was a personal friend of Prince Hal, the future Henry V, but later became a loyal subject of the king. He married into the powerful Cobham family, lords of the manor of Cobham in Kent. Oldcastle played an important role in the king's war against the Welsh rebel Owen Glendower. However, he became a Lollard – a follower of John Wycliffe who was an early Protestant reformer; among his beliefs were opposition to the corrupt practices of the papacy, and a belief in using a vernacular version of the bible – a step too far for the Holy Church. Oldcastle got into trouble as a heretic, took part in a rebellion, and was executed in 1417. By Tudor times he had become something of a Protestant hero – he features in *Foxe's Book of Martyrs*;[18] meanwhile, those who were opposed to the reformed religion preferred to highlight his misspent youth as a 'ruffian knight' with Prince Hal, before he became a reformed character.

In his youth, Sir John Oldcastle had indeed led a colourful life, and in the *Henry IV* plays Shakespeare featured him by name as a lecherous roisterer and buffoon. The insult was not wholly gratuitous, because in Foxe's book, Oldcastle is quoted in his trial as admitting to having been in his youth guilty of 'pride, wrath, and gluttony', as well as 'covetousness and lechery'. But unfortunately for Shakespeare, by ill-advisedly calling his character *Oldcastle* in his play, he ignored the fact that among the powerful descendants still living of Sir John was none other than the new Lord Cobham, whose father had been Lord Chamberlain – and the noble lord did not see the joke. In fact, it is clear that he took deep offence at his ancestor being depicted as a 'whoreson round man'.

Of course, in dramatic terms, there was good reason for Shakespeare to retain the character: he was a gift for Shakespeare's dramatic imagination: a sinful and unprincipled degenerate turned Holy Joe. Oldcastle was a ready-made comic anti-hero, and a great opportunity to have a laugh at the expense of the Puritans by deliberately depicting a Protestant hero as a drunken lecherous buffoon and hypocrite. What is certain is that Shakespeare knew what he was doing. In his imagination, the character of Jockey Oldcastle grew into a grotesque caricature to become Falstaff. Even in his cups, his repetition of fragments from the Geneva Bible revealed his gross hypocrisy. To drive the joke home, forget Wetherspoon's: he made Falstaff's centre of operations an inn called the Boar's Head in Eastcheap – a hostelry well-known to his Tudor audience. History does not record who the hostess, Mistress Quickly, may have been.

In rewriting *The Famous Victories* in this way Shakespeare was guilty of a serious error of judgement that might have cost him dear. By this time, he should have known better than to make fun of a noble lord's ancestor. This was not a good time to be making enemies at court – or to alienate a powerful Protestant faction. Some authorities suggest that it was Lord Cobham as Lord Chamberlain who was angered by the play, but it is likely that the play was written in late 1597, months after he died.[19] So it was the new Lord Cobham, Henry Brooke, who took umbrage. This alone might not have been of great moment, for Cobham as we have seen, was not particularly popular in court circles. However, there were other powerful figures in the land who were also offended. Among the cast list of Shakespeare's anti-hero's cronies was a character named *Harvey*, easily identified as Sir William Harvey who sought to marry the widowed Countess of Southampton (mother to our old friend Henry Wriothesley). Another character was given the name *Russell* (the family name of the Earl of Bedford, and thus a dig at the Lady Elizabeth). And it may well have been Lady Elizabeth, 'She Who Must Be Obeyed' who led the charge.[20]

For charge there certainly was. Shakespeare could not get away with it: too many powerful people were offended by his play. The Master of the Rolls Edmund Tilney was brought in with his blue pen, and numerous changes were made to the text, and Shakespeare was forced to change some of the names. *Sir John Oldcastle* became *Sir John Falstaff*, a cowardly knight mentioned in *1 Henry VI*. *Harvey* and *Russell* were renamed *Bardolph* and *Peto*. However, Tilney did not pick up every reference: for example, at one point, Falstaff's speech is prefixed with 'Old' instead of 'Fal.', and Prince Hal at one point refers to 'my old lad of the castle'. Shakespeare went through the motions of showing repentance, and the last line of *Henry IV* ends with this transparently unconvincing disclaimer, which simply serves to remind the audience of what had happened to the play:

> Falstaff shall die of a sweat, unless a' be killed already
> with your hard opinions, for Oldcastle died a martyr,
> and this is not that man ...

Shakespeare was playing with fire with his play. As we saw, following *The Isle of Dogs* scandal, Ben Jonson and some of his actors ended up in jail. The actors got out quite quickly, but Jonson was not released for three months.[21] Shakespeare's play was much less offensive, but even so he was lucky to have escaped fairly lightly. What saved him was the fact that many at Court, including the Queen, enjoyed the joke – and the character of Falstaff was seen as a stroke of comic genius. Sir John Falstaff deserves more than a footnote in this chapter, so in the next chapter we take a closer look at the two great plays, *1 Henry IV* and *2 Henry IV* that Shakespeare was forced to rework.

19

GAME OF THRONES

> Uneasy lies the head that wears a crown
>
> – 2 HIV III.i

Taylor and Loughnane's best guess for the dating of *1 Henry IV* is late 1597.[1] Some scholars have suggested late 1596, but the Lord Chamberlain, William Brooke, Lord Cobham, who died on March 6 1597, was far too powerful a figure to offend with a play making fun of his ancestor. So it is likely that the play was written, or at least completed, after he died – and then, as indicated in the last chapter, had to be rewritten after the uproar it caused at court. Of course, it is not known how Shakespeare reacted when his play fell victim to the censor's blue pencil. It is possible he was amused. One can imagine him laughing with his actor pals over a pint of ale. Indeed, one could say that the rewriting of the play left him laughing all the way to the bank, for it was a huge success – perhaps because of the attempt at censorship, but no doubt also because the characters of Falstaff and Hotspur were among the most popular in Shakespeare's lifetime. *1 Henry IV* was performed at court in December 1597, and was well received, and became a regular part of the repertoire of the Lord Chamberlain's Men.

It is likely that the influence of George Carey, as the new Lord Chamberlain, played a big part in having the play successfully performed at court, and saving Shakespeare from the fate of Ben Jonson over *The Isle of Dogs* fiasco. Indeed, the popularity of the Henry IV plays has endured ever since. So, if anything, the attempt at censorship backfired. But in any case, Shakespeare must have known in his bones that the character of Falstaff was an irresistible attraction: for his grotesquely overweight knight was immensely popular at all levels of society, and there were endless Falstaff jokes circulating in letters and documents of the time, and after Shakespeare's death. Reputedly, Queen Elizabeth called for another play to be written featuring Falstaff in love, which saw the genesis of *The Merry Wives of Windsor*.

1 Henry IV, Part I

This was the first in a trilogy, comprising *Henry IV* parts 1 and 2, and *Henry V*. In rewriting *1 Henry IV*, changing the names as required, he still managed to push at the boundaries of acceptability: one can sense elements of subversion. For example, the cynical treatment of 'honour': as Falstaff observes, 'What is in that word honour? What is that honour? Air.' I think too that the concept of *commodity* that came to him in the writing of *King John*, had a lasting influence on his thinking: the way greed and self-interest operate both at court, and in The Boar's Head, has the effect of tarnishing the image of the former. The scenes of power politics rubbing shoulders as it were with the picaresque scenes at The Boar's Head may interrupt the narrative drive: but one is almost forced to consider whether there is so much difference between, say, Bolingbroke who stole the throne, and Pistol, who robbed pilgrims? At least Pistol is an honest crook: he doesn't pretend to act under a cloak of so-called honour.

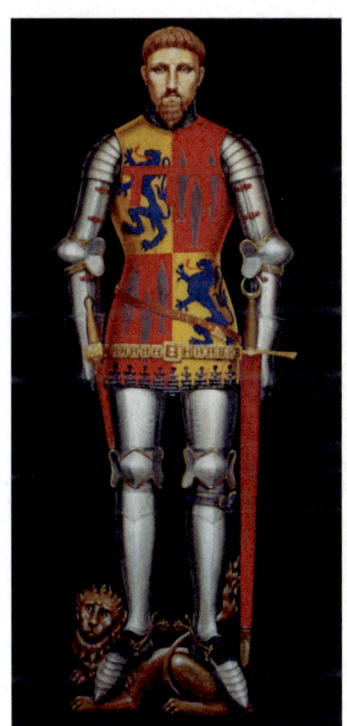

Sir Henry Percy (Hotspur) (1364-1403)

As mentioned in the last chapter, an old play *The Famous Victories of Henry V* was a major source for *Henry IV*. Other possible sources were *Chronicles of England* by John Stowe (1580) and his

Annals of England (1582), Holinshed, and Halle. It is also possible that he felt inspired to write his last great trilogy by Samuel Daniel's verse poem *Civil Wars*, which came out in 1595.[2] However, to label *1* and *2 Henry IV* as history plays hardly does justice to them. In Barbara Everett's words:

> In his history plays, Shakespeare turns chronicle into history, then history into drama, and then – in the superb *Henry IV* plays – historical drama into something almost like myth: free-standing, undocumented and legendary works of art.[3]

Myth? Perhaps. Falstaff has certainly acquired mythical status. Clearly these plays are not merely a narrative of what happened (not always following the sources), but are an implied critique of the value systems that were claimed for, or supposedly espoused by, monarchy, and which did not always correspond to reality. I don't think Shakespeare was anti-monarchist; but I believe there is a strong hint that there were aspects of monarchy, particularly the cruelty and dishonesty, that he disliked, and exposed. This was equalled by what he saw as the greed and 'vaulting ambition'[4] – the lust for power – of the nobility.

In *Richard II* we saw how Henry Bolingbroke usurped an anointed king by force of arms, and by clever manipulation of his fellow peers, thus undermining his own legitimacy. Speaking to Northumberland, King Richard made this prediction:

The role of the History play

It is interesting to consider what role history plays performed in Tudor society. To John Blundeville, writing in 1574, history plays were like morality plays, having a moral and religious purpose.[5] The old morality plays certainly had an influence on history plays – for example, Richard III had strong echoes of the favourite villain, Vice. However, for Peter Lake, history plays had a political role: 'The history plays show the way in which contemporaries actually thought about politics; that is to say, about how power has been and still is being claimed and attained, contested and legitimized, distributed and deployed, in monarchical states like Elizabethan England.'[6]

Given the degree of political awareness that the Tudor public had to acquire – even as a survival strategy – Lake is probably correct; however, the level of understanding would have varied widely, given the mixed audiences Shakespeare's plays attracted.

> ... thou ladder wherewithal
> The mounting Bolingbroke ascends my throne,
> The time shall not be many hours of age
> More than it is ere foul sin gathering head
> Shalt break into corruption: thou shalt think,
> Though he divide the realm and give thee half,
> It is too little, helping him to all;
> And he shall think that thou, which know'st the way
> To plant unrightful kings, wilt know again,
> Being ne'er so little urged, another way
> To pluck him headlong from the usurped throne.
> The love of wicked men converts to fear ...
>
> – *Richard II*, Act 1, Scene 1

These words are echoed by Falstaff's comment 'A plague upon it when thieves cannot be true to one another!' In the back of the audience's mind is a question: can or should a usurper be rewarded? In *1 Henry IV* we see the prophecy of Richard II being quickly fulfilled, as the lords who presided over the deposition of Richard II begin to jockey for power. The opening lines show Henry IV feeling cornered by rebellion on all sides:

Orson Welles plays the role of Falstaff in his 1966 film *Chimes at Midnight*, a reworking of the *Henry IV* plays. John Gielgud played the king – and Jeanne Moreau was Doll Tearsheet

> So shaken as we are, so wan with care,
> Find we a time for frighted peace to pant
>
> – HIV Act 1, Scene 1

The image is of peace as a frightened hart, pursued by hounds. To avoid 'civil butchery' in England, Henry sees the need to unite the country in a holy war to rescue 'the sepulchre of Christ' from 'pagans' – perhaps, too, hoping to salve his conscience. However, he is faced by more urgent issues: the Welsh nationalist Owen Glyndur has defeated and captured Mortimer, a thousand of whose men have been butchered – and there is a question mark over Mortimer's loyalty. Faced with this 'broil', the Holy Land must wait.

There is better news from Scotland: Northumberland's son, Harry Hotspur, has heavily defeated the Scots, and captured many lords – the source of valuable ransom money. However, Hotspur will not hand over his prisoners until the king pays his brother-in-law Mortimer's ransom. Henry refuses to do so, suspecting as he does that Mortimer has defected. This does not go down well with his erstwhile fellow-peers, and when Worcester reminds him that he only managed to become king with their help, Henry angrily dismisses him; but it is becoming obvious that Hotspur has no intention of handing the prisoners over. King Henry still refuses to ransom 'revolted Mortimer', and stalks off after issuing Hotspur with an ultimatum: 'Send us your prisoners, or you will hear of it!' Hotspur, true to his impulsive blood, hot-headedly threatens to follow him – and is adamant that he will keep the prisoners.

His father, Northumberland, persuades him to keep his powder dry, but it is plain that rebellion is brewing; and when Hotspur learns that King Richard had named Mortimer as his successor, he is aghast that Worcester and Northumberland nevertheless assisted Bolingbroke to ascend the throne:

> HOTSPUR: As both of you – God pardon it! – have done,
>   To put down Richard, that sweet lovely rose,
>   And plant this thorn, this canker, Bolingbroke?
>   And shall it in more shame be further spoken,
>   That you are fool'd, discarded and shook off
>   By him for whom these shames ye underwent.

> No; yet time serves wherein you may redeem
> Your banish'd honours
>
> – HIV Act 1, Scene 3

As these dramas at court play out, young Prince Hal is slumming it with some of his cronies. Immediately we get a thumbnail portrait of the character who, as originally named Oldcastle, so offended the powers that be, and who, in his new *persona* as Sir John Falstaff, delighted all who beheld him, from the queen down to the lowliest apprentice:

> FALSTAFF: Now, Hal, what time of day is it, lad?
> PRINCE HAL: Thou art so fat-witted, with drinking of old sack and unbuttoning thee after supper and sleeping upon benches after noon, that thou hast forgotten to demand that truly which thou wouldst truly know. What a devil hast thou to do with the time of the day? Unless hours were cups of sack and minutes capons and clocks the tongues of bawds and dials the signs of leaping-houses and the blessed sun himself a fair hot wench in flame-coloured taffeta, I see no reason why thou shouldst be so superfluous to demand the time of the day.
>
> – Act 1, Scene 2

Sir John Oldcastle being burnt for Lollard heresy and insurrection. First published in Holinshed's Chronicles (1577)

Anyone with a sense-of-humour deficit would be offended by having a distant ancestor depicted in this way. But to be fair, offence would be the more easily taken if you were a fervent Protestant, and an earl at that – especially if that distant ancestor who, as a Lollard, was a Protestant martyr and hero. No, Henry Brooke, the eleventh Baron Cobham, would not have been best pleased – even if it was actually the tenth Baron who was the original target. More influential, though, was the fervent

Cartoon of Sir John Falstaff by George Cruikshank

Protestant lobby who saw their martyr being mocked. Yes, it was inevitable that 'Oldcastle' had to be renamed.

In the badinage that follows – apparently not picked up by the censor – Prince Hal calls Falstaff 'my old lad of the castle'. Perhaps the subtlety here was lost on the censor: not just the obvious reference to 'Oldcastle' (reminding anyone who needs reminding of Falstaff's original name) but also the near anagram of *old lad* (echoes here of *Lollard*). Shakespeare would have made a good designer of crosswords. Too subtle? Not for the word-smiths of the Tudor world. Already, English was becoming a highly inventive language, and not just for the elite.

A certain parallelism is already emerging. Court politics, where all seek advantage, are depicted side by side with the drunken follies, badinage and criminality of the tavern and the brothel – equally, where all seek advantage. And Harry, Prince Hal, as Prince of Wales heir to the throne, straddles both. What is Hal playing at, slumming it with these people? In Act 1, Scene 4, he tells us, unconvincingly, that all along, he is play-acting the role of a rake, learning the argot and behaviour of the common man the better to know his ways. One day, he says, he will throw off his 'loose behaviour'.

Meanwhile at court, the king has to deal with his erstwhile allies planning to seize the country from his grasp: open rebellion has broken

Depiction of Owain Glyndur in battle by Arthur Cadwgan Michael

out. The king learns that that Mortimer has married Glyndur's daughter, and Douglas is descending with a Scottish army from the north. The real world intrudes on the goings-on at The Boar's Head, and Hal is summoned to court. However, he is in no hurry to answer the call, as he and Falstaff fool about, enjoying a role-play in which each takes it in turn to play the part of the king, and the prince, thus turning the goings-on at court into a mocking joke. For Hal, it seems, all the world is indeed a stage.

Whether a Tudor audience would have seen a parallelism between the two contrasting worlds of court and street is debatable. What is thievery at street level is seen as power-politics at court: but the vision, like a distorted mirror, is there for those who wish to see it. I think Shakespeare is developing a view of monarchy similar to that of the Bastard in *King John*: 'commodity' rules. Those competing for the crown are in Falstaff's words 'thieves who cannot be true one to another', involved as they are in a high-stakes game where lying and cheating masquerade under the cloak of 'honour'. The word constantly recurs in the speeches of the nobility, and, oddly, it is Falstaff who makes the best comment on this:

> Can honour set to a leg? no: or an arm?
> no: or take away the grief of a wound? no.
> Honour hath no skill in surgery, then? no. What is
> honour? a word. What is in that word honour? What
> is that honour? air. A trim reckoning! Who hath it?
> he that died o' Wednesday. Doth he feel it? no.
> Doth he hear it? no. 'Tis insensible, then.
> Yes, to the dead. But will it not live with the living?
> No, Why? Detraction will not suffer it.

Therefore I'll not suffer it. Therefore I'll none of it.
Honour is a mere scutcheon: and so ends my catechism.

– Act 5, Scene 1

Perhaps Shakespeare was thinking of his own newly-acquired escutcheon.

The contrast between Prince Hal of Eastcheap and Harry Hotspur is marked: Hal is a dissolute playboy, while Hotspur is macho-man *par excellence*, reminding a Shakespearian audience of England's current war hero, the Earl of Essex. Essex was an unquantifiable force to be reckoned with in the closing years of Elizabeth's reign. Like Hotspur, he was said to be 'full of humours', 'acting in fits and starts', with the temperament of a racehorse; in the words of Queen Elizabeth, Essex, like Hotspur, required 'the bridle rather than the spur'.[7] Deluded by his own ego, slow to take advice, quick to take offence, a man whose hand always hovered over the hilt of his sword, Essex bears an uncanny resemblance to Hotspur. Henry is fully aware of the differences between Hotspur and his son: just as Elizabeth was fully aware of the similarities between Hotspur and Essex – and how dangerous such a loose cannon could be. Whether Shakespeare intended it or not, the comparison was bound to be made.

Hotspur can create humour as well as testosterone. In the scene where Glyndur claims supernatural powers, Hotspur repeatedly goads him, as though seeking to provoke a quarrel, to the very limits of endurance:

> MORTIMER: Peace, cousin Percy; you will make him mad.
> GLYNDUR: I can call spirits from the vasty deep.
> HOTSPUR: Why, so can I, or so can any man;
>   But will they come when you do call for them?
> GLYNDUR: Why, I can teach you, cousin, to command
>   The devil.
> HOTSPUR: And I can teach thee, coz, to shame the devil
>   By telling truth: tell truth and shame the devil.

– Act 3, Scene 1

However, they have more important things to worry about than personal quarrels. They learn that Prince Hal has rallied to his father's cause. Yes, incredibly, overnight, Prince Hal has seemingly become a changed man. Seeking reconciliation with his father he declares he is no longer a prodigal who is 'no more worthie to be called thy sonne' as the Geneva Bible has it.

Asking forgiveness for his follies, he then denounces Hotspur's assault on the divinity of the monarch, with words that might have emanated from the old Sir John Oldcastle himself, as he became a Lollard:

> And I will call him to so strict account,
> That he shall render every glory up,
> Yea, even the slightest worship of his time,
> Or I will tear the reckoning from his heart.
> This, in the name of God, I promise here:
> The which if He be pleased I shall perform,
> I do beseech your majesty may salve
> The long-grown wounds of my intemperance
>
> – III.ii

For the rebels, the news worsens: Northumberland has fallen ill, his forces stand aloof, and Glyndur cannot produce the soldiers he promised. It is clear, at Shrewsbury, that the rebels will be fighting a losing battle: the rebels' army is heavily outnumbered by King Henry's army. The rebels resign themselves to a last throw of the dice, realising they are almost certain to lose. As Hotspur defiantly declares 'Doomsday is near: die all, die merrily'. And so they do, though they were unlikely to have been very merry. The rebels are certainly doomed, and Hotspur falls to the Prince's sword. Falstaff typically chooses to live merrily, surviving by playing dead on the battlefield. In this battle Prince Hal becomes himself, and King Henry tells him 'thou hast redeemed thy lost opinion'.

The Shakespearian audience is bound to feel that the rebels were fighting on the wrong side of history. Their proposals to divide up the kingdom between them, so that England would be taken over by warlords, would not have been popular. The country had been there, done that. But the battle of Shrewsbury is not the end of the story: there are still battles to be won.

Henry IV, Part 2

2 Henry IV, which came out in early 1598,[8] was not as popular as its predecessor, partly perhaps because of the absence of Hotspur, and possibly too because the audience would have been sad to see Falstaff getting his come-uppance, no matter how well-deserved. In *2 Henry IV* the political horizon darkens. Images of decay, and death, dominate much of the play, starting, bathetically, with Sir John Falstaff's water – his urine – which unsurprisingly yields sinister symptoms. Just as in Part 1 of the play, there is again a certain parallelism at work: this time, the diseases of the slums are echoed in the flawed and diseased body of the state. Thus, for example, in Scene 8, King Henry speaks of 'the body of our kingdom; How foul it is, what rank diseases grow'. The king is racked by guilt at the way he usurped the throne, and he remembers Richard II's prophecy:

> 'The time will come, that foul sin, gathering head,
> Shall break into corruption'
>
> – Act 2, Scene 4

To some extent, *2 Henry IV* is more of the same: it is certain that audiences could not have enough of Hal's fat friend as he cons Mistress Quickly out of her silver, canoodles with Doll Tearsheet, and again takes bribes to turn down good recruits for King Henry's army. In a later scene, no doubt much enjoyed particularly by the Inns of Court students, he is accosted by the Lord Chief Justice about the robbery in Gadshill in Part 1, and, true to form, manages to talk his way out of trouble. The Lord Chief Justice plays the 'straight man' to Falstaff's comedian, and is seemingly unaware that he is being mocked. The scene has the effect of making the law a bit of a mockery.

One senses that Shakespeare is slightly running out of steam in this play, filling it with random events that create incidents rather than develop a strong dramatic narrative. For example, take the long speech by Rumour 'painted full of tongues' in the play's Prologue. Rumour has two functions here: first, to remind the audience of what happened in *1 Henry IV:*

> I run before King Harry's victory;
> Who in a bloody field by Shrewsbury
> Hath beaten down young Hotspur and his troops,
> Quenching the flame of bold rebellion
> Even with the rebel's blood.
>
> – Act 1, Scene 1

Rumour then deliberately spreads 'fake news', as we have come to call it, of the success of the rebels. The audience is presented with a stark reminder of how London (and indeed Madrid) was constantly plagued with rumours (particularly of Armadas real or imaginary, of battles lost or won); in this case, Lord Bardolph brings to old Northumberland 'news' of the rebels' victory at Shrewsbury. For a time, the old earl believes it until he realises that he is a victim of rumour, and is overcome with grief when he hears of the death of his son: a blatant and somewhat contrived attempt to create a *coup de théâtre* – nothing like a grief-stricken earl to make good theatre ...

The rebels – Lord Bardolf, Mowbray, Hastings and the Archbishop of York – prepare again for battle. In Scene 7, Northumberland prepares to go to war, claiming 'my honour is at pawn', suggesting perhaps that honour, like Mistress Quickly's silver, can be pawned. Shakespeare's choice of words can't be accidental; surely, he again calls into question the validity of the concept of honour. Sure enough, honour gives way to self-survival, as Northumberland is easily persuaded to bide his time, flying to Scotland, to see which way the wind blows, thus signing his erstwhile allies' death warrant. With allies like Northumberland, who needs enemies ...

The honour-code is further compromised by the actions of Prince John[9] (Hal's younger brother): he gets Westmoreland to open up negotiations with the plotters – the Archbishop of York, Mowbray and Hastings. The prince agrees to deal with their grievances, and they agree to disband their army. Which done, Westmoreland promptly arrests them as traitors, guilty of high treason. One shares Mowbray's shock:

> MOWBRAY: Is this proceeding just and honourable?
> WESTMORELAND: Is your assembly so?
> ARCHBISHOP: Will not this break your faith?
> PRINCE JOHN: I pawned thee none ...
>
> – Act 4, Scene 1

Yet again commodity trumps honour – yet again 'pawned' – as the prince sends them off to be executed.

King Henry undergoes a slow decline. Racked by worry, and guilt, and appalled by the betrayal of his former allies, he finds it difficult to sleep. He is obsessed with 'the body of our kingdom/How foul it is; what rank diseases grow' and how 'foul sin' doth 'break into corruption', and how Percy (Northumberland) was once 'the man nearest my soul'. He gets some comfort from the news that Glyndur is dead, and that Northumberland

and the Scottish rebel Douglas have been defeated. Soon after the king falls into a swoon, and it is clear he has not long to live.

We turn to the famous scene where Hal finds his father asleep in his bedchamber. Thinking his father is dead, he places the crown on his head as though rehearsing for the next stage of his life – and then the king wakes up and is furious. Again a dramatic *coup de théâtre*. Persuaded that his son has made an honest mistake, father and son are reconciled in words that are at times both tender and touching. 'I never thought to hear you speak again,' says an emotional Hal. At one point, the king confesses his guilt:

> God knows, my son,
> By what by-paths and indirect crook'd ways
> I met this crown; and I myself know well
> How troublesome it sat upon my head.
>
> – Act 4, Scene 3

He then reminds Hal that in a move to unite the country in a common cause, he had a purpose 'To lead out many to the Holy Land', and gives him one last word of advice:

> Therefore, my Harry,
> Be it thy course to busy giddy minds
> With foreign quarrels ...
>
> – Act 4, Scene 1

This is, of course, a strategy long practised by political leaders throughout time, even today. So Henry V's much-vaunted divine mission to seize vast areas of France are, in truth, a political ploy masquerading as a worthy cause.[10] But that is for another chapter. When finally Prince Hal accedes to the throne, he appears in 'a new and gorgeous garment, majesty', and addresses the court in reassuring tones:

> Sits not so easy on me as you think.
> Brothers, you mix your sadness with some fear:
> This is the English, not the Turkish court;
> Not Amurath an Amurath succeeds,[11]
> But Harry Harry ...
>
> I'll be your father and your brother too;
> Let me but bear your love, I'll bear your cares ...
>
> – Act 5, Scene 15

That should be the end of the play – but guess who has to have the last word – or almost the last word? Falstaff, of course. When his old crony accosts him, calling out to him with the words 'My sweet boy!', King Henry V gives him this brutal brush off – 'I know thee not, old man. Fall to thy prayers'. He then banishes him on pain of death. Sorry, old man, there is no room for you in Shakespeare's next play: but for a Falstaff Revival, we must wait until 1599.

Several things are noteworthy about these two plays. We have noted the parallel worlds – the den of thieves at The Boar's Head, and the coterie of nobles vying for power in the palace, which has the effect of casting doubt on the concept of honour. Also remarkable is that the life of Sir John Oldcastle is much nearer that of Prince Hal than that of Falstaff; Falstaff remains unrepentant, the man he has always been, whereas it is Hal who progresses from ill-spent youth to a man with a sense of the numinous, even quoting the Bible, thus mirroring the career of Sir John Oldcastle from libertine to reformed character. But most significantly of all, in showing the infirmity of Henry IV, the diseases of the state, and the follies of the prince, Shakespeare takes a step towards undermining the mystique of monarchy – though he changes course somewhat in *Henry V*.

20

THE PRICE WE PAY FOR LOVE

> 'Fool,' said my Muse to me, 'look in thy heart and write'
> – Sir Philip Sidney, *Astrophel and Stella*

It is time to look at the next tranche of sonnets, numbers 1-60, which were written some time between the years 1595 and 1597.[1] Some of these sonnets express the emotional torment of an anguished lover. It will be recalled that Francis Meres writes in praise of Shakespeare's 'sugar'd sonnets' circulated among his private friends. For reasons to be explained, it is likely that Sonnets 1-17 were written in 1597, so we consider numbers 18-60 first.

Sonnets: 18-60

The first of these sonnets is possibly the finest Shakespeare ever wrote. It is certainly one of the most famous of his sonnets, and is probably the one that is most anthologized:

> Sonnet 18
> Shall I compare thee to a summer's day?
> Thou art more lovely and more temperate:
> Rough winds do shake the darling buds of May,
> And summer's lease hath all too short a date:
> Sometime too hot the eye of heaven shines,
> And often is his gold complexion dimmed,
> And every fair from fair sometime declines,

> By chance, or nature's changing course untrimmed:
> But thy eternal summer shall not fade,
> Nor lose possession of that fair thou ow'st,
> Nor shall death brag thou wander'st in his shade,
> When in eternal lines to time thou grow'st,
>> So long as men can breathe, or eyes can see,
>> So long lives this, and this gives life to thee.

Edmondson and Wells point out that this sonnet could be addressed to either a male or a female: most anthologists seem to assume that the addressee is a female. The jury is definitely, indeed, indefinitely, out on this, as no way can the question be decided. If Shakespeare is addressing a woman in this sonnet, it might be thought to sit oddly beside the very unromantic lustful and guilt-ridden Dark Lady sequence treated in Chapter 9. If addressed to a man, this accords with the other sonnets discussed in Chapter 12 – and those below.

These sonnets tell the story of a deeply loving, if one-sided, relationship between the writer of the sonnets and a fickle young man of noble birth – 'lord of my love' – sonnet 26. Many of them are so personal that readers may question whether Shakespeare ever intended them for publication. At the time they were written, they were probably just shared with his private friends, such as Francis Meres. It has been suggested that he may not have wanted them to be published because sodomy was, technically, against the law since at least the reign of Henry VIII; however, there were very few prosecutions.[2] In practice, close friendship between males was very common, and 'homosexuality' was not in the Tudor lexicon. One can only guess at how intimate his relationship was, and how far it existed only in his imagination. Margreta de Grazia has suggested that the sonnets are not actually homoerotic.[3] Barbara Everett also claims that the relationship was non-sexual,[4] but such arguments are tested to the limit by some of the lines quoted below:

> A woman's face with nature's own hand painted
> Hast thou, the master mistress of my passion
> A woman's gentle heart, but not acquainted
> With shifting change as is false woman's fashion ...

– Sonnet 20

> Being your slave, what should I do but tend
> Upon the hours and times of your desire?
> I have no precious time at all to spend
> Nor services to do, till you require ...
>
> – Sonnet 57

Who the young man might be is another question: a number of authorities have thought it possible that he was William Herbert, the future 3rd Earl of Pembroke, described by Duncan-Jones as 'a generous, lively highly literate young nobleman' to whom the First Folio of Shakespeare's plays was to be dedicated.[5]

Herbert, born in 1580, is the most likely candidate. However, as Greenblatt observes, there is no certainty about this.[6]

These sonnets are not only about love, but also as so often can be the case, about pain, the price we must sometimes pay for love. The relationship appears to have been all-too-short: Sonnet 33 begins a sequence of four that deal with a cooling relationship:

> But out, alack, he was but one hour mine;
> The region cloud hath masked him from me now.
> Yet him for this my love no whit disdaineth:
> Suns of the world may stain, when heaven's sun staineth[7]

By Sonnet 40 we learn the friend has taken away the poet's lover, the first of a sequence of three that lament his loss – and yet still find room for forgiveness:

> Take all my loves, my love yea, take them all
> What hast thou then more than thou hadst before?
> ...
> All mine was thine before thou hadst this more

And then to our surprise, in Sonnet 42, we find the poet's other love was a woman:

> That thou hast her, it is not all my grief
> And yet it may be said I lov'd her dearly

Who might she be? We just don't know. But this should not come as a surprise, as we have already seen (in Chapter 14) that Shakespeare was bisexual, and, no doubt, in Sir Ian McKellen's words, have, if necessary, 'got over it'.

Sonnets 1-17: the Procreation Sonnets

The standard theory has been that Shakespeare was asked to write Sonnets 1-17 to persuade a beautiful young man (often called 'the Fair Youth', presumed to be the Earl of Southampton) to get married and have children, and help to perpetuate his beauty. Why seventeen? Given the Tudor obsession with numerology, the assumption has often been made that the young man was seventeen – in Tudor times, considered the ideal time for a young man of noble birth to get married. So, a sonnet for every year. These lines give the gist:

> From fairest creatures we desire increase,
> That thereby beauty's rose might never die,
> But as the riper should by time decrease,
> His tender heir might bear his memory
>
> – Sonnet 1

And again:

> Look in thy glass, and tell the face thou viewest
> Now is the time that face should form another;
> Whose fresh repair if now thou not renewest,
> Thou dost beguile the world, unless some mother.
> For where is she so fair whose unear'd womb
> Disdains the tillage of thy husbandry?
>
> – Sonnet 3

It has often been asserted that the young earl's mother, the Countess, commissioned Shakespeare to write the sonnets, the reasoning being that he had already dedicated two best-selling poems to him. We have already noted that this is unlikely: Southampton was seventeen years old in 1590 – years before Shakespeare wrote those poems, and years before this group of sonnets was written (1595-7). It is also often assumed that the Fair Youth in the rest of the sonnets is Southampton. There is no reason to suppose that the male lover throughout these sonnets was always the same person: after 1594, as we have seen, there is no evidence that Shakespeare and the earl had any contact with each other.

Leo Daugherty, who wrote an account of the Earl of Derby's life for the *Oxford Dictionary of National Biography*, has another theory. He claims that William Stanley, the Sixth Earl of Derby (1561-1642), is the subject of these sonnets. Shakespeare, of course, became acquainted with William Stanley when he was involved in Lord Strange's Men. The problem with this theory is that Stanley wasn't very young when these sonnets were written. If, as is likely, the procreation sonnets were written for a young man in his late teens these poems would have been written many years earlier, in 1578, when Shakespeare was only about 15.

Another view propounded by Duncan-Jones,[8] J. Dover Wilson and many others puts William Herbert, the young Earl of Pembroke, in the frame. Born in 1580, for many years Herbert refused to get married, despite many attempts – at least four – to marry him off: the young man was a seriously reluctant bridegroom. In 1595, an attempt was made to arrange a marriage between Herbert and Elizabeth Carey, George Carey's daughter. The plan fell through, much to Carey's fury, because of the young man's 'not liking'. Then in 1597 another attempt was made, this time to marry him off to Bridget de Vere, granddaughter of Lord Burghley. Again, the plan failed. It

---

Mary Sidney, Countess of Pembroke, 1561-1621

One of the daughters of Sir Henry Sidney and his wife Mary Dudley, Mary Sidney's brother was the soldier/poet Sir Philip Sidney. The family were staunch Protestants.

Mary Sidney was exceptionally well-educated: she could speak or read half a dozen languages, she studied science and medicine, and was a respected poet: after her brother was killed in action after turning psalms 1-43 into poetry, she completed the remainder, displaying great technical skill. John Bodenham, writing in 1600, listed her along with Spenser and Shakespeare among England's top poets.[9]

Among her other literary words, she wrote a play, *Antonius*, on which a play by Daniel, and Shakespeare's *Antony and Cleopatra*, were based. Her house at Wilton in Wiltshire became the centre of a literary circle that included Spenser and Jonson. It appears Shakespeare was not invited, perhaps because of his anti-Puritan stance.

Mary married Henry Herbert, 2nd Earl of Pembroke (1538-1601) and had four children, one of whom died young; the others were William Herbert, the 3rd Earl of Pembroke, Anne Hutchinson, a writer, who translated Lucretius, and Philip Herbert. who became the 4th Earl on the death of William in 1630. William and Philip became the 'incomparable pair of brethren' to whom the First Folio of Shakespeare's plays was dedicated.

Mary Fitton, 1578-1641 (cropped, unknown

seems that he was simply averse to marriage, rather than women: as a twenty-year-old, he impregnated Mary Fitton, one of the queen's maids of honour, incurring Queen Elizabeth's fury. They both ended up in the Fleet prison, where the child, a boy, was still-born. Later, Herbert also had a prolonged affair with his cousin, Lady Mary Wroth, his mother's niece, and produced two children. It was not until 1604 that he finally married Lady Mary Talbot, and became a pillar of society: Lord Chamberlain (1615-1625), Chancellor of the University of Oxford, and, in 1624, a co-founder with King James of Pembroke College Oxford.

William Herbert's mother was the redoubtable Mary Sidney Herbert, Countess of Pembroke. One plausible theory is that in the late 1590s, Lady Mary was desperate for her son to marry. As sons are not famous for listening to their mothers, the suggestion is that she commissioned Shakespeare – or someone – to write the Procreation sonnets (Numbers 1-17) which urged her son William to marry. The dates fit: the sonnets were written around 1597, in time for the young man's eighteenth birthday the next year. However, the only connection we can be certain of between the countess and Shakespeare is that in the 1590s she wrote a letter in which she mentions, in passing, that 'we had the man Shakespeare with us'. This does not betoken a very intimate relationship: she makes him sound as though he was there to clean the chimney. Can one sense a note of irritation that an upstart playwright should seek to upstage her brother's poem, *Astrophel and Stella*, with two long poems of his own? She knew Shakespeare primarily as an actor/playwright, some of whose plays had in the past been performed by Pembroke's Men; and, indeed, we know that *As You Like It* was performed before King James at the countess's residence, Wilton House in December 1603.

However, how likely is it that the countess would have asked Shakespeare to write sonnets 1-17? There are three problems here. First, is it likely, in highly status-conscious Tudor England, that a countess would share a family problem with a mere actor/playwright, who is not even in her literary circle, and commission him to write seventeen sonnets to persuade her son to get married? To allow a commoner one hardly knows into the family confidence passes belief. Moreover, the poet who had written a highly erotic poem like *Venus and Adonis* would have been unacceptable to someone like the puritanical countess. Finally, if the earl knew who had written the sonnets, might he not think it an outrageous impudence?

If the countess was likely to ask anyone, it would have been someone from the Wilton Circle of writers who used to meet in her house, such as the poet Samuel Daniel, who had a far closer relationship with the Pembroke family than Shakespeare.[10] In 1592 he became part of the household in Wilton House, as well as the countess's literary circle. Having some claim to be a university man (he left Oxford without taking a degree) he was probably employed initially as a tutor to her daughter. Daniel claimed that the countess taught him how to write poetry. In 1592, inspired by Sir Philip Sidney's *Astrophel and Stella*, he wrote a sonnet sequence dedicated to the countess called *Delia, Containing Certain Sonnets: With the Complaint of Rosamond*, as well as closet drama for performance in Wilton House. He dedicated his sonnets to 'The Right Honourable Mary Countess of Pembroke'. Daniel is certainly a possibility, though the seventeen under consideration are a great deal better than his usual output. However, it should be noted that years before 1597 Daniel had parted company from Mary Sidney, and found a new patron in Charles Blount, Baron Mountjoy.

Another possibility: perhaps Shakespeare wrote them, and was not commissioned to do so by anyone? Well, if he wrote the other homoerotic sonnets, addressed to William Herbert, we have to assume that a young man in love with another would have wanted to persuade his lover to get married. Hmm, possible? Perhaps – but that is not the usual behaviour of a gay man. As C.S. Lewis observed, 'The incessant demand that the man should marry and found a family would seem to be inconsistent ... with a

The statue of William Herbert, 3rd Earl of Pembroke, outside the Bodleian Library, Oxford

real homosexual passion.'[11] Nor is writing seventeen sonnets full of unwanted advice the best way of retaining a friend. All in all, I think there is serious doubt as to whether Shakespeare was indeed the author of these seventeen sonnets.

While it is just possible that the countess asked Sam Daniel or another poet in the Wilton Circle to write these sonnets, a strong case could be made that they were written by the countess herself. Indeed, this case has been made by Robin Williams.[12] A highly accomplished poet and writer in her own right, Mary Sidney certainly had the ability to write them, the strongest motivation for writing them, and a greater emotional involvement than any poet she might have commissioned. She also had good reasons for concealing her identity. If one looks closely at these sonnets, they could easily be seen as a mother writing to her son, whom she addresses as 'love' and 'dear my love'; the author of one sonnet is 'all at war with time for love' of him. If one were to come across these sonnets for the first time, without the name of any author, and were asked who the likely author was, one would be more likely to guess 'a mother' rather than A.N. Other. Can one not sense a mother's love in lines like these?

> Thou art thy mother's glass, and she in thee
> Calls back the lovely April of her prime
>
> – Sonnet 3

> Make thee another self for love of me
> That beauty still may live in thine or thee
>
> – Sonnet 10

> ... dear my love, you know
> You had a father, let your son say so.
>
> – Sonnet 13

With Mary's close relationship with Sir Philip Sidney, it is not surprising that Katherine Duncan-Jones, in her Arden edition of *Shakespeare's Sonnets*, notes a number of echoes of Sir Philip's poems, with which, of course, the countess was very familiar. More evidence supporting her role in writing these sonnets comes in Sonnet 14. Mary Sidney had many intellectual interests, including science and astronomy. Hence:

> Not from the stars do I my judgment pluck,
> And yet methinks I have astronomy
>
> – Sonnet 14

The motivation for writing these sonnets would have been very strong for a loving mother. Her wayward son must have caused her great grief, for example, over his affair with Mary Fitton – to say nothing of the other women whose lives William Herbert may have blighted. Sadly, what may have been blighted is her relationship with her son: it is not unknown for a strong, somewhat controlling woman to overplay her hand with a wayward son, causing a rift. Anyway, it appears the sonnets were a failure, for there is no evidence that they had any effect on this reckless young man, who remained a ruthless womaniser.[13] Even so, the statue of William Herbert, Third Earl of Pembroke, still stands unstigmatised by iconoclasts outside the Bodleian Library in Oxford, and his name is perpetuated in the Oxford College.

There is a need to consider a suggestion that not all the sonnets in the 1609 publication *Shake-Speare's Sonnets* were indeed written by Shakespeare. In 1599, the publisher, William Jaggard, published an anthology called *The Passionate Pilgrim*: it contained 20 poems attributed on the title page to 'W. Shakespeare'. Most authorities believe that only five of them were by Shakespeare. (Duncan-Jones claims that only two of them – Sonnets 138 and 144, are definitely by him.)[14] We cannot assume, then, that all the sonnets in the 1609 publication – published by Thomas Thorpe – are by Shakespeare. Was Thorpe likely, after all, to determine the provenance of all the sonnets provided? Would he, in any case, have cared? More research is needed to resolve the issue.

Last word: two more theories

The case for the countess writing Sonnets 1-17 is presented very eloquently by Robin Williams, and indeed to my mind very plausibly. However, Williams then has a slightly different take; Williams suggests that the countess might have addressed these seventeen sonnets, not to her son, but to her brother, Sir Philip Sidney.[15] Mary Sidney was devoted to her brother, who entered the marriage stakes comparatively late, (he married Frances Walsingham in 1583, at the age of 29). Williams suggests as a possibility that she was concerned for his future happiness, and the future of the family name, and accordingly penned the procreation sonnets herself, urging him to marry. (She even poses the question that Sonnet 18 may have been written in mourning for her brother's untimely death at the age of 31 in the Battle of Zutphen in 1586.) This would mean that Sonnets 1-17 were written some time in the early 1580s before his marriage in 1583. Given the body of scholarship that indicates they were written some time in the late 1590s, this suggestion seems far-fetched. And why seventeen, one wonders? Our money would be on the son, not the brother. No apologies for the uncertainty! These questions are left to the reader to decide on the balance of probabilities.

Mary Herbert (née Sidney), Countess of Pembroke. Engraving by Simon van de Passe

A second theory bears much closer examination. In her book *Sweet Swan of Avon* Robin Williams makes out an even more radical, and apparently credible, case: perhaps the writer of *all* the sonnets was a woman – the Countess of Pembroke, no less. Williams points out that if the sonnets are autobiographical, they appear to fit the known facts of Mary Sidney's life – whereas we know little of the known facts of Shakespeare's private life.

What are these known facts as outlined by Williams?[16] First, in 1604, one Matthew Lister became the estate doctor at her family home at Wilton when the previous incumbent, Dr Moffet died. The countess fell deeply in love with Lister, and after her aged husband died, the doctor – ten years younger than the countess – became her constant companion. The countess had a niece, Mary Wroth, of whom she was very fond. Mary wrote a play called *Love's Secret*, with tactfully-chosen fictitious names (though Lister appears to have been 'Lineus'). The plot of the play could be interpreted as showing that the countess figure suspected that her niece was having an affair with Lister. In fact, she was not. It became apparent much later that she was, in fact, having an affair with Mary Sidney's son, William, by whom she had two children. This gives these lines from Sonnet 42 a different perspective:

> That thou hast her it is not all my grief,
> And yet it may be said I loved her dearly,
> That she hath thee is of my wailing chief,
> A loss in love that touches me more nearly.
>
> – Sonnet 42

Love's Secret was not written until 1618, long after the sonnets were published, and even longer after they were written, but that is not necessarily an objection.

The main objection to this elaborate theory is that Lister did not appear on the scene until 1604, long after most of these sonnets were written. Even so, a new reader coming fresh to the sonnets for the first time would not be surprised to be informed that the sonnets were all written by a woman. If one reads through the text of the sonnets, it is easy to imagine that they could be the voice of a woman passionately in love with a younger man. Readers might like to read these lines, making this assumption for a moment; very plausible, one might think, even though unprovable ...

> O, let me, true in love, but truly write,
> And then believe me, my love is as fair
> As any mother's child
>
> *— Sonnet 21*

> Now see what good turns eyes for eyes have done:
> Mine eyes have drawn thy shape, and thine for me
> Are windows to my breast, where-through the sun
> Delights to peep, to gaze therein on thee;
>
> *— Sonnet 24*

And if these lines were written by a woman, is there any indication that the writer is the Countess of Pembroke? Well, as has been noted, there are strong echoes of her brother's poems in the sonnets. At this point we leave the readers to make what they will of this tangled web of speculations. However, there is a strong case for the Countess of Pembroke, an accomplished writer in her own right, being the poet who wrote at least some of the sonnets. And what would have been so frustrating for the Countess was that no woman was deemed fit to write anything other than devotional poems, such as the psalms that Mary wrote with her brother. Williams suggests that she looks at the writing of poets like Spenser, and Shakespeare, and laments that she cannot hope to number herself in this pantheon, because she is a woman:

> Let those who are in favour with their stars
> Of public honour and proud titles boast,
> Whilst I, whom fortune of such triumph bars,
> Unlook'd for joy in that I honour most.
>
> *— Sonnet 25*

Mary Sidney must have felt deep frustrations in her 'outcast state' – as a woman in a man's world. This hugely talented poet would have found it so hard not to feel resentful that men could be given a voice denied to women. Was it she who in Sonnet 37 is 'made lame by fortune's dearest spite' (because she is a woman)?

Similar sentiments come in Sonnet 29:

> When, in disgrace with fortune and men's eyes,
> I all alone beweep my outcast state
> And trouble deaf heaven with my bootless cries
> And look upon myself and curse my fate,
> Wishing me like to one more rich in hope,
> Featured like him, like him with friends possess'd,
> Desiring this man's art and that man's scope,
> With what I most enjoy contented least;
> Yet in these thoughts myself almost despising,
> Haply I think on thee, and then my state,
> Like to the lark at break of day arising
> From sullen earth, sings hymns at heaven's gate;
> > For thy sweet love remember'd such wealth brings
> > That then I scorn to change my state with kings.

As a successful writer, Shakespeare, had no reason to write such lines – but a talented woman might well beweep her outcast state. Readers may or may not believe that this theory can be discounted, indeed, one could be forgiven for deciding that they are 'Much Ado about Nothing', to which we now turn.

21

MUCH ADO ON AND OFF STAGE

> Love is 'Like a fair house built on another man's ground; so that I have lost my edifice by mistaking the place where I erected it.'
> – Ford, in *Merry Wives of Windsor*, Act 2

Completed in early 1598, 2 *Henry IV* just made it into Francis Meres' list of Shakespeare's plays in *Palladis Tamia*, which appeared in September. It seems that Shakespeare may have finished writing the play in Stratford-upon-Avon – we know he was there in January and February 1598 because the town records list him as the owner of corn and malt, and a resident of Chapel Street ward, where New Place was situated.[1] He must surely have returned to London in March, to take part in a royal performance at Shrovetide – and also to see the publication of three other plays, including *Love's Labours Lost*, the first of his plays to carry his name on the title page.

Although he had been a tax defaulter in Bishopsgate for 1597, it seems he retained his lodgings there. Somehow, records show he also failed to pay taxes in 1598: the tax collectors who came knocking on Shakespeare's door (probably on 1 October 1598) left empty-handed, and 'Affid' (short for 'Affidavit') was written against Shakespeare's name.[2] It seems the tax collectors never caught up with him – perhaps he claimed to have paid tax in Stratford-upon-Avon? He does seem to have been a chronic tax-dodger.

At this time, London was buzzing with gossip: the Earl of Southampton had been having an affair with one of the queen's maids of honour, Elizabeth

Vernon, and had had a violent altercation with Sir Ambrose Willoughby. The earl, no doubt, felt that this was a good time to bolt, and in February he accompanied Sir Robert Cecil on a diplomatic mission in France, to negotiate with Henry IV. However, learning that Lady Elizabeth was pregnant, he secretly returned in August to marry her, before sailing back to France again to avoid the royal wrath. However, for him, there was no escape. The queen was furious when she heard the news: she dispatched Elizabeth Vernon to the Fleet prison, and ordered him to return. On his arrival, he was sent to join her in jail, and there, in November, she gave birth to a healthy baby girl, named Penelope, after Essex's older sister.

This was not the only drama – Southampton's friend, the Earl of Essex, was also in trouble. Essex was desperately angling to replace a visibly aging Burghley as the queen's chief minister, and not getting his own way over the appointment of a new Lord Deputy of Ireland, made an ugly face, and turned his back on the queen. Thereupon she slapped him – and he instinctively reached for the hilt of his sword. Raleigh reports that as Essex was led from the chamber, he was heard to call the queen (within her earshot) 'as crooked in her disposition as in her carcass'.[3] From now on, his days were numbered.

Around this time, Shakespeare may have written a short poem 'To the Queen'. Taylor and Loughnane suggest that it was written in February 1599, but I think that it may well have been written earlier – it is, after all, labelled 'to ye Q by ye players 1598.'[4] At this time, George Carey may have thought that *1 Henry IV* may have made too many enemies at court, particularly among the more earnest Protestants. He may have put it to Shakespeare that some fence-mending was in order by writing to ensure that the queen remained favourably disposed towards the Lord Chamberlain's Men.

George Carey,
2nd Lord Hunsdon

'To the Queen'

No other poem by Shakespeare like this exists, so he would have had a strong reason like that provided by Carey for writing it, second-rate as it is. It may have been read out at the Shrovetide entertainment in March, perhaps as an insurance policy, really. This was the result:

> As the dial hand tells o'er
> The same hours it had before,
>
> Still beginning in the ending,
> Circular account still lending,
>
> So, most mighty Queen we pray,
> Like the dial day by day
>
> You may lead the seasons on,
> Making new when old are gone,

And so it continues for another ten lines: definitely not vintage Shakespeare. As Jonathan Bate suggests, it looks as if it was written on the back of an envelope; even so, he still includes the poem in his Royal Shakespeare Company edition of the *Complete works* (2007).[5] Not everyone thinks this poem is by Shakespeare, but I think that it is, because it was found as recently as 1972 among the papers of one Henry Stanford, a member of George Carey's household.[6] The poem may have been read out as an epilogue following a performance by the Lord Chamberlain's Men. Who else would have written it but the troupe's resident playwright? In the event, it may not have been necessary, for the performance of *2 Henry IV* was well received; indeed the story goes that the queen was so delighted with the Falstaff character that she later called on Shakespeare to write another play, about Falstaff in love. Which, eventually, he did. But not yet: he probably thought that after his brush with the censor over *Henry IV*, it was best to put Falstaff into storage for the time being, and play safe with a light comedy that did not feature Sir John.

Much Ado About Nothing

The only other play completed at this time was *Much Ado About Nothing*. Taylor and Loughnane's best guess is that it was written in mid to late 1598, (just too late to appear on Francis Meres' list). The earliest printed version of the text appeared as a quarto in 1600.[7] The title page reads *Much adoe about Nothing: as it hath been sundrie times publikly acted by the right honourable, the Lord Chamberlaine his servants. Written by William Shakespeare.* The homely title could just mean 'a big fuss over nothing', or it could have a touch of the bawdy about it, in that *nothing* could be used to refer to a woman's vulva.[8] Indeed, the play is full of salacious jokes and *double entendres*, with sundry references to cuckolding. The play is possibly Shakespeare's most popular comedy, and has been performed many times, in an extraordinary range of different settings – there has been a Tex-Mex version in the US, another set in pre-Castro Cuba, and yet another in the days of the British Raj in India; a 2022 production in London's National Theatre set it in an art nouveau holiday hotel in Messina.

There is evidence that the play was written somewhat hurriedly: the quarto version appears to have been based on 'foul papers' – an early draft, or perhaps an acting copy – or even a pirated copy. Like *The Merrie Wives of Windsor*, reputably also written hurriedly, much of the play is in prose, and thus belongs to Shakespeare's 'prose period' that ends with *Twelfth Night*. The quarto version contains many errors: a number of characters appear or disappear without any stage direction – and indeed one or two

Hero being denounced at her wedding. Engraving: Peter Simon.

don't even exist. Occasionally there is a slip of the quill, and so Dogberry is named 'Kempe' at some point, though Kempe was to leave the company in 1599.

All that said, Shakespeare shows that he is as adept at prose as poetry in the exchanges between Benedick and Beatrice – which could be seen as a role reversal of Katherine and Petruchio in *Shrew*: for Beatrice constantly gets the better of Benedick, who at times struggles to keep up. We need look no further than past history to see the reasons for Beatrice's hostility – an affair, which Benedick ducked out of:

> BENEDICK: O God, sir, here's a dish I love not: I cannot endure my Lady Tongue. (*Exit*)
> DON PEDRO: Come, lady, come; you have lost the heart of Signior Benedick.
> BEATRICE: Indeed, my lord, he lent it me awhile; and I gave him use for it, a double heart for his single one: marry, once before he won it of me with false dice, therefore your grace may well say I have lost it.

Yes, the pair have a history ... One is reminded of the line 'Hell hath no fury like a woman scorned' attributed somewhat inaccurately to Congreve's 1697 play *The Mourning Bride*. Amid the badinage and bawdiness, there is an underlying but unmistakeable note of cynicism. The song Balthazar sings to Benedick gives women little comfort:

> Sigh, no more, ladies, sigh no more
> Men were deceivers ever,
> One foot in sea, and one on shore,
> To one thing constant never.
>
> – Act 2, Scene 3

Even so, the verbal duel between Benedick and Beatrice has generated great enjoyment among audiences (and indeed the actors who performed the roles) and the play has sometimes been renamed using their names. However, there are other less attractive reasons for making this play memorable. Although the play supposedly is set in Messina, Sicily, the action is seen through the lens of Tudor England: a male lens. The play starts with a messenger bringing news that Don Pedro, Prince of Aragon, is soon to return from a war (only a small war, with not many dead, and none of any note ...). He is accompanied by Count Claudio who apparently did 'the feats of a lion' in battle. Beatrice asks if one Signior Mountanto is also on his way: the messenger says he too is arriving, 'as pleasant as ever he was'. The man she calls Signior Mountanto turns out to be an old flame, Benedick. Her sardonic response casting doubt on his valour and virtue indicates hostility:

> I pray you, how many hath he killed and eaten
> in these wars? But how many hath he killed? For
> indeed I promised to eat all of his killing.

Yet why does she show any interest in whether he returns or not? We already have a sense of her ambivalence. As her uncle Leonato, the governor of Messina observes, 'There is a kind of merry war betwixt Signor Benedick and her.'

On the arrival of the soldiers, Leonato invites Don Pedro to stay, and the prince introduces his half-brother, Don John. Meanwhile Claudio is attracted to Leonato's daughter, Hero: 'That I love her, I feel,' he declares, cautiously. Prudently, he then asks if Hero has a brother, and learning that she is the sole heir to a fortune, it seems he loves her even more. Rather oddly, he asks Don Pedro to woo Hero on his behalf. One wonders if he thinks he is less persuasive and sincere than the prince could be.

Meanwhile, Benedick and Beatrice join battle in their 'merry war':

> BEATRICE: I wonder that you will still be talking, Signior Benedick: nobody marks you.
> BENEDICK: What, my dear Lady Disdain! are you yet living?
> BEATRICE: Is it possible disdain should die while she hath such meet food to feed it as Signior Benedick? Courtesy itself must convert to disdain, if you come in her presence.
> BENEDICK: Then is courtesy a turncoat. But it is certain I am loved of all ladies, only you excepted: and I would I could find in my heart that I had not a hard heart; for, truly, I love none.
> BEATRICE: A dear happiness to women: they would else have been troubled with a pernicious suitor.
>
> – Act 1, Scene 1

These verbal battles persist throughout the play, until both participants (and some of us in the audience) are exhausted. The vitriol continues at the ensuing masked ball, when Benedick yearns to be spared the company of 'Lady Tongue'. It is here that Don Pedro sets about his task of wooing Hero on Claudio's behalf, pretending to be Claudio. Don John, who appears to be motivated by nothing except malice, suggests to Claudio that Don Pedro is wooing Hero for himself. The seeds of distrust are sown: but nevertheless, the marriage between Claudio and Hero is arranged.

Benedick makes it clear that he is a committed bachelor, and in consequence, Beatrice puts on an attitude to the idea of marriage as cynical as Benedick's. 'For hear me, Hero,' she says:

> wooing, wedding, and repenting, is as a Scotch jig,
> a measure, and a cinque pace: the first suit is hot
> and hasty, like a Scotch jig, and full as
> fantastical; the wedding, mannerly-modest, as a
> measure, full of state and ancientry; and then comes
> repentance and, with his bad legs, falls into the
> cinque pace faster and faster, till he sink into his grave.[9]
>
> – Act 2, Scene 1

Methinks the lady doth protest too much. Does Hero catch the whiff of sour grapes? Possibly; but both Hero and Don Pedro suspect that despite the verbal jousting, Benedick and Beatrice have feelings for each other. In two memorably comic scenes they arrange for both to overhear

---

The Misuse of Shakespeare?

Shakespeare finds his way into many highways and by-ways of modern culture – his name, his image, his words, even, appear in countless contexts – from gin to jam, from the mass media to merchandise. It seems Shakespeare even infiltrated the US military: apparently, the medical staff working at Guantanamo Bay chose Shakespearian pseudonyms in order to conceal their identity. The *dramatis personae* of Guantanamo Bay's medical team includes Senior Medical Officer: *aka* Leonato (from *Much Ado*)

Reporting the information, Dominic Dromgoole and Human Rights activist Clive Stafford Smith[10] noted that Leonato is a man 'given to violent outbursts, usually because he allows unreliable evidence to lead him to mistaken conclusions.' They got that right, given Leonato's appalling treatment of Hero at her wedding.

As Dromgoole and Stafford Smith observe, 'It is hard to see why any of these names seemed like a good idea. When the curtain falls on these characters there isn't likely to be much applause.'

Catherine Tate (Beatrice) and David Tennant (Benedick) in Josie Rourkes's production of *Much Ado About Nothing* (2011)

conversations, indicating that each is pining for the other. The sparring couple are both delighted to learn this, but old habits die hard, and their verbal battles continue, albeit half-heartedly, as jokes at each other's expense gradually turn into flirtation – the kind of verbal mutation at which Shakespeare excelled.

Don John meanwhile sets about wrecking the wedding plans between Hero and Claudio. Iago-like, he tells Don Pedro and Claudio that Hero is unfaithful, and arranges for them to come with him one night to observe at a distance as a serving woman dressed like Hero (a servant, Margaret) appears at the window of Hero's bedchamber, chatting with one of his men (Borachio in disguise). Claudio and Don Pedro evince criminal readiness to be deceived, and his wicked plan succeeds: they are convinced that Hero is having an affair. Duly shocked, Claudio decides to publicly humiliate Hero at the wedding ceremony.

A scene almost too painful to watch ensues. At the church, Leonato agrees to give Claudio his daughter 'As freely, son, as God did give her me'. In a shocking, brutal moment in the play, when all are gathered to celebrate the wedding, in front of the altar, Claudio levels this accusation:

> CLAUDIO: What man was he talked with you yesternight
>   Out at your window betwixt twelve and one?
> HERO: I talked with no man at that hour my lord.
> PRINCE: Why then, you are no maiden ...
>
> – Act 4, Scene 4

These lines, and other references in the play, foreshadow *Troilus and Cressida*, and reflect the readiness of a patriarchal culture to perceive women as duplicitous and promiscuous.[11] Claudio then brutally rejects Hero :

> There, Leonato, take her back again:
> Give not this rotten orange to your friend;
> She's but the sign and semblance of her honour.
> Behold how like a maid she blushes here!
>   ... Would you not swear,
> All you that see her, that she were a maid,
> By these exterior shows? But she is none:
> She knows the heat of a luxurious bed;
> Her blush is guiltiness, not modesty.
>
> – Act 4, Scene 4

Her father, Leonato, not only disowns her, he threatens to tear her with his own hands in what amounts to an honour killing. Hero, appalled, and humiliated, tries to declare her innocence, and then collapses in a faint. Leonato's response? He wishes she were dead:

> O Fate! take not away thy heavy hand.
> Death is the fairest cover for her shame
> That may be wish'd for

Claudio and Don Pedro – and even Hero's own father – choose to doubt her word against that of one of Don John's serving men. On the thinnest of evidence, the men (who all almost certainly hath 'one foot in sea, the other on shore'), embark on a process of hypocritical and self-righteous slut-shaming: they denounce the poor young woman as 'an approved[12] wanton': and a 'common stale'. Benedick produces the biggest and most inappropriate understatement in the whole of Shakespeare: 'This looks not like a nuptial.' However, perhaps sensing a disapproving look by Beatrice, he expresses surprise – and doubt. Hero's only friend and ally is Beatrice.

How is this very ugly, indeed, painful, situation to be resolved? Beatrice's solution is brutally simple. In a scene fraught with drama, she demands that if Benedick loves her, he should prove it. How? 'Kill Claudio!' is her chilling reply. Suddenly, the verbal jousting we have come to expect turns murderous. Benedick reluctantly agrees to challenge his friend.

However, a friar comes up with a better solution; in a plot line reminiscent of *Romeo and Juliet*, he proposes that they should pretend that Hero has died, so causing Claudio to feel sorrow and remorse. Leonato is smitten with guilt and grief at the news, while all are shocked when Benedick, such a 'pleasant fellow', challenges Claudio to a duel, denouncing his friend as a villain who has killed an innocent and sweet lady. A moment to savour, in Shakespeare, when love for a woman trumps friendship with a man ...

The *deus ex machina* is one of the most improbable in the whole of Shakespeare: Dogberry (a seriously bad joke who only has one joke in his linguistic armoury, the malapropism) arrives, along with his crony Verges and their motley crew of constables: in a rare display of competence they have arrested Borachio and his fellow-crook, who confess everything: Hero was entirely innocent.

The play lurches to its improbable end: Leonato punishes Claudio by inviting him to marry his niece instead of his daughter. Claudio opts out of a weird musical ritual honouring the dead Hero and watches other lords perform it instead: so feeble a man, just as he asked Don Pedro to woo Hero on his behalf, he gets others to mourn her death. Benedick, on the eve of his own marriage to Beatrice, thinks it appropriate to indulge in some sexually charged badinage with Margaret, the serving woman, who somehow escapes justice for taking part in Don John's wicked conspiracy.

In a gesture of male solidarity, Benedick generously reclaims Claudio as his best friend. Leonato asks Claudio if he is still willing to settle for his niece as a substitute for the dead Hero, and Claudio stoutly declares he will marry her even if she is an Ethiope, adding a touch of racism to his other unpleasant characteristics. He then asks as the ladies appear in church

> Which is the lady I must seize I upon?

For him clearly, marriage is a process of asset acquisition, and women are there to be seized upon; and when the moment comes for the bridal veil to be raised, he discovers his bride to be Hero – surprise, surprise, not dead after all ... Unbelievably, much to the disappointment of a modern audience, Hero appears to be very happy with the arrangement and shows no sign of resentment at being publicly humiliated by this appalling specimen of manhood who is about to seize upon her.

Much Ado is a 'marmite' play: some people love it, and it has remained a popular part of the Shakespeare repertoire. Others find the badinage between Beatrice and Benedick tiresome, and the acquiescence of Hero a kind of betrayal. For the sexual politics are clear: this is a culture dominated by men, and only a brave woman (like Beatrice) can confront it. Throughout the play there are jocular references to cuckoldry, betraying an almost obsessive male anxiety about female sexuality.

For many of us, the abiding memory of this play may not be the exchanges between Benedick and Beatrice, but the cruelty of men who are all-too-ready to believe in the guilt of innocent women. They come out of this play in a very bad light. The real hero of the play is Beatrice. Certainly, the play foreshadows certain elements of modern sub-culture represented on social media by 'trolls': the victimisation of females, ill-informed judgmentalism, finger pointing, slut-shaming, virtue claiming, and spuriously claiming the high moral ground. Yet again, we should look in a mirror to consider how far modern society has progressed.

Bad news

The real dramas were taking place off-stage: three successive wet summers – and two devastating fires – had resulted in a grain shortage, and severe local hardship, in Stratford-upon-Avon. Around this time Shakespeare's friend Richard Quiney spent four months in London to petition the Court to give the town tax relief, and financial assistance. During his stay in the city, Quiney had run up debts, and short of money, in October 1598 wrote to his friend Shakespeare asking for a loan. However, it appears he never sent the letter, for it was found among his papers after he died.[13] In the event, a loan was not needed: Queen Elizabeth agreed to assist 'this town twice afflicted and almost wasted by fire', and Quiney was reimbursed his expenses for his London trip.

Meanwhile, Shakespeare and the Lord Chamberlain's Men were facing a crisis. The lease on the theatre with their landlord, Giles Allen, had expired in April 1597, and it was closed. The Lord Chamberlain's Men still put on plays at the Curtain, but the venue was run-down, and was much less popular, and revenue began to tail off. Greenblatt suggests that the situation became so desperate that the company sold off their most popular playbooks to an enterprising publisher.[14] Shakespeare and his troupe were under severe financial pressure. Perhaps he had taken a step too far with the purchase of New Place?

Worse was to come: their hostile landlord, Giles Allen, was threatening to pull down the theatre and 'to convert the wood and timber thereof to some better use.'[15] The threat of losing the theatre at Shoreditch, spelt financial ruin. Richard and Cuthbert Burbage came up with a solution: by December 1598 they had found a suitable location on Bankside, south of the river, and negotiated a lease. Time to act, there was no time to lose: Allen could start tearing the theatre down at any time. Learning that Allen had gone to his country home in Essex to celebrate Christmas, the Lord Chamberlain's Men seized their opportunity.[16]

So it was that on a snowy night in December 1598, the players gathered in Shoreditch armed with lanterns, and tools to dismantle the theatre – as well as 'swords, daggers, bills, axes and such like' to fight off anyone who tried to stop them. In the freezing temperature it was hard work, and it had to be quick, in case the landlord's men arrived to join battle. They loaded the heavy timbers onto wagons, which carted them down to the Thames;

Second Globe Theatre (detail from Hollar's *View of London*, 1647. Hollar sketched the building from life)

there was no way of rescuing the tiles. To this day, builders working nearby have found the shattered remnants of the theatre's tiles embedded in the earth – some of them can be seen in the Museum of London. The operation was very complicated: ideally, barges would have quickly transported the timbers across the river to their new site on Bankside, in Southwark, south of the river. But the Thames had half frozen over, and any attempt to slide the heavy timbers across the ice was too dangerous. Instead, the timbers were stored in a riverside warehouse. It was not until late spring that the timbers were reassembled on the new site, and the tiles of the roof replaced with thatch: the Globe Theatre was born.[17]

A furious Giles Allen sued them for trespass, but the Lord Chamberlain's Men had carried out an almost unbelievable *fait accompli*. Thanks to the efforts of the players' gifted carpenter, Peter Street, the Globe was up and running by June 1599, and a new phase in Shakespeare's life opened up. It was around this time that Shakespeare may have moved from Bishopsgate to find new lodgings on Bankside, south of the river, to be near his theatre. How long he lodged in this marshy, insalubrious area is questionable, but it is likely that he stayed long enough to ensure that his new project was taking shape, and achieving success.[18]

22

WHEREFORE WAR?

'The game's afoot, follow your spirit'

– Henry V, Act 3, Scene 1

Shakespeare spent much of the early months of 1599 in London supervising the construction of the Globe – and finalising business arrangements. He was one of the theatre's six share-holders – the other five were the Burbage brothers, John Heminges, Augustine Phillips, and Thomas Pope. (William Kempe opted out, and left the company.)[1] The Globe was situated on marshy land just south of Maiden Lane (and Park Street): the site is now nos. 67-69 Anchor Terrace, on the east side of Southward Bridge Road. It was so close to the river that it was in danger of being flooded at high tide. Shakespeare also needed to complete his next play. Taylor and Loughnane think it is probable that *Henry V* was written in the spring of this year.[2] The Globe was ready to open in late May or early June, and Shakespeare surely wanted to launch the new theatre with a blockbuster: what the audience would like was a victorious hero, lots of action, a successful war, preferably against the Spanish or French, and a burst of patriotism: nothing like a victorious campaign to entertain the London crowds.

The timing of *Henry V* was just right, for the news from Ireland was awful, made worse no doubt by our old enemy Rumour. In 1597, heavy losses had been incurred in Ireland, and in 1598, an English army was cut to pieces by the Irish rebels, led by Tyrone. Many English settlements –

plantations, as they were called – were devastated and their owners murdered or put to flight.³ The Earl of Essex was put in charge of a large army, and on 27 March 1598 cheering crowds hailed his departure from London: with him went the Earl of Southampton. A play like *Henry V* was just what was needed in 1599 to attract a big audience – to cheer up the nation by beating a patriotic drum. The Chorus at the start of Act 5 alludes to the earl's (hopefully triumphant) return, and helps to date the play:

> Were now the general of our gracious empress,
> As in good time he may, from Ireland coming,
> Bringing rebellion broached on his sword,
> How many would the peaceful city quit,
> To welcome him!
>
> – Act 5, Scene 1

The story-line of *Henry V* was a given, based as it was on Holinshed's *Chronicles* (published in 1587) and Halle's *Union* (1548), though as usual Shakespeare departed from the narratives when, and if, he thought it dramatically appropriate. The old play *The Famous Victories of Henry V* performed by the Queen's Men in the eighties also fed into the narrative, as did Samuel Daniel's poem *The Civil Wars* (1595). Shakespeare's imagination as to what the play could include went far beyond what was possible to display on the stage. His strategy for coping with this staging problem was to work on the audience's 'imaginary forces' as indicated in the Chorus's famous opening lines:

> O for a Muse of fire, that would ascend
> The brightest heaven of invention,
> A kingdom for a stage, princes to act
> And monarchs to behold the swelling scene!
> Then should the warlike Harry, like himself,
> Assume the port of Mars; and at his heels,
> Leash'd in like hounds, should famine, sword and fire
> Crouch for employment ...
> ... can this cockpit hold
> The vasty fields of France? or may we cram
> Within this wooden O the very casques
> That did affright the air at Agincourt?
>
> – Act 1, Scene 1

A few actors stumbling round the stage clutching swords and shields to represent a war between armies would no longer do: they would diminish rather than enhance the imaginative powers of the audience. Perhaps he recalled the gentle mockery of the *Henry VI* plays by Ben Jonson:

> ... or, with three rusty swords
> And help of some few foot and half-foot words,
> Fight over York and Lancaster's long jars,
> And in the tiring-house bring wounds to scars[4]

Shakespeare had to depend on a 'Muse of fire', the power of words with all the rhetorical flourishes necessary, to bring to life many different events and places in the mind's eye of the audience. Those of us who have seen films of the play – such as Olivier's 1944 classic, with Walton's stirring music find it easy to envisage what the play describes. Tudor audience had no such prompts to stretch their imaginations.

Flying the flag

1599 was not the first or the last time that *Henry V* was performed to lift the spirits of the nation. It has often been revived at times of national crisis or stress – notably the French-assisted Jacobite rebellion of 1745, and the Anglo-Boer War, 1899-1902.

Kenneth Branagh's film (1989), full of brutality and blood, had a different take: apparently, he thought that the play should be reclaimed from jingoism: not surprising that it came out after the controversial Falklands War (1982),[5] which, like the Battle of Waterloo, was in the Duke of Wellington's words 'the nearest run thing you ever saw.'

The play still resonates today. On 4 June 2004 Adrianna Huffington compares Henry's war in France with the US-led invasion of Iraq in 2003.[6] Concluding that both wars were immoral, she comments: 'I've found *Henry V* contains far more truth about our present situation than anything coming out of the White House or the Pentagon.'[7] Comparisons may be odious, but it is also hard not to compare Henry V's campaign with that of Putin's invasion of Ukraine in 2022.

Depicting *Henry V* as an anti-war drama is relatively easy: it is much harder to see it as 'pro-peace'. The British roving theatre group *Antic Disposition* set the play in World War 1 – and the opening scene showed wounded English and French soldiers being hurried to a Field Hospital to be tended. The patients (and staff) then put on *Henry V* as a kind of occupational therapy. *Antic Disposition* took the production on tour in France; a French woman came up after one production saying 'I see now. This is not a play about England and France at war. It is about peace.' *C'est incroyable*, you might think ... But it worked, and was rather moving.

The massive scale of the bloodshed inflicted on the French, the pitched battles and desperate assaults are summoned to our imagination by words alone.

If Henry has moral scruples about invading another country, they are easily dispelled by the Archbishop of Canterbury and the Bishop of Ely, who, when asked by the king 'May I with right and conscience make this claim to the throne of France?' are happy to urge him on 'with blood and sword and fire to win your right' (the tenuous claim originated from the time of Henry's great-grandfather Edward III). Henry then believes, or wants to believe, that his war has the blessing of the Almighty; it should come as no surprise that the word *God* appears 72 times in the play.[8]

The political becomes personal when the French ambassador arrives, with an insulting gift of tennis balls from the Dauphin. King Henry, no doubt inwardly furious, maintains a dignified calm:

Laurence Olivier as Henry V in his 1944 film with Renée Asherson as Princess Katherine

> We are glad the Dauphin is so pleasant with us;
> His present and your pains we thank you for:
> When we have march'd our rackets to these balls,
> We will, in France, by God's grace, play a set
> Shall strike his father's crown into the hazard
>
> — Act 1, Scene 3

This 'pleasant prince' 'hath turn'd his balls to gun-stones', and needs no further excuse to invade France. Henry then faces another test. En route to France, in Southampton, he is in the company of three men he knows to be traitors – the Earl of Cambridge, Lord Scroop, and Sir Thomas Grey. These men are dangerous, yet he talks calmly and courteously to them; and asks Exeter about a man

> That rail'd against our person: we consider
> it was excess of wine that set him on;
> And on his more advice we pardon him.
>
> — Act 2, Scene 2

He proposes to 'enlarge' the man – to set him free. However, the three traitors, keen as they are to demonstrate their love and loyalty to Henry, all urge him to show the wretch no mercy. Henry then begins to twist the knife – we know more than the three traitors what is coming – in a speech heavy with impending irony:

> Alas, your too much love and care of me
> Are heavy orisons 'gainst this poor wretch!
> If little faults, proceeding on distemper,
> Shall not be wink'd at, how shall we stretch our eye
> When capital crimes, chew'd, swallow'd and digested,
> Appear before us? We'll yet enlarge that man,
> Though Cambridge, Scroop and Grey, in their dear care
> And tender preservation of our person,
> Would have him punished.
>
> — Act 2, Scene 2

He then hands out his marching orders – 'Read them,' he says, 'and know I know your worthiness'. The three open them and are horrified to find that they are their death warrants. Yes, Shakespeare certainly knows how to create dramatic debacles! The men are marched off to be executed, as the Tudor audience, no doubt, howls derision after them.

By now, no history play was complete without some low life. Interwoven with these dramas, we have reminders of the picaresque scenes from Henry's past. They feature Messrs Bardolph, Pistol, Nym and 'Boy', not forgetting the hostess, Mistress Quickly. The audience would definitely have enjoyed their bickering and boozing, only marred by the death, off-stage, of Sir John Falstaff. In dropping him from the cast list, perhaps Shakespeare thought it better to recall him larger than life, rather than show him fading away on his deathbed.

With Henry's murky past long forgotten, we have a view in these opening scenes of a monarch, calm and in control, and in seemingly effortless command: he cooly despatches traitors, and confidently sends his ambassador, Exeter, to demand that the King of France hand over the keys to his kingdom. He also, incidentally, warns the Dauphin that he will pay for his insult. The French King tries to buy off the English: on offer, a few minor dukedoms, the hand of his daughter Katherine with a handsome dowry: to no avail – the war is on.

Oh what a lovely war it was not.[9] The scene shifts to Harfleur, billed as a triumph, but it was so nearly a disaster for Henry's army.[10] All was not going to plan: the town put up a stiff resistance. This is the scene where Henry displays his qualities of leadership, urging on his men with some reverse psychology:

> Once more unto the breach, dear friends, once more;
> Or close the wall up with our English dead.
> ...
>   The game's afoot:
> Follow your spirit, and upon this charge
> Cry 'God for Harry, England, and Saint George!'
>   – Act 3, Scene 1

Not for the last time, words have to be a substitute for action. So we don't see a Shakespearian stage army rushing onto and off the stage to attack Harfleur. Instead, we see three squaddies lying low in a fox-hole, palpably unwilling to add their bodies to the breach in the city wall: the old lags are Bardolph, Pistol and Nym, along with the Boy. Bardolph very unconvincingly urges the skivers on: 'On, on, on, on, on! to the breach, to the breach!' he exclaims, but shows no sign of leading the way, or indeed bringing up the rear. The Boy's response to this invitation is understandable:

> Would I were in an alehouse in London! I would give
> all my fame for a pot of ale and safety.
>
> – Act 3, Scene 2

Henry's choice between victory, or adding one's corpse to the breach, appears uninviting, indeed, quite mad, and certainly implies that war can easily become a kind of madness. Many of us may feel that Shakespeare gets this right, here. Nevertheless, the charge no doubt takes place, albeit off-stage. Fluellen then arrives, rounding up defaulters – 'Avaunt, you scullions!' he roars, and sends them packing. Only the Boy is left on stage, to offer the audience a succinct thumb-nail portrait of the scullions, although his word for them is *swashers*.[11] (Sadly the Boy is later slaughtered by the French – yes, he should have stayed in that ale-house).

Back to the king: attempts to reduce the town walls by mining are evidently not working out, and we soon discover that beneath the calm exterior there is cold and potentially bloody steel. He delivers this ultimatum:

>   you men of Harfleur,
> Take pity of your town and of your people,
> Whiles yet my soldiers are in my command;
> Whiles yet the cool and temperate wind of grace
> O'erblows the filthy and contagious clouds
> Of heady murder, spoil and villany.
> If not, why, in a moment look to see
> The blind and bloody soldier with foul hand
> Defile the locks of your shrill-shrieking daughters;
> Your fathers taken by the silver beards,
> And their most reverend heads dash'd to the walls,
> Your naked infants spitted upon pikes,
> Whiles the mad mothers with their howls confused
> Do break the clouds, as did the wives of Jewry
> At Herod's bloody-hunting slaughtermen.
> What say you? will you yield, and this avoid,
> Or, guilty in defence, be thus destroy'd?
>
> – Act 3, Scene 3

What happened to chivalry, his much-vaunted sense of control? Are these threats consistent with England's oldest chivalric order, the Order of the Garter? We do not know how Shakespeare's audience would have reacted to these lines, but many of them would have been aware of the massacres of townsfolk by the King of Spain's troops in the Low Countries, when they ran amok – events known as the Spanish Fury.[12] Henry does not appear in a very attractive light at this point, a definite blot on his escutcheon. The best one could say is that when the Governor of Harfleur finally surrenders, Henry places the Duke of Exeter in charge of the city, and orders him to offer mercy to all.

At this point we learn that Pistol is an 'arrant, counterfeit rascal', and Bardolf is to be hanged for robbing from a church. Henry is unmoved, and issues orders that thankfully seem at odds with his threats to the good people of Harfleur:

> We would have all such offenders so cut off: and we give express charge, that in our marches through the country, there be nothing compelled from the villages, nothing taken but paid for, none of the French upbraided or abused in disdainful language; for when lenity and cruelty play for a kingdom, the gentler gamester is the soonest winner.
>
> – Act 3, Scene 6

In the French camp, all is not well: Princess Katherine, has little faith in the military prowess of her brother, the Dauphin, and senses that a command of English might stand her in good stead. Accordingly, in a scene mainly written in French, she is seen taking an English lesson from her maid; Shakespeare has great fun turning the lesson into something of a bawdy joke.

Meanwhile, the Constable of France and other nobles meet to prepare for battle at Agincourt: they are longing for the next day to dawn, so confident are they that they can defeat the perfidious English invaders. The chauvinism of Shakespeare's vision is tempered with a certain amount of respect for the nobility, despite their arrogance; his picture of the Dauphin on the other hand is very different – he is caricatured as a fop. Instead of working out a battle plan, he starts to recite a sonnet in praise of his horse, and is interrupted by the Duke of Orleans to save him further embarrassment. As for Charles VI, he is seen as barely able to cope with events.[13]

In contrast to the French, before the Battle of Agincourt, Henry and his men are shown to be thoughtful, with no illusions about the human costs of war. Henry is humanised by moments of doubt. He asks Sir Thomas Erpingham to leave him for 'I and my bosom must debate awhile'. His experience at the tavern in Eastcheap has no doubt played a part in his recognition that

> ... the king is but a man, as I am: the violet smells to him as it doth to me: the element shows to him as it doth to me; all his senses have but human conditions: his ceremonies laid by, in his nakedness he appears but a man; and though his affections are higher mounted than ours, yet, when they stoop, they stoop with the like wing
>
> –Act 4, Scene 1

Accordingly, Henry addresses his men, nobles or commoners, as 'friends'. As he wanders, incognito, around the English camp on the night before the battle, he chats with a group of squaddies round a camp fire. When one speaks disparagingly of the king, he does his best to mount a defence, 'his cause being just, and his quarrel honourable.' 'That's more than we know,' says one, Williams, with the cynicism shared by so many soldiers in battle. He then gives Henry pause for thought:

> But if the cause be not good, the king himself hath a heavy reckoning to make, when all those legs and arms and heads, chopped off in battle, shall join together at the latter day and cry all 'We died at such a place'; some swearing, some crying for a surgeon, some upon their wives left poor behind them, some upon the debts they owe, some upon their children rawly left. I am afeard there are few die well that die in a battle; for how can they charitably dispose of any thing, when blood is their argument? Now, if these men do not die well, it will be a black matter for the king that led them to it; whom to disobey were against all proportion of subjection.
>
> – Act 4, Scene 1

We all know the outcome of the battle: Agincourt is won by Henry's army, and the flower of French chivalry perish. Estimates vary, but it is likely that some 6,000 French were killed, and only around 300 of Henry's army. Henry's archers (many of whom were Welsh) played a key part in his victory. Indeed, most prominent among his soldiers was a Welshman, Fluellen – possibly Shakespeare was doffing his cap to the Earl of Pembroke, who had strong Welsh roots. A feature of the play is the fact that all four nations were represented in Henry's army – the English captain, Gower, and captains from Wales, Scotland and Ireland. This may perhaps have indicated Shakespeare's hope that one day they might all become one. Of course, this was all grist to the mill for the World War 2 propagandists as they made the film of *Henry V*. It was just perhaps a pity that the enemy at Agincourt were French, not Nazis.

Today, we might like to think that Shakespeare was as cynical as Private Williams about the ugly face of, and motivations for, war. Shakespeare certainly underlines the brutality involved, especially when Henry orders his men to slaughter all the French prisoners, absolutely against the chivalric rules of war at the time. While it is possible to see *Henry V* through the prism of pacifist conviction, it is hard to escape the fact that he must have had some patriotic instincts, despite the reservations apparent in the play. These were probably shared by some, at least, of his audience, in the summer of 1599, when what came to be called 'the invisible armada' caused a massive war-scare in England – accompanied by widespread resentment 'at the expense and disruption anti-invasion preparations involved', as men were dragged away from the harvest to stand, poorly armed, against an enemy that never appeared.[14] In the past, some directors present the play as an exercise in patriotism, others as a call for pacifism, but both do the play a disservice: the play is yet another example of Shakespeare's capacity for creative ambiguity, and is too subtle for such simplistic interpretations.

Julius Caesar

Taylor and Loughnane think that this play was most likely written after *Henry V*, in the middle of 1599.[15] Often cited is the comment by a Swiss tourist, Thomas Platter, who records this in his diary in 1599:

> On September 21st after lunch, about two o'clock, I and my party crossed the water, and there in the house with a thatched roof witnessed an excellent performance of the tragedy of the first Emperor Julius Caesar with a cast of some fifteen people: then the play was over, they danced marvellously and gracefully together as is their wont, two dressed as men, and two as women.[16]

So the tradition of the post-performance jig lived on. With Julius Caesar we see Shakespeare extending his repertoire to what became the Roman plays. The stimulus could have come from several sources: including North's translation of Plutarch (published by his friend Richard Field in 1579) and other works by Samuel Daniel and Sir John Davies. He also may have seen an anonymous drama, *The Tragedy of Caesar and Pompey*, in 1595.

There are many reasons why this play still both puzzles and fascinates. Was Caesar a would-be tyrant, or was he a great man? Would he have abused his power if he had become Emperor, or would he have ruled wisely and well?

There is some evidence for the latter view: according to Greenblatt, Caesar admired the libraries he had seen in Greece and Asia Minor and Egypt, and he planned to provide Rome with a public library before his death.[17] Were the conspirators right to distrust him, or did they (apart from Brutus) have more unsavoury motivations? Thus there are different ways we could view both Caesar – and his assassins. Shakespeare does not make it clear at all which way the wind blows: another example of his creative ambiguity.

The play begins when two disgruntled tribunes, Flavius and Marullus, supporters of Pompey, meet workers gathering to celebrate the arrival of Caesar after his defeat of his rival Pompey. Not long before, the people had lined up to cheer Pompey: not the first time that Shakespeare has depicted crowds that are fickle. As the workers leave, the tribunes pull down the decorations that have been placed around the statues of Caesar – for which they pay the price, for we learn that later these dissidents 'are put to silence' – a sinister sign, perhaps, that Caesar has violent supporters.

Caesar meanwhile is all geared up to address the people of Rome when a soothsayer warns him to beware the Ides of March, a warning that Caesar famously disregards. As Caesar passes by to address the crowd in the Capitol, Cassius then meets Brutus, whom he knows loves Caesar. They share their concerns that Caesar could become a tyrant if he became king – fears compounded by the shouts of enthusiasm they hear as he addresses the populace. Although Caesar refuses the crown, neither Brutus nor Cassius is reassured. As the latter observes:

> Why, man, he doth bestride the narrow world
> Like a Colossus, and we petty men

> Walk under his huge legs and peep about
> To find ourselves dishonourable graves.
>
> – Act 1, Scene 2

Cassius has clearly imbibed the philosophy of Lucretius – men are not the plaything of the gods (if indeed they exist), but have free will:

> Men at some time are masters of their fates:
> The fault, dear Brutus, is not in our stars,
> But in ourselves, that we are underlings.
> Brutus and Caesar: what should be in that 'Caesar'?
> Why should that name be sounded more than yours?
>
> – Act 1, Scene 2

Cassius recalls how he once rescued Caesar from drowning in the River Tiber; he also remembers that Caesar was once weak from a fever in Spain; moreover, he had the 'falling sickness'. (He was an epileptic). He was therefore merely mortal: should such a man become king, and, in Roman terms, acquire the status of a god? It seems that Caesar has doubts about Cassius, for as he passes by, he remarks to Mark Antony:

> Let me have men about me that are fat;
> Sleek-headed men and such as sleep o' nights:
> Yond Cassius has a lean and hungry look;
> He thinks too much: such men are dangerous.
>
> – Act 1, Scene 2

Cassius then meets up with Casca, and then Cinna, and the conspiracy begins to take off: they just need the noble Brutus to join them, for 'He sits high in the people's hearts'. The scene then shifts to Brutus, agonizing in his garden, like a Roman Hamlet. Worrying about 'the abuse of greatness', he muses:

> It must be by his death: and for my part,
> I know no personal cause to spurn at him,
> But for the general. He would be crown'd:
> How that might change his nature, there's the question.
>
> – Act 2. Scene 1

However, he is still tortured by doubt and indecision. How could he square an assassination with honour? 'I love/The name of honour more than I fear death' he claims. (*Honour* occurs 41 times in this play.) He remembers the tyranny of Tarquin;[18] but

> Since Cassius first did whet me against Caesar,
> I have not slept.
> Between the acting of a dreadful thing
> And the first motion, all the interim is
> Like a phantasma, or a hideous dream
>
> – Act 2, Scene 1

Then the conspirators – Cassius, Cinna and the rest – arrive and perhaps group psychology takes over, as Brutus finally agrees to join the conspiracy. The tension in the scene when Caesar is murdered is palpable: for a moment it looks as though the conspiracy has been discovered. Metellus Cimber

Mark Antony (Marlon Brando) mourns over the dead body of Julius Caesar (Louis Calhern) in Joseph L. Mankiewicz's 1953 MGM film

tries to persuade Caesar to rescind his order banishing Cimber's brother, but Caesar refuses, claiming, with unconscious irony, to be 'as constant as the northern star'. Was this his last chance to avoid being murdered? Would he have lived if he had accepted Cimber's suit? That we shall never know, for he is then stabbed by each of the plotters in turn. 'Liberty! Freedom! Tyranny is dead!' exclaims Cinna. 'Run hence, proclaim, cry it about the streets!'

However, the conspirators make two fatal errors: first they have agreed to allow Mark Antony, Caesar's closest friend, to remain alive – and then they permit him to address the people. Mark Antony then goes into rhetorical overdrive with his famous speech:

> Friends, Romans, countrymen, lend me your ears;
> I come to bury Caesar, not to praise him;
> The evil that men do lives after them,
> The good is oft interred with their bones,
> So let it be with Caesar ... The noble Brutus
> Hath told you Caesar was ambitious:
> If it were so, it was a grievous fault,
> And grievously hath Caesar answered it ...
> Here, under leave of Brutus and the rest,
> (For Brutus is an honourable man;
> So are they all; all honourable men)
> Come I to speak in Caesar's funeral ...
> He was my friend, faithful and just to me:
> But Brutus says he was ambitious;
> And Brutus is an honourable man ...
> He hath brought many captives home to Rome,
> Whose ransoms did the general coffers fill:
> Did this in Caesar seem ambitious?
>
> – Act 3, Scene 2

And so the speech continues, growing ever more eloquent. As the conspirators wait in the wings, their daggers still bloodied, they must have recognised their own folly. Mark Antony's speech, so cleverly crafted to make them think, at first, he was speaking in their defence, became heavier and heavier with irony, as each time the word *honourable* was spat out with greater and greater sarcasm; each rhetorical question was another nail in their coffin, as the mob churned with more and more anger.

The outcome: a nation divided, torn by civil war, rather than one united under Caesar. All the conspirators paid the final price, including Brutus, described by Octavius as 'the greatest Roman of them all'. Brutus never foresaw that it was Octavius who would become the first Roman Emperor, creating a *Pax Romana* that lasted for two hundred years. The Republican ideal was dead. Brutus clearly never heard of the law of unintended consequences.

Was Shakespeare a Republican?

A final thought: virtually the whole of Shakespeare's audience would have been monarchists, and would have lived in a culture where it was almost unthinkable not to have a king or queen. Nowhere in this play is the word *republic* mentioned. So while watching *Julius Caesar*, the thought must have passed through many minds: why shouldn't Caesar be made king? The elephant in the room (or on the stage) was *republicanism*. Could Shakespeare have been a closet republican?[19] It wasn't totally unthinkable: certainly, there were Puritans, especially under the Stuarts, who thought Parliament was only answerable to God (not the monarch). Indeed, Patrick Collinson has described the Elizabethan regime as a 'monarchical republic', in which the queen ruled with the participation of both the Privy Council and Parliament.[20]

However, on the evidence of this play, I don't think one can claim that Shakespeare was a republican, even if he did see that monarchy was a flawed institution. Brutus at one point refers to the group of conspirators as a 'faction' (Act II, Scene 1) and Peter Lake observes that at this time in England the word 'faction' was almost always a term of opprobrium. Lake also comments: 'however, honourable or noble their purposes, in acting covertly against Caesar the putative defenders of republican virtue and liberty have been reduced to the politics of faction and conspiracy.'[21] One might also add 'murder'.

According to North's Plutarch, Cicero was the first man to distrust Caesar, who he saw as devious. Shakespeare chooses to ignore this characterisation of Caesar, who, indeed, is not a fully developed character in the play. Brutus, on the other hand, is beset with the best of intentions, and has some claim to be regarded as honourable. Both sides of the argument, for and against Caesar, for and against the conspirators, are evenly balanced: creative ambiguity strikes again.[22] Not for the first time, it has a double function: it enables Shakespeare to avoid being accused of subversion by being too pro-conspirators – despite any doubts expressed about kings who become tyrants. Ambiguity also has, as always, an aesthetic effect. It causes his audience to think about and discuss the play, thus making it more interesting. There is little doubt, however, that an Elizabethan audience would have approved the final outcome of the play, seeing it as a defeat for 'factionalism'.

23

FRIENDS, AND RIVALS

... the truest poetry is the most feigning, and lovers
are given to poetry, and what they swear in poetry may
be said as lovers they do feign.
– Touchstone: *As You Like It* III.iii.15–16)

In September 1599, a man wrapped in a thick cloak, riding a horse flecked with foam, arrived at the queen's palace at Nonsuch. His boots covered in mud, his clothes filthy, the man demanded audience with the queen. No one but the Earl of Essex would have made such a peremptory demand: he was desperate to get to Elizabeth before any of his enemies warned her of his arrival. Brushing past the guards, he charged into her bedroom. The queen was 'no morning woman': in *déshabillé, sans* wig, *sans* make-up, her wrinkles and blemishes were only too evident. In John Guy's words, this was the woman 'no man was ever meant to see'. She was shocked and appalled. Who was this man, muddied and breathless, bursting, unannounced, into her boudoir? Was this a coup? The queen then recognised her unwanted visitor as her erstwhile favourite, Essex – wasn't he supposed to be in Ireland, fighting the rebellious Earl of Tyrone, along with that scoundrel, who had seduced her maid of honour, the Earl of Southampton?[1] The queen did not panic: she calmed him down, and met him quietly twice later that day, listening to what he had to say. He explained that his army, originally numbering 20,000 men, had suffered heavy losses, and he had signed a truce with Tyrone. At their

> **The two mavericks: Essex and Southampton**
>
> When Essex left for Ireland, the crowds hailed his departure. No such crowds greeted his return. For this was no triumphal arrival of a victor, the Irish 'rebellion broached on his sword' (alluded to in *Henry V*): this was no Caesar being acclaimed for his defeat of a Pompey, or indeed a Tyrone.
>
> The queen was furious with Essex for several reasons: first, he had orders to defeat Tyrone, but he had dissipated his forces across Ireland, and achieved little success, meanwhile losing men through casualties, sickness, desertion – and defection.[2] Secondly, she was outraged that he had signed a truce with Tyrone. Furthermore, authorised to offer knighthoods in the field, he had handed out so many that it was tantamount to forming his own fan-club. Worst of all, returned to England without permission, he had invaded her private bedchamber where she was caught déshabillé. For months Essex was placed under house arrest. His career was quite clearly on a knife edge – if not an axe-head.
>
> Among those who accompanied Essex to Ireland was the Earl of Southampton, who showed some courage in the field. Essex appointed him General of Horse – but the queen adamantly refused to confirm the appointment.[3] He remained as a gentleman volunteer. The queen deeply disapproved of Southampton: he had not only seduced one of her maids-of-honour, he had an unsavoury relationship with the Earl of Essex.[4] He had been involved in several brawls at court, and had frittered away his fortune on gambling. It is hard to see him as offering inspiration to Shakespeare as his Muse.

third meeting, late in the afternoon, she expressed her deep displeasure, and dismissed him from her presence, and ordered him to remain in his chamber. The next day he was hauled before the Privy Council; on the queen's orders, he was committed to the custody of Sir Thomas Egerton, the Lord Keeper, in York House. His prospects could now be described as bleak.

The 'Rival Poet Sonnets' 78-86 (1598-1600)

These events were in due course to impinge on Shakespeare's life – but Shakespeare may not perhaps have been paying attention: he had other issues to deal with, for, it seems, he had fallen in love again – and he had a rival. The sonnets considered here pose two questions: who was Shakespeare's actual, or possible, loved one – a potential patron, or a lover? Secondly, who was the rival poet, 'the better spirit' competing with Shakespeare? These lines from Sonnet 80 give an indication of their content:

> Oh how I faint when I of you do write
> Knowing a better spirit doth use your name,
> And in the praise thereof spends all his might
> To make me tongue-tied speaking of your fame.

These are sometimes described as 'the rival poet sonnets' – some of them refer to another poet who is also writing about the loved one. Edmondson and Wells list them as having been written between 1598 and 1600, and note that every one of them 'could be addressed to a man or a woman.'[5] Either way, it seems that Shakespeare had become involved yet again in a strong emotional relationship, which no doubt energised and informed his Muse – unless, that is, he was, in the words of Touchstone, 'feigning' love. In the past, a number of commentators have assumed that the poet's 'sweet love' is a woman – perhaps the Dark Lady – though we should note that in Sonnet 82, the loved one is 'as fair in knowledge as in hue'. Others have assumed, wrongly, that these sonnets were addressed to the Earl of Southampton, Henry Wriothesley. However, as noted in previous chapters, Southampton was either in France, in prison with his pregnant wife, the queen's ex-maid of honour, or with Essex on his ill-fated Irish campaign; he certainly wasn't sitting round in Southampton House reading Shakespeare's sonnets. No, these sonnets were not about, or addressed to, Southampton.

There is a general consensus that the loved one was none other than Lady Mary's son, William Herbert, the future Earl of Pembroke, whom we have seen constantly refused to get married. Duncan-Jones has outlined the evidence in support of this theory. It is well-known that the young man loved the theatre, and actors: he was very generous to Ben Jonson, and when Shakespeare's old friend, James Burbage, died, he is reported to have mourned him deeply for two days.[6] Furthermore, he was named as a patron of Shakespeare's First Folio, along with his brother. His initials W.H. also appear on the front page of the sonnets when they were published in 1609, though we cannot be sure whether W.H. referred to him, or someone else.

Then we come to the rival poet: Marlowe's name almost invariably crops up. We can rule him out immediately because he was long dead. Burrow suggests that the rival poet didn't exist – he could be a composite figure – a sort of paper tiger, or 'straw man'.[7] There were poets in sixteenth-century

England that sought to praise themselves by attacking other unnamed (and possibly non-existent) poets. Not everyone is convinced by Burrow's suggestion, and names that have been proposed include George Chapman, Samuel Daniel, and John Davies of Hereford – all protégés of William Herbert. Daniel had been a tutor in the Pembroke household, and would have known Herbert well, but he had moved on since. Davies of Hereford should not be discounted – he wrote a poem *Wittes Pilgrimage* addressing the young man as 'Faire featured Soule, well-shapen Sprite; as Bate points out, he was famous for his calligraphy, hence the recurrence of words like *quill* and *pen* in these poems.'[8]

There are two other strong candidates. Several lines in this set of sonnets seem to suggest that the rival poet was in a much more exalted position than that of Shakespeare. Duncan-Jones suggests that the 'better spirit' referred to in Sonnet 80 could well be Francis Davison.[9] He was known to be a poet and indeed wrote a sonnet in praise of Pembroke's 'lovely shape'. His sonnets were not published until 1602, but they were probably circulated earlier. Davison was the son of William Davison, who had been Queen Elizabeth's Secretary of State, and had worked closely with Walsingham, the Queen's spy-master.[10] (There is a possible allusion to this in Sonnet 86, where he is 'nightly' gulled 'with intelligence'). William Davison became a scapegoat over the execution of Mary, Queen of Scots – Elizabeth blamed him, rather than accepting responsibility.[11]

Francis Davison is certainly a possibility. The other strong candidate is Ben Jonson. According to Nicholas Rowe, Jonson's play *Every Man in His Humour* had been rejected by the manager of the Lord Chamberlain's men – but Shakespeare saw its merits, and it was performed with some success in 1598.[12] Beaumont reports on the meetings between Shakespeare and Jonson at the Mermaid Tavern in Bread Street, during which, according to Fuller, there were many 'wit combats' between the two.[13] Jonson, he says, was like a great Spanish galleon, 'built far higher for learning, solid but slow in his performances', while Shakespeare was the English man-of-war, 'lesser in bulk, but lighter in sailing' who 'took advantage of all winds by the quickness of his wit and invention'.[14] The comparison is notably echoed in Sonnet 86 which refers to 'the proud full sail of his great verse', and again in Sonnet 80 which acknowledges the superiority of the rival poet, who is imagined as a massive well-armed galleon on the Spanish Main compared with Shakespeare's inferior 'saucy bark':

> But since your worth, wide as the ocean is,
> The humble as the proudest sail doth bear,
> My saucy bark, inferior far to his,
> On your broad main doth wilfully appear.
> Your shallowest help will hold me up afloat,
> While he upon your soundless deep doth ride;[15]
> Or, being wracked, I am a worthless boat
> He of tall building and of goodly pride.
>
> – Sonnet 80

To cut a long story short, we just do not know who either the loved one was – not even if male or female; indeed, the loved one could even just be his Muse who 'offers such fair assistance in my verse'. Nor do we have any way of knowing who the rival poet was. Readers may think that it makes no matter.

Ben Jonson, 1572-1637

Jonson was certainly a major rival, even if he was also what one might call a critical friend.[16] Jonson's father died two months before Jonson was born – his mother married again, and Jonson's step-father was a bricklayer, and after a brief period at Westminster School, he followed his father's trade as an apprentice. He later served as a soldier in the Low Countries before becoming a playwright. Initially, he wrote for Philip Henslowe, manager of the Rose Theatre. Jonson is listed by Francis Meres in 1598 as 'one of the best for tragedie', though none of his early tragedies has survived.

Ben Jonson: Shakespeare's friend and rival.

As we have seen, in 1597 he collaborated with Thomas Nashe in writing a satirical play called *the Isle of Dogs*. It is thought to refer to the area north of the river, opposite the Palace of Placentia, where the queen kennelled her dogs – and where the Privy Council also met. The play was denounced as seditious, and all copies of it were destroyed; Jonson and two actors – Gabriel Spenser and Robert Shaw, were arrested by Richard Topcliffe, and placed in the Marshalsea, charged with 'Leude and mutynous behaviour'. Nashe managed to escape to great Yarmouth where he laid low ...

Jonson only became established as a major playwright with *Every Man in his Humour* (1598): the four main characters each embodied one of the humours that feature in mediaeval and Renaissance medicine – choler, melancholy, phlegm and blood which were supposed to determine human character. Less successful was his follow-up, *Every Man Out of his Humour* (first performed in 1599, printed in 1600).

In 1598 Jonson was again jailed for killing Gabriel Spenser in a duel on 22 September. Henslowe was furious. In a letter to Alleyn, he wrote 'I

The Bishops' Ban

Following Jonson's *Isle of Dogs* debacle, the authorities became increasingly aware of what they perceived to be a threat to public order, as more and more printed material filled the bookstalls in St Paul's Churchyard. In June 1599, the Archbishop of Canterbury (John Whitgift) and the Bishop of London, (Richard Bancroft) signed an order banning a wide selection of printed materials unless approved by the Privy Council – including history plays. The order has been described as 'the most sweeping and stringent instance of early modern censorship',[17] though there had been several attempts to impose censorship during Elizabeth's reign.

The ban ordered the censorship not only of pamphlets ('satires' and 'epigrams') but also histories and dramatic works, all of which theoretically had to be approved by the Privy Council. However, in practice, after the first wave of acts of censorship, the ban was somewhat randomly applied.

No comfort however for those immediately affected: seven titles were ceremoniously burnt, including two by John Marston (*The Scourge of Villainie* and *The Metamorphosis of Pygmalion's Image and Certaine Satyres*, both published in 1598). A number of specific texts were named in the ban, which included all the works of Thomas Nashe and Gabriel Harvey. Shakespeare appears to have escaped intact.

The reasons for the ban remain unclear, but texts targeted included those that could be described as morally offensive – in some cases pornographic[18] – such as *The XV ioyes of Marriage* (anon) – or politically dangerous, such as works by Thomas Middleton and Marlowe.

have lost one of my company that hurteth me greatly; that is Gabriel, for he is slain in Hogsden fields by the hands of Benjamin Jonson, bricklayer.' The last word was chosen specially ... Jonson escaped hanging by pleading 'benefit of clergy' a legal loophole: leniency could be obtained by reciting a brief Bible verse (known as 'the neck-verse'). He forfeited his 'goods and chattels' and was branded on his left thumb. While in jail Jonson converted to Catholicism, which he abandoned some twelve years later.[19]

The Spanish Tragedy

The Spanish Tragedy was written sometime in the 1580s (Taylor and Loughnane suggest 1587 as a probable date), and remained popular for years,[20] so much so that it was revived in the late 1590s, with additions by various writers including Shakespeare. The play was not affected by the Bishops' Ban. The part of the protagonist 'Hieronimo' (Geronimo) was played by Ben Jonson. The original author was Thomas Kyd, whom it will be recalled, was in the wrong place at the wrong time when the authorities raided Kit Marlowe's lodgings, and found Marlowe absent, but incriminating papers present. Kyd never recovered from the torture he had suffered, and he died in 1594.

The play, also titled *Hieronimo is Mad Again*, established a new genre in theatre, the revenge play, following Seneca, the Roman Stoic philosopher and dramatist.[21] Most revenge plays tended to end with a heap of bodies piled up at the end as in the case of *Hamlet*. Indeed, many have suggested

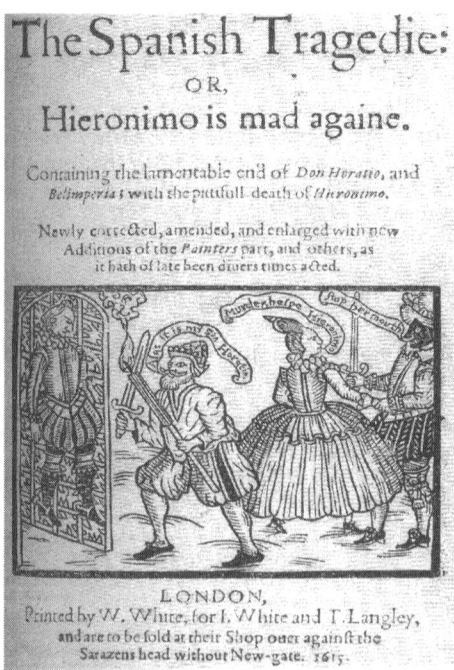

The Spanish Tragedy was reprinted several times, with Shakespeare's additions. This one was published in 1615

that Kyd wrote an early version of *Hamlet* known as *ur-Hamlet*. In *The Spanish Tragedy*, however, the bodies pile up throughout, inspired no doubt by a character called Revenge. Among the characters is a scheming lady, Bel-Imperia (daughter of the Duke of Castile), Don Hieronimo (Knight Marshall of Spain), his wife Isabella, (both of whom go mad), and their son, Don Horatio. There is also a character, an old man called Senex – an obvious reference to Seneca. Most of the plot centres on the search for, and come-uppance of, the murderers of Don Horatio. The play features a ghost, and a play within a play: like *Hamlet*. Modern taste-buds will be offended by the fact that Hieronimo bites out his own tongue to avoid revealing the truth at the end. Yes, it's a bit of a horror story, to say the least.

As Nance observes, the play contains a total of 2,637 words – 1,448 of which are additions – indeed, five additions.[22] There is considerable controversy about who wrote the additions, and when. Taylor and Loughnane suggest that Shakespeare probably wrote his contribution (Addition 4) for the revival of the play in late 1599. Another addition is by Thomas Heywood (his contributions identified by its simple style devoid of metaphor); some of the others may have been written by both in collaboration, or by others.[23] The only one that most agree is by Shakespeare is known as *The Painter* Scene, (Addition 4) in which Hieronimo, mad, converses with a painter. Hieronimo goes to an arbour, where there is a tree where his son was hanged. There he meets a painter, whose son was also murdered. Were these lines inspired by memories of Shakespeare's own lost son? These lines are from Addition 4:

> I pry through every crevice of each wall,
> Look on each tree and search through every brake
> Beat at the bushes, stamp our grandam earth
> Dive in the water and stare up to heaven
> Yet cannot behold my son Hieronimo.

Later he berates the moon – and in doing so, his words tumble over each other, so that he can barely sustain a thought:

> Where was she that same night when my Horatio,
> Was murdered? She should have shone. Search thou the book.
> Had the moon shone – in my boy's face

> There was a kind of grace, that I know, nay,
> I do know – had the murderer seen him
> His weapon would have fall'n, and cut the earth
> Had he been framed of naught but blood and death,
> Alack, when mischief doth it knows not what
> What shall we say to mischief?

To my mind, lines like these (very reminiscent of poor mad King Lear) are incomparably more compelling than those in the original play. Addition 4, and the other Additions, can be viewed in *The New Oxford Shakespeare: The Complete Works* (Modern Critical Edition, 2016), ed. Taylor, Jowett, Bourus and Egan page 1677 *et seq.*[24] Shakespeare may have been glad to finish off his work on this play, because he already had an idea for his next one – a much more cheerful affair. Perhaps the court – and the country – needed something light-hearted in view of the political events that were unfolding. It is possible, too, that with his history plays, he had been tempting fate too long, and in view of the Bishops' Ban, a change of scene was in order – for example, to the Ardennes. However, even as he started to write his next play, *As You Like It*, he was also somewhat preoccupied by another threat, this time to his new theatre, The Globe.

New Kids on the Block

The world of theatre was highly competitive, and it became even more so as the sixteenth century drew to a close, with the revival of children's acting companies. The Children of Paul's, choir boys who sang in St Paul's Cathedral, took part in drama as part of their education, and had performed at court since the Middle Ages. Their venue in the precincts of the cathedral was closed down in 1590, and they ceased to perform for a while, mainly because they could not compete with the rival theatre companies.[25]

The Children of Paul's were revived in 1599, by John Marston, with the backing of William Stanley, the 'niddicock' who appeared earlier in this book, who may have realised that little could come of Derby's Men in their tours of the north. In a letter written in November 1599 one Rowland Whyte reported that 'My Lord Derby hath put up the plays of the Children in Pauls to his great pains and charge.'[26] It seems that Marston, having been gagged by the Bishops' Ban, was looking for another, safer, medium for his talents. Marston's first play the *History of Antonio and Mellida* was put on that very November in their 'private' playhouse.[27] At a time when the Lord Chamberlain's Men were struggling to establish themselves at the opening of the winter season – in an open-air theatre – this was serious competition: the indoor performances put on by Marston's troupe of youngsters attracted the high-status, high-paying audience that the Lord Chamberlain's Men were accustomed to expect.

Another of Marston's plays put on by the Children of Paul's features a character named Sir Edward Fortune, a reference to Edward Alleyn and his Fortune Theatre, which he and the theatre manager Philip Henslowe had built in 1600, north of the river, to rival the newly opened Globe.[28] It looks as though Edward Alleyn certainly saw the Globe, and the Lord Chamberlain's Men, as a threat, for he and Henslowe seem to have formed an alliance with the Children of Paul's.

The Lord Chamberlain's Men, in turn, saw the Children of Paul's as a threat, and decided that if you can't beat them join them – or at least beat them at their own game. In September 1600 they helped to revive a rival children's company, the Children of the Chapel, who were permitted to take over the lease of the theatre in Blackfriars that Burbage had tried to develop. Their trump card was Ben Jonson, who became one of their main writers. There his brand of satire went down well, and though his first play for the company, *Cynthia's Revels* (1600) had mixed responses, he had more success with his *Poetaster* (1601), partly because of the controversy that it caused.

Nevertheless, the professionals of the Lord Chamberlain's Men were not best pleased by the emergence of these children's companies, and there are suggestions that the children, who could be as young as six, were not treated as well as they should have been. Bednarz also hints that there were suggestions that the children recruited as actors were being abused.[29] For example, Rosencrantz tells Hamlet

> There is, sir, an eyrie of children, little eyases[30] that cry out on the top of question, and are most tyrannically clapped for't. These are now the fashion, and so berattle the common stages – or so they call them – that many wearing rapiers are afraid of goose-quills and dare scarce come thither.

Hamlet replies:

> What, are they children? Who maintains 'em? How are they escoted?[31] Will they pursue the quality no longer than they can sing? Will they not say afterwards, if they should grow themselves to common players – as it is most like, if their means are no better – their writers do them wrong to make them exclaim against their own succession?

Nevertheless, the Children of the Chapel continued, and under King James became Children of the Queen's Revels.

The Poets' War

This battle of words touched on above took place in the last years of Elizabeth's reign: literary feuds, then, occurred long before those between C.P. Snow and F.R. Leavis – or for that matter, before Truman Capote had a run-in with Gore Vidal, with Mailer joining the fray. The origin of the spat that became known as the Poets' War, or Poetemachia, is somewhat murky, and there are elements of 'which came first, the chicken or the egg?' It could be said to have started with a dress-rehearsal in which Marston saitirizes Jonson's pride through the character of Chrisoganus in his play *Histriomastix*. Ben Jonson gets his own back, satirizing Marston's pomposity in *Every Man out of His Humour* in 1599. Jonson was clearly gifted, but he was full of self-regard, and could be very abrasive, if not aggressive, and he easily provoked resentment. He was the central figure in the Poets' War.

From a quarrel between individuals the feud developed into what also came to be called the War of Theatres – as the rivalry between the writers for the two children's groups of players developed. Writing for the Children of Paul's, Marston responded to Jonson with his play *Jack Drum's Entertainment* (1600) which seemed to depict Jonson as a cuckold. In response, the Children of the Chapel performed Jonson's *Cynthia's Revels* (1600), which attacked both Marston and Dekker. And so it went on: Marston retaliated with his production of *What You Will*, eliciting Jonson's satirical comedy *The Poetaster* (1601) which had the Marston character vomiting ridiculous words. Dekker was not one to be left out and his *Satiromastix* (1601) mocked Jonson as an arrogant hypocrite. The play was performed by both the Children of Paul's and the Lord Chamberlain's Men.

As time went on, it appears that all those involved seem to have made peace with each other: perhaps the whole episode was a publicity stunt? Shakespeare stayed clear of the fray, despite Jonson's 'Mustard' crack, although I think he found the verbal jousting of the Poets' War both amusing if somewhat tiresome. It was impossible to ignore the fact that Jonson was jealous of Shakespeare, and in *Every Man out of His Humour* there was more than one element of spitefulness. Particularly spiteful was the character of Sordido, a farmer who, at a time of bad harvests, hoped to extort money from the starving – an allusion to the fact that Shakespeare had been accused of hoarding ten quarts of malt in Stratford[32]. No wonder, then, that thereafter Shakespeare and the Lord Chamberlain's men kept Jonson at arm's length, especially after his duel with Spencer. It was not until 1603, with the dust settled, that Shakespeare's company put on *Sejanus, His Fall* at court, in which Shakespeare played one of the parts. This play was hissed off the stage at The Globe in a later performance.

Even so, Shakespeare did get his own back with *As You Like It*, the subject of the next chapter.

24

FROM COMEDY TO TRAGEDY

Present mirth hath present laughter. What's to come is still unsure.
— *Twelfth Night*

It is hard to imagine how difficult it must have been for Shakespeare to concentrate on his writing given what was going on in London – the Bishops' Ban, the Poets' War, and the competition from the Children's groups; moreover, London was abuzz with rumours, as the saga of the Earl of Essex continued. Shakespeare may well have felt uneasy, having published two poems dedicated in fulsome terms to Essex's best friend, the Earl of Southampton. Now under house arrest after the disgrace of his dishonourable truce in Ireland, Essex was in deep trouble. Nor was he helped by would-be supporters: the poet and dramatist George Chapman dedicated his translation of Homer to Essex, ill-advisedly describing him as 'the embodiment of Achillean virtues'.[1] Worse than that, the historian John Hayward's book *The First Part of the Life and Raigne of King Henrie IIII* came out in early 1599. It dealt with the deposition of Richard II and the accession of Henry IV, and was dedicated to – the Earl of Essex! 'Great art thou in hope, and greater in expectation,' he eulogised – and in the book he twice raised the question of monarchical power.[2] No second book emerged for years: the book was suppressed, and no one was surprised when Hayward ended up in the Tower.

Although Essex was for a time freed from house arrest in August 1600, he remained in deep trouble; seen as a very serious security threat, his

Portrait of Robert Devereux, 2nd Earl of Essex, 1565-1601 By Marcus Gheeraerts the Younger

meetings – and correspondence– were closely monitored, as Cecil built up a dossier; Essex desperately tried to regain his standing at court, but he completely failed in all attempts to meet the queen and plead his case. Elizabeth had banished him from court forever. The earl then made his own bid for popularity by commissioning an engraving from Thomas Cockson that can still be viewed in the British Museum.[3] It depicts Essex, clad in full armour, astride a horse. In the background are images of his famous 'victories'. As if glorifying him as a powerful warrior were not bad enough, beneath the engravings were the words: 'Virtue's honour, Wisdom's nature, Grace's servant, Mercy's love, God's elected'. If this were meant to be a PR exercise, it badly backfired: surely, he must have realised that only one person in England could claim to be 'God's elected' – the queen. It was a serious case of lèse-majesté. If Essex's enemies wanted more ammunition, they need look no further.

The man in whose charge the earl was placed, Sir Thomas Egerton, gave him friendly advice to eat humble pie, but Essex was too proud to listen. In a defiant letter to Egerton, he asked 'Why, cannot princes err? Cannot subjects receive wrong? Is an earthly power or authority infinite?'[4] This was more ammunition for Essex's enemies. In February 1600 he was called to appear before the Court of Star Chamber. The earl at last realised how deep in trouble he was, and he wrote to the queen acknowledging his offence, begging 'that this cup may pass' – an echo from Christ's words on the

Robert Devereux, 2nd Earl of Essex in armour, 1599 (Engraving: Thomas Cockson)

cross. Elizabeth, typically indecisive at this stage of her life, agreed to postpone – but not to cancel – the trial.

Essex was not going to go down without a fight; he had a pamphlet printed, praising his military victories. This was the last straw: his attempt to gain fame and popularity merely reminded the authorities of how dangerous a threat he was. As Cecil brought him in to be tried in June 1600, the queen did not intervene: perhaps she recalled how Bolingbroke had removed Richard II? Charged with failing to carry out his orders in Ulster, agreeing to a dishonourable truce with Tyrone, and leaving his post without permission, he was stripped of the Garter, and all state offices, and placed under house arrest, to await the queen's pleasure. When in October, his monopoly of the sweet wine trade, the mainstay of his finances, was not renewed by Elizabeth, he grew desperate. For Essex, it was now a battle for survival.[5]

Shakespeare's reactions

In the past, many scholars have assumed that Shakespeare admired Essex. John Dover Wilson found it impossible to doubt that 'Southampton's poet had Essex in mind while writing his historical plays.'[6] How certain is this? The fact that Hotspur, for example, resembled Essex in character does not by any means imply that Shakespeare was a fan of his, nor should one forget that Hotspur came to a sticky end, albeit 'bravely'. By this stage in his career, Shakespeare must have become very aware of the political pitfalls one could fall into, and he was in the business of surviving and prospering: there is nothing to suppose that he was prepared to take risks by revealing hazardous political inclinations – if indeed he had any. He certainly had no wish to join John Hayward in the Tower. In addition, judging by his portrayal of Achilles sitting sulking in his tent in his play *Troilus and Cressida*, (see Chapter 27) he did not share Chapman's view of Essex's 'Achillean virtues'. However, as already noted, his former close association with Southampton, the close friend of Essex, and those poems with their embarrassingly fulsome dedications, would have been a worry.

With all the machinations at court going on, history plays that might invite dangerous political comparisons were definitely to be avoided. Thus his attitude to the Bishops' Ban was subtly ambiguous. On the one hand we have Celia's observation in *As You Like It*: 'the little wit that fools have was silenced' (probably a comment on Marston). On the other hand, these remarks, from Jaques, in *As You Like It*, could be said to be a criticism of the Bishops' Ban:

> I must have liberty
> Withal, as large a charter as the wind
> To blow on whom I please ...

And Jaques goes on:

> Give me leave
> To speak my mind, and will through and through
> Cleanse the foul body of the infected world
>
> – Act 2, Scene 7

As for the Poets' War, Shakespeare had no wish to add fuel to the fire, although perhaps he could not himself resist a gentle satirical depiction of Ben Jonson in the persona of Jaques.[7]

As You Like It

If the sonnets treated in the last chapter did indeed refer to a love affair with a woman, then she is definitely Rosalind in *As You Like It* – or someone very similar. Perhaps, after all, his new loved one was a woman? Taylor and Loughnane consider it likely that the play was written in early 1600 – but there is a question mark about why it was entered on the Stationers' Register within months – in August 1600 – along with *Henry V* and *Much Ado About Nothing*.[8] However, it did not appear in print, as far as we know, until the Folio of 1623, so it is possible it was registered swiftly to avoid being pirated. The idea of the play comes from *Rosalynde* by Thomas Lodge, though some have detected the influence of Edmund Spencer's *The Faery Queene*.[9] Lodge's piece is a thin tale, also set in the forest of Arden, written in prose from around 1590: it was in its time extremely popular. Shakespeare rewrites his story as a pastoral comedy, with a few name changes, and a touch of melancholy – the latter being fashionable at the time in court circles. Many of the characters in both Lodge and Shakespeare have French names, and some of them are occasionally addressed as *Monsieur*.

At the start of the play, we learn about two brothers, Oliver and Orlando and his wrinkled retainer, known as Adam, allegedly once played by Shakespeare himself. Orlando has been deprived of his inheritance by his older brother, Oliver, who tries to get rid of him by getting him to challenge Charles the Wrestler in Duke Frederick's court. We have this early insight into Orlando's character from Oliver:

> I hope I shall see
> an end of him; for my soul, yet I know not why,
> hates nothing more than he. Yet he's gentle, never
> schooled and yet learned, full of noble device, of
> all sorts enchantingly beloved, and indeed so much
> in the heart of the world, and especially of my own
> people, who best know him, that I am altogether
> misprized[10]
>
> – Act 1, Scene 1

Is Jaques a portrait of Jonson?

In *Every Man in his Humour,* Jonson seeks to present a picture of the 'deeds and language' of Elizabethan London, showing 'an image of our times'. In fact, he presents a series of pretty negative caricatures: Captain Bogadil is a braggart; Wellbred is definitely Illbred, 'full of lascivious jests'; Brainworm is a conman. All in all, an unsavoury picture – you could say Jonson is a verbal Hogarth.[11] Yet he himself has a murky past, twice imprisoned, once for murder, narrowly escaping the gallows with his branded thumb. Are these lines that Duke Senior addresses to Jaques a gentle satire on Jonson?

Most Mischievous, foul sin, in chiding sin
Or thou thyself hast been a libertine   – Act 2, Scene 7

Jonson's cynical view of humanity certainly suggests he is a depressive, or is at least one who revels in melancholy. Does that make Jonson Jaques? Well, 'I can suck melancholy out of a song as a weasel sucks eggs,' comments Jaques, as he listens to Amiens singing:

Under the greenwood tree
Who loves to lie with me
And turns his merry note
Unto the sweet bird's throat

– Act 2, Scene 5

He then sings his own version, which insults both patrons, and those they support, as 'gross fools' – sour grapes, if you will, for Jonson was very jealous of poets like Daniel who were much favoured by influential people at court. It is interesting to see that at the end, Jaques oddly refuses to return to court, but instead decides to return to a monastery – reminding one of Jonson's unexpected conversion to Catholicism when in prison.

He makes Orlando sound a bit of a wet – but not a bit of it. In an altercation with Oliver, Orlando has him by the throat; and when it comes to the wrestling match, where everyone is betting on Charles, who has already destroyed two challengers, Orlando lays him out, and the Champion is ignominiously carried off the stage. It is in this scene that Orlando and Rosalind first meet, and it seems to be a case of love at first sight: Orlando, overcome, is rendered speechless. Strong physically, then, but weak when it comes to emotional relationships.

The conflict between Oliver and Orlando is mirrored in the conflict between Duke Frederick and Duke Senior, also brothers: the latter is forced out of office by Frederick, and takes to the woods with his supporters, including the melancholy philosopher Jaques. When Duke Frederick finds out that Orlando is one of his brother's supporters, he orders Oliver to find his brother and bring him in – dead or alive. Warned of this, Orlando also escapes to the woods. Meanwhile, Frederick banishes Rosalind, Duke Senior's daughter, and she also takes to the woods, accompanied by Celia her cousin and best friend. Rosalind decides to dress up as a young man, for safety's sake, while Celia disguises herself as a shepherdess. With them goes 'Clown' – Touchstone, a part created for a newcomer to the company, Robert Armin, replacing Will Kempe, who by this time had left the company.

As You Like It is a play full of charm: gently satirizing the follies and foibles of love, it is both life-affirming, charming and melancholy: life-affirming because it celebrates the power of love, which wins through despite human folly; charming, both in the music and in the delightful exchanges between Orlando and Rosalind/Ganymede; and melancholy through the commentaries on life provided by Jaques, who thinks in his famous *Seven Ages of Man* speech that

> All the world's a stage
> And all the men and women merely players,
> They have their exits and their entrances
> And one man in his time plays many parts ...
>
> – Act 2, Scene 7

Touchstone provides the witty jokes. The music, provided by Thomas Morley, a sometime neighbour of Shakespeare's in St Helen's, Bishopsgate,[12] adds a touch of almost post-coital wistfulness to the play.

The play depends heavily on the audience's suspension of disbelief. How are these urbanites to survive in the forest? Is the forest as idyllic as it seems? Touchstone as usual provides the shrewd comment 'And now am I in Ardenne, the more fool I. When I was at home I was in a better place.' It seems Ardenne is almost a magic place – so many of the characters seem to fall in love with each other (perhaps there is something in the water). That may explain Orlando's urge to pin his love poems to trees, telling the trees what he can't say to Rosalind. 'Hang there, my verse, in witness of my love,' he says. However, one suspects he was a better wrestler than he was a poet, and he seems to have had some trouble finding words that rhyme with *Rosalind*: does her name rhyme with *wind*, or *mind*?

> From the east to western Ind
> No jewel is like Rosalind.
> Her worth being mounted on the wind,
> Through all the world bears Rosalind.
> Are but black to Rosalind.
> Let no face be kept in mind
> But the fair of Rosalind.
>
> – Act 3, Scene 2

And by this means Rosalind learns of his love. She is delighted, despite the quality of the verse – but then realises she has a problem: 'Alas the day, what shall I do with my doublet and hose!' What would he think of her, saying she loves him while flashing her legs at him? She decides to speak to him 'like a saucy lackey, and under that habit play the knave with him.' There ensues a series of scenes that have them flirting with each other without him at least seemingly being aware of it. Ganymede, as we must

---

Cross-dressed courtship

A suspension of belief becomes impossible in the mock-courtship scenes between Orlando and Rosalind/Ganymede: oddly, these scenes become even more ludicrously incredible, and funnier, when acted by an all-male cast. This was seen in a notable performance of *As You Like It* by The Lord Chamberlain's Men at the Literary Festival in Hay-on-Wye in 2022. This troupe, newly reformed in 2004, claims to be 'the UK's premier all-male theatre company', and attracts enthusiastic audiences as it tours the country.

now call her, tells him that 'Love is merely a madness', and offers to cure him: as part of the cure, he must address her not as Ganymede, but 'Rosalind', and must come every day to woo her.

In parallel scenes, Touchstone flirts with Audrey, a goatherd, and a passing pastor, Sir Oliver Martext, agrees to marry them on the spot – though Touchstone then thinks better of it, if only because the vicar is obviously a Puritan. Meanwhile, Silvius, a shepherd, is wooing Phoebe, a shepherdess: bad luck, Silvius, she has fallen in love with Ganymede, and sends him/her this parody of a love poem:

> *Art thou god to shepherd turned,*
> *That a maiden's heart hath burned?*
> *Why, thy godhead laid apart,*
> *Warr'st thou with a woman's heart?*
> *Whiles the eye of man did woo me,*
> *That could do no vengeance to me.*
>
> – Act 4, Scene 3

A scene from *As You Like It* as performed by the all-male Lord Chamberlain's Men at the Hay Festival, 2022

The play develops into a joyful farce. Surely Orlando must realise that Ganymede is his Rosalind? Once again, we have to suspend our disbelief. One is tempted to think that indeed he does, and their exchanges are an elaborate flirtatious game, as Ganymede tries to teach Orlando wooing strategies. She rehearses possible exchanges with him – she pretending to be herself:

> ROSALIND: Well, in her person, I say I will not have you.
> ORLANDO: Then in my own person I die.
> ROSALIND: No, faith, die by attorney. The poor world is almost six thousand years old, and in all this time there was not any man died in his own person, *videlicet*, in a love cause.
>
> – Act 4, Scene 1

This is but one instance of Shakespeare using this play to laugh at the mythos of courtly love, more aptly described as romantic love, perhaps, for the term *courtly love* was not widely used until the nineteenth century.[13] In Chrétien de Troyes' courtly romance *Lancelot*, the lover is a slave to his mistress and obeys her every command, however unreasonable. Love was frequently referred to as a sickness. Petrarch's sonnets to Laura contributed to the mythos. Much of the inspiration of romantic love comes from Ovid's *The Art of Love*,[14] in which the lover is pale and listless, indeed, almost dying. Jaques' Seven Ages of Man speech depicts the lover

> Sighing like furnace, with a woeful ballad
> Made to his mistress' eyebrow
>
> – Act 2, Scene 6

Rosalind laughs at the idea of a lover 'sighing every minute, groaning every hour'. But even she has caught the virus: 'O coz, coz, coz, my pretty little coz, that thou didst know how many fathom deep I am in love!' she tells Celia. But it still does not stop her from casting cold water over the standard idea of what a lover should look like and how he should behave. She realises that he is love-struck, yet teases him by pretending to prove he is not; for a true lover should have

> A lean cheek, which you
> have not; a blue eye and sunken, which you have
> not; an unquestionable spirit, which you have not; a
> beard neglected, which you have not – but I pardon

> you for that, for simply your having in beard is a
> younger brother's revenue. Then your hose should
> be ungartered, your bonnet unbanded, your sleeve
> unbuttoned, your shoe untied, and everything
> about you demonstrating a careless desolation. But
> you are no such man. You are rather point-device in
> your accoutrements, as loving yourself than seeming
> the lover of any other.
>
> – Act 3, Scene 2

Here there are echoes of Polonius' description of the love-sick Hamlet. And Orlando? He bears the name of Ariosto's heroic knight – the embodiment of chivalry in the Old French romance *The Song of Roland*. When Celia finds him resting under a tree she describes him as 'a wounded knight' – and laughingly likens him to 'a dropped acorn', enjoying a joke at his expense and offering a side-swipe at 'chivalry'. For in this play the roles of Knight and Lady seem to have become reversed. The initiative stays with Rosalind: Orlando is more like a squire to Rosalind's knight. She upstages him by being a good deal more skilled in wooing than he is, and indeed does most of the talking – hers is the largest female role in the whole of Shakespeare. He is cast not as a knight, but as a pupil.

This play entertains yet tantalizes in equal measure: for *As You Like It*, more perhaps than any other of Shakespeare's comedies, demonstrates his capacity for creative ambiguity *par excellence*. What are we to make of a boy actor acting the part of a woman pretending to be a boy, and developing a flirtatious exchange with a young man? As Bate observes, 'On both the public stage of the Globe and the private stage at Blackfriars, nothing seems to have given audiences more pleasure than the image of a boy actor dressed as a girl dressed as a boy.'[15] The play is fraught with sexual frissons, if not tensions. The play is perhaps Shakespeare's way of reconciling himself to a love-affair that turns out badly, as perhaps seen in the sonnets discussed in Chapter 23.

Shakespeare also hints at other issues, particularly the contrast between urban and rural living. His largely newly-urbanized audience almost all had a rural background, or came from families that lived in the country. Even in the poorer areas of London there were town-dwellers who kept livestock, including pigs and even the occasional cow. There were those who lived in the town, and farmed in the nearby countryside. A Tudor audience would have enjoyed the exchanges between Touchstone and Corin, the shepherd, who points out that

> Sir, I am a true labourer. I earn that I eat, get that I wear, owe no man hate, envy no man's happiness, glad of other men's good, content with my harm, and the greatest of my pride is to see my ewes graze and my lambs suck.
> – Act 3, Scene 2

The two of them compare town life (or rather court life) with country life:

> Those that are good manners at the court are as ridiculous in the country as the behaviour of the country is most mockable at the court. You told me you salute not at the court but you kiss your hands. That courtesy would be uncleanly if courtiers were shepherds.
> – Act 3, Scene 2

The good shepherd's practical comments are in stark contrast with the foolish 'witty' talk of the court generated by Touchstone. However, this play reminds Shakespeare's audience that all is not well in the so-called idyllic countryside: Touchstone calls the forest a desert – and indeed what was left of the forest of Arden near Stratford had been largely taken over by farmland. In Warwickshire, tenant farmers were losing their land and even their livelihood with enclosures, the land being bought up by the local gentry.[16] When Touchstone asks Corin if he has any 'philosophy', Corin replies

> No more but that I know the more one sickens, the worse at ease he is, and that he that wants money, means, and content is without three good friends; that the property of rain is to wet, and fire to burn; that good pasture makes fat sheep; and that a great cause of the night is lack of the sun; that he that hath learned no wit by nature nor art may complain of good breeding or comes of a very dull kindred.
> – Act 3, Scene 2

The reference to fire was also apt: thatched houses easily caught fire, and Stratford had been badly affected by fires on several occasions.[17] Yes, country-folk were in the hands of the elements – in the late 1590s, there had been three successive summers of bad harvest because the weather had been unusually cold and wet: as a result, there was a shortage of grain, inflated prices and hoarding. Corin is so impoverished that he cannot even offer food and lodging to Orlando: he is 'shepherd to another man/And do not sheer the fleeces that I graze.' Even worse, the 'cote' where he lived and the 'flocks and bounds of feed/Are now on sale.' There is a good chance that Corin might have to drift off to the city to join the unemployed day labourers who gathered there in ever greater numbers.

Even so, the play is determinedly optimistic; *As You Like It*, as the title suggests, winds up as an elaborate exercise in wishful thinking in which we are invited to suspend our disbelief as all turns out well – happy ever after: Ganymede promises to bring back Rosalind, and slips away in order to return in her own clothes. Oliver becomes a reformed character and signs over the estate to Orlando; Frederick has a rush of blood to the head, hands his Dukedom back to Duke Senior, and becomes a hermit, followed by Jaques. Best of all, the play ends with multiple marriages: Orlando to Rosalind, Oliver to Celia, Touchstone to Audrey, and Silvius to Phoebe. Yes, all's well that ends well. And, typically (in this play) Rosalind has the last word, as she delivers the epilogue before the final curtain.

The End for Essex

Robert Devereux, Earl of Essex, too, would soon have to face his own final curtain. Deprived of all his positions at court, and of his main source of revenue, he was now desperate, and almost deranged. In a final throw of the dice he planned rebellion. By this time, the earl was now almost obsessed with his own sense of entitlement. To further his plan, he ordered some of his men to approach Shakespeare's company, The Lord Chamberlain's Men, to put on a performance of *Richard II* at the Globe the day before his march on the city of London. In the fantasy world that Essex now occupied, putting on a piece about a deposed monarch would somehow in some mysterious way be a seedbed or catalyst for a rebellion. The company's business manager, Augustine Phillips, may have had serious doubts about the wisdom of acceding to his request – but the offer was tempting: the usual fee for a command performance was £10.00. Essex's men offered him an additional 40 shillings – 'more than the ordinary'.[18]

The next day, on Sunday 8 February, 1600 Essex broke cover to lead 300 'captains and men of quality' to rally London against the court. His plan was to arrest Raleigh and Cecil, thereby 'rescuing' the aged queen, who would then, in his dreams, make him regent. Shouting 'the Crown of England has been sold to Spain!', the rebels set off down Cheapside.[19] It was like the 2021 assault on the Capitol Building in Washington, D.C. – though at least Essex led the charge in person. However, he had seriously misjudged the mood of the nation. The people who had cheered him on his way to Ireland in March 1599 now closed their doors and windows on him, and resolutely failed to respond. The attempted coup petered out, and most of his supporters melted away. Of the three hundred who rode out from Essex House, only fifty rode back, but, surrounded, there was nothing to do but surrender. The whole project was doomed from the start, and Essex and his supporters were arrested, and put on trial in Westminster Hall, the very place where Richard II had been deposed, as featured in Shakespeare's play. The rebels paid a heavy price: five were executed, including Southampton's friend, Sir Charles Danvers: Others were fined. After pleas from his mother, Southampton was sentenced to life imprisonment in the Tower, but there was no way out for Essex: he was sentenced to death.

What were the repercussions for Shakespeare and the Lord Chamberlain's Men? Shakespeare himself escaped censure: perhaps he was safely in Stratford-upon-Avon at the time: a good place to be for a man who only seven years earlier had effusively devoted himself to Southampton, one of the main conspirators. It was Phillips who had to face the music – and fast talking was needed: he explained that they put on the play for the money. He 'and his fellows' had been very reluctant to perform the play – it was 'so old and so long out of use that they should have small or no company at it'.[20] Phillips was very lucky to escape punishment. No doubt the fact that the Lord Chamberlain's Men were sponsored by the queen's relative, George Hunsdon, saved him and the other actors from censure. Perhaps, too, the queen recalled Shakespeare's poem 'To the Queen'.

On Shrove Tuesday 1601, the same day Elizabeth signed Essex's death warrant, the Lord Chamberlain's Men were ordered to perform before her in court. Robert Sharpe suggests that the play they had to put on was none other than *Richard II*.[21] Even though Elizabeth once exclaimed 'I am Richard II. Know ye not that?'[22] she was entirely capable of this act of grim humour. The next morning, on Ash Wednesday, 25 February, Robert Devereux, 2nd Earl of Essex, was beheaded in the yard of the Tower of London. On the scaffold, he confessed to having been 'puffed

The Earl of Southampton in the Tower of London with his cat (From The Buccleuch Collections/*Boughton House*. By kind permission of His Grace, the Duke of Buccleuch and Queensbury, KT. (Attributed to John de Critz)

up with pride, vanity and love of this wicked world's pleasures', and asked for God's forgiveness. Three strikes, and he was out.

The life of the Earl of Essex was like that of a Shakespearian tragic hero: a man with so many gifts, destroyed by a tragic flaw – or, in this case, flaws. A charming, handsome man who from birth developed a sense of entitlement, which caused him to be proud, arrogant, and totally self-absorbed, his ambition far outreached his ability. Although he was personally very brave, his military prowess was massively overrated, as can be seen by his performance particularly in Ireland; and he showed very poor political judgement, as evidenced by his bizarre attempt at a coup: tragedy that turned to a brutal farce. The tragedy that Shakespeare never wrote.

25

HUMOURING THE QUEEN

'With mirth and laughter let old wrinkles come.'
– *The Merchant of Venice*

Where was Shakespeare at this time, before, during and after the Essex debacle? It is often claimed that he lived in the Clink parish of St Saviour's, Southwark from 1599, to be near the Globe. However, Marsh asks why would a man who aspired to being a gentleman, the proud owner of the second biggest house in Stratford, have chosen to leave an upmarket, respectable area like St Helen's in order to live in the low-lying marshland of Southwark, south of the river, an area with an unsavoury reputation?[1] It is likely that if Shakespeare did move to Southwark, this was only temporary, to be near the Globe while it was being constructed, and perhaps for its opening performances around June. It is also possible that having bought New Place in 1597, he may have persuaded the authorities that his tax should be paid in Stratford-upon-Avon.[2] As we have seen, it is possible that at the time of Essex's mad adventure, Shakespeare was safely in Stratford-upon-Avon (or claimed to have been there ...) and so avoided involvement with the investigations following the performance of *Richard II*.

England in peril

If Shakespeare was for a time removed from the maelstrom of political events, the same was not true of the queen and her court. Elizabeth was stressed by the events in Ireland, and the shocking Essex debacle. She was also, in any case, subject to moods of deep depression. Commenting on her chronic ill health she once remarked, mirthlessly, '*Mortua sed non sepulta!* Dead but not yet buried.'[3] Apart from the aches and pains of old age, many other causes for concern were accumulating: the Earl of Essex crisis, bad as it had been, was comparatively only a minor distraction.

During this period, the threat of invasion by Spain became ever more serious: Philip II had died in September 1598, and Philip III had made peace with France, enabling him to concentrate on regaining the Dutch republic and invading England.[4] This was not an idle threat – in June 1595 the Spanish had carried out a raid on Cornwall, destroying much of Penzance,[5] and in 1600 panic swept through England at news of the approach of yet another Spanish Armada – the fourth: county militias were put on alert, and a huge fleet was deployed to patrol the Channel and the coast of Ireland. Dozens of small ships filled with ballast were scuttled in the Thames estuary, in case London was attacked, and coastal defences were strengthened. Wild rumours circulated – at one point, the queen took refuge in St James Palace.[6] It turned out that the armada had been destined for Ireland, but at the last minute was diverted to the Azores to protect the treasure ships from the New World. The fact that the fourth Armada – known as 'the invisible armada' was a 'no show' was no cause for complacency – for a fifth armada set out in August 1601, and was yet again scattered by storms. However, Spain still posed a serious threat: a force of some 3,400 soldiers landed at Kinsale, south-west of Cork, to support Tyrone. Fortunately, Mountjoy, Essex's successor in Ireland, saw them off.[7]

There were numerous other worries facing Elizabeth and her ministers: the religious divisions in England, social unrest caused by low wages, high taxes and inflation, and worries about her successor, were all compounded by the death of so many of her former trusted ministers, particularly Walsingham, Hunsdon and Burghley. In short, the Queen needed a respite from these problems: what was certainly required was a play – several plays – to raise her spirits.

By now it must have become obvious to Shakespeare that momentous events were taking place, and this was not the time to act out on the stage anything that was remotely political. In his role as Lord Chamberlain in charge of royal entertainments, George Carey must also have been aware that the queen was in urgent need of a distraction from her political pressures, so he may have called on Shakespeare to whip up a quick play to offer her some respite.

The Merry Wives of Windsor

As we have seen, *As You Like It* featured characters from two different worlds – from the aristocratic world of a duke's court to the world of common folk. Perhaps Shakespeare thought it was time to come down to earth, to the day-to-day concerns of ordinary people, people whose troubles were more about marriage and money, rather than power and ambition. And if you want to please both ordinary people and the court, where better to set it than in street-wise (or street-foolish) Windsor, where ordinary people acted out their own homely comedies and tragedies.

The Merry Wives of Windsor, written in mid-to late 1600, found its way into print as early as 1602, with Shakespeare named as the author.[8] It was unusual for a play to be published so quickly, and there is a lingering doubt about the date: the play could well have been written earlier. It has been suggested that it was partly derived from a lost play by Henry Porter called *The Merrie Wives of Abingdon* – completed before Porter's death in 1597.[9] The title page claims that 'this most pleasant and excellent conceited comedy ... had been divers times acted ... both before Her Majesty and elsewhere.' Shakespeare's play has been very popular, both in England and many other countries, ever since. It was Nicholas Rowe, writing in 1709, who claimed that the queen was so well pleased with 'that admirable character Sir John Falstaff' that 'she commanded him to continue it for one play more, and to show him in love.' If that is the case, then Coleridge said that this proves her to be 'a gross-minded baggage.'[10] We don't know where Rowe's story originated, or if there is any truth in it.

Many authorities have suggested that it looks as though the play was written in a hurry: it uses off-the-peg plot-lines derived from throw-away folk tales, and is almost entirely written in prose. However, this overlooks that fact that inn-keepers, loafers, tricksters, housewives and hangers-on seldom speak in blank verse – the dialogue in the play has an earthy quality that makes it clear that these are ordinary folk going about their business, criminal or otherwise, using the language they share with the bulk of a Tudor audience. The dialogue degenerates into sub-standard blank verse at the end, when the play almost becomes a masque, and the characters are, in practice, play-acting.

The play is well within a tradition of comedy dating back to classical times, and can be said to be part of a virtually universal tradition of so-called trickster tales: whether it be continent-wide African and Asian folklores, or the tales of trickster animals in Native American stories. They are a common feature of mediaeval drama – for example Bocaccio's *Decameron*, and Chaucer (*The Miller's Tale, The Reeve's Tale*). Many books of anecdotes depicting tricksters were popular in Tudor times, known as 'Merrie tales', often about cheating wives and lecherous monks. A probable source for Shakespeare's play is Giovanni Fiorentino's *Il Pecorone*, written in the late fourteenth century, published in England in 1558.[11] There are many similarities, including the 'hero' Bucciola hiding in a pile of dirty clothes, just as Falstaff tries to avoid detection by hiding in a laundry-basket. In another scene, also similar, Falstaff mistakenly tells a disguised husband about his plan to seduce the man's wife.

The Merry Wives of Windsor is the only comedy that Shakespeare wrote that is set wholly, and unmistakably, in England. I think it is more than likely that Shakespeare wrote at least some of it while enjoying living in his new house in Stratford, and he possibly derived a lot of his inspiration from all the local scandal and tittle tattle that went on there. Accordingly, the cast list of *The Merry Wives of Windsor* includes not just the stock characters you will find in any small-town comedy or folk-tale. In Shakespeare's hands, they become flesh and blood people: his cast list includes the local gossip (Mistress Quickly), the foolish local justice (Master Shallow), his clueless stooge (his cousin, Slender), the jealous husband, (Master Ford), and the local doctor (who becomes rather oddly a dotty French physician), and the buxom wench (Anne Page). To add a bit of spice, and some easy laughs, the Parson is Welsh – Sir Hugh Evans, who 'makes fritters of English'. (In Tudor England, racist stereotypes were not yet a crime.) To these must be added the Host of the Garter Inn, along with the usual pub cronies (Pistol and Corporal Nym) and of course, the trickster – none other than our fat old friend, Sir John Falstaff, and his targets, the

Merry Wives themselves – Mistress Page and Mistress Ford. However, unlike the women in *1 Henry IV*, who were easy targets, easily fooled, the wives of Windsor are of sterner, and indeed, somewhat surprisingly, chaster, stuff. Finally, perhaps to accommodate the Children of the Chapel, the young folk of Windsor are given parts to play, in the denouement of Falstaff towards the end of the play.

In the opening scene, we meet Shallow, a justice of the peace in Gloucestershire, and his nephew, Slender, who boasts that his family could sport a dozen white luces on their coat of arms – as did the Stratford's local Catholic-hunter, Sir Thomas Lucy, who, it will be recalled, had named Shakespeare's father on a list of recusants in 1592. The Welsh parson, Sir Hugh Evans, adds to the fun by rubbing salt into the wound by calling the luces 'louses' – an example of what Falstaff calls 'Welsh flannel'. Is Shakespeare having a joke at the expense of local Warwickshire JP Sir Thomas Lucy, whose deer he (allegedly) once poached? With the Tudor love of word-play and puns, the family adopted the luce, a freshwater fish, as their heraldic device.

> SIR JOHN: Now, Master Shallow, you'll complain of me to the King?
> SHALLOW: Knight, you have beaten my men, killed my deer, and broke open my lodge.
> SIR JOHN: But not kissed your keeper's daughter?
> SHALLOW: Tut, a pin. This shall be answered.
> SIR JOHN: I will answer it straight: I have done all this. That is now answered.
>
> – Act 1, Scene 1

Sir John pulls rank: Shallow is a mere 'esquire', and Falstaff is a knight who also claims to have influence with the king (a reference of course to *Henry IV*). Yes, he admits guilt to all charges – and his reply adds up to 'So what?' Game, set and match to Falstaff.

It is, I suppose, possible that Shakespeare could still nurse a grudge against Sir Thomas after so many years have passed, and the reference to deer reinforces the old myth that Shakespeare had done a bit of poaching. However, there are two other possible targets for gentle mockery by Shakespeare. First, Thomas Lucy's son, a second Sir Thomas, had made himself extremely unpopular in Stratford by supporting another JP, Sir

Edward Greville, in his seizure of common land in Stratford ('The Bancroft')[12] – an area near the river where locals grazed their cattle. (Today it is the site for a residential home; nearby is the Royal Shakespeare Theatre.) Sir Edward had outrageously imprisoned some of Shakespeare's friends for riot for opposing the seizure. Furthermore, in 1602, some of his son's thugs beat up Richard Quiney, causing his death.[13] All this could certainly have evoked scurrilous responses, with crude ballads. To add doubt to confusion, Leslie Hotson suggests that another more probable target was a corrupt JP, William Gardiner, who was widely detested in Southwark. and who tried to close down the Swan Theatre: his heraldic device also contained luces.[14] Perhaps, after all, Shakespeare was simply casting aspersions on all JPs, who were (unlike today) not notoriously even-handed in administering justice. Or perhaps he was being deliberately ambiguous, so no one could definitely pin any accusation on him.

Whoever the target was, he was not the only person guyed in this play. At one point, Mr Ford disguises himself as one Master Brooke – a joke at the expense of Lord Cobham and his family. No room for ambiguity here! Cobham was not the most popular character at court, and the queen would have taken mischievous delight at seeing a little joke at his expense, especially when he is greeted by Falstaff with the words 'Such Brookes are welcome to me, that o'er flows such liquor.' In this play, Shakespeare avoids the cardboard caricatures representing Vices that the satirists such as Marston and Nash include in their plays: his targets are not individual vices, they are the foibles of real people. In this exchange, he has a laugh at the expense of the Welsh schoolmaster who applies his Welsh flannel to Latin as well as English – for him, *hic, haec, hoc* becomes 'hig, hag, hog'. He is giving a Latin lesson to a young man named Will whom Mistress Page, accompanied by Mistress Quickly, has brought to school. Who might Will be, one wonders ... The lesson turns into a series of bawdy jokes:

> EVANS: What is the focative case, William?
> WILLIAM: O–*vocative*, O–
> EVANS: Remember, William, focative is '*caret*'.[15]
> MISTRESS QUICKLY: And that's a good root.
> EVANS: 'Oman, forbear.
> MISTRESS PAGE: What is your genitive case, plural, William?
> WILLIAM: Genitive case?

EVANS: Ay.

WILLIAM: *Genetivo 'horum, harum, horum'.*

MISTRESS QUICKLY: Vengeance of Jenny's case! Fie on her! Never name her, child, if she be a whore.

EVANS: For shame, 'oman.

MISTRESS QUICKLY: You do ill to teach the child such words. He teaches him to hick, hack, which they'll do fast enough of themselves, and to call 'whorum'. Fie upon you!

– Act 4, Scene 1

However, of course, the real target is Falstaff and his ludicrous machinations. This chapter will not attempt to describe all the details of the convoluted plot of *The Merrie Wives.* There are two narratives running alongside: one has been mentioned already – who will marry Anne Page? Her parents are not agreed: her mother's choice is Dr Gaius the French doctor; her father's choice is Master Abraham Slender, whose candidacy is supported by the Welsh parson, Sir Hugh Evans. Lastly, there is a young gentleman, Fenton. We only know whom she runs off with at the end of the play. Readers are invited to make an educated guess on who was the lucky man.

The main story-line features the multiple attempts of Sir John Falstaff to seduce Mistresses Ford and Page. Queen Elizabeth, allegedly wanted Shakespeare to depict Falstaff falling in love, but he is in love only with

---

A Warwickshire Scandal

A scandal that took place in Stratford-upon-Avon in 1600 involving the Lucy family may well have influenced the sub-plot of this play. Sir Thomas Lucy, JP, had a favourite grand-daughter, Elizabeth Aston, who had a substantial dowry. In 1600 she eloped with one John Sambach, a sometime servant of Sir Thomas. Sir Thomas strongly disapproved of the marriage, and it may even have contributed to his death, for he died within the year. As detailed by Sokol (2009)[16] the story has similarities to the sub-plot of *The Merry Wives of Windsor*, in which Anne Page runs off with one of her suitors, Fenton, against the wishes of her father, who wanted her to marry Slender. There is no doubt that Shakespeare would have known about this scandal on his doorstep, and it is possible that it explains the reference to the Lucy coat of arms.

Was Shakespeare making fun of Sir Thomas? He would have been well-advised to remember that a luce grows into a pike, an aggressive carnivorous species ...

money in this play, for it is Page's and Ford's money he is after – and he has recognized that the two wives control the purse-strings. He seems at first to be taken with Mistress Ford, and thinks she will be easily won over. 'I spy entertainment in her,' he asserts:

> SIR JOHN: She discourses, she curves, she gives the leer of invitation. I can construe the action of her familiar style, and the hardest voice of her behavior, to be Englished rightly, is 'I am Sir John Falstaff's'[17]
> PISTOL: He hath studied her will, and translated her ill: out of honesty, into English.
>
> – Act1, Scene 2

Why stop at one? He has Mistress Page in his sights, too. He makes the mistake (the first of many) of sharing the details of his cunning plan with his cronies, Pistol and Nym. He aims to woo both women at the same time, with two love letters so crude they would have to be seen to be believed – though he is convinced they will be irresistible. And, of course, they will not be believed, and are definitely resistible. Nevertheless:

> SIR JOHN: I have writ me here a letter to her – and here another to Page's wife who even now gave me good eyes too, examined my parts with most judicious oeillades; sometimes the beam of her view gilded my foot, sometimes my portly belly.
> PISTOL: Then did the sun on dunghill shine
>
> – Act 1, Scene 3

Pistol and Nym will have nothing to do with his manoeuvres, and refuse to deliver the letters. They decide to warn Masters Ford and Page of Falstaff's intentions. Falstaff's plan is clearly heading for side-splitting disaster, made even more certain by the second mistake he makes: the letters he has written to the two women are identical, only the names are different. Naturally, as so many women have always done throughout the centuries, they compare notes – literally: and are outraged by the 'greasy knight'. Mistress Ford exclaims

> What tempest, I trow, threw this whale, with so many tons of oil in his belly, ashore at Windsor! How shall I be revenged on him? I think the best way were to entertain him with hope till the wicked fire of lust has melted him in his own grease. Did you ever hear the like?
>
> – Act 2, Scene 1

The two women then join forces – and the audience knows that Falstaff's goose is cooked, especially as the husbands also have him in their sights: one of them, Ford, a jealous husband, disguises himself as Brooke,[18] and pretends to enlist Falstaff's help in seducing his own wife: only Shakespeare could make this up ... So we draw a veil over much that ensues: needless to say Falstaff gets his come-uppance; first having hidden in a laundry basket to escape detection, he ends up being dumped into an extremely filthy River Thames. On another occasion, disguised as a woman, he is cudgeled 'into all the colours of the rainbow'. At the end, as instructed, he appears in Windsor Forest disguised as Herne the Hunter (a sort of spirit of the forest, according to local folklore). Looking like a Windsor stag, complete with huge antlers, still in hope of 'a good rut time', he finally gets his assignation – but more than he bargained for. Both women arrive to confront him – and of course, he remains unfazed, issuing an invitation he is convinced cannot be refused:

The Merry Wives dumping Falstaff in the laundry-basket, by Johann Heinrich Füssili

Divide me like a bribed buck, each a haunch.

But then there is an invasion, seemingly of wood sprites hobgoblins and fairies – the Children of the Chapel in masquerade mode. They all wreak their revenge on the 'cuckoldly knave', tormenting him as they surround him as he collapses like a wounded stag.

So if *A Spanish Tragedy*, *Titus Andronicus* and *Hamlet* are revenge tragedies, *The Merry Wives of Windsor* is a revenge comedy, and was a huge success. Phyllis Rackin reports that between 1701 and 1750 it was performed over two hundred times,[19] and while it was less popular in the prudish nineteenth century, it has been repeatedly revived since – especially by the RSC in Stratford: a scene where the wives meet in a hair-dressers, and plot their revenge, their hair in curlers under massive 1950s hair driers, is particularly memorable. Local references are one of its appeals: perfumes based on local herbs were said to be on sale in Bucklesbury, a London street. The Garter pub is set in Windsor,[20] and Windsor Castle – and the park – get a couple of mentions, as does the nearby village, where Frogmore Cottage was once occupied by Prince Harry and Meghan Markle.[21] There are many other homely references to Tudor England: linen bleachers ('whitsters') operate in Datchet Mead; Mistress Quickly gives a long list of her household tasks; Mistress Ford has a 'buck-basket' for her laundry, and a 'cowl-staff' for the servants to carry it. The menfolk scarcely figure in keeping activities in the town functioning.

Phyllis Rackin also wonders why feminist critics have focused so much attention on *The Taming of the Shrew* (which was not particularly popular in Shakespeare's time) while *Merry Wives* is largely neglected.[22] For this play gives a much clearer picture of how Shakespeare saw women – and indeed how women saw women in Tudor times – than *Shrew*. Mistresses Page and Ford are strong women who manage their husband's financial affairs, and easily make a fool of Falstaff. That was one good way, one might think, of dealing with sexual harassment. Mistress Quickly easily outwits Falstaff in this play, and lures him into the traps set by the wives. These women could be ideal role-models for our daughters and granddaughters – even though they had to live within the constraints of Tudor England. Margaret Cavendish, writing in the seventeenth century, was full of praise for Shakespeare's representation of women. We should be happy to give Mistress Cavendish the last word.

One would think he had been Metamorphosed from a Man to a Woman, for who could Describe *Cleopatra* Better than he hath done, and many other Females of his own Creating, as *Nan Page, Mrs Page, Mrs Ford,* the Doctor's Maid, *Bettrice, Mrs Quickly, Doll Tearsheet,* and others, too many to relate?[23]

26

THE FOOD OF LOVE

> Some are born great, others achieve greatness, and some have greatness thrust upon them
>
> – Malvolio, *Twelfth Night*

In 1601 Shakespeare had strong reasons for spending time in Stratford, among them, the decline of his father, who died in September. His father's death meant that Shakespeare was now the most senior member of the family, so his house in Henley Street automatically passed into his possession – with his mother Mary retaining the right of abode. Shakespeare also inherited the title of gentleman. As has been noted, this may also have been a good time for Shakespeare to lie low in Stratford, because his poems with their fulsome dedications to the Earl of Southampton had been reprinted several times, and were still in circulation – a dangerous embarrassment with the earl now imprisoned in the Tower after Essex's abortive rebellion.

Twelfth Night

Shakespeare may not have needed to worry about those dedications, because the queen clearly enjoyed his plays. The first recorded performance of *Twelfth Night* was in Middle Temple Hall on 2 February 1602. The play was probably written in late 1601.[1] One source Shakespeare used was a sixteenth century play *Gl'Ingannati*, ('The Deceived'), which was published in Venice in 1592. Whether Shakespeare read it in Italian is doubtful, but various versions of the play appeared in English – and John Florio may have told Shakespeare about the play, too. Like *The Comedy of Errors*, the play also owes something to the *Menaechmi*, by Plautus – the comic confusions arising from identical twins: always good for mistaken identity jokes.

We can be fairly sure of the date: the play does not appear on Francis Meres' 1598 list, but Act III, Scene ii alludes to a description of the Arctic Voyage of William Barentz published in June 1598. There is also a reference to a new map showing the Indies published in Hakluyt's *Voyages*, published in 1599. In addition, in the early 1600s there was widespread interest in the visit (1598-1601) by the traveller and adventurer Sir Anthony Shirley to the court of the Sophy in Persia, referred to in the play. These references help to date the play fairly accurately.[2]

So did the queen watch *Twelfth Night* in January 1602? One would hope so, for the old queen needed some respite from real life, including trying to forget the Essex saga. Queen Elizabeth was not in a good place. To the pains of old age (she died on 24 March 1603) were added huge financial problems – the war-chest was virtually empty – causing arguments with parliament about taxation. There were also complaints about the monopolies she had created as rewards for loyalty, and widespread social unrest continued.[3] It would be surprising if George Carey, her Lord Chamberlain, did not offer her Shakespeare's new play to raise her spirits. It was customary for the queen to hold a banquet, followed by an entertainment, for Epiphany. Elizabeth had already enjoyed *The Merry Wives*: so it is plausible that she looked forward to another jolly evening with the Lord Chamberlain's Men performing a play by Shakespeare. Remarkably, on 6 January 1601, the queen's guest of honour was Don Virginio Orsino, Duke of Bracciano, and it seems likely that a year later Shakespeare's duke in *Twelfth Night, Orsino*, was named after him.[4] *Twelfth Night* is generally recognised as being Shakespeare's best comedy, and yet again features a boy acting the part of a girl, disguising herself as a boy.

The play opens famously in the ducal palace with Orsino love-sick (as was the fashion, in the tradition of courtly love) musing:

> **Boys will be girls**
>
> Scholars have shown great interest in the role of cross-dressing in Shakespeare's plays. Not only Shakespeare: Shapiro has listed eighty plays involving cross-dressing, and there may well be many more.[5] To the modern eye, it seems odd, especially as in other European countries, women played women's parts.
>
> The effect of cross-dressing has been seen mainly in homo-erotic terms: Lisa Jardine sees cross-dressing 'for a male audience's appreciation', pandering to homo-erotic tastes.[6] In his pamphlet *Anatomy of Abuses* (1585) Philip Stubbes loudly complained that playgoers were tempted 'to play the sodomites or worse.'[7] Yet the general public – from apprentices to the queen – seem not to have batted an eyelid at cross-dressing.
>
> Nor should we forget that many women were in Shakespeare's audience.
>
> So in *As You Like It*, the epilogue addresses men and women – and indeed addresses women first. Rackin points out that women too enjoyed the cross-dressing.[8] She notes that Olivia eschews men's company – until Malvolio describes the messenger from Orsino ('Claudio') as 'Not yet old enough for a man, nor young enough for a boy ... One would think his mother's milk were scarce out of him.' She immediately shows an interest. Perhaps her dream partner is a slim, effeminate youth – she does fall in love with 'Claudio'. Similarly, in *As You Like It*, Phoebe is attracted to Rosalind. So female fantasies, as well as male, were perhaps at work.
>
> Today, it seems outrageous that women in England were not permitted to act on the stage, but as Rackin and others have pointed out, there was a positive side. Theatre created the illusion that eventually became reality: women could play parts on stage, as in life, as well as men. Boys dressed as women who then played characters pretending to be men could be seen as empowering women: Portia could never have been accepted as a lawyer if her true gender had been revealed – and there she was, a woman dominating a courtroom with her legal expertise. Yes, she can do it!

> If music be the food of love, play on
> Give me excess of it, that surfeiting,
> The appetite may sicken, and so die
> That strain again, it had a dying fall
> O, it came o'er my ear like the sweet sound
> That breathes upon a bank of violets,
> Stealing and giving odour ...
>
> – Act 1, Scene 1

It emerges that the object of his love is Olivia; he recalls that the first time he set eyes on her,

> That instant was I turned into a hart
> And my desires, like fell and cruel hounds,
> E'er since pursue me.[9]

Unfortunately for him, Olivia remains isolated in her house. She has, it seems 'abjured the company and sight of men' in order to mourn a dead brother for seven years. A caricature of the courtly lover, Orsino, wallowing in self-pity, wanders off to lie amid 'sweet beds of flowers'. One wonders whether Duke Orsino Bracciano would have been flattered by having his name borrowed for the occasion, for it is very difficult to take Orsino seriously in this first scene.

In many productions of *Twelfth Night*, the play opens with Act 1, Scene 2 – the shipwreck scene, when Viola and the sea captain are cast on the coast of Illyria (present day Croatia). There is hope that her identical twin brother Sebastian may yet be alive: the sea captain claims he saw Sebastian riding the waves 'like Arion on a dolphin's back'. (Arion was a magician who could calm the seas). However, Viola bestirs herself, not to look for him, but to seek her fortune in Orsino's court, disguised as a young man. Nothing like a bit of cross-dressing to keep an audience amused ...

In Scene 3 we move on to Olivia's house, and meet the lady of the house, her maid – and two very unwelcome visitors, her disreputable kinsman, Sir Toby Belch, a less boisterous version of Falstaff, much given to the bottle, and his very dim crony Sir Andrew Aguecheek, who arrives in the hope of making Olivia his bride. Some hope: he claims to be able to 'cut a caper', but is clearly a buffoon. Sir Toby encourages Sir Andrew in his deluded ambition, all the while extracting money from him.

Back at the palace, Viola, now dressed as Cesario, has stretched credibility to the full by having gone from nought to sixty in about two seconds: she has become Orsino's favourite. Orsino gives him/her the task of courting Olivia on his behalf. Cesario/Viola gains entrance to Olivia's house, and is as *persona grata* as Orsino is not. Mayhem ensues: Olivia falls for Cesario, Viola falls for Orsino, and Aguecheek spends a lot of time falling flat on his face, metaphorically speaking, while hoping to marry Olivia. Perhaps the character who suffers the agony of love most is Viola. Although now in love with Orsino, she is required to court Olivia on his behalf; dressed as she is as Cesario. She is powerless to do much about it. Meanwhile, she now finds that she has to be friendly to Olivia without offering encouragement, as she realises that Olivia is falling in love with her. Tortuous, painful exchanges take place:

OLIVIA: Stay! I prithee, tell me what thou think'st of me.
VIOLA: That you do think you are not what you are.
OLIVIA: If I think so, I think the same as you.
VIOLA: Then think you right; I am not what I am.
OLIVIA: I would you were as I would have you be
VIOLA: Would it be better, madam, than I am?

– Act 3, Scene 1

The situation is only resolved when, eventually, unbeknown to Viola, her twin brother, Sebastian, shows up, having survived the shipwreck: confusion follows, as Viola is mistaken for Sebastian, and vice versa, with a series of mistaken identity jokes. For Sebastian, the outcome is bewildering, as he is seized on by Olivia, who believes him to be Cesario, and ends up as her husband. But why, he wonders, does she insist on calling him Cesario? Anyway, it seems he falls instantly in love with her, without even knowing about her bank balance.

Malvolio

It is time to meet Malvolio, Lady Olivia's steward. A law student, John Manningham, wrote about the performance on Candlemas in the Middle Temple in his diary, remarking particularly on the Malvolio episode:

> At our feast we had a play called 'Twelfth night or what you will'. Much like the *Comedy of Errors*, or *Menaechmi* in Plautus, but more like and near to that in Italian called *Inganni*. A good practice in it to make the steward believe his lady widow was in love with him, by counterfeiting a letter, as from his Lady, in general terms, telling him what she liked best in him, and prescribing his gesture in smiling, his apparel, etc. and then when he came to practice, making him believe they took him to be mad.[10]

In the opening scenes, Malvolio is a stern, and pompous puritanical. There are suggestions that Malvolio is meant to be a caricature of Sir William Knollys, Controller of the Queen's Household, a hard-line Puritan who had made himself very unpopular. His ancestral sign was an elephant – no surprise then that he was also thick-skinned.[11] Sir William Knollys definitely did need a thick skin: for Malvolio could well be based on him. As a guardian of Mary 'Mall' Fitton, one of the Queen's Maids of Honour, Knollys felt it was his duty to keep a watchful eye on her welfare; sadly, his watchful eye became lustful. Born in 1545, he was old enough to know better than to fall for a young woman, Mall Fitton. In a pathetic attempt to appear youthful, and spry, he dyed his beard in line with the current fashion: a yellow moustache was counterbalanced by a varicoloured long beard; his legs were covered in yellow cross garters.[12] At court, and indeed on the streets of London, he became a cruel joke. Could it be his face, or Malvolio's, that is described by Maria as smiling with 'more lines than is in the new map with the augmentation of the Indies'?[13] Sadly for the old knight, where he failed, the young Earl of Pembroke, William Herbert, a notorious womaniser, succeeded: he made Mistress Mall pregnant, and as a result ruined her. Sir Toby Belch asks 'Wherefore are these things hid? ... Are they like to take dust like Mistress Mall's picture?' The lechery of Sir William is hinted at in the name given to Shakespeare's character 'Mall voglio' – 'I want Mall'.[14]

Incidentally, Mary Fitton has sometimes been on the 'Dark Lady' list of candidates, but she was hardly into her teens when the Dark lady sonnets were written. However, as she was born in 1578, she might conceivably have been the woman referred to in Sonnets 40-42 (date 1595-7). Is this about William Herbert, The Earl of Pembroke, stealing Mary Fitton from Shakespeare?[15]

Malvolio meeting the Countess (detail, unknown artist)

That thou hast her, it is not all my grief,
And yet it may be said I loved her dearly ...
– Sonnet 42

Our detective work is not yet over, for there is one other very promising candidate guyed in the character of

Malvolio: another Puritan, Sir Thomas Posthumous Hoby, the son of Countess Elizabeth Russell, the woman who destroyed Burbage's dream of an indoor theatre. (See Chapter 18) According to A.L. Rowse, as a local magistrate, Hoby 'had made himself obnoxious in Yorkshire by interfering with the jollities of his Catholic neighbours.'[16] In fact, worse than that, he took pleasure in rooting out Catholic dissenters in the county, and made arch-enemies of the Catholic Ewre family among others. In August 1600 there was a scandalous episode in Hoby's house, Hackness Hall in Yorkshire. The house was gate-crashed by a mob of revellers, armed to the teeth, claiming to be hunters, led by Sir William Ewre. It was as if the Bullingdon Club invaded a private house. The unwelcome guests became fearsomely drunk, man-handled Hoby's servants, threatened to geld Hoby's chaplain, and even invaded Hoby's wife's bedroom – allegedly, Ewre threatened to rape her. They left at last, breaking windows and vandalising property. The whole episode is described graphically by Laoutaris,[17] and Hoby brought the case before the Star Chamber.

The events above are echoed by scenes in *Twelfth Night*. In Act 1, Scene 3 Sir Toby Belch turns up uninvited at the house of his kinswoman, Olivia, and with his chum Sir Andrew starts carousing. It gets worse: in Act 3, Scene 3, they again get riotously drunk, and even Maria, the long-suffering maid, complains about their 'caterwauling', and warns them that Olivia may throw them out. 'My lady's a Cathayan,' replies Sir Toby (meaning 'a Catharan – 'pure' – a term often used to describe Puritans – nothing to do with China.)[18] Sure enough, Olivia dispatches Malvolio to order them to moderate their behaviour or quit the house. 'Do ye seek to make an alehouse of my lady's house?' he says, and gives them their marching orders. A personality clash between him and Sir Toby Belch was inevitable. 'Dos't thou think, because thou art virtuous, there shall be no more cakes and ale?' demands an inebriated Sir Toby.

Malvolio's passing shot is at Maria, whom he blames for encouraging the dissolute men. The unwelcome visitors would certainly have shared the view expressed by H.L. Mencken, that Puritans 'had the haunting fear that someone, somewhere, might be happy',[19] and decide to have their revenge. Maria comes up with a cunning plan to trick Malvolio, whom she describes as 'some kind of Puritan.' There follows one of the cruellest practical jokes in literary history. A cryptic message is left for him to discover – 'some obscure epistles of love', purporting to come from Olivia. Of course, he is completely fooled as he reads the envelope:

> By my life, this is my lady's hand! These be her very *c*'s, her *u*'s, and her *t*'s, and thus she makes her great *P*'s. It is in contempt of question her hand.
>
> – Act 2, Scene 5

He reads on: *To the unknown beloved, this, and my good wishes*, and then opens the letter and reads:

> *Jove knows I love*
> *But who?*
> *Lips, do not move*
> *No man must know*

Then comes the killer as he reads:

> *But silence, like a Lucrece knife,*
> *With bloodless stroke my heart doth gore;*
> *M. O. A. I. doth sway my life*
>
> – Act 2, Scene 5

He reads on: '*I may command where I adore*'.

And his urgent desire for love overcomes any sense of incredulity: his puritanical pride and prejudice succumbs to self-persuasion:

> Why, she may command me;
> I serve her; she is my lady. Why, this is evident to any formal capacity. There is no obstruction in this. And the end – what should that alphabetical position portend? If I could make that resemble something in me! Softly! 'M.O.A.I.'

He notes that M could stand for Malvolio – and then notes that every letter is in his name – the right vowels, though in the wrong order. Even so, he has an urge to confirm what he hopes and thinks he has learnt, as he reads on:

'If this fall into thy hand, revolve. In my stars I am above thee, but be not afraid of greatness. Some are born great, some achieve greatness, and some have greatness thrust upon 'em. Thy fates open their hands. Let thy blood and spirit embrace them. And, to inure thyself to what thou art like to be, cast thy humble slough and appear fresh. Be opposite with a kinsman, surly with servants. Let thy tongue tang arguments of state. Put thyself into the trick of singularity. She thus advises thee that sighs for thee. Remember who commended thy yellow stockings and wished to see thee ever cross-gartered. I say, remember. Go to, thou art made, if thou desir'st to be so. If not, let me see thee a steward still, the fellow of servants, and not worthy to touch Fortune's fingers. Farewell. She that would alter services with thee, The Unfortunate-Unhappy

Then comes the persuasive postscript:

> Thou canst not choose but know who I am. If thou entertain'st my love,
> let it appear in thy smiling; thy smiles become thee well.
> Therefore in my presence still smile, dear my sweet, I prithee.
>
> – Act 2, Scene 5

We must wait until Act 3, Scene 4 to see the outcome ... Olivia asks her maid Maria to bring Malvolio to see her, and Maria warns her that he is behaving very strangely – 'tainted in's wits' – and it would be best to have a guard nearby. He now appears in a bizarre outfit, yellow stockings and all, grinning like a Cheshire Cat, and leering suggestively. This exchange follows:

> OLIVIA: How now, Malvolio!
> MALVOLIO: Sweet lady, ho ho!
> OLIVIA: Smil'st thou? I sent for thee upon a sad occasion.
> MALVOLIO Sad, lady? I could be sad: this does make some obstruction in the blood, this cross-gartering but what of that? If it please the eye of one, it is with me, as the very true sonnet is: 'Please one, and please all'.
> OLIVIA: Why, how dost thou, man? What is the matter with you?
> MALVOLIO: Not black in my mind, but yellow in my legs ...
> OLIVIA: Wilt thou go to bed, Malvolio?
> MALVOLIO (*kissing his hand*): To bed? Ay, sweetheart, and I'll come to thee.
>
> – Act 3, Scene 4

Poor Malvolio. Not the first time a man has misread the signals. It does not take long before they pretend to think he is mad, and lock him up. In a comedy, this development strikes an uncharacteristically sour note, but this was a time when Tudors used to pay to watch the antics of poor deranged people in lunatic asylums. No one likes to think that Shakespeare was unkind, but it is likely here that the potential for creating great onstage drama trumped any scruples we would like to think he may have had at making a complete mockery of a fellow human being. One can only say that Shakespeare was much kinder when he came to the character and plight of King Lear. With the enlightened views on mental illness in the 21st century, modern audiences may find the final degradation of Malvolio hard to take, and the only way to make it acceptable to a modern audience is by turning the situation into farce, for example, as performed in a National Theatre production in London in 2020 of *Twelfth Night* with the extraordinary performance of Tamsin Greig as a Lesbian Malvolia.

What if laughter were really tears?

This question, by Soren Kierkegard, leads us to another lens through which we might see the Malvolio sub-plot. Duncan-Jones unpicks many elaborate hidden jokes in these scenes:[20] she notes that at this time in 1601 Sir William Dethick, the official who handed out coats of arms, in his position as Garter King of Arms, was put on trial accused of corruption: in particular, handing out honours to those who did not deserve them – among those listed, John Shakespeare. This meant that Shakespeare's inherited position as a gentleman was now being challenged, as Sir William Dethick tried to face down his accusers in the Royal College of Heralds. This could have been seen as a humiliation for the Shakespeares, especially after Ben Jonson's mocking crack about 'Not without mustard.'[21]

Perhaps Shakespeare even subconsciously saw a bit of Malvolio in himself – not, of course, the sober-suited Puritan, but a man who had both social and amorous aspirations: Shakespeare's undistinguished origins, and current position as a man of the theatre, in Tudor eyes made it hard, if not impossible, for him to be seen as a gentleman, and this claim now rested on shifting sands. This placed him in a position similar to that of Malvolio, who also aspired to a step up in the social hierarchy.

Furthermore, he shared with Malvolio the experience of failing in the amorous stakes. We have a strong hint in Sonnets 40-42, which, though dated between 1595-7, may well have been written a little later:

> Take all my loves, yea take them all
> What hast thou then more than thou hadst before?

As we have seen, this could well refer to William Herbert, 3rd Earl of Pembroke, a young blade well known for his numerous love affairs. In 1601 he was imprisoned for impregnating Mary Fitton – perhaps the woman Shakespeare claims he loved 'dearly' in Sonnet 42 – and indeed insists in line 14: 'She loves but me alone'. Does this make Shakespeare – still only 36, but beginning perhaps to show signs of age – another Malvolio/Sir William Knollys? It may be too fanciful to think that if the lady in Sonnets 40-42, was indeed Mall Fitton, perhaps *Mall voglio* applied not to Sir William only, but to Shakespeare himself. Maybe both Sir William, and William Shakespeare, were defeated by William Herbert. We are on shifting sands here, with perhaps too many *ifs* and *maybes*.

However, Katherine Duncan-Jones even suggests that Shakespeare (perhaps as a self-defence mechanism) turned the joke on himself in a process of self-mockery, although her suggestion that he might even have played the part of Malvolio himself seems far-fetched.[22] However, she notes that the yellow stockings reflect the colour of the impresa that the College of Heralds awarded the Shakespeares (in theory, gold, in practice, yellow paint); the cross garters were seen as a huge joke, recalling the bend sinister on the shield of his coat of arms. Cross-garters were definitely the fashion of the 1580s or even earlier. By 1600, cross garters 'were worn chiefly by old men, Puritans, pedants, footmen, and rustic bridegrooms'.[23] In 1601, they would have been seen as hopelessly unfashionable, a joke.

Readers, the sub-title of *Twelfth Night* is *What You Will*. So it is down to you to decide if this theory can hold any water. What is certain is that when Malvolio appeared on the stage at the Inns of Court, dressed in his yellow finery, he was greeted with howls of mirth. It is interesting that John Manningham singles out this sub-plot to recall in his diary. He is not alone: when we remember *Twelfth Night*, who do we most remember? Do we recall Feste, who one could say represents the spirit of festival and joy? Or Malvolio?

So although *Twelfth Night* is definitely meant to be a comedy, there is a certain underlying melancholy in there, too. In the first four lines of the play, there are two references to death, or dying, and one to sickness. Perhaps the death of his father reminded Shakespeare of his own mortality, and so began an extended period of melancholy in his life, as reflected in his plays. The process has already begun in *Twelfth Night*. Caroline Spurgeon notes that from this play onwards, the number of references to disease, and the plague, increases: ' ... after 1600, every one of (his plays) is serious and used in a way that the gravity and horror of the disease are emphasised.'[24] Even one of the best-known songs in *Twelfth Night* carries on the refrain:

> Come away, come away, Death
> And in sad cypress let me be laid;
> Fly away, fly away, breath,
> I am slain by a fair cruel maid.
>   My shroud of white stuck all with yew,
>   O prepare it!
> My part of death, no one so true
> Did share it.
>
> – Act 2, Scene 4

At one point in Act 2, Scene 3 Sir Toby starts to sing a song:

> Farewell, dear heart, since I must needs be gone

And Feste finishes it:

> His eyes do show his days are almost done.

Does Shakespeare, too, think that the days of loving are indeed gone? Not quite: Sonnets 104-126, written any time between 1600 and 1609, express, or are about, love. Only two of them are clearly addressed to a male: the others could be addressed to either a male or a female. As usual, Shakespeare remains ambiguous. But I think it is likely they were written quite early on, because his next play, *Troilus and Cressida*, could hardly be described as a celebration of love.

27

WAR AND LECHERY

Lechery, lechery, still wars and lechery! Nothing else holds fashion.
— Thersites, *Troilus and Cressida*, Scene 8

Shakespeare already had in mind his next play *Troilus and Cressida* while writing *Twelfth Night*, because at one point, the Fool tells Viola/Claudio that 'I would play Lord Pandarus of Phrygia, sir, to bring a Cressida to this Troilus.' Perhaps Shakespeare felt it was time to change genres from comedy to re-establish his standing as a serious playwright; it was not until after his death, that Ben Jonson commented (in his encomium in the 1623 Folio) that Shakespeare had 'smalle Latine and Less Greeke', but perhaps Shakespeare felt that he still had something to prove, not least that he had more than a superficial knowledge of the classics. So it was to the classics he returned, with *Troilus and Cressida*, written in 1602.[1]

Shakespeare may have had personal reasons for writing this play in the way that he did: sometime during 1602, it is likely that he moved to Silver Street in north-west London, where he lodged with a Huguenot family, the Mountjoys, near the lodgings of his colleagues Heminges and Condell.[2] Did he do this to avoid paying tax? That is possible. There may have been another reason, for his landlord Christopher Mountjoy had an attractive wife who it seems was no better than she ought to have been. The quack and astrologer Simon Forman records visits from Marie Mountjoy that are suggestive; another visitor was one 'Master Wood' who asked on behalf of Mistress Marie Mountjoy 'whether the love she bears him will be altered or not.'³ Lodge also adduces evidence that the Mountjoy marriage was not a happy one – Christopher Mountjoy also consulted Forman to enquire if his two apprentices were 'honest'. Was he concerned about his wife's fidelity? Then the husband was himself censored by the French Church elders for 'lewd acts and adulteries' which had resulted in the pregnancy of at least one servant girl.⁴ It seems more than possible that Shakespeare himself had dealings with Marie that caused him to develop a jaded view of women. How else do we explain his depiction of Cressida in his next play?

The Trojan War⁵ was definitely *à la mode* in the early 1600s: the first of George Chapman's *Seven Books of the Iliad of Homer* had been entered on the Stationers' Register in April 1598, and was an immediate hit, and continued to be so, despite (or because of), the fact that it was dedicated to

---

The Inkhorn Controversy

At this time, Shakespeare was being criticised on stylistic grounds. There was in the late Mediaeval times, and well into the Jacobean period, the so-called Inkhorn controversy.⁶ The English language was undergoing, not exactly birth-pangs, but certainly development pangs – if one may describe the enrichment of a language as a pang. Many scholars questioned whether coinages (invented words – neologisms), and borrowed words, or words with Latin roots, should be permitted in English. Such words became known as *inkhornisms*, and those who used them (such as Shakespeare) were labelled 'neologisers' by the 'Purists'. Thus we have Sir John Cheke (1514-1557) arguing that 'I am of this opinion that our own tung should be written cleane and pure, unmixt and unmangeled with borrowing of other tunges ... '

In recent times we have had campaigns in favour of 'Plain English' – indeed the Plain English Campaign was founded in 1979⁷ with a ritual shredding of verbose central and local government documents. However, as early as 1553 Thomas Wilson (1524-1571) launched into his own Plain English campaign with his *Arte of Rhetorique,* calling on all to use 'our speech as most men doe':

Among all other lessons this should be learned, that we never affect any straunge ynkhorne terms, but to speak as is commonly received⁸

Thus Shakespeare was criticised for borrowing words from other languages, and using Latinisms. The Purists also hated the use of prefixes and suffixes added to words of classical origin, as in *protractive, accommodation* and *amazement*. Shakespeare was attacked, too, for coinages such as *dwindle* and *embrace*; and portmanteau words such as *farmhouse* and *gentlefolk*. Also targeted were hyphenated words such as *lack-lustre* and *green-eyed*. During the Tudor period, the neologisers were regarded as 'barbarous' and 'rude' by their opponents. Why borrow or make up words when there was already a perfectly good English lexicon to draw on? Unfortunately, this was not true, for as Ralph Lever observed in his *Art of Reason* (1573) there were 'more things than there are words to express them.'

the Earl of Essex. Henslowe's diary records that Henry Chettle and Thomas Dekker were writing a play inspired by Chapman in the following year.[9] Only a fragment of this play survives in the British Library.[10] Shakespeare would certainly have been familiar with Chaucer's verse romance *Troilus and Crisseyde* (drawn from Boccaccio) and the story of the star-crossed lovers was well known. That Shakespeare chose to retell this story of love and infidelity suggests that he nurtured an ugly perspective on human nature, based perhaps on his own recent emotional experience. Neither the Greeks nor the Trojans come out well in this play – and nor does Cressida; human nature is viewed through a very unfavourable lens.

Troilus and Cressida

At this time, people still remembered the Earl of Essex and his execution, and there were many who still saw him as a hero and mourned his death. Inevitable perhaps, then, that Shakespeare's depiction in this play of the character of Achilles, sulking in his tent, and resentful of authority, should be sometimes identified with the earl, brooding in Essex House. Achilles is depicted as something of a bully and a spoilt brat.[11] Even so, given the other unsavoury features of this play, it is unlikely that Shakespeare's play was ever acted before the queen, nor is it known whether it was ever performed for King James. Its performance history is

Simon Forman – the Tudor equivalent of a psychiatrist: described as a quack, a womaniser and an astrologer – and the voice of his age

murky: two different editions were printed in 1609: one claiming that it was acted at the Globe, the other that it was 'never staled with the stage, never clapper-clawed by the hands of the vulgar.'[12] It seems more than possible that it was acted at one of the Inns of Court: law students would have appreciated its Latinate language, its classical references, its bawdiness, and a number of legal or legalistic terms – for example, *in witness thereof, in reversion, to be cited, derive, appertainments, underwrite, self-admission,* and *fee-farm* (used about land-tenure). There must be some doubt about whether it was ever intended for the Globe in front of 'the vulgar', for the play is extraordinarily wordy – thus adding fuel to the fire in the Inkhorn controversy.

Shakespeare's play was first entered in the Stationers' Register in early February 1603 with, on its title page, the words 'as it has been acted by my Lord Chamberlain's Men'. However, this appears to have been a 'blocking entry'[13] designed to stop piracy. When in 1609 it appeared in print, two versions were entered in the Stationers' Register. There may have been a dispute over ownership, for in the Folio edition of 1623, it was squeezed in at the last minute between Histories and Tragedies but was not even mentioned in the list of contents.[14] The debate continues whether it should be classified as a History, a Comedy, a Tragedy, or a Satire. It is often put down as one of Shakespeare's so-called Problem Plays. In the Epistle at the start of the play, it is referred to as a comedy eight times, and the dark humour would have had a cynical appeal in some circles; yet if you go to a performance of it today, you will find few in the audience are laughing, even though there are some very funny lines. One may only realise that a dirty joke is meant by the leering body-language of the actors; but to enjoy the humour you would need to be almost as cynical as Thersetes, 'a scurrilous Greek', who provides a grim commentary as events take place.

The Greeks, led by Agamemnon, King of Mycenae, are besieging Troy, where Helen, the runaway wife of Menelaus, King of Sparta, lives with Paris. In Troy,[15] Troilus, one of King Priam's sons, is in love with Cressida, whose father Calchas, believing that the war is a lost cause, has defected to the besieging Greeks. Cressida's uncle, the lecherous Pandarus, with the mentality of a voyeuristic brothel-keeper, encourages the romance and acts as a go-between. There is no doubt that Troilus suffers the painful pangs of love he fears is unrequited. He tells Pandarus that he is 'mad [for] Cressid's love', but his hopes 'lie drowned.' (Scene 1, lines 43 *et seq.*)

Later, an exchange between Cressida and Pandarus is full of gossip, badinage and sexual innuendo, all of which suggests that she may be no better than she ought to be. Cressida comes over as cynical, manipulative, and calculating, as she decides to play hard to get:

> Things won are done. Joy's soul lies in the doing.
> That she beloved knows naught that knows not this:
> Men prize the thing ungained more than it is.
> That she was never yet that never knew
> Love got so sweet as when desire did sue
> Therefore this maxim out of love I teach:
> Achievement is command; ungained, beseech;
> Then though my heart's contents firm love doth bear
> Nothing of that shall from mine eyes appear.
> – Act 1, Scene 3

To be fair, Cressida knows her worth, but is not sure that men share her view. For both Greeks and Trojans appear to have in common a seriously misogynistic culture – though they can hardly be blamed for having negative views about Helen. As Hector says, 'She is not worth what she doth cost the keeping.' In modern parlance, she is seen as damaged goods. The Greek commander Diomedes is more scathing: 'For every false drop in her bawdy veins/A Grecian's life hath sunk ... ' (Scene 4). All somewhat unfair, really. As Pascal has it, 'The heart hath its reasons that reason does not know.'

Abruptly, the love affair between Troilus and Cressida becomes a relative sideshow, as the scene changes to the besieging Greeks, where all is not well. Agamemnon complains that 'after seven years siege, yet Troy walls stand'; Ulysses observes that 'great Hector's sword had lacked a master' – an attack on the Greek champion Achilles who has refused to fight. Achilles' problem is he resents the fact that the leadership lies with an ineffectual Agamemnon, rather than the obvious choice – himself; while in the Grecian camp

> ... look how many Grecian tents do stand
> Hollow upon this plain: so many hollow factions.[16]
> – Act 1, Scene 3

Ulysses has an explanation: 'Troy in our weakness lives, not in her strength.' The reason for the failure in their campaign is the divisions in the Greek camp, and the collapse in authority. He then expatiates (at some length) on the importance of what he calls 'degree', without which 'The unity and married calm of states' is destroyed:

> ... O, when degree is shaked,
> Which is the ladder of all high designs,
> The enterprise is sick. How could communities,
> Degrees in schools and brotherhoods in cities,
> Peaceful commerce from dividable shores,
> The primogeneity and due of birth,
> Prerogative of age, crowns, scepters, laurels,
> But by degree stand in authentic place?
> Take but degree away, untune that string,
> And hark what discord follows.[17]
>
> – Act 1, Scene 3

The root cause is then identified: the great warrior Achilles, too proud to accept the leadership of Agamemnon, refuses to go out on the field of battle, and sulks in his tent, relaxing with his friend Patroclus. There, says Ulysses, the 'Great Achilles'

> Grows dainty[18] of his worth, and in his tent
> Lies mocking our designs, with him, Patroclus
> Upon a lazy bed the livelong day
> Breaks scurrile jests ...
>
> – Act 1, Scene 3

Ulysses angrily describes how, in Achilles' tent, Patroclus acts out satirical imitations of the leadership to entertain his lover: thus Agamemnon becomes 'a strutting player', and old Nestor is 'the scene of mirth' as he displays 'the faint defects of age', stroking his beard, and fumbling as he tries to put on his armour – all seen as 'Stuff for these two to make paradoxes,' until 'Sir Valour'[19] cries

> O, enough Patroclus,
> Or give me ribs of steel! I shall split all
> In pleasure of my spleen
>
> – Act 1, Scene 3

Achilles may be doubled up with laughing, but no one else in the Greek camp sees the joke. Ulysses and his fellow commanders are appalled at Achilles' insubordinate behaviour and arrogant dereliction of duty. But Achilles may have a point about Agamemnon's leadership, for he does not have that air of authority one expects to find in a leader: thus when Aeneas appears under a flag of truce, he fails to recognise him at first, and Agamemnon is visibly irritated. Aeneas' purpose in arriving at the Greek camp is to offer a challenge for someone to come armed to contest Hector's claim that

> He hath a lady wiser, fairer, truer
> Than ever Greek did compass in his arms
>
> – Act 1, Scene 3
>
> ...
> If none, he'll stay in Troy when he retires.
> The Grecian dames are sunburnt, and not worth
> The splinter of a lance. Even so much.
>
> – Act 1, Scene 3

Here the classical meets the culture of the mediaeval court, where knights would enter the lists wearing their lady's gauge on their helmet. Hector clearly expects the Greeks to nominate Achilles as their champion, but Ulysses has 'a young conception' in his brain which he shares with Nestor. He has thought of a subtle way of putting proud Achilles in his place: rather than nominate him as the obvious responder to Hector's challenge, he suggests they put forward the name of Ajax, thus to 'pluck down Achilles' plumes' and upstage him.

While the Greeks carry out their plan to confront Hector with Ajax, the scene shifts to the palace of King Priam. He calls for a meeting of his commanders, and reads out this message from the Greeks:

> *Deliver Helen and all damage else –*
> *As honour[20], loss of time, travail, expense*
> *Wounds, friends, and what else dear that is consumed*
> *In hot digestion of this cormorant war*
> *Shall be struck off. Hector, what say you to it?*
>
> – Act 2, Scene 2

'No man lesser fears the Greeks than I,' replies Hector, but goes on to say that Helen is 'not worth what she doth cost the holding.' One would think that the Trojans would jump at the chance to end the war on the terms offered. However, Paris is reluctant to part with his wife; and Troilus, in an echo of the famous line from Marlowe,[21] while questioning the value of Helen, (turning her into a commodity), argues strongly for continuing the war:

> Is she worth keeping? Why, she is a pearl
> Whose price hath launched above a thousand ships
> And turned crowned kings to merchants.
>
> – Act 2, Scene 2

Troilus is clearly swayed by his belief in the importance of love, but he cites 'Manhood, Honour:'[22] he points out that the Trojans all applauded Paris when he abducted Helen – so how can they now change, without losing face?

> If you'll confess he brought home worthy prize –
> As you must needs, for you all clapped your hands
> And cried 'Inestimable' – why do you now
> The issue of your proper wisdoms rate
> And do a deed that never Fortune did,
> Beggar the estimation which you prized
> Richer than sea and land?
>
> – Act 2, Scene 2

Troilus insists that to agree to the generous terms offered by the Greeks would dishonour Helen, and indeed themselves. Then Cassandra, a priestess of Apollo and Priam's daughter, enters, distraught:

> Cry, Trojans, cry! Practise your eyes with tears
> Troy must not be, nor goodly Ilium stand,
> Our firebrand brother O Paris burn us all!
> Cry, Trojans, cry! A Helen and a woe!
> Cry, cry! Troy burns, or else let Helen go!
>
> – Act 2, Scene 2

Cassandra has been cursed by the gods with the gift of seeing the future – but the torture of knowing that no one would ever believe her; as always, her prophecies remain unheeded. Yet another hysterical woman, no doubt ... as men have through the ages always commented whenever women are right ... Hector sees the arguments of Troilus and Paris as based on passion rather than reason: he calls on the Trojans, for once, to listen to Cassandra:

> Paris and Troilus, you have both said well,
> And on the cause and question now in hand
> Have glozed but superficially, not much
> Unlike young men, whom Aristotle thought
> Unfit to hear moral philosophy.
> The reasons you allege do more conduce
> To the hot passion of distempered blood
> Than to make up a free determination
> 'Twixt right and wrong, for pleasure and revenge
> Have ears more deaf than adders to the voice
> Of any true decision
>
> – Act 2, Scene 2

Troilus says Cassandra is 'brainsick'. He reminds Hector that he is about to achieve glory in his forthcoming battle with a Greek champion, and Hector, relishing the idea, can no longer resist. And so, against his better judgement, he gives in to the eloquence of Troilus, and the war goes on. Little does Troilus realise that in insisting that the war should continue, he dooms both his love affair, as well as the future of Troy.

From high politics to low life, or, as Thersites would have it, from war to lechery. The folly of the Trojans' decision is underlined in Scene 7, where Pandarus encounters Paris and Helen, and uses heavy sarcasm to underscore his own thoughts on what is going on.

In this scene, Pandarus calls Helen *Sweet Queen* fifteen times – including for good measure *honey-sweet Queen*, and *very very sweet Queen*. Paris and Helen seem to be unaware of the heavy sarcasm of Pandarus, which is full of sexual innuendo. (The word *queen* was another term for *prostitute*). He then sings a bawdy song, more fit for the brothel than a boudoir, and thus sets the tone for Scene 8, in which he acts and sounds like a pimp as he brings his niece Cressida, modestly veiled, to Troilus so they can consummate their love for the first (and last) time. The mood changes to one of grotesque comedy in which he plays the part of a brothel-manager. 'Come. Come, what need you to blush?' he leers, as Cressida puts on a show of reluctance. Eventually, Cressida unveils, and Pandarus urges Troilus 'So, so; rub on, and kiss the mistress.'[23] Any attempt at intimacy is seriously hampered by the lurking presence of Pandarus, who becomes *voyeuriste extraordinaire*. The occasional kiss is heavily punctuated, if not punctured, by an outpouring of verbiage that sounds more like philosophizing than love-talk, until what sounds like truth at last emerges:

> CRESSID: Boldness come to me now, and brings me heart Prince Troilus,
>   I have loved you night and day for many weary months
> TROILUS: Why was my Cressid then so hard to win?
> CRESSID: Hard to seem won; but I was won, my lord
>   With the first glance that ever – pardon me,
>   If I confess much, you will play the tyrant.
>   I love you now, but not, till now, so much
>   But I might master it ...

She goes on to explain:

> See, we fools!
> Why have I blabbed? Who shall be true to us
> When we are so unsecret to ourselves?
> But though I loved you well, wooed you not
> And yet, good faith, I wished myself a man
> Or that we women had men's privilege
> Of speaking first.
>
> – Act 3, Scene 2

And she then makes a comment that is revealingly prophetic:

> I have a kind of self resides with you;
> But an unkind self, that itself will leave,
> To be another's fool. Where is my wit?
> I would be gone; I speak I know not what.
>
> – Act 3, Scene 2

That said, Cressida produces what sounds like a promise of loyalty, but is more a statement of hope than conviction, undermined by her ambivalence even about exchanging a kiss. But then it seems she feels the occasion needs to be marked by a statement of faith: 'If I be false or swerve a hair from truth,' she exclaims, 'then let men say "As false as Cressid."' As Queen Gertrude says in *Hamlet*, 'Methinks the lady doth protest too much.'[24]

Despite the dampening presence of Pandarus, who is no doubt listening at the door, their love is consummated for a night – and then dread news is announced: a prisoner exchange initiated by Cressida's father Calchas, has been agreed with the Greeks. A captured Trojan commander, Antinor, is to be exchanged for Cressida. During a brief truce, miserably, the two lovers give each other love tokens before Troilus accompanies a visibly upset Cressida to the Greek camp, and hands her over to Diomedes. There Cressida shows little sign of grief, and submits without protest as the Greek commanders give her kisses. Ulysses comments:

> Fie, fie on her!
> There's language in her eye, her cheek, her lip
> Nay, her foot speaks. Her wanton spirits look out
> At every joint and motive of her body
> O, these encounterers, so glib of tongue
> That give accosting welcome 'ere it comes
> And wide unclasp the tables of their thoughts
> To every ticklish reader! Set them down
> For sluttish spoils of opportunity
> And daughters of the game.[25]
>
> – Act 4, Scene 6

Then a trumpet sounds, signalling the arrival of Hector and other Trojans to witness the fight between Hector and Ajax. On hearing this, Greeks all call out 'The Trojans' trumpet'. (it is not clear whether this is meant be an unpleasant pun (on *strumpet*), but could well be. The two sides are enjoying the brief truce, as though two football teams were catching up at half time. They look on as the duel between the two warriors begins – and then, to everyone's disappointment (including, no doubt, that of a Tudor audience) the fight ceases when Hector declares that he refuses to continue as he and Ajax are cousins. For a night, the truce holds, as the Greeks and Trojans fraternise.

In the Grecian camp, Troilus befriends the Greek commander, Ulysses, who guides him to Calchas' tent, to witness a scene where Cressida is called to meet Diomedes. Ajax's cynical slave Thersites (described as 'a scurrilous Greek') quietly follows them. Incidentally, the characterisation of Thersites as a social critic might be seen as Shakespeare's last shot in the Poets' War: for many commentators have suggested Jonson is being satirized. (In *Tristram Shandy*, Laurence Sterne describes Thersites as an exemplar of abusive satire, 'as black as the ink it is written with.')

Arriving at Calchas' tent, Ulysses and Troilus are then shocked when they hear Cressida address Diomedes as 'Sweet honey Greek'. Appalled, they watch as Cressida and Diomedes begin to flirt: the signals Cressida gives off are very mixed, signalling *No, Yes, No, Yes, Possibly* – men have a rude word for this kind of behaviour. The final straw is when she gives the Greek the sleeve that Troilus gave her as his love-token. A moment of remorse, as she snatches it back – too late, Diomedes snatches it again, and says he will wear it in his helmet in his next battle. As Thersites comments, her mind has 'now turned whore'. No wonder Troilus angrily destroys the letter, unopened, that Cressida later sends him. To him they are 'Words, words, mere words.'[26]

Troilus's loss is overshadowed by the battle that follows: at one point he engages both Ajax and Diomedes, and in doing so, loses his horse, which Diomedes captures. He instructs his servant:

> Go, go, my servant, take thou Troilus' horse;
> Present the fair steed to my lady Cressid:
> Fellow, commend my service to her beauty;
> Tell her I have chastised the amorous Trojan,
> And am her knight by proof.
>
> – Act 5, Scene 5

He probably intends to indicate to her that Troilus is dead. We never hear how Cressida responds. But Troilus survives, as does Diomedes. The main casualties in the last battle are Patroclus, the 'masculine whore' of Achilles. His death at last provokes Achilles into joining in the battle, to kill Hector in a cowardly fashion. What happens to both Troilus and Cressida is left to the imagination. Neither he, nor the play, finds closure.

Last words

Possibly the Purists who joined battle in the Inkhorn controversy also disliked the view of human nature depicted in the play. For it was not just womanhood that was impugned: the great heroes of Greece and Troy are repeatedly insulted by Thersites. Here, the hyphenated words that the Inkhorn Purists hated so much come into their own as a means of delivering insults: Thersites calls Ajax *a mongrel beef-witted lord, a scurvy-valiant ass,* or *a sodden-witted lord,*[27] and takes his life in his hands by calling Achilles an *idol of idiot-worshippers*; Ulysses might have taken as a compliment being called *a dog-fox*. Thersites diminishes the bloody battles between Greek and Trojan as *clapper-clawing*. Poor old Nestor is called *that stale old mouse-eaten dry cheese*.[28] Perhaps Shakespeare uses hyphenated words deliberately, in defiance of the Purists?

What caused Shakespeare to write such a dispiriting play, full of filthy jokes and language, and offering such a bleak view of human nature? As we have seen, the text of *Troilus and Cressida* is studded with words from a bawdy register – or items you might hear in an ale-house: for example, *belly, plackett,* and even items like *do, will,* and *thing* which in common use had, and are given, sexual meanings. The imagery is that of the brothel and the sewer, and there are unmistakable references to syphilis.[29] The feeling of disgust with sex is palpable. Both Helen and Cressida are depicted as little less than whores. To Ulysses, Cressida is just a daughter of the game. And Helen? The view of Diomedes is likely to be shared by most except Paris:

> She's bitter to her country. Hear me, Paris:
> For every false drop in her bawdy veins
> A Grecian's life hath sunk; for every scruple
> Of her contaminated carrion weight
> A Trojan hath been slain. Since she could speak,
> She hath not given so many good words breath
> As for her Greeks and Trojans suffered death.
>
> – Act 4, Scene 1

Shakespeare appears to be steeped in misogyny and disillusionment: perhaps he had had an unhappy love affair; perhaps he was suffering the syphilitic after effects – there was a lot of syphilis around in Tudor England.[30]

Perhaps he was merely experiencing a mid-life crisis. These words may tell us something of his problem:

> TROILUS: That is the monstrosity in love, lady: that the will is infinite and the execution confined, that the desire is boundless and the act a slave to limit.
> CRESSID: They say all lovers swear more performance than they are able, and yet reserve an ability that they never perform vowing more than the perfection of ten, and discharging less than the tenth part of one ...
> – Act 3, Scene 2

There is a feeling of sadness on behalf of Troilus who is described as a young man of great worth and promise – and how he ended remains unanswered

> Not yet mature, yet matchless, firm of word.
> Speaking in deeds, and deedless in his tongue;
> Not soon provoked, nor being provoked, soon calmed;
> His heart and hand both open, and both free,
> For what he has, he gives, what thinks, he shows;
> Yet gives he not till judgement guide his bounty
> Nor disfigures an impair thought with breath;
> Manly as Hector, but more dangerous ...
> – Act 4, Scene 6

The last speech in the play is not a positive reaffirmation of the triumph of the human spirit, or an eloquent attack on the futility of war, but an extremely cynical speech from Pandarus. He addresses 'Good traders in the flesh' their eyes 'half-out' from venereal disease, and asks 'Why should our endeavour be so desired, and the performance so loathed?' His final words are unlikely to endear him to any audience:

> Brethren and sisters of the hold-door trade
> Some two months hence my will shall here be made,
> It should be now; but that my fear is this:
> Some gallèd goose of Winchester would hiss[31]
> Till then, I'll sweat and seek about for eases
> And at that time bequeath you my diseases.
> – Act 5, Scene 7

28

THE QUEEN IS DEAD, LONG LIVE THE KING!

> A workaday regnant queen, shorn of her glitter and her gold, her glamour and her greatness, with a false face, a disturbed psyche, a heart of stone, a barren womb and feet of clay; and as such a woman trying to do a man's job, but not always doing it very happily or well.
>
> – David Carradine[1]

In the months following the death of Essex, Queen Elizabeth suffered more than usual from melancholy. However, she struggled on, as she went from one royal palace to another, and managed to hold on to the reins of government, even as they began to slip through her fingers. On 2 February 1602 the Lord Chamberlain's Men performed – but not in one of her palaces. Unusually, she went to the Middle Temple to watch a performance of *Twelfth Night*. The hall, and the table where she presided over the banquet, can still be seen today. Throughout the spring and summer of 1602, she remained active, spending time in her palaces at both Greenwich and Richmond, where she celebrated May Day. That year she visited the homes of some twenty of her courtiers in and around London. In a moment of uncharacteristic optimism, Cecil wrote in a letter to Carew: 'Blessed by God! I saw not Her Majesty so well these dozen years!'[2]

However, in October there were signs that her memory was beginning to fade. She still managed to entertain foreign envoys, including the new French ambassador, and she was well enough to open Parliament, the thirteenth and last of her reign. Members of Parliament were greatly exercised over the monopoly system – monopolies were in the queen's gift, and were being scandalously abused, as they became cash-cows for the lucky holders. When the queen announced an immediate end to the system,[3] a deputation of 159 MPs went to express their thanks, and on 30 November, she received them in the Council Chamber at Whitehall, and it was here that she made what became known as her 'Golden Speech':

> I do assure you, there is no prince who loves her subjects better. There is no jewel, be it of never so rich a price, which I set before this jewel: I mean your love. For I do more esteem it than any treasure or riches ... [4]

The queen put on a brave show over Christmas, despite bouts of serious depression. As the Earl of Worcester observed at the time, 'Irish tunes are at this time most pleasing but in winter, 'Lullaby', an old song of Mr Byrd's, will be more in request, as I think.'[5] That Christmas, the queen was not dancing. She was however well enough to enjoy a play: records show that on 2 February 1603, 'John Hemynges and the rest of his company, servauntes to the Lorde Chamberleyne's Men' gave their last ever performance before the queen at the royal palace of Richmond.[6] History does not record what play was performed. Somehow, Elizabeth continued to deal with affairs of state: on 6 February 1603, she had an audience with the Venetian ambassador, in which she spoke fluent Italian. She was cheered by the news that just before Christmas, Lord Mountjoy had won a great victory against Tyrone, and the Spanish troops that had landed at Kinsale had ignominiously surrendered. On 17 February, she authorised Mountjoy to negotiate a peace process, agreeing to accept the rebel earl's submission as long as hostilities ceased.[7]

Even so, it was clear that her days were numbered, and she was greatly saddened by the illness of her closest friend, Kate Carey, Countess of Nottingham, George Carey's daughter: at the age of 57, on 25 February, the countess died. Grief-stricken, the queen ordered a state funeral, but now she went into a steep decline. The coronation ring she had worn since being crowned had become embedded in her finger, and had to be removed with a file. This caused her great distress, for with the removal of this ring, she felt that the sacred bond between her and her people had been broken.

The death of Kate Carey seemed to remind her of Mary, Queen of Scots.

Sir Robert Carey, Kate's younger brother, reported that 'She shedd many tears and sighs, manifesting her innocence that she never gave consent to the death of that queene.'[8] She ate and slept little in her last days, and at the end lost the power to speak. But she did manage to whisper to Cecil that her kinsman, the King of the Scots should succeed her – or so Cecil said.[9] On the evening of 23 March, Archbishop Whitgift, who himself only had a year to live, for hours knelt his aching old limbs in prayer at her bedside. She died at 3.00am on Thursday 24 March. In the words of John Manningham:

> The morning about 3 at clock, her Majesty departed this life, mildly like a lamb, easily like a ripe apple from the tree, *cum leve quadam fibre, absque gemitu*.[10]

Beside her bed, her women found a packet of letters, tied up with a ribbon, 'the writing slightly blotted with her tears'. On the back of one of them, a letter from Robert Dudley, the Earl of Leicester, she had written 'his last letter.'[11]

The nation may have mourned, but breathed a sigh of relief when order and calm were preserved. Elizabeth's courtiers, including Cecil, anxious for an orderly succession, had already started to jockey for position with James VI of Scotland, soon to become James I of England. Camden notes that 'as the report now grew daily stronger and stronger, that her sickness increased upon her, it was astonishing to behold with what speed the Puritans, Papists, ambitious persons and flatterers posted night and day by sea and land to Scotland, to adore the rising sun and gain his favour.' Cecil and the Privy Councillors proclaimed James king before daybreak, less than three hours after the old queen had died. The proclamation was read out at key locations around the city, to be swiftly printed and distributed. Rumours were rife of a Catholic plot to install Archduke Albert and the Infanta on the throne, and to avoid civil disorder, the Privy Council banned all public gatherings, and theatres and ports were closed. The proclamation had a positive effect: by the evening, bonfires were lit, and church bells rang out, as the citizenry welcomed a new era; soon, elaborate preparations were being made to welcome King James – unfortunately, to be much delayed because of a serious outbreak of the plague.

Queen Elizabeth's body was brought by barge from Richmond Palace, and lay in state for a month at Whitehall. Her funeral took place on 28 April. The cortege was attended by over a thousand black-clad mourners; many more lined the funeral route. Stowe recorded that 'there was such a general sighing, groaning and weeping as the like hath not been seen or known in the memory of man'. Her body was lowered into a vault in the north aisle of the Henry VII Chapel in Westminster Abbey, joining that of her Catholic sister, Mary Stuart.

Shakespeare would have heard every rumour of the queen's decline and death – Rumour was in overdrive through this period – to be replaced by Sorrow when the queen died, and the mythos of Good Queen Bess began again to take root. Her shortcomings were quickly forgotten, as the nation mourned, and realised that she had been a major factor in maintaining the nation's stability. A number of eulogies were written in her memory – efforts to achieve a balance between mourning the queen and welcoming the king proving a challenge to some of them.[12] One anonymous ballad-writer called on

> You poets all, brave Shakespeare, Jonson, Greene
> Bestow your name to write for England's Queen.
> Return your songs and Sonnets and your ways
> To set forth sweet Elizabeth's praise.[13]

Greene would have had some difficulty in following the ballad writer's advice, having died in 1594. Perhaps his name was selected because it rhymed with *queen*? It surely could not have referred to Shakespeare's distant cousin, a lawyer called Greene,[14] who did indeed write an appalling poem in a vain attempt to court preferment.[15]

Seemingly, not a word from Shakespeare, though some detect a reference to her demise in Sonnet 107. We do not know exactly how he felt about the queen – but he was notably absent from the list of those who wrote a poem to mark her passing. In his booklet *England's Mourning Garment* (1603), Henry Chettle made a thinly-veiled attack on Shakespeare for failing to write an encomium. But Shakespeare was not the only poet who failed to do so. Others are attacked in Chettle's poem, all, incidentally, provided with pseudonyms. Various authorities have identified among the offenders

Ben Jonson, Sam Daniel, George Chapman, Michael Drayton, Thomas Lodge, Thomas Dekker and John Marston – some of whom did indeed write a few lines – but mainly in praise of James even while the nation was still in mourning for Elizabeth.

Many authorities have speculated on the reasons why Shakespeare did not join in Elizabeth's plaudits. It is often assumed that Shakespeare met the queen, but there is no evidence that he did so, even though the Lord Chamberlain's Men were clearly her favourite acing company. She certainly saw him acting on the stage – perhaps even as Malvolio, and knew of his authorship. So while Shakespeare did not dance on her grave, he does not seem to have mourned her passing. Some have suggested that he was distressed by the imprisonment of Southampton, and the execution of Essex – as many were – there was a feeling among the populace that the earl did not deserve to be executed. However, I think Shakespeare had few illusions about either of them.

Indeed, it is likely that he had few illusions about the queen, either: for he had direct experience of how brutal her rule could be. Even if he did not choose to speak ill of the dead, he probably knew enough about what was going on in England to realise that the 'golden words' of Elizabeth's speech to Parliament were a PR exercise, and her promises on monopolies were likely to be empty. He must have known, as the queen apparently did not, that 'the overwhelming majority of her people were struggling with the crippling effects of high prices, harvest failures, poverty and disease.'[16] He knew, too, of poor people who died of starvation, and must have seen the mariners and soldiers, many bearing the grievous scars of war, returning from defending their country, denied not just pensions, but even their wages. One group limped into London demanding their pay: the queen ordered her privy councillors to arrest and hang them. 'The gallows are the pay they give us for going to the wars!' shouted one as he awaited his fate. Then – as now – many an ex-serviceman could be seen begging, and sleeping rough, on the streets of London. They could be forcibly dragged off and re-enlisted to fight again in the Netherlands, or in Ireland, along with any thought to be 'rogues and vagabonds' found 'loitering' in the streets.[17] Having once been robbed by a highwayman, the infamous Gabriel Ratsey, he knew, too, how social conditions had created a dangerously violent element in society, No doubt he had some sympathy with Cecil's edict that those judged to be 'incorrigible or dangerous Rogues' could be banished to 'The New-found Land, the East and West Indies', and sundry countries on the European mainland.[18]

Above all, perhaps, he would have found abhorrent the brutality of Elizabeth's government in dealing with suspected enemies of the state – including, of course, Edward Arden, Dr Lopez, and many innocent priests such as Father Southwell – and the gruesome methods of torture and execution. We do not know what he thought of (or even knew about) the scheme, mooted in 1596, to deport people of black African descent found living in England to Spain and Portugal to be sold as slaves – some were to be used to exchange for English prisoners of war.[19] Nor do we know how much he knew of the endless political machinations and disinformation campaigns by both the regime, and those (especially on the continent) who opposed it, as described by Lake.[20] So he might well have found distasteful the hypocrisy and flattery involved in writing the final obsequies to the queen, and thus helping to propagate the cult of 'Gloriana'.[21]

Sonnets 104-126

Judging by Sonnets 104 – 126, the last group of sonnets Shakespeare wrote in the period 1600-1604,[22] he was much more concerned with private joys and griefs than public issues. In any case, he may well have thought that a sonnet was not the way to mark the passing of a monarch. In these sonnets, most of which could be addressed to a male or a female, Sonnet 119 refers to 'siren tears' which may imply that the poem is addressed to a female. But these poems are about love, so who cares about the gender of the person or people, involved? As Shakespeare says in Sonnet 121:

> Or on my frailties why are frailer spies,
> Which in their wills count bad what I think good?

One of the best of all his sonnets, still a favourite reading at weddings, really says it all – life is, or should be, all about love:

> Let me not to the marriage of true minds
>   Admit impediments. Love is not love
> Which alters when it alteration finds,

>   Or bends with the remover to remove:
> O no! it is an ever-fixed mark
>   That looks on tempests and is never shaken;
> It is the star to every wandering bark,
>   Whose worth's unknown, although his height be taken.
> Love's not Time's fool, though rosy lips and cheeks
>   Within his bending sickle's compass come:
> Love alters not with his brief hours and weeks,
>   But bears it out even to the edge of doom.
>   If this be error and upon me proved,
>   I never writ, nor no man ever loved.

– Sonnet 116

Sic transit gloria regina

The whole country felt relief at the peaceful transition from Elizabeth to James, and it is likely that Shakespeare also felt the same, even if he did not join in the crowds who so ecstatically greeted James on his arrival in London some nine days after the old queen's funeral. Politically, it looked as though the threat from Spain was at last declining; the war in Ireland had come to a halt with Tyrone's surrender, and (it was hoped) this meant the tax burden would be lightened; the threat of civil disorder was reduced with the execution of Essex; the plots against the crown seemed to be in abeyance – though shocks were in store ... Above all, the arrival of a new king, the father of two sons and a daughter, with no apparent opposition, and the succession thus assured, meant that the future seemed stable and secured.

On a more personal level, the burden of anxiety was now largely lifted: with his father dead and buried, and his Catholic sympathies forgotten, Shakespeare no longer had reason to fear harassment by the authorities, especially as Topcliffe was increasingly side-lined by the authorities. Many fellow thespians had died in penury, or of disease, and some had been murdered or imprisoned, but Shakespeare had survived, and prospered, despite the poisoning of one former patron (Lord Strange), and the imprisonment in the Tower of another (Southampton). He had survived near bankruptcy when the lease on the Blackfriars Theatre ran out; and the Globe Theatre was thriving. A successful playwright, poet, and shareholder in the company, Shakespeare's professional reputation was high, indeed, his career was at its peak. Furthermore, he was financially very secure: he owned the second biggest house in Stratford-upon-Avon, and was able to invest in property and other businesses. His wife remained healthy, and had proved very capable both as a business woman and a home builder – she was largely responsible for the restoration of New Place. She would not die until August 1623 – possibly just in time to see the First Folio. Shakespeare's only serious regret would have been the death of his only son, and in the early 1600s, the fact that his daughters were not yet married off may have caused Shakespeare some concern.[23]

The welcome arrival of King James, then, was a time of hope, while Elizabeth was now becoming a legend. And we know what Shakespeare thought of legends, from his treatment of the Trojan War in *Troilus and Cressida* – a war that the Tudors had seen as one of heroic courage and valour, but which he saw as a war of unrelieved brutality and hypocrisy. Despite this, Shakespeare seems to have managed to retain a residue of optimism. Most authorities recognise that Sonnet 107, despite its topical opacity, refers to the year 1603, which saw the eclipse, or death, of Elizabeth, the 'mortal moon', and the 'balmy time' – the peaceful accession of King James. There was however, a sting in the tale – the reference to 'tyrants' in the last line. For in his plays it is clear Shakespeare knew about tyrants. Time would tell whether this was a comment on the Tudor dynasty – or, if it was a warning, as the Stuarts took over the reins of power:

The Chariot in Queen Elizabeth I's Funeral Procession
From a Drawing of the Time, supposed to be by the Hand of William Camden (Society of Antiquaries, 1791). Part of a folding panorama nearly 29 feet long.

Not mine own fears, nor the prophetic soul
   Of the wide world dreaming on things to come,
Can yet the lease of my true love control,
   Supposed as forfeit to a confined doom.
The mortal moon hath her eclipse endured
   And the sad augurs mock their own presage;
Uncertainties now crown themselves assured
   And peace proclaims olives of endless age.
Now with the drops of this most balmy time
   My love looks fresh, and Death to me subscribes,
Since, spite of him, I'll live in this poor rhyme,
   While he insults o'er dull and speechless tribes;
     And thou in this shalt find thy monument,
       When tyrants' crests and tombs of brass are spent.

                                      Sonnet 107

Select Bibliography

Bate, Jonathan, *Mad About Shakespeare* (London: William Collins, 2023)

Bate, Jonathan *How the Classics Made Shakespeare* (OUP, 2019)

Bate, Jonathan, & Rasmussen Eric, (eds.) *William Shakespeare and Others: Collaborative Plays* (Basingstoke: Palgrave Macmillan, 2013)

Callaghan, Dympna (ed.) *A Feminist Companion to Shakespeare* 2nd Edition (Wiley-Blackwell: Oxford, 2016)

Duncan-Jones, Katherine *Shakespeare: An Ungentle Life* (London: Methuen Drama, 2010)

Duncan-Jones, Katherine *Portraits of Shakespeare* (Oxford: the Bodleian Library, 2015)

Edmondson, Paul, and Wells, Stanley (eds.) *All the Sonnets of Shakespeare* (CUP, 2020)

Edmondson, Paul, & Wells, Stanley (eds.), *The Shakespeare Circle An Alternative Biography* (CUP, 2015)

Edmondson, Paul, & Wells, Stanley (eds.), *Shakespeare Beyond Doubt: Evidence, Argument, Controversy* (CUP, 2013)

Fletcher, Loraine *Honour Killing in Shakespeare* (London: Greenwich Exchange, 2019)

Gallagher, John *Learning Languages in Early Modern England* (OUP, 2019)

Greenblatt, Stephen *Will in the World* (New York: W. W. Norton & Company, 2004)

Greenblatt, Stephen *Tyrant: Shakespeare on Power* (NY: W.W. Norton & Co. Inc, 2018)

Greer, Germaine *Shakespeare's Wife* (London: Bloomsbury, 2007)

Guy, John *Elizabeth: The Forgotten Years* (London: Penguin/Viking/Random House, 2016)

Honigmann, E.A.G. *Shakespeare: The 'Lost' Years* 2nd Edition (Manchester University Press, 1998)

Jackson, Claire *Devil-Land: England Under Siege 1588-1688* (London: Allen Lane, 2021)

Karim-Cooper, Farah *The Great White Bard: Shakespeare, Race and the Future* (London: Oneworld, 2023)

Kastan, Scott & Stallybrass, Peter (eds.), *Staging the Renaissance: Reinterpretations of Elizabethan and Jacobean Drama* (NY & London: Routledge, 1997)

Lake, Peter *How Shakespeare Put Politics on the Stage* (New Haven & London: Yale University Press, 2016)

Laoutaris, Chris *Shakespeare and the Countess: The Battle That Gave Birth to the Globe* (London: Penguin, 2014)

Loughnane, Rory, & Power, Andrew *Early Shakespeare 1588-1591* (CUP, 2020)

Manley, Lawrence & Maclean, Sue-Beth *Lord Strange's Men and Their Plays* (New Haven: Yale University Press, 2014)

Marsh, Geoffrey *Living with Shakespeare* (Edinburgh University Press, 2020)

Milward, Peter, SJ, *Shakespeare's Religious Background* (London: Sidgwick & Jackson, 1973)

O'Neill, James *The Nine Years War, 1593-1603: O'Neill, Mountjoy and the Military Revolution* (Dublin: Four Courts Press, 2018)

Orlin, Lena Cowen *The Private Life of William Shakespeare* (OUP, 2021)

Rackin, Phyllis *Shakespeare and Women* (OUP, 2014)

Schoenbaum, Samuel *William Shakespeare A Compact Documentary Life* (New York, Oxford: OUP, 1987)

Shapiro, James *1599: A Year in the Life of Shakespeare* (London: Faber & Faber, 2005)

Shapiro, Stephen *Contested Will: Who Wrote Shakespeare?* (London: Faber & Faber, 2010)

Shapiro, James *Shakespeare and the Jews* (New York & Chichester: Columbia University Press, 1996)

Shapiro, James *Shakespeare in a Divided America* (London: Faber & Faber, 2020)

Shapiro, Michael *Gender in Play on the Shakespearian Stage: Boy Heroines and Female Pages* (Ann Arbour: University of Michigan Press, 1996)

Smith, Emma *The Making of Shakespeare's First Folio* (Oxford: The Bodleian Library, 2015)

Taylor, Gary, Jowett, John, Bouros, Terri & Egan, Gabriel (eds.) *The New Oxford Shakespeare: The Complete Works: Modern Critical Edition* (OUP, 2016)

Taylor, Gary, & Egan, Gabriel *Shakespeare Authorship Companion* (OUP, 2017)

Thompson, Ayanna (ed.), *The Cambridge Companion to Shakespeare and Race* (CUP, 2021)

Wells, Stanley *Shakespeare For All Time* (London: Macmillan, 2002)

Wells, Stanley *Shakespeare, Sex and Love* (OUP, 2010)

Wood, Michael *In Search of Shakespeare* (London: BBC, 2003)

NOTES

PREFACE

[1]Dawson, C.M. *The Story of Greenwich* (Blackheath: Heathvale Press, 1977), p34

[2]Winkler, Elizabeth *Shakespeare was a Woman and Other Heresies: How Doubting the Bard Became the Biggest Taboo in Literature* (NY: Simon & Schuster 2023)

[3]Knights, L.C. who wrote a famous essay called 'How many Children had Lady Macbeth' in *Explorations Essays in Criticism Mainly on the Literature of the Seventeenth Century* (NY: George W. Stuart Publishers, 1947).

INTRODUCTION

[1]Steevens, George, & Johnson, Samuel *The Plays of Shakespeare with the Corrections and Illustrations of Various Commentators* (10 vols., 1773)

[2]Edmondson, Paul, & Wells, Stanley *Shakespeare Beyond Doubt* (Cambridge University Press, 2013)

[3]Quoted in Harries, Susan *Nicholas Pevsner: The Life* (London: Chatto & Windus, 2011), p87

(Hegel in *Phenomenology of the Spirit* (1807) uses the term *Geist der Zeiten* 'spirit of the times')

[4]A Spanish expedition invaded Cornwall in 1595 with the help of a local Catholic, and destroyed Penzance and several villages. Colin Martin and Geoffrey Parker's Book *Armada* casts fresh light on Philip II's 'Enterprise of England' in 1588 (Yale University Press, 2023)

[5]Lake, Peter *Bad Queen Bess? Libels, Secret Histories, and the Politics of Publicity in the Reign of Queen Elizabeth I* (OUP, 2016)

[6]Quoted in Stephen Alford's review article 'On a Par with Nixon' in *LRB* Vol 38 No 22 17 November 2016

[7]Bloom, Harold *Shakespeare: The Invention of the Human* (NY: Riverhead Books, Penguin Putnam Inc, 1998)

CHAPTER 1 WHO WAS SHAKESPEARE?

[1]Marsh, Geoffrey *Living with Shakespeare* (Edinburgh University Press, 2020)

[2]Edward Malone (1741-1813) was an Irish lawyer who became a great Shakespearian scholar. A friend and colleague of Samuel Johnson, he edited *The Plays and Poems of William Shakespeare*. Quoted in Schoenbaum Samuel. *William Shakespeare: A Compact Documentary Life* (NY, Oxford: OUP, 1987), p26

[3]Rutter, Carol Chillington 'Schoolfriend, publisher and printer Richard Field' in *The Shakespeare Circle: An Alternative Biography* (eds) Paul Edmondson & Stanley Wells (CUP, 2015), pp164

[4]Michell, John *Who Wrote Shakespeare* (London: Thames & Hudson 1996), pp13-14; Lacy reports that Sir Walter Raleigh's surname was spelt in 73 different ways. See Lacy, Robert, *Sir Walter Raleigh* (Weidenfeld & Nicolson London, 1973), p11

[5] Guy, John, *Elizabeth: The Forgotten Years* (London: Penguin/Viking/Random House UK, 2016), p32

[6] Fallow, David 'His father John Shakespeare' in *The Shakespeare Circle* (eds) Edmondson & Wells (CUP, 2015) gives a detailed account of his business activities.

[7] Quoted in Fripp, E.I. *Shakespeare's Haunts near Stratford* (Oxford & London, 1929). Leland's Itinerary notebooks are in the Bodleian Library, MSS Topgen. e.8-15; other fragments are in the British Library, or surviving only as later transcripts

[8] Fripp, Edgar *Shakespeare Studies* (OUP, 1930)

[9] *The Shakespeare Circle* (eds) Edmondson, Paul & Wells, Stanley (CUP, 2015)

[10] Greer, Germaine *Shakespeare's Wife* (London: Bloomsbury, 2007)

[11] Schoenbaum, *op cit.*, p17 Aubrey, John *Brief Lives* Aubrey (1626-1697) See also Aubrey, John *Brief Lives*, (ed) O.L. Dick London 1949 Aubrey was a pioneer archaeologist, folklorist, local historian (Wiltshire and Surrey), writer – and biographer.

[12] Bearman, Robert 'John Shakespeare: A Papist, or Just Penniless?' in *Shakespeare Quarterly*, Vol 56 No 4 (Winter 2005), pp411- 433

[13] Greenblatt Stephen, *Will in the World* (NY: W.W. Norton & Company, 2004), pp92 *et seq.*

[14] Greer, *op cit.*, p32

[15] Duncan-Jones, Katherine *Portraits of Shakespeare*, (Oxford: the Bodleian Library, 2015), pp55 *et seq*. She cites two references: May Edmond's 'It was for Gentle Shakespeare Cut' in *Shakespeare Quarterly* 42.3 (Autumn 1991), See also Edward Town, 'A Biographical Dictionary of London Painters 1547-1625, Walpole Society 76 (2014), p75

[16] Duncan-Jones *op cit.*, pp75 *et seq.*

[17] Fleming, Juliet 'The Ladies Shakespeare', pp3-4 in Callaghan, Dympna (ed). *A Feminist Companion to Shakespeare* 2nd Edition (Wiley-Blackwell: Oxford, 2016)

[18] Duncan-Jones *op cit.*, p9

[19] Wilson, John Dover *The Essential Shakespeare: A Biographical Adventure.* (CUP,1932), p5

[20] Orlin, Lena Cowen *The Private Life of William Shakespeare* (OUP, 2021). Orlin, a Professor at Georgetown University, Washington DC, adduces evidence that Shakespeare commissioned the monument himself.

[21] Grant, Stephen H. *Collecting Shakespeare: The Story of Henry and Emily Folger* (Baltimore: Johns Hopkins University Press, 2014)

[22] Somerset, Anne *Unnatural Murder: Poison at the Court of James I* (London: Weidenfeld and Nicholson, 1997), pp309 *et seq*

[23] Elton, Ben *The Upstart Crow* (London: BBC Publications, 2019) The book gives the script of the three-part BBC series: but is no substitute for viewing the series.

[24] Jeffrey David, Ian 'Shakespeare's empathy: enhancing connection in the patient-doctor relationship in times of crisis' in *The Journal of the Royal Society of Medicine* 2021 Vol 114(4), pp178-181

CHAPTER 2 THE EARLY YEARS

[1] Duffy, Eamon *The Stripping of the Altars* (New Haven & London: Yale University Press, 1992)

[2] Fripp (a) *op cit.*

[3] Stone, Lawrence *The Crisis of the Aristocracy 1558-1641* (Oxford: The Clarendon Press, 1965), p128

[3] Recusants were English Catholics who refused to attend Anglican services, as laid down by law, and were thus at risk of incurring penalties such as fines

[4] Fripp (a) 1928 *op cit.*

[5] Schoenbaum, S. *op cit.*, pp 35-6

[6] Wood, Michael *In Search of Shakespeare* (London: BBC, 2003), p7

[7] Wells, Stanley *Shakespeare For All Time* (London: Macmillan, 2002), p11

[8] Greenblatt *op cit.*, p26

[9] Rowse, A.L. *William Shakespeare: A Biography* (NY: Barnes & Noble Inc, 1995), p47.

[10] Bate, Jonathan *Soul of the Age* (London: Viking 2008), pp79 *et seq.*

[11] Burrow, Colin *Shakespeare & Classical Antiquity* (OUP, 2013). His discussion of Ovid's influence pp92 *et seq.* is particularly interesting

[12] Taylor, Gary, and Wells, Stanley *The Oxford Shakespeare: The Complete Works* 2nd Ed. (OUP, 2005)

[13] Edmondson, Paul, and Wells Stanley (eds) *All the Sonnets of Shakespeare* (in the order in which they were written 'so far as current scholarship allows', p2) (CUP, 2020)

[14] The reference to 'a seething bath' raises a question here: the phrase reminds one sharply of a book by William Clowes published in 1579 on how to cure *Morbis Gallicus* (syphilis) by bathing in hot water. It is unlikely that an innocent country boy like Shakespeare would have read Clowes' book at this time. Perhaps he revised this poem some years later?

[15] Miola, Robert *Shakespeare's Reading* (OUP *Topics* series, 2000), p2

[16] Rutter, Carol Chillington 'Shakespeare and school' in Edmondson, Paul, and Wells Stanley *Shakespeare Beyond Doubt* (CUP, 2013), pp133-144. *Ethopoeia* means the ability to put oneself in the place of other people so as to both understand and express their feelings better.

[17] Jeffrey, *op cit.* See Note 24, Chapter 1. *Ethopoeia* is necessary for doctors as well as actors (and playwrights)

[18] Greenblatt *op cit.*, p36

[19] Wilson, Ian *Shakespeare: The Evidence* (London: Hodder Headline Publishers, 1998), pp70-71

[20] *Ibid.*, p65

[21] A dumbshow was a mime designed to indicate, or comment on, the main plot line of a play. It was 'an allegorical survival of the mediaeval morality play' (Dobson, *Oxford Encyclopedia of Theatre and Performance* in *Shakespeare Works*)

[22] Rowe, 1709, ppii-iii. Quoted in Schoenbaum *op cit.*, p73. Rowe (1674-1718) was an English poet and dramatist, and an early editor of Shakespeare's works.

[23] Wilson, *op cit.*, p51

[24] Fallow, *op cit.* in *The Shakespeare Circle*, pp35-6

[25] Schoenbaum, S. *op cit.*, p32

[26] Bearman, Robert *Shakespeare's Money* (OUP, 2016), pp10-21

[27] Duncan-Jones, Katerine *Shakespeare: An Ungentle Life* (London: Methuen Drama, 2010), p16

[28] Fallow *op cit.*, p35

[29] Schoenbaum *op cit.*, pp39-41

[30] Quoted in E.K. Chambers, *The Elizabethan Stage,* 4 Volumes, (Oxford: Clarendon Press, 1923) Vol. 2, pp87-8; spellings modernized. See also Lee, Sidney (ed). 'Whitgift, John' in *Dictionary of National Biography. Vol. 61.* (London: Smith, Elder & Co, 1900)

[31] Ackroyd, Peter *Shakespeare: The Biography* (London: Chatto and Windus, 2005), p60

[32] Greenblatt, pp95 *et seq.* Debdale was later re arrested, and executed, in 1586.

[33] Aubrey, John *Brief Lives.* Quoted in E.A.G. Honigmann *Shakespeare: The 'Lost' Years* 2nd Edition Manchester University Press, 1998, p2. See Bodleian Library, MS. Aubrey 6 folio 109, recto; see online at Shakespeare documented.folger.edu/Aubrey

[34] Honigman *op cit.*, p8 *et seq.* See also Fr Peter Millward, SJ 'Shakespeare's Teachers' in Dutton, A.R., Finlay A.G. & Wilson, R. *Theatre and Religion: Lancastrian Shakespeare* (Manchester University Press, 2003), p58 *et seq.*

[35] Schoenbaum *op cit.*, pp114-115

CHAPTER 3 THE FAMILY MAN

[1] Horsler, Val *Shakespeare's Church: A Parish for the World* (London: Third Millennium Publishing, 2010), p49

[2] Burgess, Anthony *Nothing Like the Sun: A Story of Shakespeare's Love Life* (London: Heinemann, 1964)

[3] Burgess, Anthony *Shakespeare* (London: Jonathan Cape, 1970), pp56-58

[4] *ibid.*

[5] O'Farrell, Maggie *Hamnet* (London: Bloomsbury, 2020)

[6] Greenblatt, Stephen *Will in the World* (NY: W.W. Norton & Company, 2004), p123

[7] Ingram, Martin *Church Courts: Sex and Marriage in England 1570-1640* (CUP, 1987), p286

[8] Greer *op cit.*, p80

[9] Greenblatt *op cit.*, p123

[10] Duncan-Jones, Katerine *Shakespeare: An Ungentle Life*, p19

[11] Greer, Germaine *op cit.*, p47

[12] *ibid., p46*

[13] Greenblatt *op cit.*, p125

[14] Edmondson and Wells *op cit.*, p49

[15] Gurr, Andrew 'Shakespeare's First Poem: Sonnet 145', *Essays on Criticism* xxi, 1971, pp 221-6

[16] Williams, Robin *Sweet Swan of Avon: Did a Woman Write Shakespeare?* (Sante Fe: Wilton Circle Press, 2012), p212

[17] Wilson *op cit.*, p56

[18] Wells, Stanley *Shakespeare For All Time* (London: Macmillan, 2002), pp19-20. There is no documentary evidence that 'Anne Whateley' ever existed.

[19] Greer *op cit.*, pp94-96

[20] Mackinnon, Lachlan 'His daughter Susana Hall', *The Shakespeare Circle, op cit.*, p77

[21] *cf* Scheil, Katherine 'His wife Anne Shakespeare and the Hathaways', *The Shakespeare Circle op cit.*

[22] Greer *op cit.*, pp217-9

[23] *ibid.*, p343

[24] Author's translation.

CHAPTER 4 MORE LOST YEARS: LEICESTER'S MEN

[1] Greenblatt, Stephen *op cit.*, pp161-162

[2] Greer, *op cit.*, p142

[3] Manning, Roger B. *Village Revolts: Social Protest and Popular Disturbances in England* 1509-1640 (Oxford: Clarendon Press 1988), p4

[4] Greer *op cit.*, p139 Greer gives details of a case involving common land in Shottery being enclosed – an area that had been used as common land for hundreds of years

[5] Greenblatt *op cit.*, p93

[6] Schoenbaum *op cit.*, p104-5

[7] Fripp, Edgar I. *Shakespeare's Stratford* (OUP, 1928), p10

[8] Holden, Anthony *William Shakespeare* (London: Little Brown and Company, 1999), pp48-50

[9] Hutchinson, Robert *Elizabeth's Spy Master* (Weidenfeld & Nicholson 2005), pp101-102. See also Jessie Childs, *God's Traitors: Terror and Faith in Elizabethan England* (The Bodley Head, 2014).

[10] Guy, John *Elizabeth: The Forgotten Years* (London: Penguin/Random House, 2016), p171

[11] Shapiro, James *1599* (London: Faber & Faber, 2005), p160

[12] Gristwood, Sarah *Elizabeth & Leicester* (London: Random House/Transworld Publishers Bantam Press, 2007), p324

[13] Wood, Michael *In Search of Shakespeare* (London BBC Worldwide, 2003), p74

[14] *Ibid.*, pp94-5

[15] Duncan-Jones, Katherine *Shakespeare: An Ungentle Life* (London: Methuen Drama, 2010), p40

[16] *Ibid.*, p41

[17] Schoenbaum *op cit.*, p255

[18] Falconer, Alexander *Shakespeare and the Sea* (London: Constable New York: Frederick Ungar, 1964)

[19] Cooper, Rt Hon Alfred Duff *Sergeant Shakespeare* (London: Rupert Hart-Davis; Republished M.S.G. Haskell House, 1977)

[20] Duncan-Jones *op cit.* describes the whole episode, pp36-40

[21] This information was revealed by the archivist in Kronborg Castle in the BBC programme *Who do you think you are?* Series 18.2 with Dame Judi Dench

[22] Loughnane, Rory 'Shakespeare and the Idea of Early Authorship', pp23 *et seq.* in Loughnane & Power *Early Shakespeare 1588-1591* (CUP, 2020)

[23] Fallow, John 'His Father John Shakespeare' in *The Shakespeare Circle op cit.*, p38

CHAPTER 5 THE QUEEN'S MEN

[1] McMillin, Scott & Maclean Sally-Beth *The Queen's Men* (CUP, 1998), p67

[2] John Julius Norwich *The Popes*. (London: Random House, 2012) Gregory rescinded the 1570 Papal Bull in 1580, persuaded by English Jesuits.

[3] Hutchinson, Robert, *Elizabeth's Spy Master* (Weidenfeld & Nicolson: London, 2006), p64. See also John Cooper's *The Queen's Agent* (London: Faber, 2012)

[4] Duncan-Jones, *op cit.*, p46

[5] Quoted in Plowden, Alison *Danger to Elizabeth: The Catholics under Elizabeth I* (New York: Stein & Day, 1973)

[6] Lake, Peter *How Shakespeare Put Politics on the Stage* (New Haven and London: Yale University Press, 2016), p23. (Duncan-Jones says they visited Edinburgh and Dublin in the year after the Spanish Armada.)

[7] Wilson, Ian *op cit.*, p6

[8] Hutchinson *op cit.*, pp49 et seq. See also *Invisible Power: The Elizabethan Secret Services 1570-1603* by Alan Haynes (Alan Sutton Publishing Ltd, 1992)

[9] Lake *op cit.*, p43

[10] Shapiro, James *1606: Shakespeare and the Year of Lear* (London: Faber & Faber, 2016)

[11] Duncan-Jones *op cit.*, p44

[12] Shapiro *1599*, pp98-9

[13] Duncan-Jones *op cit.*, pp47-48

[14] Jonson, Ben *Timber: or Discoveries Made upon Men and Matter* (1641) in *Ben Jonson, Workes*, (1640 title page), pp97-8. Quoted in Schoenbaum *op cit.*, p259

[15] Duncan-Jones *op cit.*, p44. She reports that in 1589 one group of the Queen's Men did indeed visit these cities.

[16] Duncan-Jones *op cit.*, p47

[17] Bate, Jonathan, *Soul of the Age* (London: Penguin, 2008), p354

[18] Bate, Jonathan, & Rasmussen Eric, pp16-17 'General Introduction' to *William Shakespeare and Others: Collaborative Plays* (Basingstoke: Palgrave Macmillan, 2013), p74

[19] In blank verse, each line contains ten syllables, each stressed syllable following one unstressed: thus: thus: ti-TUM ti-TUM ti-TUM ti-TUM ti-TUM. This rhythm is known as 'iambic' – hence the term iambic pentameter (Greek *pente* meaning five.)

[20] Shapiro, James *1606: Shakespeare and the Year of Lear* (London: Faber & Faber, 2016), p18. In the Christmas period of 1591, the Queen's Men performed only once at court; while the Admiral's Men and Strange's Men performed six times.

CHAPTER 6 LONDON

[1] Rye, William Brenchley *England as seen by foreigners in the days of Elizabeth and James the First* (London: John Russell Smith, 1865) New edition (Adamant Media Corporation, 2005)

[2] Grimble, Ian *The Harington Family*

(London: Jonathan Cape, 1957) In the US, the toilet is called John' – in memory of Sir John Harington?

[3] *Paul Hentzner's Travels in England, During the Reign of Queen Elizabeth*, trans. Richard Bentley 1797, p16. The title page mistakenly states that Horace Walpole was the translator. (See Schoenbaum *op cit.*, p340)

[4] The towers were built by Hawksmoor. Money intended for the church was diverted to St Paul's – hence the phrase 'robbing Peter to pay Paul'.

[5] Stowe, John 'Notes: Volume 2, pp1-100', in *A Survey of London. Reprinted from the Text of 1603*, (ed) C.L. Kingsford (Oxford, 1908) (Reprinted in Orlin, Lena Cowen (ed). *Material London ca 1600* Philadelphia, 2000), pp356-374.

[6] Kenyon, John & Ohlmeyer, Jane 'The Background to the Civil War in the Stuart Kingdoms' in *The Civil Wars* (eds) Kenyon & Ohlmeyer, (OUP, 1998), p4

[7] Porter, Stephen *Shakespeare's London* (Stroud: Amberley Publishing, 2011), p199

[8] Jenner, Mark S.R. 'The Great Dog Massacre' in *Fear in Early Modern Society* (ed) Naphy W.G., & Roberts, Penny (Manchester University Press, 1997), p48

[9] Blank, Paula, 'The Babel of Renaissance English' Chapter 8 In *The Oxford History of English* (ed) by Lynda Mugglestone (OUP, 2006), p231

[10] Porter *op cit.*, p44

[11] Erichsen, Gerald, 'What Is the 'Jewish' Spanish Language?' ThoughtCo, 26 August, 2020, thoughtco.com/what-is-the-jewish-spanish-language-3078183.

[12] Wood, Michael *In Search of Shakespeare* (London: BBC, 2003), p154. This ugly note may have been inspired by Marlowe's plays (it was signed 'Tamburlaine').

[13] Guy, John *op cit.*, p193. He reports that 'younger Huguenots were rediscovering their national identity as Frenchmen,' and discriminating against native Englishmen.

[14] Weir, Alison *Elizabeth the Queen* (London Jonathan Cape, 1998), pp327-328

[15] Schoenbaum *op cit.*, pp169-170.

[16] Gallagher, John *Learning Languages in Early Modern England* (OUP, 2019)

[17] Hudson, John *Shakespeare's Dark Lady* (Stroud: Amberley Press, 2016), pp43-44

[18] Farmer, Alan B. and Lesser, Zachary 'Vile Arts: The Marketing of English Printed Drama, 1512-1660', *Research Opportunities in Renaissance Drama 39 (2000)*, pp77-165. https://doi.org/10.1017/CB09780511581892.

[19] Duncan-Jones, 2010 *op cit.*, p326.

[20] Wells, Stanley *Shakespeare For All Time* (London: Macmillan 2002), p146

[21] The First Folio can be viewed on line at Bodleian Library Arch. G c.7. For Cop-specific notes, visit https://solo-aleph.bodleian.ox.ac.uk/?func=direct&doc_number=011811163&format=999&local_base=HOL60

[22] E.K. Chambers, *The Elizabethan Stage*, 4 Volumes (Oxford, Clarendon Press, 1923) Vol. 2, pp411-14

[23] Schoenbaum *op cit.*, pp138-140

[24] In 1737, this task was handed over to the Lord Chamberlain; this only ended in 1968

[25] Laoutaris, Chris *Shakespeare and the*

Countess: The Battle That Gave Birth to the Globe (Penguin: London, 2014)

[26] For the original version of this anecdote, visit the British Library MS. Harley 5353, f.29^v; SS, item 115, p152.

[27] Rackin, Phyllis *Shakespeare and Women* (OUP, 2014), p72

[28] Greenblatt, Stephen *Will in the World: How Shakespeare Became Shakespeare* (W. W. Norton & Company, 2004), p74

CHAPTER 7 ENTER, SHAKESPEARE

[1] Fallow, David, 'His father, John Shakespeare' in *The Shakespeare Circle*, pp26-39

[2] From *The Trimming of Thomas Nashe*. Quoted in Ackroyd, Peter, *Shakespeare: The Biography* (London: Chatto & Windus, 2005), p162

[3] Bodleian Library, MS. Aubrey 6 folio 109, recto; see online at Shakespeare documented.folger.edu/Aubrey. See also Aubrey, John *Brief Lives*, (ed). O.L. Dick London, 1949

[4] The image can be viewed in the Folger Digital Image Collection. File name: 53314. Source Call Number: V.a.230https://luna.folger.edu/luna/servlet/detail/FOLGERCM1-6-6-669518-145864: Archaionomia

[5] University of Toronto Library holds a large collection of Hollar's etchings. The map can be accessed via: Parthey Pennington Number P1000, ID J Hollar k 0967. See also Gillian Tindall's *The Man Who Drew London* (London: Chatto & Windus, 2002)

[6] Fuige, F.M. *The History of Parliament: The House of Commons 1558-1603* (ed). P.W. Hasler (London: Boydell and Brewer, 1981)

[7] Quoted in Baker, John *English Law under Two Elizabeth: The Late Tudor Legal World and the Present* (CUP, 2021)

[8] Dawson, Giles E. 'A Seventh Signature for Shakespeare' in *Shakespeare Quarterly*, Vol 43 No.1 Spring 1992 pp72-79. See also Dawson's article in *English Institute Annual* 1942

[9] Easton, Roger E. Jr. 'Spectral Imaging of Shakespeare's "Seventh Signature"' Folger Shakespeare Library: *The Collection: Research and Exploration at the Folger* 19 March 2012. Dawson's article can be viewed on https://luna.folger.edu/luna/servlet/detail/FOLGER. See also https://collation.folger.edu/2012/03/spectral-imaging-of-shakespeares-seventh-signature/

[10] Shakespearian studies have been dogged by a number of frauds including those of Samuel Ireland, and John Payne Collier, See Wilson *op cit.*, pp21-22. See also William Jaggard's *Literary Forgeries and Mystifications* (Shakespeare Press, 1911), pp1 *et seq.*

[11] Loughnane, Rory 'Shakespeare and the idea of Early Authorship' in Loughnane, Rory, & Power, Andrew J *Early Shakespeare 1588-1594* (CUP, 2020), pp26-29

[12] See also McInnis, David & Steggle, (eds) Matthew *Lost Plays in Shakespeare's England* (Basingstoke: Palgrave Macmillan, 2014

[13] From his poem 'The Tables Turned'.

[14] Jackson, MacDonald P. 'Determining Authorship: A New Technique', *Research Opportunities in 12 Renaissance Drama* 41: 2002, pp11-14

[15] Jackson, MacDonald P. 'A Supplementary Lexical Test for *Arden of Faversham*' pp182-193, in Taylor, Gary and Egan, Gabriel *The New Oxford Shakespeare Authorship Companion* (OUP, 2017), p499

[16] Jackson, MacDonald P. 'Shakespeare's Early Verse Style' in Loughnane & Power 2020 *op cit.*, pp102-120

[17] Pruitt, Anna 'Refining the LION Collocation Test: A Comparative Study of Authorship Test Results for *Titus Andronicus* Scene 6' in Taylor & Egan *op cit.*, pp 92 et seq.

[18] In particular, Taylor, Gary, & Loughnane, Rory 'The Canon and Chronology' particularly pp487 *et seq.* in Taylor & Egan, *Authorship Companion* (OUP, 2017) *op cit.*, p487. See also Vickers, Brian *Shakespeare, Co-Author: A Historical Study of Five Collaborative Plays* (OUP, 2004), p2

[19] Taylor and Loughnane's 'Best Guess' is late 1588. *Companion*, p487

[20] Wells, Stanley *Shakespeare For All Time* London (Basingstoke & Oxford: Macmillan, 2002), p147

[21] Warren, Roger (ed). *William Shakespeare's* Two Gentlemen of Verona. (OUP: The Oxford Shakespeare, 2008), pp24-25

[22] Sharpe, Will argues that this was his first play. See 'Collaboration and Shakespeare's Early Career' in Loughnane and Power 2020, *op cit.*

[23] Bate, Jonathan & Rasmussen, Eric *William Shakespeare & others Collaborative Plays Introduction* (Basingstoke: Palgrave Macmillan, 2013), p1? Note: the pagination of this work is odd.

[24] *Companion*, p487

[25] Jackson, Macdonald P. *Determining the Shakespeare Canon:* Arden of Faversham *and* The Lover's Complaint (OUP, 2014)

[26] *Companion*, 2027, p490

[27] Wiggins, Martin 'The unknown author of *Arden of Faversham*' in *A Woman Killed with Kindness and Other Domestic Plays* (ed). Martin Wiggins (OUP, 2008), pp284-287

[28] Bourus, Terri 'Arden of Faversham, Richard Burbage and the Early Shakespeare Canon' pp200 et seq. in Loughnane & Power, 2020, *op cit.*

[29] Sharpe: See above, Note 20

[30] Vickers, Brian *op cit.*, p148-243

[31] Wilson, *op cit.*, p75

[32] Seneca (4BCE-65CE) *(Before Common Era* and *Common Era*; avoiding the religious connotations of BC and AD): he was a Roman Stoic philosopher. His revenge tragedies derived from the same Greek myths used by Euripedes, Sophocles and Aeschylus, and heavily influenced Tudor and Jacobean drama.

[33] *Companion*, pp490-491

[34] Thompson, Ayanna, (ed)., *The Cambridge Companion to Shakespeare and Race.* (CUP, 2021)

[35] Bartels, Emily C. 'Too Many Blackamoors: Deportation, Discrimination, and Elizabeth I.' *Studies in English Literature* 46.2 (Spring 2006): 305-22. *Plus ca change* ... Memories still alive of the *Windrush* scandal. Undaunted, in 2021, the British Conservative government proposed to deport unwanted immigrants to Rwanda.

[36] Nubia, Onyeka *Blackamoores: Africans in Tudor England* and *England's Other*

Countrymen. (Nottingham: Narrative Eye, 2013). See also Miranda Kauffman's *Black Tudors* (London: One World Publications, 2017)

[37] Manley, Lawrence & Maclean, Sue-Beth *Lord Strange's Men and their Plays* (New Haven: Yale University Press, 2014), p58

CHAPTER 8 LORD STRANGE'S MEN

[1] Bate, Jonathan, 'Introduction' in *William Shakespeare and Others: Collaborative Plays op cit.* 2013, p12

[2] Manley, Lawrence & Maclean, Sue-Beth *Lord Strange's Men and their Plays* (New Haven: Yale University Press, 2014), p58

[3] Starkey, David *Elizabeth: Apprenticeship* (London: Chatto & Windus, 2000), p243. Lord Strange was not an enemy, but as a Catholic he was a potential threat; though no doubt the queen had never read Sun Tzu's *The Art of War* which contained the famous aphorism 'Keep your friends close, but your enemies even closer.'

[4] Manley & Maclean *op cit.*, p246

[5] This suggests that the letters were genuine: but it is just possible that the letters were concocted by Burghley to incriminate Ferdinando, *cf* Wilson *op cit.*, p108

[6] Wilson *op cit.*, p109

[7] Weir, Alison *The Wars of the Roses* (London: Jonathan Cape, 1995), p196. There is a splendid painting of this imaginary event in the Parliamentary Art Collection.

[8] Duncan-Jones, Katherine *op cit.*, paints a somewhat unsavoury picture of the bard. However, to quote *Hamlet*: 'Use every man according to his deserts, and who would 'scape whipping?'

[9] In another letter, Persons writes him off as a 'niddicock' who spends his time writing plays for in-house performance.

[10] Manley, Lawrence 'From Strange's Men to Pembroke's Men: *2 Henry VI* and *The First Part of the Contention* in *Shakespeare Quarterly*, vol 54 No 3 Autumn 2003, pp253-287

[11] Sharpe, Will 'Collaboration and Shakespeare's Early Career' in Loughnane and Power, (eds) *op cit.*, pp54-58 & 64-51

[12] *Companion* (2017), p491

[13] Rhind, Neil *The Heath* (Blackheath, London: Bookshop Blackheath Ltd & Warwick Leadlay Gallery, 1987), p10

[14] Lake, Peter 2016 *op cit.*, p104

[15] McNulty, Charles commented: 'All that's missing are the Confederate flags and selfies' in an article 'What *Hamlet* has to say about Trump's impeachment trial', *LA Times*, 8 February 2021. There is a Cade Road, in Greenwich, and a Cade Street in Heathfield, East Sussex. Can one foresee a Trump Street in Washington?

[16] Lee, Sidney (1890). 'Hacket, William' In Stephen, Leslie; Lee, Sidney ((eds)). *Dictionary of National Biography.* (London: Smith, Elder & Co), p4

[17] Kaufman, Alexander L. *The Historical Literature of the Jack Cade Rebellion* (Burlington: Ashgate, 2009), *passim*. See also Harvey, I.M.W. *Jack Cade's Rebellion of 1450.* (Oxford: Clarendon Press, 1991), pp80-81; p186-191

[18] Guy, John 2016 *op cit.* (The 1601 Poor Law remained in force until 1834)

[19] Sharpe, James 'Social Strain and Social Dislocation 1585-1603.' in J. Guy (ed), *The Reign of Elizabeth I: Court and Culture in the Last Decade.* (CUP, 1995), pp192-211. Sharp points out that by 1600, many villages in England were polarised between the rich and poor.

[20] Cited in Shapiro, James 2015 *op cit.,* p195. In Puttenham's mind, perhaps was the story of Croesus, King of Lydia. The oracle of Delphi told him if he attacked Persia a great empire would be destroyed: True – the Lydian Empire was destroyed. (In this case, destructive ambiguity.)

[21] Cf. John Keats' concept of negative capability – 'being in uncertainties, mysteries, doubts' as an important part of the aesthetic; surely inspired by Shakespeare.

[22] *Companion*, pp493 *et seq.*

[23] Macmillan, Margaret *War: How Conflict Shaped Us* (London: Profile Books, 2020), pp133-5. The horror of the battle was remembered for generations

[24] *Companion*, pp513- 517

[25] Guy, John 2016 *op cit.,* 135 Essex challenged Raleigh to a duel in 1588, pp128-129

CHAPTER 9 THE BATTLE OF THE SEXES

[1] Hirrel, Michael J. 'Thomas Watson, Playwright: Origins of Modern English Drama' pp 187-207 in McInnis & Steggle, (eds) *Lost Plays in Shakespeare's England* (Basingstoke: Palgrave Macmillan, 2014). Not a single play by Watson has survived.

[2] Nicholl, Charles *A Cup of News: The Life of Thomas Nash* (London & Boston: Routledge & Kegan Paul, 1984)

[3] Rackin, Phyllis *Shakespeare and Women* (OUP, 2005), pp51-52

[4] Bean, John 'Comic Structure and the Humanizing of Kate in *The Taming of the Shrew,*' in *The Woman's Part,* edited by Lenz, Greene, and Neely, Urbana: University of Illinois Press, 1980, pp65-78 looks at *Shrew* as seen as a romantic comedy. Rackin suggests that perhaps more than half of a Tudor audience could have been women.

[5] *Companion* (217), pp499 *et seq.*

[6] Morris, Brian (ed) *William Shakespeare's The Taming of the Shrew* (The Arden Shakespeare London: Methuen, 1981)

[7] *Companion.* p500

[8] Nance, John 'Early Shakespeare and the Authorship of *The Taming of the Shrew*' in Loughnane & Power *Early Shakespeare 1588-1591* (Cambridge: CUP, 2020), pp261-283

[9] Rackin, *op cit.,* offers a nuanced view, p55.

[10] Packer, Tina *Women of Will* (NY Vintage Books: Penguin Random House, 2015), p12

[11] Wells, Stanley *Shakespeare, Sex and Love* (OUP, 2010)

[12] Me Too is a social movement against sexual abuse and sexual harassment. It was started in 2006.

[13] Henderson, Diane E. 'A Shrew for the Times' in *Shakespeare: The Movie, Popularizing the Plays on Film, TV and Video* edited by Lynda E. Boose & Richard Burt. (London: Routledge, 1997), p161. See also for example Brock Brower's review 'Shakespeare's "Shrew' With No Apologies" in *NY Times,* 6 August 1978.

[14] Inspired perhaps by writers such as Yarrow, Allison *90s Bitch: Media, Culture and the Failed Promise of Gender Equality* (NY: Harper Collins Publishers, 2018).

[15] Williamson, Marilyn *The Patriarchy of Shakespeare's Comedies* (Detroit, Ill: Wayne State University Press, 1986)

[16] Rackin *op cit.*, p53

[17] Schoenbaum *op cit.*, pp 41-2. The report is reproduced in page 41 of his book. Fortunately, no further action was taken

[18] *samizdat*: originally used to describe underground literature in Russia, often circulated in manuscript

[19] Edmondson, Paul & Wells, Stanley (eds) *All the Sonnets of Shakespeare* (CUP, 2020)

[20] Jackson, MacDonald P., 2001 'Vocabulary and Chronology: The Case of Shakespeare's *Sonnets*.' *Review of English Studies*, New Series, 52 pp59-75. See also Jackson 2002 'Dating Shakespeare's Sonnets: Some Old Evidence Revisited' *Notes and Queries* 247, pp237-241

[21] Lee, Sidney *Dictionary of National Biography* vol 51 (New York, 1897), p363. This approach to literary text has been a cardinal principle of hermeneutics. Historical and cultural context, biographical information, psychological interpretation, and authorial intention were off the table, as would be this book! cf. L.C. Knights, who wrote a famous essay called 'How many Children had Lady Macbeth' in *Explorations Essays in Criticism Mainly on the Literature of the Seventeenth Century* (NY: George W Stuart Publishers 1947). This approach has been labeled 'the New Criticism'. *The Meaning of Meaning* and *Practical Criticism* by I.A. Richards helped to develop the methodological approach.

[22] Bate, Jonathan *The Genius of Shakespeare* (London: Picador Classic, 2016), p53

[23] Greenblatt, Stephen *Will of the World: How Shakespeare Became Shakespeare* (London: Jonathan Cape, 2004), p23, p249

[24] Shapiro, Stephen *Contested Will* (London: Faber & Faber, 2010), pp303 *et seq.*

[25] Bate, Jonathan *Soul of the Age: The Life Mind and World of William Shakespeare* (London: Penguin Books, 2009), p225

[26] In his poem *Scorn not the Sonnet*

[27] Rowse, A.L. *Shakespeare, the Man* (Revised edition) (London: Macmillan 1988), pp74-99. See also *The Poems of Shakespeare's Dark Lady* Introduced by A.L. Rowse (London: Jonathan Cape, 1978). David Bevington, is one of a number who have questioned Rowse's claims. See his 'A.L. Rowse's Dark Lady' in *Aemilia Lanyer, Gender, Genre and the Canon* (ed) Marshall Grossman, (Lexington: The University Press of Kentucky, 1998), pp1 *et seq.*

[28] Lasocki, David and Prior, Roger *The Bassanos* (Burlington VT, Ashgate Publishing, 1998), pp1-3

[29] Woods, Suzanne (ed) *The Poems of Aemilia Lanyer* (OUP, 1993). See also Woods, S. *Lanyer: A Renaissance Woman Poet* (OUP, 1999)

[30] Rowse *op cit.*, p100

[31] Bate, Jonathan 2009 *op cit.*, p210

[32] Duncan-Jones, Katherine (ed) *Shakespeare's Sonnets* (London: Bloomsbury Methuen Drama 2010), pp404, 408. As noted in Chapter 4, Sonnet 154's 'seething bath which yet men prove/ against strange maladies a sovereign cure' could also be so interpreted.

CHAPTER 10 POWER PLAY

[1] *Companion*, 503-506

[2] Guy, 2016 *op cit.*, p368 notes that Cecil used Nicholson as a spy, describing him as a 'pigeon'. Could this be the origin of the word *stool-pigeon*?

[3] Archer, Harriet 'Poetry Counsel and Coercion in the History Plays', p150 in Loughnane and Power *op cit.*, 2020

[4] *ibid.*

[5] The 'Most Noble Order of the Garter', was the order of chivalry founded by Edward III in 1348.

[6] Taylor, Gary et al. *The New Oxford Shakespeare Complete Works* Modern Critical Edition (OUP, 2016), p479

[7] Sumption, Jonathan *The Hundred Years War 1: Trial by Battle* (Philadelphia: The University of Pennsylvania Press, 1991), pp239 et seq. The war was indeed brutal.

[8] *ibid.*, p327

[9] le Bel, Jean *The True Chronicles of Jean le Bel.* trans. Nigel Bryant (CUP/Boydell & Brewer, 2011), p155-6

[10] *Companion*, 2017, p506-7

[11] Tillyard, E.M.W. *Shakespeare's History Plays* (London: Chatto and Windus, 1945)

[12] Jowett, John (ed) *The Oxford Shakespeare Richard III* (OUP, 2000)

[13] Jowett *op cit.*, p80

[14] Greenblatt, Stephen *Tyrant: Shakespeare on Power* (NY: W.W. Norton & Co, 2018), pp 53-54

[15] Tay, Josephine *The Daughter of Time* (1951) (Republished Brooklyn, NY: Important Books, 2013)

CHAPTER 11 FRIENDS, AND ENEMIES

[1] Guy, John *op cit.*, pp152-153

[2] The ruins (Grade 1 listed) are still worth visiting

[3] Guy *op cit.*, pp154-155

[4] Wilson *op cit.*, p123

[5] *Ibid.*, p122

[6] Devlin, Christopher S.J. *The Life of Robert Southwell, Poet and Martyr* (London: Longmans Green, 1956). The family tree is on page 264

[7] Guy *op cit.*, pp172-173

[8] Schoenbaum *op cit.*, p150

[9] Kewes, Paulina (ed), *Plagiarism in Early Modern England* (London: Palgrave Macmillan, 2003). The issue is discussed in more detail in Chapter 15

[10] Newcombe, L.H. (2004) 'Greene, Robert (baptised 1558, d 1592)'. *Oxford Dictionary of National Biography* (online ed.) Oxford University Press. doi:10.1093/ref:odnb/11418

[11] Works of Gabriel Harvey, I p168 quoted in Charles Nicholl, *Cup of News: The Life of Thomas Nashe* (London & Boston: Routledge & Kegan Paul, 1984), p49

[12] Wilson, Ian *op cit.*, p119

[13] Westley, Richard 'Computing Error: Reassessing Austin's Study of *Groatsworth of Wit*', Literary and Linguistic Computing, Volume 21, Issue 3, Sept. 2006, pp363-

378, https://doi.org/10.1093/llc/fqi044. Duncan-Jones *Shakespeare: An Ungentle Life op cit.* agrees with Austen p48

[14]Bate, Jonathan *Soul of the Age op cit.*, pp40-41

[15]Burgess, Anthony *Shakespeare* (London: Jonathan Cape, 1970), p119

[16]Hurstfield, Joel *The Queen's Wards: Wardship and Marriage under Elizabeth I* (London: Longmans, 1958) discusses the issues *passim*

[17]Duncan-Jones *op cit.*, p75

[18]*Companion*, p508

[19]Schoenbaum *op cit.*, p177

[20]Guy, John 2016 *op cit.*, pp194-5

[21]The whole episode is treated in detail in Nicholl, Charles *The Reckoning: The Murder of Christopher Marlowe* (Chicago: University of Chicago Press, 1995)

[22]Guy, John *op cit.*, p195

[23]Wells, Stanley *Shakespeare for all Time*, p56

[24]Duncan-Jones *op cit.*, p67

CHAPTER 12 UNTO SOUTHAMPTON DO WE SHIFT OUR SCENE

[1]Burrow, Colin *Complete Sonnets and Poems* (OUP, 2002), p126

[2]Quoted in Nicholl, Charles *A Cup of News: The Life of Thomas Nash* (London & Boston: Routledge & Kegan Paul, 1984)

[3]Schoenbaum *op cit.*, p178, which contains the quotation from Rowe.

[4]Devlin, Christopher *The Life of Robert Southwell: Poet and Martyr* (London: Sidgewick & Jackson, 1967). See also Michael Wood's *In Search of Shakespeare* (London: BBC Publications, 2003), pp151-154

[5]Edmondson & Wells *All the Sonnets of Shakespeare, op cit.*

[6]Duncan-Jones, Katherine (ed), *Shakespeare's Sonnets* (London: Bloomsbury, 2010), p41

[7]Edmondson and Wells *op cit.*, pp92-125. This includes all Shakespeare's sonnets. The 1609 book did not include sonnets in Shakespeare's plays, some of which are among his best.

[8]Lee, Sidney *Dictionary of National Biography* vol 51 (New York, 1897), p363

[9]Duncan-Jones *Shakespeare: An Ungentle Life op cit.*, p50

[10]Praz, Mario *The Romantic Agony* trans. A. Davidson (OUP, 1978, first published 1933)

[11]*The Janus Report on Sexual Behavior*, published in 1993, concluded that 5 per cent of men and 3 per cent of women considered themselves bisexual. A survey in 2002 found that 1.8 per cent of men aged 18-44 claimed to be bisexual

[12]Bowie, David Interview in *Playboy* Magazine, 1976

[13]Shapiro, James *Contested Will: Who Wrote Shakespeare?* (London: Faber & Faber, 2010), p307

[14]McKellen, Ian quoted in *Sunday Mercury*, 8 January 2012

[15]Wells, Stanley President of the Shakespeare Birthplace Trust, *ibid*

[16]Burrow, Colin (ed) *The Oxford Shakespeare Complete Sonnets and Poems* (OUP, 2002), p506

[17]Ian Wilson *op cit.*, p.96 gives an account of the execution. On the scaffold, Southwell expressed loyalty to the Queen, and the crowd were so impressed that they demanded that he be quickly hanged, rather than suffer the torture of being disembowelled. Lord Mountjoy, who presided over the execution, tugged at Southwell's legs to hasten his death. Mountjoy subsequently became a Catholic.

[18]Daugherty, Leo *The Assassination of Shakespeare's Patron: Investigating the Death of the Fifth Earl of Derby* (NY: Amherst Cambria Press, 2011). This book offers a solution to the mystery.

[19]For more information on the earl, see Hammer, E.J. *Polarisation Elizabethan Politics: The Political Career of Robert Devereux, 2nd Earl of Essex, 1585-1597* Cambridge Studies in Early Modern British History (CUP, 2008). For a more accessible account, see Sarah Beth-Watkins, *Elizabeth's Last Favourite: Robert Devereux, 2nd Earl of Essex* (London: Chronos Books, 2021)

[20]His father was a *converso*, a Jew who publicly recanted the Jewish faith and adopted Christianity under the pressure of the Spanish inquisition. Perez claimed to be a Christian even on the scaffold – a claim greeted by mockery by the crowd.

[21]Guy, John *op cit.*, pp228 *et seq.*

[22]The Bullingdon Club was a secret society started by well-heeled students at Oxford University. It was notorious for its destructive binges. (Boris Johnson was a member.)

[23]Guy, *op cit.*, pp 260 *et seq.* gives an account of this ill-planned expedition

CHAPTER 13 A LITTLE LIGHT RELIEF

[1]See Tassinari, Lamberto *John Florio: The Man Who Was Shakespeare* (Montreal: Giano Books 2009). Another edition, in French, by the same author: *John Florio alias Shakespeare* (Lormont, Bordeaux, Nouvelle-Aquitaine, 2016)

[2]Michell, John *Who Wrote Shakespeare?* (London: Thames and Hudson, 1996)

[3]Hudson, John *Shakespeare's Dark Lady* (Stroud: Amberley Publishing, 2016), p53, pp124-5

[4]Waugh, Alexander 'Edward de Vere as Shakespeare' in Eddi Jolly, (ed) *Great Oxford II*, for the de Vere Society 2021. Many of Shakespeare's greatest plays were written after de Vere died in 1604. He is known to have been in Italy in the 1570s – but his knowledge of Warwickshire was negligible. Few give this theory any credence. See also Michel, *op cit.*

[5]Schoenbaum *op cit.*, p169

[6]Simonini, R.C. *Italian Scholarship in Renaissance England.* University of North Carolina Studies in Comparative Literature. (Chapel Hill: University of North Carolina, 1952), p68

[7]Yates, Francis *John Florio: The Life of an Italian in Shakespeare's England.* (CUP, 1934), p127

[8]Rossi, Carla *Italus Ore, Anglus Pectore.* (London: Thecla Academic Press, 2018), p231

[9]Bate, Jonathan *The Genius of Shakespeare* (London: Picador Classic, 2016), pp56-58

[10]Schoenbaum *op cit.*, p161

[11]*Companion*, pp509-510

[12] See Schoenbaum *op cit.*, pp185-6 for a full account of the evening's riotous festivities.

[13] Ian Wilson suggests that the play was one of Shakespeare's 'prentice-pieces'. *Shakespeare the Evidence*, p92

[14] Wallis, Helen M. 'The First English Globe: A Recent Discovery', *The Geographical Journal 117* 1951, pp275-90

[15] See for example *Acts 19* verses 13-20

[16] Wilson *op cit.*, p90

[17] Milward, Peter SJ *Shakespeare's Religious Background* (London: Sidgwick & Jackson, 1973), pp52-3

[18] Also the name of Aemilia Lanier: a coincidence?

[19] See Tofte's poem 'Alba, the Month's Minde of a Melancholy Lover' (1598). Original copies of Tofte's book of poems are held in the Folger Library's collection, and in the Huntingdon Library

[20] *Companion*, 2017, p510

[21] It has been suggested that the play was inspired by Pierre de la Primaudaye's *The French Academy*, translated into English in 1596: but the play was written before this translation appeared.

[22] Greenstreet James G. 'A Hitherto Unknown Noble Writer of Elizabethan Comedies', *The Genealogist* April 1891 pt 4, 295ff

[23] Pendergast, John *Love's Labour's Lost: A Guide to the Play* (Westport CT: The Greenwood Press, 2002)

[24] Smallwood, Robert 'Twentieth-century Performance: The Stratford and London Companies' in Wells, Stanley, & Stanton, Sarah *The Cambridge Companion to Shakespeare on Stage*, Ch 6, pp98-117 (CUP, 2002; online edition, 2006)

[25] Florio, John *First Fruites*. Its full title was *Florio his firste fruites which yeelde familiar speech, merie prouerbes, wittie sentences, and golden sayings. Also a perfect induction to the Italian, and English tongues, as in the table appeared.* Microfilm of the original can be seen in King's College, Cambridge. (Lacks title-page.) It is also available in the Open Library Id. OL15080317M

CHAPTER 14 THE LORD CHAMBERLAIN'S MEN

[1] Marsh, Geoffrey *Living with Shakespeare* (Edinburgh University Press, 2020), pp4-5

[2] Rutter, Caroline 'Schoolfriend, publisher and printer Richard Field' in Edmondson & Wells, (eds) *The Shakespeare Circle* (CUP, 2015), p171

[3] Burrow, Colin *Shakespeare and Classical Antiquity* (OUP, 2013), p97. A copy of *De Arte Amandi* is in the Huntingdon Library.

[4] Duncan-Jones *op cit.*, p132

[5] Price, Diana *Shakespeare's Unorthodox Biography* (Westport, CT, Greenwood Press, 2012), pp134-135 (Price casts doubt on Shakespeare's authorship on these and other grounds.)

[6] Shapiro, James *A Year in the Life of William Shakespeare: 1599.* (New York, HarperCollins, 2005), p133.

[7] Duncan-Jones *op cit.*, p133

[8] Wilson, Ian *Shakespeare: The Evidence*, p176. 'Niddicock' means a foolish person

[9] Manley, Lawrence, & MacLean, Sally-Beth *Lord Strange's Men and Their Plays* (New Haven & London: Yale University Press, 2014), pp 325-327. William Stanley formed another troupe 'Derby's Men', but it became a little-known touring company in the north of England.

[10] Greenblatt, *Will of the World*, p273

[11] van Es, Bart *Shakespeare in Company* (OUP, 2013)

[12] McMillin, Scott, and MacLean, Sally-Beth *The Queen's Men and Their Plays*. (CUP, 1998), p179

[13] Chambers, E.K. IV *op cit.*, pp164-5

[14] *Companion*, pp511-512

[15] Guy *op cit.*, pp368 *et seq.*

[16] *Companion*, pp512-513

[17] Tillyard E.M.W. *Shakespeare's History Plays* (London: Chatto and Windus, 1944)

[18] *Companion*, p513.

[19] Holinshed, Raphael *The Chronicles of England, Scotland and Ireland*, London, [1587]. Published online by the Schoenberg Center for Electronic Text and Image, University of Pennsylvania Libraries. http://sceti.library.upenn.edu/sceti/. Accessed April 2021. Holinshed differs in many respects from Shakespeare. Holinshed records that Mowbray carried out the deed, on the orders of the king

[20] 'A trueborn Englishman' Bolingbroke, later to become Henry IV, was the first English ruler since the Norman Conquest whose mother tongue was English rather than French

[21] Of the 46.5 million eligible voters, only 72.2 per cent voted. 51.9 per cent voted to leave the EU; 48.1 per cent voted to remain (BBC figures). Most such referenda require a 60 per cent majority either way

[22] Some of the details of the ritual come from Hall, Edward *The Union of the Noble and Illustre Famelies of Lancastre and York* (London, 1590). See British Library Richard II fols. vii^b-ix. The relevant section is quoted in Ranald, Margaret Loftus *Shakespeare & His Social Context* (AMS Press, NY, 1987), p208

[23] Guy *op cit.*, p248

[24] Lake, Peter *op cit.*, pp270-271

[25] *ibid.*, pp236-237

[26] Forker, Charles (ed) *Richard II* (London: Arden Shakespeare, 3rd edition, 2002) has one of the best commentaries on this play.

[27] A detailed account of Essex's madcap attempt to seize power can be found in Guy *op cit.*, pp 333 *passim*. See also Chapter 24 of this book.

[28] Guy *op cit.*, pp344-345

CHAPTER 15 WHAT FOOLS THESE MORTALS BE

[1] Duncan-Jones *op cit.*, p172

[2] Schoenbaum *op cit.*, pp230-1

[3] de Somogyi, Nick (ed) *Shakespeare on Theatre* (London: Nick Hern Books, 2012)

[4] Grant, Stephen H. *Collecting Shakespeare: The Story of Henry and Emily Folger* (John Hopkins University Press, 2014). This book tells the story of the biggest collection of Shakespeariana in the world. It is situated in Washington DC. cf. folger library: www.edu

[5] *Companion*, pp517-8

[6] Holmer, Joan Ozark, 1985 'Draw, if You Be Men: Saviolo's Significance for *Romeo and Juliet*', *Shakespeare Quarterly* 45: 163-89; cited in *Companion*, p517. It is possible that Shakespeare picked up such terms from chatting to Italian fencing instructors in London

[7] Brooke, Arthur, *Romeus and Juliet, Being the Original of Shakespeare's* Romeo and Juliet (ed) J.J. Munro (NY: Duffield & Company, 1908), p58. Quoted in Evans, G. Blakemore (ed) *Romeo and Juliet* (CUP, 2003)

[8] Kewes, Paulina (ed) *Plagiarism in Early Modern England* (London: Palgrave Macmillan, 2003)

[9] Horace *Epistles* 1.3., lines 9-20

[10] Bate, Jonathan *How the Classics Made Shakespeare* (Princeton and Oxford: Princeton University Press, 2019), p59. Echoes here of Francis Meres' favourite trope.

[11] *ibid.*, p61

[12] Greene, Thomas L. *The Light in Troy: Imitation and Discovery in Renaissance Poetry* (New Haven & London: Yale University Press, 1982)

[13] Scott-Warren, Jason, 'Commonplacing and originality: Reading Francis Meres' in *The Review of English Studies, Vol* 68 No. 287 November 2017, pp902-923, Oxford OUPhttps//academic.oup.com/res

[14] Taylor & Loughnane *op cit.*, p520

[15] Duncan-Jones *op cit.*, p100

[16] Barton, Anne *The Shakespearian Forest* (CUP, 2017). See also Bernheimer, Richard, *Wild Men in the Middle Ages* (New York: Octagon Books, 1979).

[17] *gaslighting* is a term meaning to cause someone to question their sanity; the expression comes from the 1944 film *Gaslight*: a husband causes his wife to think she has a mental illness by dimming their gas-fuelled lights

[18] Boehrer, Bruce *Shakespeare Among the Animals: Nature and Society in the Drama of Early Modern England* (New York: Palgrave Macmillan, 2002). Quoted in Taylor *et al*, (eds) *The New Oxford Shakespeare: The Complete Works* Modern Critical Edition (OUP, 2016), p1080

[19] Gibson, Marion 'Witchcraft in the Courts', in Gibson, Marion (ed), *Witchcraft And Society in England And America, 1550–1750* (Continuum International Publishing Group, 2006), pp1-9

CHAPTER 16 COURTING CONTROVERSY

[1] McGlynn, M. 'From Charter to Common Law: The Rights and Liberties of the Pre-Reformation Church' in Griffith-Jones, R. & Hill, M. (eds), *Magna Carta, Religion and the Rule of Law* (CUP, 2015), p57

[2] Translations of *Magna Carta* in this book are by Henry Summerson of the Magna Carta Barons Association founded in 2013, and are from *The Magna Carta Barons* ed Peter Sinclair (Front Line States, Royston Herts, 2016). It is sometimes claimed that Magna Carta is the origin of Habeas Corpus; in fact, Habeas Corpus dates back to the Assize of Clarendon, enacted by Henry II in 1166

[3] Guy, John *Tudor England* (OUP, 1990), p14

[4] Lipscomb, S. *1536: The Year that Changed Henry VIII* (London, 2009), p166

[5] Thompson, F. *Magna Carta: Its Role in the*

Making of the English Constitution (Minneapolis: The University of Minnesota Press, 1972), p140.

[6]Baker, J. 'Magna Carta and Personal Liberty' in Griffith-Jones, R. & Hill, M. (eds), *Magna Carta: Religion and the Rule of Law* (Cambridge: CUP, 2015), p98

[7]*ibid.*, p100 Robert Cawdry argued this in 1591, and Robert Beale followed suit in 1593, both were ignored

[8]Lake, Peter 2017 *op cit.*, p194

[9]See for example Duncan-Jones *op cit.*, pp77-79

[10]Vicars, Brian 2004 *'The Troublesome Raigne,* George Peele, and the Date of King John' in *Words that Count: Essays of Early Modern Authorship in Honor of MacDonald P. Jackson,* (ed) Brian Boyd, pp72-79

[11]Taylor & Loughnane *op cit.*, p521

[12]Incredibly, half of Shakespeare's plays did not appear in print until the First Folio of 1623.

[13]According to Duncan-Jones *op cit.*, p326 a unique record of the relative popularity of Shakespeare's plays can be found in the Bodleian Library: the two most popular plays consulted by the young men were *Romeo and Juliet,* and *Julius Caesar.* The Tragedies were the most popular, the Histories the least. Bottom of the list among the histories was *King John*

[14]Most of Europe saw Elizabeth as a bastard, the daughter of an illegal marriage to Anne Boleyn. In contrast, Mary Stuart was legitimate. Mary's great-grandfather was Henry VII, making Henry VIII her great uncle. Henry VIII had removed Elizabeth from the line of succession. Many English Catholic exiles believed Mary had a better right to the throne than Elizabeth.

[15]Guy, John *op cit.*, pp 84-91. The audience would also recall the murder of Thomas a Becket.

[16]*op cit.*, p90

[17]The Earl of Essex appears in Act 1, Scene 1, and thereafter is nowhere mentioned. See next chapter.

[18]Holinshed *op cit.*

[19]Greer, *op cit.*, p197

[20]O'Farrell, Maggie *Hamnet* (London: Bloomsbury, 2020)

[21]Peery, William, 'The Hamlet of Stephen Dedalus', *The University of Texas Studies in English,* vol. 31, 1952, pp109-119. JSTOR, www.jstor.org/stable/20776053. Accessed 27 April 2021.

[22]Rowse, A.L. *William Shakespeare: A Biography* (NY: Barnes & Noble, 1963), p242

[23]*All is True* Sony (Pictures Classics, 2018). Written by Ben Elton, starring Kenneth Branagh as Shakespeare, Judi Dench as Anne Hathaway, and Sir Ian McKellen as an aged Earl of Southampton.

[24]*Companion*, p522

CHAPTER 17 BAD NEWS

[1]Guy, John *op cit.*, p259

[2]*ibid.*, pp 260-262. Guy describes these events, and the poor judgement of Essex.

[3]Wernham, R.B. *The Return of the Armadas: The Last Years of the Elizabethan War Against Spain 1595-1603* (OUP, 1994), pp139-140. Unbelievably, a total of five armadas set out, all of which ended in failure

[4] Guy, *op cit.*, pp272 *et seq.*

[5] Essex had an affair with Elizabeth Stanley, unhappily married to William Stanley, 6th Earl of Derby

[6] Barnett, Correlli *Britain and Her Army* (London: Penguin Book, 1974), pp49-50. Barnett points out that the Crown's wartime income was only 300,000 a year – and the cost of maintaining 7,600 men in the Low Countries alone was 126,000. Tyrone's rebellion in Ireland cost almost 2 million.

[7] Barnett, *op cit.*, pp31-37, gives an account of the seriously inadequate Elizabethan militia system.

[8] Duncan-Jones, 2014, p103. To spin wheels, you had to be in at the hub.

[9] Wilson, Ian *op cit.*, p222

[10] Quoted in McKerrow (ed) *The Works of Thomas Nashe* in 5 volumes. vol 5 p194 2nd edition (ed) F.P. Wilson (OUP, 1995); also quoted in E.K. Chambers *The Elizabethan Stage op cit.* Vol 1, p23

[11] *Companion op cit.*, p522

[12] Granville-Barker, Harley *Prefaces to Shakespeare* Vol. 4 (NY: Atlantic Publishers & Distributors, 2005 New edition.) Originally published by Batsford 1927-1947

[13] Bloom, Harold *Shakespeare The Invention of the Human*, p171 (NY: Penguin Putnam, 1998)

[14] Lasocki & Prior, *op cit.*, p93

[15] Shapiro, James *Shakespeare and the Jews* (NY & Chichester, West Sussex: Columbia University Press, 1996). This book goes into great detail about the status of Jews in England at the time.

[16] Lawson, Philip *The East India Company: A History*, p2 (London: Longman, 1993) The East India Company received a royal charter on 31 December 1600, giving them a monopoly on all trade to the east. See also Keay, John *The Honourable Company: A History of the English East India Company* (London: Harper Collins, 1991)

[17] 'Early European Settlements' *Imperial Gazetteer of India*, II, 1908, p454

[18] Irigaray, Lucy 'Women on the Market', pp174-89 in Alan D. Schrift (ed) *The Logic of the Gift: Towards an Ethic of Generosity* (London: Routledge, 1997)

[19] Roth, Cecil *History of the Jews in Venice* (Philadelphia: Jewish Society of America, 1930)

[20] Wesker, Arnold *The Merchant*. Later renamed *Shylock* (London: Penguin, 1976)

[21] As reported in the *New York Times*, 27 July 2016

[22] Shapiro, James *Shakespeare in a Divided America* (London: Faber & Faber 2020), p.7

[23] Kaplan, M Lindsay 'Others and Lovers in The Merchant of Venice' pp341-357 in *A Feminist Companion to Shakespeare* (ed) Callaghan, Dympna Blackwell (Malden Mass. & Oxford, 2000), pp341 *et seq.*

[24] Kaplan, *op cit.*, p344

[25] Shapiro, 1996, *op cit.*, p121

CHAPTER 18 PRIDE COMES BEFORE A FALL

[1] An imprese was a heraldic device, or picture, including the motto, of a noble of learned personage; hence the word *impress*.

[2] Schoenbaum, op cit., p228

[3] Duncan-Jones, op cit., pp110 et seq.

[4] Schoenbaum, op cit., pp234 et seq.

[5] Guy, op cit., pp279-281. Guy provides a detailed account of these events.

[6] Laoutaris, Chris *Shakespeare and the Countess: The Battle that Gave Birth to the Globe*, pp281 et seq. (London: Penguin, 2014).

[7] Nelson, Alan 'Neighbours; Petition Against the Blackfriars Playhouse November 1596', in Hannah Lea Crumme (ed) *Shakespeare on the Record: Research of an Early Modern Life* (London: Bloomsbury, 2019)

[8] Laoutaris, op cit., p283

[9] Guy, John, op cit., p201

[10] Laoutaris, op cit., p284

[11] ibid., p286

[12] Lee, Christopher *1603: A Turning Point in British History* (London: St Martin's Press 2003) This book gives a picture of Henry Brooke as being a man of little brain, and not very popular. His poor judgment was shown by his involvement in the ludicrous 'Main Plot' against King James in 1603, which meant he ended his days in the Tower

[13] The company was reborn in 2004, permission having been given by the Lord Chamberlain at Buckingham Palace to use the name. It claims to be the UK's premier all-male theatre company

[14] Shapiro, James *1599: A Year in the Life of Shakespeare*, p13 (London: Faber & Faber, 2005)

[15] Chambers E.K. *The Elizabethan Stage*, Vol IV, (Oxford: The Clarendon Press, 1923), pp322-3

[16] Ward, B.M. 'The Chamberlain's Men In 1597', *Review of English Studies,* ix, 1933, pp55-58

[17] Schoenbaum, op cit., p165

[18] John Foxe *Actes and Monuments of matters happening in the Church*, 1563, p266. This work is commonly called *Foxe's Book of Martyrs*, a book of Protestant history and martyrology.

[19] *Companion*, p522

[20] *She Who Must Be Obeyed* – Lady Russell, of course. The is a phrase first used in Henry Rider Haggard's 1886 novel *She: A History of Adventure*. It has become a slang term for 'my wife' implying she is in charge. The phrase was sometimes used about former British Prime Minister Mrs Thatcher.

[21] Ackroyd, op cit., p307

CHAPTER 19 GAME OF THRONES

[1] *Companion*, p523

[2] *The New Oxford Shakespeare: The Complete Works (Modern Critical Edition)* (ed) Taylor, Jowett, Bouros & Fgan, (OUP, 2016), pp1278

[3] Everett, Barbara 'Shakespeare and the Elizabethan Sonnet', *London Review of Books*, Vol 30 No 9, 2008

[4] This phrase occurs of course in *Macbeth*

[5] John Blundeville's *True order and method of writing and reading histories* (London, 1574). He claimed there were three reasons for reading history: 'To acknowledge the

providence of God ... by the examples of the wise, to learn ... how to behave ourselves in all our actions, as well private as public, both in times of peace and war'; and to be 'stirred by example of the good to follow the good, and by example of the evil to flee evil.'

[6]Lake, Peter *How Shakespeare Put Politics on the Stage* (Yale University Press, 2016), p41

[7]Quoted in Guy, John *Elizabeth: The Forgotten Years*, p143

[8]*Companion*, p523

[9]Prince John of Lancaster later becomes Duke of Bedford – the man who has Joan of Arc burnt at the stake. An ugly character (See *1 Henry VI*).

[10]Readers will no doubt be reminded of Putin's invasion of Ukraine in 2022

[11]A Turkish sultan, Amurath murdered his brothers on succeeding to the throne in 1574; his successor in 1596 did the same.

CHAPTER 20 THE PRICE WE PAY FOR LOVE

[1]Edmondson, Paul & Wells, Stanley (ed) *All the Sonnets of Shakespeare* (CUP, 2020)

[2]Nicholas Udall, a schoolmaster who wrote a play called *Ralph Roister Doister* was convicted for sodomy with his pupils – and sentenced to a year in prison. It seems to have done his career little harm, he continued as a schoolmaster, and it is believed his play was performed before Queen Mary.

[3]de Grazia, Margreta 'The Scandal of Shakespeare's Sonnets' in *Shakespeare Survey*, 46 (1994)

[4]Everett, Barbara 'Shakespeare and the Elizabethan Sonnet', *London Review of Books*, Vol 30 No 9, 2008

[5]Duncan-Jones, *op cit.*, p154

[6]Greenblatt, *Will of the World op cit.*, p232

[7]As noted in the previous chapter, these lines have been taken to refer to the death of Hamnet.

[8]Duncan-Jones (ed) *Shakespeare's Sonnets* (London: Bloomsbury Arden Shakespeare, 2010), pp52-69

[9]For an account of the life and works of this remarkable woman, see Hannay, Margaret P *Philip's Phoenix: Mary Sidney, Countess of Pembroke*, (OUP, 1990)

[10]Daniel had a strong influence on Shakespeare: He used the 'Shakespearian sonnet form' before Shakespeare did, and evidence of his influence may be found in *The Rape of Lucrece*, and a number of Shakespeare's history plays – and *Antony and Cleopatra*. For an account of his life and work, see Rees, Joan *Samuel Daniel: A Critical and Biographical Study*. (Liverpool: Liverpool University Press, 1964)

[11]Lewis, C.S. *English Literature in the Sixteenth Century* (OUP, 1954), pp503-5

[12]Williams, Robin *Sweet Swan of Avon: Did A Woman Write Shakespeare?* (Santa Fe: Wilton Press, 2006), p86 *et seq.*

[13]Mary Fitton was not the only one of his conquests. Others included Elizabeth Carey, Sir George Carey's daughter, Bridget Vere, Lord Burghley's granddaughter, his cousin Lady Mary Wroth, and the Earl of Nottingham's niece.

[14]Duncan-Jones, *op cit.*, p124. The other three come from *Love's Labours Lost*.

[15] Williams, *op cit.*, pp88 *et seq.*

[16] Williams, *op cit.*, pp77 *et seq.*

CHAPTER 21 MUCH ADO ON AND OFF THE STAGE:

[1] Schoenbaum, 1987 *op cit.*, p236

[2] Marsh, *op cit.*, p146

[3] Guy, *op cit.*, p284

[4] *Companion*, pp524-5. The only original copy is held by Cambridge University Library Ms.Dd.5.75, folio 461

[5] Bate, Jonathan, & Rasmussen, Eric (eds) *The Complete Works of William Shakespeare* The Royal Shakespeare Company Complete Works. (Basingstoke: Macmillan, 2007)

[6] May, Stephen M. *Henry Stanford's Anthology: An Edition of Cambridge University Library* Manuscript Dd. 5.75

[7] *Companion, op cit.*, p524

[8] Pruit, Anna (ed) 'Much Ado about Nothing' in Taylor, Jowett, Bouros & Egan (eds) *The New Oxford Shakespeare: The Complete Works Modern Critical Edition* (OUP, 2016), p1441

[9] A *cinque pace* is a five-step dance ending with a leap every five steps: when it ends, the dancers are exhausted.

[10] Dromgoole, Dominic, & Stafford Smith, Clive *London Review of Books*, 7 November 2013, p27

[11] The name 'Hero' comes with 'baggage' attached, for Shakespeare has deliberately named her after a character in a Greek legend, who features in Marlowe's unfinished poem *Hero and Leander*. Hero was a priestess of the Goddess of love, Aphrodite, and was dedicated to chastity until she met Leander. He swam across the Hellespont to be with her, guided by the lamp in her tower; when it went out, he lost his way and was drowned. Hero was thus perceived to be an unchaste *femme fatale* by Shakespearian audiences.

[12] 'approved'- proven

[13] Schoenbaum, *op cit.*, pp238-9

[14] Greenblatt, Stephen *Will of the World* (London: Jonathan Cape, 2004), p291 (*Richard II, Richard III* and *Romeo and Juliet* came out in quick succession. *I Henry IV* and *The Merchant of Venice* came out in the following year.)

[15] Wood, Michael *op cit.*, p218

[16] Holden, Antony *William Shakespeare* (London: Little Brown and Company, 2004), p167

[17] Shapiro, James *1599: A Year in the Life of Shakespeare* (London: Faber & Faber, 2005), pp4 *et seq.*

[18] Marsh, Geoffrey *op cit.*, pp441-442

CHAPTER 22 WHEREFORE WAR?

[1] In Act 3, Scene 2 of *Hamlet*, Hamlet complains about clowns who 'steal the show' by their improvisations. This may explain why Kempe left the Lord Chamberlain's Men. In 1600, he performed his famous 'Nine Days' Wonder' – Morris dancing from London to Norwich, commemorated by a wood carving in Chapelfield Gardens in Norwich.

[2] *Companion*, pp 526-7

³O'Neill, James *The Nine Years War, 1593-1603: O'Neill, Mountjoy and the Military Revolution* (Dublin: Four Courts Press, 2018). Among those who were forced out was the poet Edmund Spenser, whose castle at Kilcolman was destroyed.

⁴From the prologue to Jonson's play *Everyman in his Humour* (1598)

⁵A 2012 production of *Henry V* was set in the Falklands War, complete with camouflage nets and sandbags. (The Falklands War saw Argentina's attempt to seize the Falklands Islands [Los Malvinas], foiled by a British task force: a bloody, brutal war.)

⁶https://www.salon.com/2004/06/04/bush_and_shakespeare/

⁷London's National Theatre's production of *Henry V* in 2003 (director Nicholas Hytner) was set in the Iraq war. It was not designed to raise the nation's spirits.

⁸The word *Dieu* only appears 11 times. No surprises here.

⁹*Oh, What a Lovely War!* is a musical developed by Joan Littlewood and her ensemble at London's Theatre Workshop in 1963. It is a satire on World War I, and indeed on war in general.

¹⁰Shakespeare does not mention that up to a quarter of Henry's army died from dysentery at Harfleur.

¹¹ie swashbucklers: swaggering swordsmen

¹²There was also another massacre, called the English fury, again at Mechelen, in 1580. The massacre at Maastricht (1579) left only 400 people alive from a population of 30,000.

¹³In France he was known as Charles the Beloved, but he did suffer from mental illness, and apparently had psychotic episodes

¹⁴Longmate, Norman *Defending the Island: From Caesar to the Armada* (London: Pimlico, 2001), p496

¹⁵*Companion*, pp528-9

¹⁶Platter, Thomas *Travels in England,* trans. from German by Clare Williams, (London: Jonathan Cape, 1952), pp166-7

¹⁷Greenblatt, Stephen *The Swerve: How the Renaissance Began* (London: the Bodley Head 2011), p281. The burning of Alexandria's library when Caesar was trying to maintain control of the city was accidental.

¹⁸Tarquin was the tyrannical seventh and last King of Rome. His son was the villain of Shakespeare's poem *The Rape of Lucrece* (See Chapter 13)

¹⁹Hadfield, Andrew *Shakespeare and Republicanism* (CUP, 2005), p1 *et seq*

²⁰Collinson, Patrick 'The Monarchical Republic of Queen Elizabeth I' Ch.4 in Guy, John (ed) *The Tudor Monarchy* (London: Hodder Education Publishers, 1997).

²¹Lake, Peter *op cit.*, p480

²²As Farah Karim-Cooper notes, 'Shakespeare often challenges us to hold two contradictory views simultaneously – it was how his mind worked.' Karim-Cooper, Farah, *The Great White Bard: Shakespeare, Race and the Future* (London: Oneworld, 2023)

CHAPTER 23 FRIENDS, AND RIVALS

[1] Guy, *op cit.*, pp320-321

[2] *ibid.*, pp309-310

[3] *Ibid.*, p310.

[4] Duncan-Jones, *Shakespeare: An Ungentle Life*, pp92-93

[5] Edmondson, Paul and Wells, Stanley, *op cit.*, pp189-197

[6] *ibid.*, p237

[7] Burrow, Colin (ed) *The Oxford Shakespeare: Complete Sonnets and Poems*, p536 (OUP, 2002)

[8] Bate, Jonathan *Soul of the Age*, pp233-5. Note that *Wittes Pilgrimage* was not published until 1605.

[9] Duncan-Jones, Katherine (ed) *Shakespeare's Sonnets* (London: Bloomsbury, The Arden Shakespeare, 1997) rev 2010 pp 63-64

[10] Hutchinson, Robert *op cit.*, pp196 *et seq.* See also Conyer Read's *Mr Secretary: Walsingham & the Policy of Queen Elizabeth*, 3 vols (Oxford: Clarendon Press, 1825; reprinted NY, Brooklyn: AMS Press, 1967)

[11] Guy, *op cit.*, pp85-88

[12] Schoenbaum, *op cit.*, pp203-204

[13] Fuller, Thomas *History of the Worthies of England* 1662 – the first attempt at a dictionary of national biography.

[14] Beaumont, Francis *POETICAL pieces, chiefly social, and some political.* Several refer to events at Oxford. Repository: The British Library Add. MS 30982, fols. 75v-76r ca.161.

[15] The word *ride* in this context is usually used in the expression 'ride at anchor'

[16] Bevington, David 'Jonson and Shakespeare: A Spirited Friendship' in *Ben Jonson Journal*, May 2016 Vol 23 No 4, pp 1-23 (Las Vegas: Department of English University of Nevada)

[17] Donaldson, Ian 'Life of Ben Jonson'. *The Cambridge Edition of the Works of Ben Jonson Online* (Cambridge University Press). Accessed 11 June 2021

[18] Shuger, Debora 'Civility and Censorship in Early Modern England', in *Censorship and Silencing: Practices of Cultural Regulation*, (ed) Robert C. Post (Los Angeles: Getty Research Institute for the History of Art and the Humanities, 1998), p89

[19] Boose, Lynda 'The 1599 Bishops' Ban: Elizabethan Pornography, and the Sexualization of the Jacobean Stage', in *Enclosure Acts: Sexuality, Property and Culture in Early Modern England*, (ed) Richard Burt and John Michael Archer (Ithaca: Cornell University Press, 1994), p197.

[20] *Companion*, p528

[21] Watling, E.F. 'Introduction', *Four Tragedies and Octavia*, p9 (London: Penguin Books 1966) Seneca was regarded as a crypto-Christian in the Middle Ages, possibly because of his alleged relationship with St Paul.

[22] Nance, John 'Shakespeare and the Painter's Part' in *Companion* (2017), p261 *et seq.*

[23] Taylor, Gary 'Did Shakespeare Write *The Spanish Tragedy* Additions?' In *Companion* (2017) *op cit.*, pp246-260

[24] The whole play, including the five

additions, can be found in *William Shakespeare & Others Collaborative Plays*, pp207 *et seq*. Jonathan Bate & Eric Rasmussen (eds) (with Jan Sewell and Will Sharpe) (Basingstoke: Palgrave Macmillan, 2013)

[25] Wilson, Ian *op cit*., pp264 *et seq*.

[26] Historical Manuscripts Commission, Lord de L'isle and Dudley (Penshurst Place) II, 415. Quoted in Wilson *Ibid*., p265

[27] Geckle, George L. *John Marston's Drama: Themes, Images, Sources*, (Rutherford, NJ: Fairleigh Dickinson University Press, 1980), p34. Their 'private space' was in fact a church - St Gregory's, attached to the cathedral.

[28] They also bought leases to several other sites to create bearbating venues

[29] Bednarz, James B. *The Poets' War* (NY: Columbia University Press, 2000) Recruited? Some of the boys were even kidnapped and put on the stage

[30] *eyases:* baby eagles *clapped:* beaten

[31] *escoted:* treated, maintained

[32] Duncan-Jones, *op cit*., p140

CHAPTER 24 FROM COMEDY TO TRAGEDY

[1] Chapman's famous *Seven Books of Homer's Iliades* was also dedicated to Essex, whom he claimed was the embodiment of 'Achillean virtues'.

[2] Chisholm, Hugh, (ed) (1911). 'Hayward, Sir John'. *Encyclopædia Britannica*. Vol. 13 (11th ed.). (CUO, 1911) 1p6. See also Bate, *Soul of the Age*, pp261 *et seq*.

[3] Guy, *Elizabeth: The Forgotten Years op cit*., p324

[4] *Ibid*., p325

[5] Ibid., p328

[6] Wilson, J. Dover *The Essential Shakespeare* (CUP, 1932), pp96-103

[7] It has been suggested that Jaques is based on the character of Malevole in John Marston's play *The Malcontent*. However, Marston's play was written at least two years after *As You Like it*

[8] *Companion*, pp531-531

[9] Lodge's *Rosalynde, Euphues' Golden Legacy* edited by Edward Chauncey Baldwin, is published as an ebook (17181) by Project Gutenberg

[10] *misprized*: despised

[11] Readers will recall Hogarth was the famous pictorial satirist in 18th century London.

[12] Marsh, *op cit*., p294

[13] *cf The Allegory of Love* by C.S. Lewis. Courtly Love was not quite the same as romantic love. The defining characteristics of Courtly Love were Courtesy, Chastity, Adultery, and 'Religion of Love': adultery was in the mind only, for chastity was also required.

[14] Bate, Jonathan *How the Classics Made Shakespeare* (Princeton University Press, 2018), p187

[15] Bate, Jonathan *Soul of the Age*, 2008 *op cit*., p218

[16] Schoenbaum, *op cit*., p281-282

[17] *ibid*., p.240. The queen agreed to help

to relieve 'the town twice afflicted and almost wasted by fire'.

[18] Schoenbaum, op cit., p218

[19] The whole episode is described by Guy op cit., pp328 – 332; also Bate 2008 op cit., pp249 et seq. The queen's ministers were trying to negotiate a peace treaty with Spain: Essex was all for outright war.

[20] Duncan-Jones Shakespeare: An Ungentle Life op cit., p147

[21] Sharpe, Robert B. The Real War of the Theatres: Shakespeare's Fellows in Rivalry with the Admiral's Men 1594-1603 (D.C. Heath & Co, Oxford UP), p.183

[22] Guy, op cit., p345. See her meeting with Lambarde in Chapter 14.

CHAPTER 25 HUMOURING THE QUEEN

[1] Marsh, Geoffrey op cit., p146

[2] Ibid., p162

[3] Guy, op cit., p319

[4] Jackson, Claire Devil-Land England Under Siege 1588-1688 (London: Allen Lane 2021), p83

[5] Ibid., p78

[6] Guy, op cit., pp312-3

[7] Ibid., pp349-350

[8] Companion, pp533-535

[9] Hibbard, G.R. (ed) The Merry Wives of Windsor (London: Penguin Books, 1973), p52

[10] Nicholas Rowe from Life, in Works of Shakespeare 1709, quoted in W.K. Chambers William Shakespeare: A Study of Facts and Problems 1930 vol II I ppviii-ix . However, a talk given by Chris Wakefield at the Coleridge Memorial Trust's Anniversary Lunch of 2011 states the case for Coleridge's highly developed sense of humour.

[11] Hibbard, op cit., pp19 et seq.

[12] Ackroyd, Peter Shakespeare: The Biography (London: Chatto & Windus, 2005), p371.

[13] Greer, Germaine 'His daughter Judith and the Quineys' in The Shakespeare Circle (eds) Paul Edmondson & Stanley Wells (CUP, 2015), pp114-5

[14] Hotson, Leslie Shakespeare and Shallow (Boston: Nonesuch Press, 1931)

[15] caret: To Evans, it means 'missing'. To Quickly it means 'carrot', a root. It was also a slang word for 'penis'. Focative is also meant to be suggestive.

[16] Sokol B.J. (2009) 'A Warwickshire Scandal: Sir Thomas Lucy and the Date of The Merry Wives of Windsor in Shakespeare 5 pp355-71 cited in Taylor & Loughnane, op cit., p533

[17] John Jowitt (and team), who wrote the notes for the play edited by Sarah Ellis, in The New Oxford Shakespeare Complete Works: Modern Critical edition (ed Taylor, Jowett, Bourus & Egan, p1770) The glosses are as follows: discourses – (perhaps with the implication 'glances meaningfully'); carves – cuts and serves meat (perhaps with a sexual innuendo, 'serves at her own pleasure'; makes inviting gestures; Englished rightly: translated properly. (translated in the sense understood)

[18] Early version had Broom instead of Brooke – Shakespeare originally playing safe?

[19] Rackin, Phyllis *Shakespeare and Women* (OUP, 2005), p64

[20] Now reinvented as a posh spa hotel, *The Harte and Garter Hotel*

[21] A Royal Mausoleum for Queen Victoria and Prince Albert is also situated in Frogmore.

[22] Rackin, *op cit.*, p64

[23] Cavendish, Margaret 'Letter CXXII' in *Sociable Letters* (London: William Wilson, 1664) Quoted in Rackin, *op cit.*, p64

CHAPTER 26 THE FOOD OF LOVE

[1] *Companion*, p534

[2] *Ibid.*, p535

[3] Guy, *op cit.*, pp350-2. The unrest was caused by the numerous social issues already alluded to. Anxiety over who would succeed Elizabeth also played a big part. Senior members of the government were already secretly in touch with James VI of Scotland, in the hope of holding on to their positions

[4] *Companion* p535

[5] Shapiro, Michael *Gender in Play on the Shakespearian Stage: Boy Heroines and Female Pages* (Ann Arbour: University of Michigan Press, 1996). Shapiro provides an extensive survey of crossdressing on the Renaissance stage.

[6] Jardine, Lisa 'Boy Actors, Female Roles, and Elizabethan Eroticism' in *Staging the Renaissance: Reinterpretations of Elizabethan and Jacobean Drama*, edited by David Scott Kastan and Peter Stallybrass (NY & London: Routledge, 1997), p74

[7] See entry in the 1911 edition of *Encyclopedia Brittanica*. Not to be confused with John Stubbes, whose right hand was severed in 1579 for attacking the possible marriage of the queen to the Duc d'Alençon

[8] Quoted in Rackin, Phyllis *Shakespeare and Women* (OUP, 2005)

[9] A reference to the story from Ovid about the young hunter Actaeon who saw Diana, goddess of hunting (the Greeks called her Artemis) bathing naked in a mountain stream. As a punishment, she turned him into a stag, and set his own dogs on him

[10] Sorlien, Robert Parker (ed) *The Diary of John Manningham of the Middle Temple 1602-3* (Hanover: The University Press of New England, 1876), p48. Manningham's Memorandum book is in the British Library collection: MS Harley 5353, (folio 10)

[11] Guy, *op cit.*, p168

[12] Duncan-Jones, *op cit.*, explains why cross-gartering was so unfashionable that it was a joke, p179

[13] This refers to a map published in 1600 by Richard Wright, Richard Hakluyt and John Davis

[14] The story can be found in Brown, I *Dark Ladies* (London: Collins, 1957). See also E.L. Chambers, *Shakespeare's England,* Vol 1. (Oxford: The Clarendon Press, 1923), p89

[15] Burl, Aubrey *Shakespeare's Mistress* (Stroud: Amberley Publishing, 2012) reviews all the 'Dark Lady' candidates. For Mary Fitton, see pp162-175

[16] Rowse, A.L. *William Shakespeare: A Biography* (NY: Barnes & Noble Books, 1995), p335

[17] Laoutaris, Chris *Shakespeare and the Countess* (London: Penguin Random House UK, 2015), pp354-9

[18] Sir Toby, being drunk, gets the name wrong. The word *Cathar* meant 'religious puritan' (implied in Catharism). In France, the Cathars were much persecuted by orthodox Catholics.

[19] Quoted in *The American Mercury*, January 1925, under the title 'Clinical Notes'. The magazine was hi-jacked in the 1950s, and steered towards 'the fever swamps of anti-Semitism' and Nazism.

[20] Duncan-Jones, *op cit.*, pp180-181

[21] Readers may recall Jonson mocking the Shakespeare motto 'Not without right'. See Chapter 18

[22] Duncan-Jones, *op cit.*, p180

[23] Linthicum, M. Channing *Costume in the Drama of Shakespeare and his Contemporaries* (OUP, 1936), p264

[24] Spurgeon, Caroline *Shakespeare's Imagery and What it Tells Us* (CUP, 1935). See also Wolfgang Clemen *The Development of Shakespeare's Imagery*, 1951. Reprinted by Routledge 2013

CHAPTER 27 WAR AND LECHERY

[1] *Companion*, pp536-537

[2] Nicholl, Charles *The Lodger: Shakespeare on Silver Street* (London: Allen Lane, 2007), pp51-53

[3] Cook, Judith Dr Simon Forman (London: Chattor & Windus, 2001), p116. See also A.L. Rowse's *Casebooks of Simon Forman*. Burl, *op cit.*, discusses Marie's role as a possible 'Dark Lady'.

[4] Nicholl, *op cit.*, pp116-117

[5] Described in Homer's *Iliad*: the Greeks try to seize back the wife of the Spartan King, Menelaus, Helen, who was abducted by the Trojan prince Paris.

[6] An inkhorn was a small container, often made of horn, for ink

[7] The Campaign was launched in 2011. A famous example: the Met Office talked of 'the probability of precipitation' instead of simply saying 'rain is likely'

[8] Medine, Peter E. (ed) produced a critical edition of his work *Thomas Wilson: The Art of Rhetoric (1560)*. (University Park, PA: Pennsylvania State University Press, 1993).

[9] Taylor, Gary *et al* in Taylor et al *op cit*. (*The New Oxford Shakespeare: Complete Works*), 2016, p.1906

[10] British Library Add. MS 10449, folio 5

[11] Ackroyd, *op cit.*, p389. A comparison is sometimes made of Achilles' relationship with Patroclus, and Essex's with Southampton.

[12] Taylor *et al* (eds), *op cit.*, (OUP, 2016), p1906

[13] Wells, Stanley *Shakespeare: An Illustrated Dictionary* (London: Kaye and Ward, 1978), p177

[14] Bate, Jonathan *The Soul of the Age*, p436

[15] Troy was also called Ilium; King Priam's palace was also called Ilium.

[16] The tents are hollow because of the heavy loss of life; the factions are hollow because they have developed over trivial issues. Eg, Achilles' resentment of the authority of Agamemnon.

[17] Many authorities have claimed that Ulysses' views were also those of Shakespeare they certainly reflect the general view of most of Tudor society.

[18] *Dainty*: it means something like *fastidious*; many words have changed in their meaning over time. So *naughty* was much nearer *wicked* in Tudor times

[19] *Sir Valour*. Here, Ulysses refers mockingly to Achilles. The Greeks were furious at his refusal to take part in battling the Trojans. Could this be Essex failing to engage Tyrone in Ireland?

[20] 'Honour' is thus replaced by 'commodity'

[21] Readers will recognise this as a reference to Marlowe's *Dr Faustus* finally published in 1604: 'Was this the face that launched a thousand ships?'

[22] 'Honour' is mentioned 31 times in this play. As so often, an alibi for folly

[23] *rub on*: this double entendre comes from bowling: the expression is used to describe a ball that rolls on, slowing down, to stop when it touches another bowl.

[24] Queen Gertrude in Act 3, Scene 2 of *Hamlet*

[25] *daughters of the game*: a hunting metaphor, meaning a woman pursuing sex, a prostitute

[26] 'Words, words, words'. ie They mean nothing. Cf Hamlet's same comment.

[27] There have been suggestions that Shakespeare is having a gentle dig at Ben Jonson when he has Cressida's servant describing Ajax as being 'valiant as the lion, churlish as the bear, slow as the elephant.'

[28] A very good study of the language of *Troilus and Cressida*, and Shakespeare's other plays, can be found in Hussey, S.S. *The Literary Language of Shakespeare*, 2nd Edition (Harlow: Addison Wesley Longman Ltd, 1997)

[29] Duncan-Jones, Katherine in *Shakespeare: An Ungentle Life*, p255, points out that this would have been very close to the knuckle

[30] Duncan-Jones, *op cit.*, p305, is just one of several commentators who have speculated that Shakespeare may have had syphilis. If so this would have been a deeply personal cause of anxiety

[31] *A Winchester goose* was a nickname for a prostitute – the Bishop of Winchester owned several houses of ill repute in Southwark

CHAPTER 28 THE QUEEN IS DEAD, LONG LIVE THE KING!

[1] Quoted in Stephen Alfords article 'On a par with Nixon' in *London Review of Books*, Vol 38 No 22, 17 November 2016,

[2] Guy, *op cit.*, p273

[3] More easily said than done. Robert Cecil had a monopoly on starch; Sir Walter Raleigh had a monopoly on tin. Guy (pp359-361) indicates how empty this promise was (he describes the queen's 'weasel words.')

[4] Weir, Alison *Elizabeth the Queen* (London: Jonathan Cape, 1998), p473

[5] Lodge, E. (ed) *Illustrations of British History, Biography and Manners*, 2nd edition 3 vols. London 1838 Vol. ii p578; quoted in Guy *op cit.*, p373

[6] Wilson, Ian *Shakespeare: The Evidence op cit.*, p292

[7] Jackson, Clare *Devil-Land England Under Siege 1588-1688* (London: Allen Lane, 2021), pp86-7

[8] Borman, Tracey *Elizabeth's Women: The Hidden Story of The Virgin Queen*. (London: Vintage Books, 2009), p389

[9] Camden colluded in retelling this story in his *Annales* published in 1617 – but clearly he had a vested interest in not displeasing King James. But Guy (*op cit.*, pp382-3) insists that this is a fairy tale, and quotes a much more reliable source.

[10] Duncan-Smith, Katherine, *op cit.*, p184. Translation from the Latin: 'With some light fever and some groaning.' For Manningham, see Chapter 26, footnote 5.

[11] National Archives State Paper 12/215, no.65

[12] Duncan-Smith, *op cit.*, pp189-191

[13] Quoted in Wilson, *op cit.*, p295

[14] Bearman, Robert 'Thomas Greene: Stratford-upon-Avon's Town Clerk and Shakespeare's Lodger' *Shakespeare Survey 65* Holland (ed) (CUP, 2009), p98

[15] See Duncan-Smith, *op cit.*, pp188-191 for samples of Greene's verse

[16] Guy, *op cit.*, p357. See also Guy, pp199 *et seq.*

[17] Guy *op cit.*, pp119-120, 187, 201, 402

[18] Lee, Christopher *1603: A Turning Point in British History* (London: Hodder Headline, 2003), pp45-46

[19] Guy, op cit., pp205-206. But we do know that Shakespeare had liberal views on both immigrants and people of colour – as Farah Karim-Cooper has pointed out, Aaron in *Titus* is not a stereotype. Nor indeed is Shylock. One could add Othello.

[20] Lake, Peter *Bad Queen Bess? Libels, Secret Histories and the Politics of Publicity in the Reign of Queen Elizabeth I* (OUP, 2016)

[21] Guy, *op cit.*, pp5, 23, 145, 158, 267.

[22] Edmundson & Wells, *op cit.*, 2020

[23] Greer, 2015, *op cit.*, pp118-119

INDEX

Alleyn, Edward, 93, 95, 190, 315, 319

Amphibologia, see creative ambiguity,

Arden, Edward, 21, execution 66, 72, 74, 150-1, 380

Arden, Mary, 29 - 31, 46, 85

Arden of Faversham, 72, *98, 102-105*

Armada, 19, 22, 72, 86, 122, 150, 218, 229, 245, 265, 303, 339

As You Like It, 52, 61, 70, 274, 310, 318, 326 *et seq.*, 330, 340

Audibert, Justin, 127

Babington Plot 69, 76, 80, 176

Bassano, Emilia see Lanier

Blake, William, 211

Bloom, Harold, 14, 22, 231-2,

Bodleian Library, 35, 158, 166, 207, 275, 277

Bourus, Terri, 15, 104, 105, 318

Bowie, David, 169

Branagh, Kenneth, 227, 296

Brando, Marlon, 306

Brooke, Henry, 246, 248, 252, 259

Brooke, William, Lord Cobham 230, 246,

248, 251-2, 254, 343

Burbage, Cuthbert, 96, 292, 294,

Burbage, Richard 79, 94, 96, 109, 112, 191, 292, 294

Burbage, James, 44, 93, 110, 190, 203, 208, 216, 245-6, 247-8, 250, 312, 319, 355

Burghley, Lord see Cecil, William

Burrow, Colin, 163, 171, 312

Carey, Henry, 1st Lord Hunsdon, 13, 190, 191, 209, 216, his mistress, Emilia Lanier 13, 129, 133

Carey, George 2nd Lord Hunsdon, 190, 191, 201, 216, 218, 225, 230, 247-8, 249, 254, 272, 282, 283, 340, 350, 376

Catholic connections, 21, 29, 38, 39-40, 47, 128, 137, 149-150, 158, 180, 342

Cecil, Robert, Sir, 173, 229, 230, 246, 282

Cecil, William, First Lord Burghley, 24, 75, 98, 110, 112, 137, 155-6, 159, 161, 171, 174. 176, 199, 229, 272, 282, 324, 325, 335, 375, 377, 380,

Censorship 20, 43, 73, 93, 230, 248, 250, *et seq.*, 254, 260, 283, Bishops' Ban 315,

& Richard II, 333-4

Chamberlain's Men, the Lord, 103, 114, 120, 188 *et seq.*, 202-3, 217, 230, 248-9, 254, 282-3, 291-3, 314, 318-9, 320-1, 329 (at Hay Festival), 334-5, 350, 364, 375, 379

Chandos Portrait, 32-4, 35

Chettle, Henry, 153-4, 363, 378

Cobbe Portrait, 34-5

Coleridge, Samuel Taylor, 340

Comedy of Errors, The, 179 *et seq.* 350, 353

'commodity' 221 - 226, 235, 255, 261, 265, 368

Computer research, 14, 99, 100, 103, 114, 125, 153, 154

Creative ambiguity, 20-1, (*Amphibologia* 118), 121, 128, 134, 192, 215, 223, 139, 226, 303, 304, 309, 325, 332, 343

Cross dressing, 351, 352

Daniel, Samuel, 193, 256, 272, 273, 274, 275, 295, 303, 313, 327, 379

Dark Lady [of the sonnets] 13, 14, 55, 106, 128 *et seq.*, 137, 168-9, 170, 178, 269, 312, 354

Dekker, Thomas, 320, 363, 379

Dench, Judi, 71,[21] 227[23], 239, *277*

Devereux, Robert, 2nd Earl of Essex, 120, 122, 155, 158, 164, 173-4, 194, 199, 201, and Cadiz expedition 228-9, 231, and Azores expedition, 244-5, and Hotspur 262, 282, 295, 310, 312, his end 322, *et seq.*

Droeshout Portrait, 32-33,

Dudley, Robert, 1st Earl of Leicester, 65, 68, 69, 71, 72

Duncan-Jones, Katherine, 33, 34, 46, 54, 67, 69, 71, 74, 77, 79, 80, 155, 160, 168, 173, 190, 202, 209, 270, 272, 276, 312. 313, 358, 359

Edmondson, Paul, 18, 28, 41, 42 & *passim*, 55, 56, 129, 167-8, 170, 269, 312

Edward III, 136 *et seq.*

Egan, Gabriel, 15, 99, 100, 318

Eliot, George, 102

Eliot, T.S., 21

Elizabeth 1, 19, advisers 76, 110, 155, 191, 199, 230, anger, 229, 273, 281-2, 309-10, 323, portrait 24, 86, birth 13, claim to the throne 109, 220, aging & death, 173, 191, 192, 339, 350, 375-7, 381, funeral 378- and Essex 262, 282, 339, 310, 324-5, 335-7, 339, excommunicated 74, 222, favourites, 164, 199, 262, image 74, 86, 201, 379, knowledge of languages 89, 376, & Mary Q. of Scots 69, 224, 212, 313, 376, poverty, 117, 291, 378, 379, refusal to marry 75, & *passim*, religion 19, 30, 37, 38, 39, 40, 43, 151, 218, 222, 225, 339, rule 37, 219, 308, 339, 376, 379-380 self-description 20, 335, 338, succession, 112, 192, 199, 200, 220, 376, smallpox 27, 191, threats, 19, 20, 30, 39, 65, 69, 74, 201, 262, 377

Emilia, (play), 13, 133

Ethopoeia, 42-43,

Falstaff, Sir John, 22, 37, 45, 71, 79, 251 *et seq.*, 264-7, 283, 299, 340-7

Field, Richard, 62-3, 97, 158, 189, 190, 247, 303, 360

First Folio, 14, 18, 23, 26, 33, 79, 90, 91, 100, 124, 137, 138, 188, 270, 272, 312 382

Fitton, Mary 273, 276, 353-4, 359

Florio, John, 155, 176-8, 188, 350

Folger Library, 15, 35, 97, 203

Forman, Simon, 133, 361-3

Foxe's Book of Martyrs, 64, 219, 251

Greenblatt, Stephen, 30, 40, 45, 53, 54, 60, 67., 130, 146, 226, 238, 270, 291, 304

Greene, Robert, 97, 109. 123, 149 *et seq.* 158, 179, 206, 378

Greenwich, 13, 15, 19, 83, 88, 90, 98, 103, 192, 201, 228, 375

Greer, Germaine, 28, 31, 53, 54, 58-60, 62, 226

Hamlet, 22, 31, 43, 44, 70, 77, 81, 95, 96, 108, 162, 196, 226, 233, 305, 316-7, 319, 320, 332, 347, 371

Hamnet, 26, 59, 61, 67, death 226-7

Hamnet, (novel) 52, 226

Hathaway, Anne, 50–51, marriage, 56, & malt-making 59-60, 281, as mother 60; 128, 202, 226, 244, 249

Henry IV Part 1 250 *et seq.*, 254 *et seq.*

Henry IV Part 2 250, 264 *et seq.*,

Henry V, 22, 78, 89, 95, 255, 266-7, 294 *et seq.*

Henry VI Part 1, 113, 147, 120-2, 147, 252

Henry VI Part 2 113, 114-118, 137, 145

Henry VI Part 3 112, 116,

Henry VI plays revised 1595, 192

Henslowe, Philip, 81, 93, 124, 153, 190, 230, 314, 315, 319, 363

Herbert, Mary, Countess of Pembroke

See Mary Sidney

Herbert, William, Earl of Pembroke, 27, 33, 270-2, 273, 274-6, 313, 354, 359

James 1 & VI 377

Jew, 88, 106, 133, 137, 174, 231, 232, 233, 236-240, 241, 300

Jonson, Ben, 17, 18, 21, 26, 79, 91, 243, 248, 249, 252, 254, 272, 296, 312, *Everyman in his Humour* 313, 314, and *Isle of Dogs* 311-315, 316, 319, 320-321, and Poets War 320-1, 326, 327, 358, 361, 372, 378, 379

Jowett, John, 15, 144-145, 318

Joyce, James, 169, 227

Kempe, William, actor, & Kronborg Castle 71; 79, 109, 125, 146, 191, 285, 294, 328

King John, 208, 216-7, 219 *et seq.* 215, 261

Knights. L.C., 14

Kyd, Thomas, 81, 92, 103, 107, 109, 123, 138, 153, 159, 172, 317, and The *Spanish Tragedy*, 81, 316

Lake, Peter, 75, 77, 117, 199, 200, 218, 256, 308, 380

Lambarde William, 97-98, 201

Lanier, (Bassano) Emilia, 13, 14, 129, 131-3, 191, 232,

Larkin, Philip, 13, 134

Leicester, Earl of, 65, 69, 82, 112, 377

Leicester's Men, 44, 68 *et seq.*, 76-7, 78, 82, 96, 109, 192,

Locrine, 80-1, 98

Lopez, Dr., 174, 231, 232, 380

Loughnane, Rory, 99, 100, 103, 106, 124, 136, 144, 179, 182, 203, 254, 282, 283, 294, 303, 316, 316, 317, 326

Love's Labours Lost, 56, 70, 176 *et seq.*, 192, 202, 212, 281

Lucy, Sir Thomas, 63-4, 66, 74, 128, 150, 342, 344

Macbeth, 14, 22, 91, 104, 243, 244

Magna Carta, 217-9

Marlowe, Christopher, 36, 81, 88, 92, 96, 98, 103, 106-7, 109-111, 114, 118, 120, 123, 124, 125, 136-138, 151-5 passim, death 159; 192, 231, 232, 312, 315, 316, 368, *Dr Faustus,* 124, 137, *The Jew of Malta* 36, 137, 231, 232, *Tamburlaine,* 81, 106

Marston, John, 315, 318-320, 326, 343, 379

Mary I (Mary Tudor), 29, 37, 39, 76, 110, 191, 200

Mary Stuart (Queen of Scots), 65, 69, 107, 110, 112, 121, 200, 224, 313, 376, 378

McKellen, Sir Ian, 169, 226[23], 271

Merchant of Venice, 36, 83, 169, 174, 208, 227, 231 *et seq.*, 338

Meres, Francis, 130, 136, 207 *et seq.*, 219, 231, 232, 268, 269, 281, 283, 314, 350

Merry Wives of Windsor, 255, 281, 284, 340 *et seq.*

Much Ado About Nothing, 126, 283 *et seq.*

Nashe, Thomas, 97, 103, 120, 123, 137, 151, 152, 159, 163, 218, 230, & *Isle of Dogs* 248-9, 315

Norden, John, 84

Othello, 22, 24, 36, 45, 89, 106, 177, 178

Overbury, Sir Thomas, 35

Packer, Tina, 126

Papp, Joseph, 127

Passionate Pilgrim, The, 277

Perry, Grayson, 110

Petrarch, 92, 129, 131, 134, 139, 140, 168, 330

plagiarism 152, 206,

Plots, 19, 20, 30, Ridolfi 39; 46, Somerville, 65; Throckmorton 64-65, 74; Babington 69, 76, 80, 176; Lopez, 174, 176, 231; 199

plague, 15, 20, 21, 27, 30-1, 81, 86-87, 94, 149, 159-160, 162, 178, 189-190, 226, 230, 244, 246, 265, 360, 377

Queen's Men, 44, 72, 73 *et seq.*, 96, 98, 100, 110, 191, 295

racism, 106, 174, 232, 239, 290, 380

Rackin, Phyllis, 124, 125, 128, 347, 351

Raleigh, Sir Walter, 88, 194, 282, 335

'strangers' (foreigners), 28, 88, 97, 177

Rape of Lucrece, The, 162 *et seq.*, 189, 208

Richard II, 45, 189, 193 *et seq*, 203, 216, 242, 249, 256-7, 264, 322, 325, 334, 335, 336, 338

Richard III, 45, 84, 94, 110, 113, 115, 136, 137, 144 *et seq.*, 149, 191-2, 197, 249

Romeo and Juliet, 22, 203 *et seq.*, 207, 208, 210, 213, 249, 290,

Rowse, A. L., 41, 131, 355,

Royal Shakespeare Company, 239, 283,

Rowe, Nicholas, 45, 63, 163, 313, 340,

Russell, Elizabeth Cooke/ Hoby – Dowager Countess of Bedford, 246 *et seq.*, 355

Shakespeare Authorship Coalition [SAC], 18

Shakespeare, John, business activities 28, 29, 45, wool-dealer 45, 48, whittawer, 31, 45-6, family 30, career 39-40, property, 46, & religion 29, 39, 47, 64, 66, 150, 342, role in Stratford, 39-40, 44, 151, & his son's move to London 62, decline, 242 and coat of arms 242-4, death 349, 360, 381

Shakespeare, Susanna, 26, 58-9, 60

Shakespeare, William, birth 26, children 26, 58-59, first lost years 48-9, courtship & marriage 26, 50 *et seq.*, & Dark Lady 13, 14, education 40 *et seq*, family life 31, 31, rewriting plays, 80, second lost years, 61 *et seq.*, upbringing 30-1, knowledge of Italian 89, 176 *et seq.*, and death of son Hamnet 226-7 & 242, and father's coat of 242-3, buys New Place 244, as share-holder, 294, and death of father 360, 381

Shakespeare's Sonnets (1609) 276

Authorship issues 276, 280 *et seq.*

Sonnet Nos. 153-4, 41-42,

Sonnet No. 145, 55-56.

Nos. 127-144, 146-152 (including the Dark Lady Sonnets,) 128 - 135.

Nos. 61-77, & 87-103, 167 – 171.

Nos. 18 – 60, 268- 271.

Nos. 1-17 (the Procreation Sonnets) 167 & 271-27.

Another take on *Nos. 42, 20, 25 & 29,* 278-280.

Nos. 78 – 86 (The "Rival Poet" Sonnets), 311 -314.

Nos. 104 – 126, 380 - 381

Shapiro, James, 18, 77, 81, 118, 130, 169, 189, 238, 241, 351

Sidney, Mary, Countess of Pembroke, 272 *et seq.*

Sidney, Sir Philip, 27, 69, 71-2, 82, 113, 129, 130, 155, 268, 272, 274, 276, 277

Sir Thomas More, 73, 84, 88, 148

Southampton, Henry Wriothesley, 3rd. Earl of, 112, 154-6, 158, 160, 161-5, 168-171, 177, 178, 182, 191, 271, 281, 295, 310, 311, 312, 322, 325, 334, imprisoned 335, 336; 379; 381; an embarrassment to Sh. 349

Southwell, Robert, SJ, 151, 166-172, 380

Stanley, Ferdinando, Lord Strange, later 5th Earl of Derby, 108, 109–114, 120, 151, 153, 154, 160, death 171-2

Stanley, William, later 6th Earl of Derby, 112, in house plays 114, involvement with *Love's Labours Lost* 182 *et seq.* 190; 272, 318

Stationers' Register, 43, 80, 90, 114, 118, 124 153, 162, 326, 362, 364

Strange's Men, 81, 109 -122, 149, 190, 192, 272

Stuart, Mary (Queen of Scots), 39, 65, 69, 107, 110, 112, 121, 224, 313, 376, 378

stylometric analysis, 99, 104

syphilis, 27, 87, 373

Taming of the Shrew, 49, 119, 124-128, 149, 187, 285, 347

Tarlton, Richard, 77, 100, and his dog 100, 146, 247

Taylor, Gary, 15, 41, 99, 100, 103, 106, 124, 136, 144, 179, 182, 203, 219, 231, 254, 282, 283, 294, 303, 316, 317, 318, 326,

Tilney, Sir Edmund, Master of the Revels, 73, 230, 252,

Titus Andronicus, 99, 105-108, 109, 110, 153, 208, 347

Topcliffe, Richard, 65, 66, 149, 151, 166, 249, 315, 381

Troilus and Cressida, 289, 325, 360-373

Twelfth Night, 53, 89, 90, 91, 130, 177, 284, 322, 349-360, 361

Two Gentlemen of Verona, 59, 62, 98, 100-102, 109

Vagabonds Act, 43-4, 379

Venus and Adonis, 80, 155-158, 162, 166-7, 189, 208, 274

Walsingham, Sir Francis, 24, 64-65, 74-7, 159, 229, 277, 313, 339

Welles, Orson, 257

Wells, Sir Stanley, 18, 28, 41-42, 55, 56, 58, 91, 100, 126, 129, 160, 167, 168, 169, 170, 269, 312

Wesker, Arnold, 238 – 239

Williams, Robin, 57, 276, 278 – 280.

Winter's Tale, The, 48-49

IMAGES

All images taken from Wikimedia Commons apart from the following:

p51 Holy Trinity Church (courtesy of Neville Grant)

p105 Peacham drawing of a scene from *Titus Andronicus* (reproduced by permission of the Marquis of Bath, Longleat House, Warminster, Wiltshire)

p125 The clown and dancer Will Kempe from Kempe's *Nine Daies Wonder* 1600 (courtesy Mary Evans Picture Library)

p205 A scene from Zeffirelli's film *Romeo and Juliet* with Olivia Hussey as Juliet and Leonard Whiting as Romeo (courtesy of Bridgeman Art)

p233 In 1946 the New Yiddish Theatre Company staged *The Merchant of Venice* at the Adler Hall, Whitechapel in the heart of London's East End. Here, Meier Tzelniker (as Shylock) and his daughter Anna Tzelniker (as Portia), with director Robert Atkins in their dressing room (courtesy of The Jewish Museum, London)

p239 Judi Dench as Portia and Polly James as Nerissa in the Royal Shakespeare Company production of *The Merchant of Venice*, 1971 (courstesy Alamy Images)

p257 Orson Welles plays the role of Falstaff in his 1966 film *Chimes at Midnight*, a reworking of the *Henry IV* plays. John Gielgud played the king – and Jeanne Moreau was Doll Tearsheet (courtesy of ArenaPAL)

p275 The statue of William Herbert, 3rd Earl of Pembroke, outside the Bodleian Library, Oxford (courtesy of Neville Grant)

p288 Catherine Tate (Beatrice) and David Tennant (Benedick) in Josie Rourkes's production of *Much Ado About Nothing*, 2011 (courtesy of ArenaPAL)

p297 Laurence Olivier as Henry V in his 1944 film with Renée Asherson as Princess Katherine (courtesy Bridgeman Arts)

p306 Mark Antony (Marlon Brando) mourns over the dead body of Julius Caesar (Louis Calhern) in Joseph L. Mankiewicz's 1953 MGM film (courtesy of Bridgeman Art)

p260 Cartoon of Sir John Falstaff (courtesy of Look and Learn)

p330 A scene from *As You Like It* as performed by the all-male Lord Chamberlain's Men at the Hay Festival, 2022 (courtesy of Neville Grant)

p336 The Earl of Southampton in the Tower of London with his cat (from The Buccleuch Collection/Boughton House. By kind permission of His Grace, the Duke of Buccleuch and Queensbury, KT.

p382 The Chariot in Queen Elizabeth I's Funeral Procession. From a drawing of the time, supposed to be by the hand of William Camden (Society of Antiquaries, 1791). Part of a folding panorama nearly 29 feet long (courtesy of Bridgeman Art)

All efforts have been made to trace copyright. If there are any errors please inform the publishers for correction/attribution in future editions.